IN
DEMOCRACY'S
SHADOW

IN DEMOCRACY'S SHADOW

THE SECRET WORLD OF NATIONAL SECURITY

Edited by

Marcus G. Raskin and A. Carl LeVan

NATION BOOKS
NEW YORK

IN DEMOCRACY'S SHADOW
The Secret World of National Security

Published by
Nation Books
An Imprint of Avalon Publishing Group
245 West 17th St., 11th Floor
New York, NY 10011

AVALON
publishing group incorporated

Nation Books is a co-publishing venture of the Nation Institute
and Avalon Publishing Group Incorporated.

Library of Congress Cataloging-in-Publication Data is available.

ISBN 1-56025-696-6

9 8 7 6 5 4 3 2 1

Book design by Pauline Neuwirth, Neuwirth & Associates, Inc.
Printed in Canada on recycled paper
Distributed by Publishers Group West

I dedicate this book to Ann and Dick Barnet:
scholars, advocates, and dear friends.
—MARCUS G. RASKIN

I dedicate this book to the loving and
living memory of my mother.
—A. CARL LEVAN

CONTENTS

PREFACE

This book offers a vigorous defense of democracy's ideal and an unapologetic critique of our drift from it. The Cold War is largely responsible for this drift and we believe it was pivotal to the construction of a framework of political power put in place long before the horrible events of September 2001. The essays on our recent and present past all make this clear.

Most of the book's contributors are drawn from a group of regular participants in a monthly seminar on the National Security State at George Washington University convened by Marcus G. Raskin. A few other contributors were participants in a conference at the National Press Club in 1999 hosted in connection with the seminar, and several became involved through their affiliation with the Institute for Policy Studies in Washington, D.C. Participants included current and former members of Congress, current and former cabinet officials, and scholars recognized as leaders in their academic fields. Anabel Dwyer served as the initial rapporteur for the seminar before A. Carl LeVan served in that position for most of the remaining six years.

The debates in the seminars and at these various affiliated events over the years were extraordinary. Participants disagreed on matters such as the need to rewrite the National Security Act of 1947 as the centerpiece of the strategy for dismantling the National Security State. Differing views on the relationship between capitalism and American expansionism also led to lively debates. However, everyone involved in this book is devoted to challenging the assumptions of the National Security State and engaging in a debate on fundamental issues related to the institutional and intellectual betrayal of American democracy. It is our collective hope that *In Democracy's Shadow* and the collection of alternatives it contains will offer a powerful tool for inciting the citizenry to action and restoring accountability to government.

MARCUS G. RASKIN and A. CARL LEVAN

January 2005

INTRODUCTION

NO DEMOCRACY, NO SECURITY

Marcus G. Raskin and A. Carl LeVan

The popular understanding of democracy in America has been betrayed by a reorganization of power and authority that contradicts and undermines the very purpose of constitutional government. The formation of the "National Security State" represents the triumph of a philosophy of governance that has shaped our federal government for at least a hundred years. This philosophy takes for granted accepted notions of hegemonic foreign policy and national defense based on permanent war. Since at least 1947 it has deeply embedded itself in the attitudes of the bureaucracy, the major political parties, and the educational system. This means that changes in the American government since the tragic attacks on September 11, 2001, are profound but not necessarily new. This book traces those changes back to the early years of the twentieth century and follows them step-by-step through the Cold War. With that war behind us and a new "war on terrorism" in the making, democracy is becoming a shadow of itself. Our purpose with this book is to show why and how at the dawn of another century we have a responsibility to build a new framework for public policy based on participation, openness, and accountability. The contributors describe the operational modalities of the National Security State, which we believe is now a fundamental organizing principle of the modern American political system.

The United States emerged from World War II the preeminent Western power, and policy planners were astutely aware of this. The U.S. adopted a foreign policy embracing elements of self-preservation as well as strategies of antagonism that it justified through a bipolar worldview, which characterized and frequently caricatured the Soviet Union as an ominous and omnipresent global rival. The resulting Cold War was waged abroad through proxy armies, undeclared wars, propaganda, and tools of the free market. At home, the war imposed limits on political freedom, challenging and even subverting the constitution. While this forty-five-year period is significant because of the international struggles that served as theater in a search for global order, it is also remarkable because it entailed a transformation of the American government.

The National Security State continues to grow and expand even as the Cold War fades into memory. Today some see global empire as the best insurance against terrorism, while others view the Democratic and Republican parties as acceptable fig leaves for nationalist triumphalism. These attitudes have enabled a fundamental reordering of the American state and empowered it to act outside of the public interest, often with the help of structures that only appear to be beyond government influence. This is most apparent when the idea of democracy is used to veil the activities of global capitalism, which has primarily served the interests of a very small group of people. The book treats this question separately because the contributors differ on the nature and effect of the free-market model on national security. It is clear, though, that global capitalism American–style is important to the emergence of the National Security State, and at other times functions at cross-purposes with global economic strategies.

The authors included in this book are mostly drawn from a group of scholars, senior policy officials, and members of Congress who participated in a monthly seminar on the National Security State (NSS) at the George Washington University over the course of nearly seven years. A few other contributors were participants in a conference at the National Press Club hosted by the seminar in 1999, and the remainder became involved through their affiliation with the Institute for Policy Studies. Despite their political differences, each author is devoted to challenging the assumptions of the NSS and engaging in a debate on fundamental issues related to the institutional and intellectual betrayal of democracy through the construction of a framework of political power embedded within the state.

THE ORIGINS OF THE NATIONAL SECURITY STATE

The book is divided into four sections, beginning with a collection of essays on the origins of the National Security State. The opening chapter by Marcus Raskin, the convener of the GWU seminar, and Carl LeVan, the seminar's rapporteur for many years,[1] describes the development of the NSS over the course of the twentieth century, describing its institutional characteristics and everyday manifestations. They propose a broad set of features that define the National Security State. This chapter confronts questions such as: Is the best way to understand the NSS as a conscious or unconscious mode of organizing? As a political pathology? As an autonomous transbureaucracy defined not by department but by ideology? How does self-interest come into play?

The next two chapters of this section expose how the defining events of the Cold War are little more than celebrated myths accepted as history. If we once accepted aggressive Soviet behavior in Europe and the need to use and maintain atomic weapons as the legitimate, truthful, and moral justification for America's early postwar posture, these authors shatter those illusions. Gar Alperovitz and Kai Bird write, "The advent of nuclear weapons gave Washington an alternative to constructing a European peace in cooperation with the Soviet Union." The American monopoly on atomic technology lowered the costs of going it alone, and this was an unprecedented opportunity to advance American interests singularly. "At Yalta, Washington had essentially agreed to a neutralized Germany. With the bomb, however, U.S. policy-makers realized they could afford the risks of acting unilaterally." Policy elites also calculated that the bomb would address the expected problem of being unable to generate domestic support for a long-term deployment; the troops could come home and America's atomic umbrella would protect Europe.

America unfolded the umbrella over Germany in order to protect Western civilization from Soviet ambitions. The U.S. demonstrated its commitment to the people trapped on the other side of the Iron

Curtain through the Berlin airlift's daring supply of humanitarian aid. The official story, as told in *Documents of American History*, describes the airlift as a victory over oppression and a response to unprovoked aggression:

> At the Potsdam Conference a four-power command was set up to govern Berlin. Although Berlin was surrounded by Soviet occupied territory, the city itself was divided into four zones occupied by American, British, French, and Russian troops. On June 20 and June 22, 1948, the Soviet occupation officials declared that they considered Berlin an integral part of the Soviet zone of Germany and would henceforward govern the city on a unilateral basis. On June 24, they halted all land and water traffic between the Western zones of Germany and Berlin. The United States and Britain responded with an airlift of food, coal, etc., to the beleaguered [*sic*] citizens of the Western zones . . . On May 12, 1949, the Soviets abandoned their blockade and normal traffic was restored between the Western zones of Germany and Berlin.[2]

During a seminar on "National Security and the War System" at the National Press Club, Professor Carolyn Eisenberg of Hofstra University offered compelling evidence that the United States made a calculated decision to divide Germany by 1947. She argues that the U.S. accomplished this by misrepresenting Soviet actions in Berlin and exaggerating the extent of the blockade. The U.S. prevented the United Nations from playing a constructive role in ending the blockade and provoked the Soviets by printing an allied currency that excluded them. It also utilized its atomic monopoly as the instrument to establish a permanent and superior military presence in Europe at a time when keeping American troops there was politically difficult in the United States. All of this occurred, she notes, without significant participation of elected officials and in violation of the Potsdam and Yalta agreements.

Birnbaum's chapter opens by describing Soviet behavior in Berlin as a "blockade" but argues that by this point the Cold War was already firmly in place in the beliefs of policy planners and in geopolitical constraints. "The U.S. role in the Cold War, far from representing a break in an isolationist or self-contained national history, was entirely compatible with our expansionist and imperial past," he writes. World War II and the subsequent independence movements weakened the British and French empires, and the U.S. was eager to fill the void.

The final chapter in this section, by Terrence Paupp, describes how the technology of the atomic age precipitated a moral and legal crisis. Atomic weapons had an immediate and enduring effect on the moral boundaries that had served as constraints on the conduct of war for generations. The "nuclear crucible," says Paupp, "is the negation of our common humanity." It set up a clash between policies of force and coercion and policies based on international law and popular moral precepts. Various religious conventions in the 1930s articulated a program of opposition to weapons of mass destruction, forming a basis for ethical and theological positions on the pressing issues of modern warfare. Paupp states that under current international law there is no color of legitimacy to their first use. Nuclear weapons are indiscriminate by nature. The 1996 World Court decision questioning the legality of nuclear weapons as an instrument of war set international law as a bar to their legal use.

Paupp maintains that the connections between the legal and the moral basis for opposition unequivocally points to the necessity of the abolition of nuclear weapons. This position is now supported by former members of the American military establishment, notably the former chief of the Strategic Air Command, General George Lee Butler. It is tragic that the Bush administration has emphasized exactly the reverse of nuclear abolition. It set the nation on the course of building, justifying, and using nuclear weapons as Weapons of First Use (WFU) against any targets deemed necessary for any purposes. While the so-called Mutual Assured Destruction (MAD) policy has been the publicly stated policy of the U.S., the Bush policy has blown open the nuclear curtain for the world to see that MAD was the policy of the United States with its fingers crossed. It does not take Carl von Clausewitz or Machiavelli to see that the American nuclear policy now ensures the rekindling of the arms race with other nations scrambling for their own nuclear "charges." The Bush policy makes clear that the U.S. will use nuclear weapons against nonnuclear powers.[3] Of course this will drive countries such as North Korea to seek a nuclear deterrent against the U.S.

DECONSTRUCTING OUR RECENT AND PRESENT PAST

The second section is called "Finding Our Recent and Present Past" because it deals with the creation of our present predicament. Proclamations about the end of the Cold War and America's "victory" in it conceal the very real discrepancy between the changes in the world and the permanence of the National Security State. In this section, essays by Richard Falk, Peter Weiss, John Steinbruner and Jeffrey Lewis, and William Blum establish continuity between Cold War policies and the present day. Two of these chapters discuss how to restore the lost hope of the United Nations. Richard Falk, professor emeritus of political science at Princeton University, discusses security policy in the context of international cooperation, personal accountability, and disarmament. He outlines a new foreign policy that includes the fortification of international institutions in the context of world security and human rights. Peter Weiss from the Center for Constitutional Rights describes a plan for restoring the basic principles of international cooperation contained in foundational documents such as the UN Charter and the Universal Declaration of Human Rights. They advocate a very different defense system that surrenders the role of Pax Americana, an inherently unstable model for security.

As Falk and Weiss make clear, America abandoned other options. Following World War II, the nations of the world recognized the horror of that war as the kind of "cataclysmic trauma" that made a peaceful world order based on the rule of law a reasonable possibility. The problem was that the U.S. did not take a risk for a new system promulgated by President Roosevelt. The U.S. desired stability but it knew a multilateral system based on the United Nations conflicted with its own vision of postwar foreign policy where the UN is often reduced to an inconvenient conscience that sugarcoats the cold realities of power politics.

The origins of the UN reflect this ambivalence. It was trumpeted as the single most important international institution that the United States and other nations would recognize and participate in. It was the place to air disputes and provide international security. It was to be the people's place internationally, mediated through sovereign states. The first three words "We the Peoples" begins a statement of ideals, hopes, and needs for a world that had just gone through two grotesque world wars in twenty years, as well as violent civil wars. It was not surprising that this sense of hope and ideals would be the central part of what the UN was about. But could it ever withstand the drive toward unilateral triumphalism that rejected international security and disarmament? The United States and other nations made clear that they were reluctant to adopt a different formulation of international affairs that seemed possible in 1944; the UN charter did not contemplate the existence of nuclear weapons.

In the initiating meeting of the UN, a few weeks after President Roosevelt died, the United States went about tapping the phones of all the delegations that came to the UN meetings. (The UN served as a gathering place for spies.) The UN Charter gave veto power to the Big Five (Great Britain, France, China, the U.S., and the Soviet Union) over all security matters. But the UN, through the General Assembly, debated issues and set the framework for the solution to a host of problems such as finance, refugees, human rights, and later the decolonization process.

The U.S. pulled away from the UN when it became clear that it could not command a majority in the UN General Assembly. During the Cold War, the U.S. was not above treating the UN cavalierly, much the way a rich relative complains about his nieces and nephews because they don't follow his every command. During the Cold War, Soviet and U.S. negotiators could not agree on what to do about nuclear weapons. The Soviets demanded that the U.S. give up its nuclear weapons before an international authority that would have free access in the Soviet Union to ensure compliance. (Both sides would have been better off had each accepted the other's plan!) The U.S. asserted that "serious" ideas about the control of finances and banking would reside in the International Monetary Fund and the World Bank. These institutions saw no need or interest in viewing themselves as part of the UN framework. Indeed, they have often operated against the underlying purpose of closing the gap between rich and poor and do not take account of human rights and security issues. This separation from the UN remains foolish because it means that the world's poor have no voice. Of the period following the Cold War, Phyllis Bennis wrote, "There can be little doubt that at all levels the U.S. dominates, and when it chooses to exercise its power controls the workings, the actions and inactions, the successes and the failures of the United Nations."[4]

George W. Bush has taken this withdrawal further with his expressed willingness to wage a war on behalf of UN resolutions but without the support of the Security Council. The 2003 Iraq War led to a paradoxical situation of the UN avoiding war as a means of supporting its resolutions. American nationalists took this as an example of the weaknesses of alliances, presaging a change in U.S. foreign policy.

For security questions, the North Atlantic Treaty Organization (NATO) became the multinational organization of choice, and it competed with the UN for this status from its inception. Its original attractiveness resided in its geographic place, seemingly shared values, and business opportunities. The UN came into being before the atomic bombs were used, which gave the impression that the UN was outmoded from its beginning. Throughout its history, the U.S. has been adroit in using the UN as a fig leaf, from the "police action" in Korea that was legitimated in the UN Participation Act of 1944 to the "sanctions enforcement" policies crafted for Iraq after the 1991 Gulf War. The current Bush strategy of abandoning sanctions for all-out war with Saddam Hussein in 2003 is consistent with a historical pattern in the Third World. A war for policy planners and ideologues is fought and then other nations are invited to share the cost of reconstruction after the war. The U.S. offers blandishments to them that may not be quite enough.

This brings up the question: which will the U.S. identify with in the future, an expanding NATO or the UN? President Clinton's choice of NATO, played out in Yugoslavia, is a curious kind of patriarchy in which NATO, the military and hunter arm, is to take care of security and peacekeeping on the ground. The UN, the maternal element of international affairs, is left picking up the pieces (refugees, food, and health services) with insufficient funds from the NATO states, the father. This is a very dangerous situation in world affairs. The National Security State system is comfortable with this arrangement but that system does not bode well for modern democracy, human rights, or economic justice.

Both during and since the Cold War, atomic pathologies served as the centerpiece of this security model. As Steinbruner and Lewis carefully document in their chapter, the nightmare of the Cold War is far from over. Nuclear weapons are deeply entrenched in our bureaucracy and military strategy. The U.S. and Russia still operate rapid reaction forces for deterrence of mass attack that would have lethal effects if they were actually used. Military planners still deem too many possible scenarios as acceptable for triggering nuclear war plans. One scenario derives from the danger of chemical and biological weapons. Another is the danger of disintegration of the Russian armed forces. Russia cannot afford a large military anymore, and this fiscal constraint encourages a reliance on nuclear weapons to compensate for the weaknesses of its conventional forces. At home, Americans are still at great risk. Since 1945, the government has lost eleven nuclear weapons, including one that was misplaced in a Georgia swamp. Military officials saw this incident "less as a security, safety, or ecological problem," says investigative journalist Jeffrey St. Clair, "than a potential public relations disaster that could turn an already paranoid population against their ambitious nuclear project."[5] Safety standards for nuclear weapons (including the management of plutonium and highly enriched uranium) fall far below those set for nuclear power.

Steinbruner and Lewis warn that, far from the Bush administration's stated intention to liquidate the legacy of the Cold War, the "underlying reality is that U.S. military forces are being prepared for extended confrontation, not political accommodation." They note that the Moscow Treaty permits both Russia and the U.S. to retain large arsenals of nuclear weapons in excess of any conceivable purpose. In the meantime, the United States is heavily investing in defense transformation that will dramatically increase the capacity of the United States to engage in preemptive military operations to support an increasingly nationalistic security agenda outlined by the Bush administration.

As they made clear at the University Seminar, these policies set the United States on a collision course with the other major societies in the world, particularly Russia and China. Although both countries appear to be pursuing short-term strategies of incremental accommodation toward the United States, Steinbruner and Lewis warn that continued neglect toward the legitimate security interests of other states may eventually result in more forceful reactions. They are particularly worried that Washington's plans for expanded military activities in outer space, including missile defenses, could catalyze international opposition to U.S. security policies. China, in particular, may view Washington's pursuit of missile defenses and advanced space-based war-fighting capabilities as provocative and, in response, pursue "asymmetric" military actions aimed at U.S. assets in space.

Avoiding a calamitous confrontation will require changes that extend beyond those anticipated in the Moscow Treaty in order to address the real legacy of the Cold War: the inequitable distribution of security within the international system. Although new rules governing military activity in outer space are a necessary first step, this chapter makes clear that achieving fundamental political accommodation will require an adjustment in U.S. security policy of historic proportions.

In the final chapter of this section, William Blum, a former State Department analyst, argues that there is a remarkable continuity to American foreign policy. He claims that its assumptions cannot be found in its self-definition. Despite the disintegration of the Soviet Union, interventions in the recent past and the military adventures of today reveal proclamations of multilateralism and humanitarianism as rhetoric accompanying other purposes. Conventional accounts of history hold that countless American interventions throughout the world were based on containment of communism. Blum argues that from 1945 onward this claim has been misleading. "For in real, nonpropagandistic terms, American interventions throughout the world, time and again, had but the most precarious or only imagined connection to the Soviet Union and its alleged expansionism."

SUBSTRUCTURES OF AUTHORITY
IN THE NATIONAL SECURITY STATE

Analysis of the organization of power and privilege that undergirds the National Security State requires analysis of government institutions and bureaucratic practices, but it also requires a glance beyond government structures. Essays by Seymour Melman, Saul Landau, and Anabel and David Dwyer explore how the National Security State has become embedded in our domestic and international economic policy, in courts and universities, and in the media.

Dwyer and Dwyer approach institutions as both formal and informal structures. Institutions are a domain where legitimation and socialization occurs within a context of goals, roles, and practices. Within this type of framework, we are able to examine particular laws as well as their sources within the Cold War culture. Court decisions that reinforce arbitrary powers, limit freedom, or allow law to be subservient to force should be viewed in the context of this larger network of institutions. As the dissenting view in the International Court of Justice's opinion on the legality of nuclear weapons stated, "No legal system can confer on any of its members the right to annihilate the community which engenders it and whose activities it seeks to regulate." Judge Weeramantry insisted the ability to rule the people and the ability to destroy the people contradicts the most obvious notions of legitimacy. "The legal system which accommodates that rule, itself collapses upon its foundations, for legal systems are postulated upon the continued existence of society." The legal rationale for nuclear weapons was not and is not based on law. It is based on another set of institutions and assumptions that are violent in nature. President George W. Bush's willingness to use nuclear weapons first and in any kind of conflict tells us that the restraints that Judge Weeramantry claimed in the terms of international law do not exist in the world of power politics, but not because they can't be governing. Rather, governments don't want law to govern.

    Like the judiciary, the independence of universities may be more apparent than real. For decades, institutions of higher learning have been a critical arena where knowledge can be enlisted in service of power. Before the Cold War, the prominent anthropologist Franz Boas attacked his colleagues for involving themselves in a military-scientific-industrial complex by accepting government funding. "They have not only shaken the belief in the truthfulness of science," he wrote in a 1919 letter, "but they also have done the greatest possible disservice to scientific inquiry." During the Cold War, the acceptable boundaries of independent academic inquiry shifted significantly. The cooperation of the universities is "an essential ingredient of the nation's rearmament program," the Pentagon Defense Science Board told Congress in 1982. "Military, intelligence, and propaganda agencies provided by far the largest part of the funds for large research projects in the social sciences," explains American University communications professor Christopher Simpson. Federal funds, frequently provided covertly, funded more than three-fourths of the budgets for social science research institutes at Columbia University, Princeton University, and MIT. At such institutions, "state and corporate security agencies frequently *initiated* social science concepts and projects, and the campus experts *followed*—not the other way around."[6] It is not news that such studies did not challenge the assumptions of these agencies.

Less surprising is how economic elites tend to share the assumptions of the NSS and collaborate in policies that serve their interests. Landau's chapter argues this is true both in domestic and in international economic policy. He argues that promoting the free flow of goods and capital is part of the National Security State's operations. In the globalized economy, immigrants and migrant workers have become a means to make the labor pool more flexible. This is facilitated by coercive programs and policies that permit manipulation of the labor market and control over subject populations. Between 1993 and 1999, the Immigration and Naturalization Service's budget for border patrol increased from less than $1 billion to $2.56 billion. After September 11, 2001, President Bush requested a 14.5 percent increase in its budget, from $5.5 billion to $6.3 billion.[7] Immigration's untold stories are grim. In 1999 alone, 356 migrants died trying to elude the patrol while crossing the border. Ironically, NAFTA, which was meant as a legislative measure to increase commerce between the United States and Mexico, has declined in influence since September 11 in part because of American security measures taken at the border.

In the last essay of this section, Melman describes the integration between military planning and domestic economic policy. In particular, military Keynesianism and military corporatism prevented America from capturing the peace dividend at the end of the Cold War, instead allowing military budgets to surge after a brief decline. More than a decade after the disappearance of the Soviet Union, U.S. military spending remains more than six times larger than Russia's, the country with the second largest military budget in the world. The Pentagon's budget remains guided by outdated assumptions of military planning. While other federal agencies fight for funding, military spending continues to account for a majority of all discretionary spending (the funding bills debated annually by Congress). The Pentagon receives increases even if they violate congressional budget resolutions. According to the Center for Defense Information, America's military budget is twenty-three times larger than the *combined* spending of the seven countries the Pentagon itself has identified as the most likely adversaries (Cuba, Iran, Iraq, Libya, North Korea, Sudan, and Syria). This occurred during a period in which military spending declined globally from $1.2 trillion in 1985 to $809 billion in 1999. During that time the U.S. share of the world's military spending rose from

31 percent to 36 percent. One of Melman's main points though, is how the military industrial complex simply adapted to this post–Cold War environment, despite a shrinking workforce during a period of economic growth.

ACCOUNTABILITY AND DEMOCRACY

The fourth section of the book discusses some of the major obstacles to holding the National Security State accountable. The NSS has facilitated concentration of power by ceding constitutional checks and balances to unelected bureaucrats. It has operated on an assumption of secrecy, establishing broad criminal liability for anyone who threatens those assumptions. And it has looked the other way as intelligence officers engaged in highly illegal activities abroad at a rate of "several hundred times a day" according to one congressional report.[8] These modalities raise the costs of participation in politics and have had the effect of rewarding citizen passivity. Essays by Peter Raven-Hansen and Marcus Raskin and A. Carl LeVan analyze the role of the bureaucracy, the judiciary, and Congress on these terms. Historian Anna Nelson looks carefully at the problem of secrecy, a common theme among all of these essays for the role it plays in undermining accountability.

Secrecy not only makes the government less accountable, as so many misguided covert operations show, it also limits policy choices in important ways. There are, of course, alternatives to secrecy. Greater openness would ensure major decisions in the name of the U.S. would better reflect the will of the nation and help ensure that accountability is possible when policy strays from the publicly stated objectives. Insisting on the consent of the governed will restore legitimacy to operations that should require public debate and consent in the first place. Another advantage of reducing secrecy is that open-source information is frequently more accurate than secret information. For example, the CIA told Congress in 1979 that the U.S.S.R.'s per capita national output was comparable to Italy, the United Kingdom, and Japan combined, when open-source information showed that it was only about a fifth of that.[9] And as Mel Goodman, a former CIA analyst, has pointed out, open sources did a better job of predicting India's nuclear tests. Secrecy protected and unnecessarily prolonged misguided policies. For example, a great deal of executive secrecy evolved from nuclear weapons and policies related to protecting them and planning how to use them. The American people embraced "deterrence" as a guardian, even participating in massive (and absurd) fallout shelter programs that mobilized millions of people into a false sense of security or even hysteria.

The use of secrecy in formulating national security doctrines has had a pernicious effect on democracy. Both the public and the Congress are denied relevant information and face a "rationality deficit," where they are told they do not have sufficient information to make rational judgments, or that they are not entitled to make those judgments at all. This kind of excessive secrecy is by no means unusual. A House of Representatives subcommittee in 1988 found that national security decision directives were often issued without Congress being informed, "thereby, preventing any review or monitoring of the directives themselves or their impact on executive branch operations and organizations."[10] George Washington University law professor Raven-Hansen argues that these changes have produced greater secrecy, veiled the sources of authority for many of these activities, and increased the likelihood of the use of force without benefit of public and legislative debate. He shows how much of the NSS's expanded authority comes from executive orders, presidential decision directives, and far-reaching administrative regulations instead of through public laws. Most alarming, perhaps, is how this embedded unaccountability has been accelerated within criminal law since September 11. This has occurred through the use of military tribunals and new laws imposing limitations on the public's knowledge of judicial proceedings. Reforms in the name of fighting terrorism or the drug war sacrifice important civil liberties and fundamentals of due process without making the nation any more secure, and the wall between domestic and foreign disappears—yet the possibilities of internalizing international law are ignored. He makes a strong case that "terrorist" has proven to be a term of convenience and discretion for state managers rather than a term evenly applied under the rule of law.

In another chapter, Anna Nelson, a professor of history at American University, shows how the wall of secrecy was erected during the Cold War, and how it was perpetuated afterwards. This occurred through attacks on the Freedom of Information Act, new criminal sanctions on those who attempt to blow the whistle, the weakening of the Presidential Records Act by the attorney general, and other modifications to the NSS architecture. Through legislation such as the Homeland Security Act and the Patriot Act, Congress was a willing partner in perpetual war and protecting the wall of secrecy between the government and the people it supposedly serves. Secrecy failed to serve democracy most convincingly in the recent Iraq War, where the president coyly misled the public.

The chapter by Raskin and LeVan is concerned specifically with Congress, for it stands at the locus where the first set of brakes should be applied to the National Security State. However, this has rarely happened. "Congress stands almost helplessly outside of the departments," Woodrow Wilson once explained. "Even the special, irksome, ungracious" investigations which it from time to time institutes . . . do not afford it more than a glimpse of the inside of a small province of federal administration . . . It can violently disturb, but it cannot often fathom, the waters of the sea in which the bigger fish of the civil service swim and feed. Its dragnet stirs without cleansing the bottom."[11] Congressman Ron Dellums, who served as chair of the House Armed Services Committee, accused Congress of abrogating its responsibilities: "The result has been a blind acceptance of misinformation, exaggeration, and hyperbolic pronouncements about the nature of U.S. security needs and a generally enthusiastic endorsement of a jingoistic, interventionist approach to developments in the Third World."[12] In her presentation to the GWU seminar, Congresswoman Elizabeth Furse described similar obstacles during her tenure on the House Armed Services Committee. The military establishment went to great measures to prevent Congress from reining it in. Through her criticism of overblown military spending on such weapons platforms as the C-17 military transport plane, Furse discovered how formidable the obstacles to her agenda of peace through disarmament and economic conversion were. These barriers were often enlarged by her status as a woman in a male-dominated policy arena.

CONCLUSIONS: PREVENTING PAST AS PROLOGUE

We have titled this important collection of essays *In Democracy's Shadow* because we are concerned that the institutions, policies, and habits of the

Cold War have cast too long a shadow over democracy's ideals. The title captures the culture and mindset that rationalized such undemocratic institutions and perpetuated so many dangerous Cold War policies that continue into the twenty-first century. Every national intelligence estimate prepared by the CIA on the development of the Soviet military between 1974 and 1986 overestimated the rate at which Moscow would modernize its strategic forces.[13] Such errors, of course, fueled dangerous weapons buildups and steered energies domestic toward military needs instead of more productive outputs.

"In intelligence the gravest problem and the source of . . . the most dramatic intelligence failures is an established mindset," says former Secretary of Defense (and former Director of Central Intelligence) James Schlesinger. The problem is not simply a particular prevailing ideology because it concerns how knowledge is organized. "Senior officials reach judgments about policy that become fixed convictions in their minds, indeed axioms that become unchallenged and begin to influence intelligence assessments. It is these axioms, drawn from the policymakers, that lie at the root of the most dramatic (so-called) intelligence failures."[14] Schlesinger describes the symptoms of political pathology, where the bureaucracy preserves itself by leaving fundamental axioms and assumptions unexamined. However, it would be a mistake to conclude that the problem lies simply with intelligence analysts, policy makers, or a particular institution such as Congress. The creation of transbureaucracies such as the new Department of Homeland Security reveals how integrated the institutional infrastructure of the NSS has become, and how the Bush administration views any sort of dissent not as a part of checks and balances, but rather as a threat to the security of our nation.

What happens to individuals who challenge these political pathologies? Hazel O'Leary, another presenter at the GWU seminar, encountered both masculine and military pathologies firsthand as President Clinton's secretary of energy. She outlined how the truth about nuclear weapons has survived thanks to whistleblowers in the bureaucracy and devoted citizens groups on the outside who remain committed to an informed public. They all demonstrate that citizenship is action with deliberation, especially at a time when freedom hangs by a thread. This book is a first step toward students, citizens, and a few bold voices in the state apparatus becoming armed with the knowledge necessary to participate in restoring the promise of democracy.

INTRODUCTION

NOTES

1 George Washington University seminar's first rapporteur was Anabel Dwyer, who coauthors a chapter in this book.
2 Henry Steele Commager, *Documents of American History*, Vol. 2, Eighth Edition (New York: Appleton-Century-Crofts, a division of Meredith Corporation, 1968).
3 David G. Savage, "Nuclear Plan Meant to Deter," *The Los Angeles Times* , March 11, 2002, A1. "Nuclear Plan Creates Shockwaves Worldwide" *The Los Angeles Times* March 12, 2002, B12. See White House Nuclear Policy Review, submitted to Congress December 31, 2001.
4 Phyllis Bennis, *Calling the Shots: How Washington Dominates Today's UN* (New York: Olive Branch Press, 1996, 233).
5 Jeffrey St. Clair, "The Case of the Missing H-Bomb," *In These Times*, August 20, 2001.
6 Jonathan Feldman, *Universities in the Business of Repression: The Academic-Military-Industrial Complex and Central America* (Boston: South End Press, 1989). Christopher Simpson ed., *Universities and Empire: Money and Politics in the Social Sciences During the Cold War* (New York: W.W. Norton & Co, 1998).
7 Alison Solomon, "War at the Door." *The Village Voice* February 26, 2002.
8 House Permanent Select Committee on Intelligence, *IC21: The Intelligence Community in the 21st Century*, 1996, 205.
9 Daniel Patrick Moynihan, "End the Torment of Secrecy," *The National Interest*, Spring 1992.
10 Cited in Frederick Kaiser, "Impact and Implications of the Iran-Contra Affair on Congressional Oversight of Covert Action," *Intelligence and Counterintelligence* 7, no. 2 (summer 1994), 205–234.
11 Woodrow Wilson, *Congressional Government* (Boston: Houghton Mifflin Company 15th Edition, 271). It should be noted that as president he relished this power.
12 Ronald Dellums with R. H. Miller and Lee Halterman, *Defense Sense: The Search for a Rational Military Policy* (Cambridge, MA: Ballinger Publishing Co., 1983, 55).
13 Speech by George Tenet, Princeton University Conference on the CIA's Analysis of the Soviet Union, March 8, 2001.
14 Former Secretary of Defense and former Director of Central Intelligence James Schlesinger in testimony before the Senate Select Committee on Intelligence, February 20, 1992.

★ **P A R T** ★

1

COLD WAR
BEGINNINGS

1

THE NATIONAL SECURITY STATE AND THE TRAGEDY OF EMPIRE

Marcus G. Raskin and A. Carl LeVan

American democracy is decaying because freedom has been
mortgaged to bear the costs of empire. The present organization,
assumptions, size, and character of the American state is a product of
its emergence as a world power (now "superpower") at the beginning
of the twentieth century and the end of the Spanish–American War.
Throughout the century, with the possible exception of President
Herbert Hoover and some administration officials in the New Deal,
the leadership class has been surprisingly comfortable with this brew
of national triumphalism. It accepted the idea that the American state
could never be at rest. In its nature and imperial responsibility it was
taken for granted throughout the twentieth century that it is in continuous conflict with other nations, whether for markets, resources,
ideology, tutelage, or national prestige. And geopolitically, it must
never be second.

These activities are both expensive and difficult to maintain. Contrary to propaganda, modern wars are very expensive and dangerous
for technologically dependent states. They can lead to wars without
end and imprudent foreign and national security policies, which in
their very fiber promote the idea of American invincibility even as the

country's infrastructure decays. As part of this system of invincibility the society cedes to the corporate economy the planning and regulatory function. While the state can, if it so chooses, intervene directly, the decision-making system is a coordinated effort between the national security budget and the largest corporations. That is to say, dominant factors in American politics are the largest corporate units and the national security establishment. Their power greatly circumscribes the issues that separate the two parties, and while substantial differences were present in the first years of the Cold War, the distinctions have grown smaller as the colossi of American life have increased their power and reach without bothering to ensure their legitimacy. The unenviable task of politicians has been to ride these runaway horses.

The presumed end of the Cold War—the fall of the Berlin Wall—was surely a victory for the people of Eastern Europe, but this posed a problem for the one remaining world empire that was not resolved until the terrible tragedies of September 11, 2001. After twelve years of seeking purpose, the American government entered a new stage of rationalizing a greatly expanded National Security State. The attacks in New York, Washington, and Pennsylvania had a profound effect on the Bush presidency. Before September 11, Bush faced a considerable crisis since the winner of the popular vote in the 2000 election came in second place. Discussions that raised doubts about his legitimacy and intellectual capacities ended with the attacks. Similarly, discussion about reexamining the assumptions of the National Security State and cutting defense budgets ended. In other words, the United States had entered a new stage in its Icarus–like political flight. It became acceptable for the state managers and the leader-president to expand the "needs" of the state. And both agreed that the state's purpose would be best fulfilled through the instruments of continuous war. Thus, in fairness to George W. Bush, it is not likely that Al Gore or the state apparatus would have reacted any differently to the horrendous attack on the U.S. by zealots from Saudi Arabia. Vice President Gore had also promised the relevant corporations and state managers huge increases in defense expenditures.

In the face of the present crisis the American system of government continues to be labeled a democracy or a republic whose practices are irreproachable. Ordinary citizens of all classes are expected to rally behind triumphal symbols and rituals. But in reality these are merely cover stories for the actual operations of political power in a state whose important decisions are secret and whose actions undermine individual and collective freedom.

The state employs a ladder of violence from economic and political destabilization to assassination to the first use of nuclear weapons. Its operations have included spying on U.S. citizens and using them as unwitting guinea pigs in so-called national security experiments. It includes ways to play on the insecurity of people and their willingness to suspend independent judgment. Indeed, President Bush has made clear that the Constitution is not a "suicide pact," and if what is required, as the attorney general and other members of the administration believe, is a curtailment of freedoms in a war which can last for a generation or longer, then so be it. The American state must act for itself and for the world against those who we deem as enemies. Virtually all of these activities and assumptions are grounded in past identifiable laws, rules, secret regulations, and bureaucratic structures that determine the present, and the future. In other words, President George W. Bush did not have to start *de novo*. Republican and Democratic administrations alike operated a National Security State through countless regulations, secret memoranda, defense contracts, wiretaps, and hardware acquisitions, which laid the groundwork for the current Bush administration's response. From FDR forward, American political, economic, and military elites shared in the creation of the Central Intelligence Agency (CIA), the National Security Agency (NSA), the Department of Defense (DoD), the Department of Energy (DoE), the National Reconnaissance Office (NRO), and dozens of other bureaucracies. They collaborated in extending the power and reach of the Federal Bureau of Investigation (FBI). This framework is woven into America's social fabric, including its educational institutions, corporations, scientific enterprises, and the media. It constrains the actions of American leaders and elites and serves as the means to ensure a stable distribution of power and authority according to the judgments of political and economic elites, including national security managers who work within a grammar of power designed to ensure that the U.S. can operate as the paramount power in the world, coming and going as it pleases, with whatever weapons it chooses. What was once hidden is clear for all to see. President

George W. Bush is the new steward to manage and use the state as a warrior instrument, whether at home or abroad. The national security state is the form that protects, umpires, and expands American economic interests. The Bush administration took power as a coalition of religious and business forces that would craft a faith-based business civilization to create and dominate markets under the guise of free enterprise and low tariffs. Republicans believed that resurrecting a traditional belief in God and patriarchy could be linked to an aggressive business civilization, which in turn stood on the ground of revolutionary technology, innovation, and powerful forms of propaganda and self-congratulation. But the realities of American national life were such that the Bush administration found it was far easier to govern an expanding state that had powerful warrior and authoritarian aspects than a liberal, relatively freewheeling culture of individualism and experimentation of the kind the Republican party claims to represent. The actual nature of the American state involves inertial forces, which have moved uninterrupted, either at a slower or faster pace under different administrations, but always forward. This has been the strength of the National Security State, which merely entered a new stage following September 2001.

The question is how to address the resiliency of the National Security State in the face of extraordinary international changes, criminal activity, and real and manufactured threats. For those who questioned the NSS, the journey has been difficult, fraught with failure. Through the espionage controversies of the 1990s, the Iran–Contra scandal of the 1980s, and the congressional investigations of the 1970s, those who sought to rein in the secret agencies accomplished little. The 1975 investigative committees headed by Congressman Otis Pike and Senator Frank Church uncovered illegal domestic spying programs, assassination plots, and torture training, but to little practical avail. Congress failed to curb the National Security State's power. It was co-opted and simply failed to exercise its oversight responsibility. But why did Congress fail? One answer is that Congress, through its committee structure, is co-opted into the operations of the NSS. Congress does not review the fundamental missions of the National Security State, or its assumptions, nor how it can be changed within a free society.

In order to understand the operational modalities and principal features of the National Security State that account for this resiliency, it is first important to appreciate how they are rooted in important struggles of the twentieth century. The essays here also discuss more recent events and policies as evidence of continuity and a long-established trajectory. The conclusion to the introduction summarizes the problems at hand. The conclusions to the book will analyze the meaning of responsibility for the citizenry, including government officials and knowledge workers, in this dark time. We will also touch on why the radical shifts in the calculus of world power are not necessarily to the U.S.'s benefit. Being the "single superpower with world responsibilities" may prove to be a poisoned pill as American policy makers respond to direct assaults on American power and ideas with conventional National Security State nostrums. Democratic rhetoric could not mask the actual operations of state power, whether in explaining the American selection process for its president, a failed coup in Venezuela, or the arming of Iraq during its war with Iran.

THE EARLY ORIGINS OF THE NATIONAL SECURITY STATE

The transformation of the state did not occur over a few days or years. The continental powers and the British empire were the Americans' teachers, each nation having its own brand of imperialism, but all believing in their cultural superiority and their right to take what they wanted from the poor sectors and nations of the world. The imperial nations would compete with each other without concern for the colonized, who were objects but not subject actors except in certain struggles (Spain, Cuba), but then only as "associates" without voice or power to be heard in the disposition of their land, resources, or people. In the nineteenth century, the Monroe Doctrine became widely accepted, and by 1890 Americans chose to play the imperial game abroad in earnest much to the dismay of anti-imperialists such as Mark Twain, William James, and Carl Schurz.

By the time the United States entered World War I, it had occupied the Philippines and intervened in Central America and the Caribbean no less than forty-five times. Members of the Senate, such as Albert Beveridge, argued that God had given the United States a triumphal mission to civilize minorities around the world, undertake imperial ventures continuously, and protect the profit margins of American corporations through trade and investment outside of the United States.

With such activism came questions about the nature and shape of the American government.

After the war against Spain the United States gave serious thought to reorganizing the government to accommodate the needs of its worldwide economic, political, and social interests. American leaders studied the British Council of Imperial Defense as a model for their state structure. In 1911, Congressman Richmond Pearson proposed the establishment of a council of national defense dominated by the military secretaries and six committee chairmen from Congress. His bill excluded the president because Congress has the power under the Constitution to regulate the armed forces.[1] These proposals, it should be noted, occurred in the age of progressive reform, which sought to rationalize rules of the economic and corporate system. President Theodore Roosevelt considered military power to be an important quiver in the bow of progressive reform and world economic dominance.

During World War I, the Overman Act gave preference and "guidance" wherever necessary to ensure American military power and fighting capacity. The act fell into disuse when the war ended in 1918, but its assumptions did not fade away. In 1919–20, the Palmer Raids expelled thousand of immigrants and radicals in the name of internal security. They were the "terrorists" of their time. The attorney general under Woodrow Wilson, A. Mitchell Palmer, was the intellectual forebear to Attorney General John Ashcroft, who also wishes for the expulsion of undesirables.[2]

In the 1920s, General Hugh A. Drum proposed the creation of a council of national defense to manage military-political relations and develop plans for a nationwide transportation and mobilization infrastructure. He thought the council should have the power to recommend to the president reorganization of the executive branch in peacetime and its expansion in wartime. The proposal was shelved out of concerns raised in the War Department that Drum's ideas would threaten the military's autonomy, and it would be better to work with a president who was more cooperative.

The organization of other states was closely studied by elites who openly considered how the authoritarian model might inform solutions to the increasingly dire economic and social situation in America. In 1931, Chicago's mayor, "Wild" Bill Thompson, told Congress that if the federal relief net was not forthcoming, the government would have to send in troops. When the Bonus Army, consisting of thousands of veterans from World War I, marched on Washington in 1932, the federal government did just that. In response to their demands for advance payments on their pensions, General MacArthur's troops tear-gassed them and burned down their shantytown, outraging a sympathetic American public. "What does a democracy do in a war?" asked Roosevelt's former political mentor, Al Smith, in 1933. "It becomes a tyrant, a despot, a real monarch. In the World War, we took our Constitution, wrapped it up and laid it on the shelf and left it there until it was over." The same year Walter Lippmann counseled the president, "The situation is critical, Franklin. You may have no alternative but to assume dictatorial power."[3]

After these turbulent events, Roosevelt began to seriously consider how to organize the American bureaucracy for crisis and war. In 1934–35, he organized the Civilian Conservation Corps, which, in addition to advancing conservation, removed young men from urban areas so they could be organized and taught military discipline. The urban, unemployed young men were transformed from revolutionary rabble to the pillars of a future army. In 1936, President Roosevelt asked Louis Brownlow, one of the administrative geniuses behind the New Deal, if he had the power to manage the economy. Brownlow told him that the Council of National Defense had never ceased to exist, meaning that the president could still commandeer the economy for a national purpose through an advisory committee on defense. In 1937, Assistant Secretary of War Louis Johnson began drafting what later became an Industrial Mobilization Plan. It was a brokered agreement between big business and the military. The plan collapsed because it excluded farmers and unions, and President Roosevelt in 1938–40 became vulnerable to charges that he was surrendering the economy to military and big business.

Through World War II, the United States took for granted that as a superpower it had to reorganize itself for continuous conflict and economic stability even during peacetime. The Soviet Union had been an ally of expedience and served as a counterbalance against imperial Japan. It was recognized by the Roosevelt administration but was held in bad odor by the Department of State. The Soviet Union became a threat because of what it stood for even before its

actions hinted at any real danger. (The repressive actions of the Bol-
sheviks at home were an entirely different matter.) The Soviet Union's
propaganda gave the appearance that it championed economic and
social justice and would solve the problem of widespread unemployment. During the Wilson administration, the International Labor
Organization (ILO) was formed partly in response to this concern. As
Steve Schlossberg, a former director of the Washington Office of the
ILO, noted, "The slogan became poverty anywhere is a threat to
prosperity everywhere." Indeed, poverty was thought to be the seedbed
for communism and nationalist leaders who had their doubts about an
international economy directed by the United States. By the 1990s, the
end of the Cold War meant the West was finally off the hook on the
question of economic justice because it no longer had to counter
Soviet propaganda.

Throughout the Cold War (and before) the Soviet policy was a cautious one. Indeed, it was prepared to negotiate arrangements with the
West at the expense of local communist parties, although it was not
prepared to give up its notions of secure borders, sovereignty, and
socialism. In other words, the Soviets stayed out of the American
sphere of influence where American policy makers hoped to engage
and develop a middle class that would be loyal to American values and
the supposed stability that came from capitalist enterprise. The Soviets had no illusions about their situation compared to American power.
The U.S. had emerged from the war as "top dog," in the words of Paul
Nitze, and it intended to maintain that position without negotiating
with either the Soviets or European Communist parties. Furthermore, Stalin had made clear that the Comintern was an instrument of
Soviet foreign policy, not vice versa.

THE "TOP DOG" BARKS IN EUROPE

Victory over Germany, Japan, Italy, and fascist collaborators such as
Romania and Hungary reconfigured the balance of power in Europe.
The U.S. was the key player in redrawing the map in Europe, and
Under Secretary of State Dean Acheson suggested to Congress in 1947
that the Monroe Doctrine should be extended to any part of the
world the U.S. deemed worthy. A new map of the world was being
drawn, and American leaders wanted to be the principal mapmakers.

But they knew that with isolationism's popularity, the American people would have to be dragged into war "kicking and screaming," as Dean Rusk later put it. FDR's policies were aimed at confronting a dying colonialism through new rules. Thus, American policies did not favor the Dutch's "right" to keep Indonesia as their colony. Similarly the U.S. had no interest in restoring the British Empire to its early twentieth-century grandeur. India, the jewel of the crown, was to be independent of British political control.

Under eighteenth-century ideas borrowed from Newtonian physics, the question during the Cold War was whether, if there was a power vacuum politically in these areas of the world, it would be far better that they fell under American tutelage than struggle for neutrality and independence. If these nations were to fall under the political and economic spell of the United States, the U.S. would need an activist foreign and national security policy that could only emerge from new security institutions. As the economic depression changed the character of American government, so it was that American imperial responsibility brought stunning domestic changes to the character of the American government. Redrawing the world's political map thus required the reorganization of the state and a new posture toward the Soviet Union, America's only potential rival, whose presence in Europe was still substantial.

Yet the Soviet Union was not the threat the U.S. claimed it was. There was arguably no evidence (then or now) that the Soviets intended to attack the Western countries or Germany following Hitler's defeat. But the United States had resolved to "keep the Germans down, the Russians out, and the Americans in," as the diplomatic mantra of the day put it. Two key events proved crucial and led to a rethinking of the U.S. relationship with postwar Germany. One involved the recruitment of Reinhard Gehlen, who oversaw all of Hitler's military-intelligence operations in Eastern Europe and the U.S.S.R. Once Gehlen believed the U.S.–Soviet alliance would collapse, he surrendered himself to the U.S. and persuaded Allen Dulles and others that his hatred of Communism had always been above his commitment to the Nazis. "Washington was in a Cold War mode sooner than most people realize," says journalist Martin Lee. "The Gehlen gambit also belies the prevalent Western notion that aggressive Soviet policies were primarily to blame for triggering the Cold

War." A year before the CIA was officially created (1947), Gehlen recruited thousands of former Gestapo and SS officials who had been under his command as part of the Nazi armed forces. Gehlen was an important planner and intelligence officer for Operation Barbarossa, the invasion of the Soviet Union on June 22, 1941. His intelligence network eventually supplied the North Atlantic Treaty Organization (NATO) with two-thirds of its intelligence on the Warsaw Pact.[4]

The second event was the Berlin Airlift, one of the most celebrated Western narratives of the Cold War. With the blink of an eye, the status of Berlin had changed and so had America's posture toward Moscow. In popular culture a few years before, the Germans were presented as ogres and the Soviets admired. Films such as *Mission to Moscow* praised the Soviets as America's most important ally because they were on the frontline against Nazism. Like an Orwellian novel the picture had changed for the citizenry. A senior CIA analyst who designed the president's daily intelligence brief summed up his 1949 analytic training: "Whatever you do, just remember one thing—the Soviet Union is up to no good!"[5] George Kennan famously labeled this new strategy "containment," and the self-deceptions it generated made the world a much more dangerous place, as did his support of covert operations in Eastern Europe. This is not to take away from Kennan's analysis that the internal contradictions within the Soviet Union would cause it to change if not collapse. It is important to remember that there were those in high places who wanted a preventive war against the Soviet Union virtually immediately after the war with the Germans ended. One such person was President Truman's secretary of the Navy, John Sullivan. Kennan's views were subtler, urging instead a program of covert operations in Eastern Europe and the Soviet Union.

Until mid-1947 a significant number of politicians continued to believe that Germany was the primary enemy even though it lost World War II. The American military government in Germany believed that Germans had to be reeducated and de–Nazified and so did the American people. This point of view was marginalized and considered heretical with the reelection of Truman in 1948. It was already taken for granted that the use of the atomic bomb had won the war for the United States and the West in the Pacific. In Germany the United States was more likely to depend on former Nazis for advice on rebuilding the German army while ensuring that anti–Nazis who had a left-wing past would be tolerated but not encouraged in any efforts that would impede German rearmament. For example, the left's mövement in West Germany against nuclear armaments on the continent of Europe was thought to be either a Soviet plot or naïve. In either case the United States would have none of such thoughts as part of a dominant policy thrust, whether in Germany or elsewhere, such as Great Britain.

THE DAWN OF THE ATOMIC AGE

The immediate effect of the atomic bomb was to pacify (and devastate) Japan, but it was also central to the American policy in Germany. First of all, as Alperovitz and Bird point out, the bomb revolutionized American foreign policy by allowing for unilateral action and reducing the domestic political costs of troop deployment, since, with a nuclear umbrella, fewer American troops would be needed in Europe.

Second, the precedent of the bomb's first use has not only scared others, it has served as an instrument for the transformation of the American state to a perpetual war status in the postwar period. The bomb itself has been more than a piece of ordnance tucked away in a military depot. Nuclear weapons brought a changed social system as a result of their making, testing, and execution. A huge network was required to protect the bomb and its secrets (from the public and most of Congress) and a military-scientific-industrial complex to maintain its viability. The nuclear bomb social system needed missiles, antimissiles, and bombers to deliver nuclear weapons even though nuclear scientists knew, and said as much from the beginning of the nuclear age, that some nuclear weapons could be carried in suitcases. Further, national leaders came to believe that having nuclear weapons was not only prestigious but also necessary to counteract the activities of other nations.

Ironically, in the United States, the buildup of nuclear weapons—eventually adding up to more than 50,000 among the nuclear powers—stimulated a buildup of conventional forces as well. At first, military planners concentrated on ensuring that the Air Force, the Navy, and the Army had the ability to use nuclear weapons in either a tactical or a strategic war. By the 1960s they decided that nuclear weapons alone were an insufficient guarantee of security. General Maxwell Taylor was concerned that overreliance on nuclear weapons prevented the U.S. from protecting its interests throughout the world; only multiple levels of escalation with conventional weapons could accomplish this. Thus a doctrine of "flexible response" was required to make threats credible in ordinary military and diplomatic engagements. This policy was added to massive retaliation, a policy that had lovingly been referred to as a "wargasm." That is to say, there would be no discrimination as to where the bombs and missiles would fall. That line was already crossed in World War II. What was new and indeterminate would be the effect nuclear weapons would have on diplomacy and the preparations underway for the National Security State.

UNRESOLVED DEBATES

After the radioactive dust over Hiroshima and Nagasaki settled, and the borders were redrawn in Europe, another set of issues awaited American leaders. Elites were arguing over what role the military should play in postwar society and how to deal with another potential economic crisis as millions of troops returned home. The Depression still loomed in the nation's consciousness. According to General William Y. Smith, a former deputy chief of staff at NATO, the struggle for control over the economy had not been resolved during World War II. "The military departments constantly pressured the president for more control over the economy," claims Smith. "He met their demands by insuring them important positions in mobilization agencies."[6] In fact, after World War II (1945–1950), the military held all assistant secretary of state positions.

The ostensible purposes of the National Security Act of 1947 were to unify the military and address the intelligence failure at Pearl Harbor but its larger purpose was to resolve the debate over the new "machinery" for controlling domestic and foreign policy. An important part of the act's solution involved articulating a new discourse on "national security" that created an ambiguous nexus between domestic civilian life in peacetime and a permanent military infrastructure. This nexus spawned a new kind of bureaucrat: the civilianized military official and the militarized civilian.

THE NATIONAL SECURITY ACT OF 1947

The act legitimated and articulated an overarching concept of national security, setting in concrete by legislation and executive order the state apparatus that is still in place. Of course concrete takes time to dry and this occurred in stages, but the laying of the foundation was a seminal event in American history. "The United States has attained an unprecedented ascendancy among nations," said one senator during the debates. "Willing or not, we have acquired new and awful obligations. A large part of the responsibility for the future of peace of the world rests with us. The world looks to us for our cooperation, but even more it depends upon our willingness and ability to back cooperation with the military power to preserve the peace."[7]

The first proposals for military unification began to take shape in 1944, and Truman addressed Congress on the idea in December 1945. His plan was largely based on the Army's recommendations. Secretary of the Navy James Forrestal objected to a single large department and recruited his former business colleague Ferdinand Eberstadt to help formulate an alternative. They both favored something along the lines of the British Committee of Imperial Defense, where the secretary of defense would be the principal assistant related to national security. In May of 1946, Secretary of War Robert Patterson and Secretary of the Navy Forrestal wrote to President Truman proposing the establishment of a Council of Common Defense, a National Security Resources Board, a Central Intelligence Agency, and a statutory Joint Chiefs of Staff.[8] According to Anna Nelson, the National Security Council was a product of the controversy between the Truman and the Forrestal–Eberstadt camps: "Rather than the carefully conceived idea its later prominence would indicate, the NSC was a creation of compromise."[9]

After the bill was introduced, most of the debate in Congress, the military establishment, and the executive branch was limited. It centered on unification and issues related to the controversial creation of a new Department of the Air Force, the status of the Marines, and the authority a secretary of defense would have over the services. Congress was not informed about the intelligence collection or the covert action functions of the CIA, aside from a few private conversations Truman had with individual members.[10] Limiting referral of the bill to committees overseeing the armed services further distorted the fact that the bill would have far-reaching ramifications throughout the executive branch. Congress as a whole had delegated its authority to a congressional defense committee system, which served as the champions and goads of the national security institutions to usurp more authority.

The bill went much further than military unification and the creation of a Council on Common Defense along the lines of the Patterson–Forrestal proposal. It set in place the permanent structures of war planning to "provide adequate security measures at all times, rather than only when hostile nations threaten," in the words of Senator Liston Hill (D-AL). "If we are to be prepared at all to meet the speed of future attack, we must prepare in peacetime," he told the Senate during the floor debates. This meant, as Senator Raymond Baldwin (R-CT) pointed out, "a need for wider civilian participation in the national security." He reassured his colleagues that the National Security Council would serve as an advisory panel "on national security matters alone." But even the act's adherents were unable to clarify exactly what this meant. The original language of S. 758 sought to establish the National Security Council to "advise the president with respect to the integration of domestic, foreign, and military policies." Senator Robert Taft (R-OH) successfully insisted that the phrase "and their functions relating to the national security" be added in order to clarify that the NSC would be prohibited from advising on questions not related to national security. Senator Brien McMahon (D-CT) had the foresight to point out that his colleague's second degree amendment would not remedy the problem: "I can think of no policy having to do with our national existence, our government, or our national life that would not come within that language." It was the conservatives who feared an overly broad definition of national security.

THE TRIUMPH OF THE MCMAHON POSITION

Invented terms such as "the drug war" or "the war on terror" offer fungibility to policy planners and hollow reassurances to the public that its interests are being served. These vagaries carry more political currency for the NSS than McMahon ever anticipated. A National Security Council planning document published in 1997 identified ozone depletion, environmental disasters, organized crime in Russia, climate change, and global diseases as threats to national security.

According to one widely circulated intelligence estimate on the threat of disease, "Along with having a large civilian and military presence and wide-ranging interests overseas, the United States will remain at risk from global infectious disease outbreaks." The military, the civilian population and U.S. "equities" abroad are all in danger. "In addition to their impact on the U.S. population," the estimate states, "infectious diseases will add to the social, economic, and political strains in key regions and countries in which the United States has significant interests or may be called upon." Several months later, the White House called AIDS a "security threat of the greatest magnitude."[11] It is unlikely that any of these situations can be ameliorated better through the lens of national security rather than being treated as public health threats (with the emphasis on "public"). Yet we see attempts made to stretch traditional ideas of national security through unproven and dangerous law enforcement assumptions and methods. It is important to note that concerns for infectious diseases, environmental disasters, and starvation are not primary, secondary, or even tertiary concerns for national security managers. Their task as defined by the Cold War and practice is to maintain American dominance as the "superpower." AIDS, starvation, and environmental disasters are *not* organizing instruments to change the behavior of American society. Thus, there may be an environmental disaster in the making as a result of flagrant use of resources, but no national security manager claims that the mores and habits of Americans change.

Throughout the Cold War, framing an issue in national security terms afforded executive agencies wide latitude, which resulted in special exemptions for the secret agencies. With this latitude government officials were able to package and repackage issues that, depending on the popular mood, or that of a new administration, might require a shift in bureaucratic categories on a program budget without changing the original underlying purpose of the policy. This we could refer to as rhetorical manipulation of the public mood without shifting policies.

For example, the U.S. historically believes that the Monroe Doctrine means that Latin America is its "backyard," which from time to time must be policed. Thus the U.S. commitment to the drug war is recategorized as a fight against terrorism. This recategorization allows the U.S. to intervene with great zeal and moral force especially since the official claim is that terrorists in Colombia are involved with an international network of terrorists. The drug war and the supply and demand of drugs are grafted onto an expanded counterinsurgency program meant to assert dominance over the Andean nations. Of course, such policies are not without risk. Sometimes they stem from the fight over drugs and their use as an international currency. It is to be remembered that the American police and military engagement in Vietnam began as an attempt to stop the sale and export of drugs that may or may not have had a relationship with the Trotskyists of Indochina after World War II.

18   From the early days of the CIA and its predecessor, the OSS, drugs were used by secret agencies as an important means of enticing criminal gangs to support American government policies, especially those that began from the premise of patriotic anticommunism. Drug dealers received "get out of jail free" cards if they successfully claimed that they were involved in their activities either as assets for the CIA or direct agents. It is clear that there are profound effects from antidrug policies that are in fact based on the use of drugs for political purposes. The Indochina war ended with thousands of American soldiers exposed to lifelong physical damage because of their use of drugs while the CIA was implicated in the use of drugs as an instrument of control and strategy in the anticommunist war in Asia.

Immigration offers another example of how recategorization has reframed an issue in terms of national security. Today the military is playing an ever-increasing and dangerous role in border enforcement. The precedent for this was the use of the Union military after the Civil War (until 1877) as a means of confronting guerrilla war waged against freed slaves by former Confederate soldiers. The expanded involvement of the military and the intelligence agencies in law enforcement has stretched the limits of existing posse comitatus laws that date back to the Civil War, with serious implications for protection of individual rights and basic civil liberties.

OPERATIONAL MODALITIES OF
THE NATIONAL SECURITY STATE

The policies falling under the guise of national security have become as vast as Senator McMahon predicted. These policies have given rise to four mutually reinforcing characteristics which form the template of the NSS: (1) organizing for war and limited war; (2) control of the public sphere; (3) limiting or undermining individual rights; and (4) the concentration of authority. These characteristics have a permanence that survived the occasional congressional scrutiny, numerous media scandals, and most notably the end of the Cold War. One reason for this resiliency is the *integration of domestic and foreign policy*, rewarding an economic dependence on the war system. As shown below, organizing for war was part of maintaining the military-industrial complex. Partnerships between unions and anticommunists undermined the independence of civil society, and corporate America cooperated with a federal desire to invade consumer privacy. All of these efforts served the NSS by securing the economy for national security purposes and eroding the distinctions between peace and war.

Organizing for war, Cold War, and limited war

Distinctions between war and peace in terms of planning and preparation for war and conflict disappeared in various ways. This multi-layered policy includes instructions for how to build, use, and perpetuate nuclear weapons, fight limited wars, and maintain a permanent economic infrastructure for national security purposes. The military industrial complex created a system whose purpose for war and its preparation overwhelmed advocates for disarmament. In 1991 Greg Bischak wrote, "the forty-five year legacy of the Cold War leaves in place a formidable array of military institutions which block the way to disarmament and an alternative framework for international security," not the least of which was President Reagan's $2.25 trillion defense buildup in the 1980s.[12] As a result of campaign promises made by George W. Bush in his 2000 presidential campaign and September 11, the national security and internal security budgets are virtually boundless, especially given the inability of the Democratic Party and many advocacy groups to challenge the assumptions and purposes of the budget. It is foolish to believe that unlimited defense and security expenditures do not have negative effects on the civilian economy.

However, the relationship between the economy and national security is a complex one. Economic growth under President Clinton and budget constraints meant that military spending accounted for a

19

diminishing share of the gross domestic product and therefore had a decreasing share of the labor force. In 1987 U.S. defense spending was at a post–Vietnam War high of 7.2 percent of GDP. By 1996 this figure was only 4.6 percent, and in 1998 the Department of Labor estimated it would remain there until about 2006.[13] Ironically, this situation enabled the military to protect its budgets remarkably well and ask for larger defense budgets unrelated to strategic needs. This shadow economy continues to impose its costs on social programs, whose budgets are squeezed by military expenditures.

Nuclear weapons were one of the less visible and more costly components of the shadow economy. Stephen I. Schwartz's Nuclear Weapons Cost Study Project determined that nuclear weapons have cost $5.5 trillion since 1940. His committee's calculations include costs of developing, fielding, and maintaining the nuclear arsenal and defending against attack. At one point the Federal Reserve maintained more than $2 trillion in currency to be used after a nuclear war. Literally hundreds of millions of pages pertaining to the nuclear network are still classified.[14] These costs seem reasonable if one believes nuclear weapons prevented World War III. This dubious assertion has proved to be less than compelling. As former Strategic Air Command (SAC) Commander General George Lee Butler has stated on a number of public occasions, deterrence does not deserve credit for preventing world war. "We were faced with an array of circumstances that were left over from a forty-year buildup of systems and beliefs that, in many respects, had been just as murderous as a real war." War was not avoided, says General Butler. "In a sense, the Cold War was a war in all its aspects."[15] The total destructive capability of nuclear weapons rendered them impractical for intervention and small conflicts, but intermediate forms of violence were widely employed as a substitute.

Limited war meant paramilitary wars, presumed "police actions," low-intensity conflicts, and covert activities. Many of these were carried out under the CIA's so-called "fifth function," outlined in the National Security Act, authorizing it to "perform such other functions and duties related to intelligence affecting the national security as the National Security Council may from time to time direct." Clark Clifford, the act's principal drafter, made the language to authorize covert operations deliberately vague. "We did not mention them by name because we felt it would be injurious to our national interest to advertise the fact that we might engage in such activities," which were supposed to be unusual but limited in scope. In retrospect, he admits that this was clearly a bad idea. "Over the years, covert activities became so numerous and widespread that, in effect, they became a *self-sustaining* part of American foreign operations. The CIA became a government within a government, which could evade oversight of its activities by drawing the cloak of secrecy around itself."[16]

The lawlessness of the covert apparatus involved bombing Cambodia in 1969 and mining Nicaraguan harbors in 1984 when the U.S. was officially at peace with those countries, supporting death squad governments in El Salvador and Guatemala, and financing religious extremists in Afghanistan simply because they professed a hatred for the Soviet Union. We are far from escaping the terrible legacy of these interventions. The Afghan rebels' hatred for Moscow, for example, was not commensurate with a love for democracy in any sense. The most stridently anti–American rebels ironically received approximately half of the weapons provided by the CIA. Two things about this aid must be mentioned. First, it began not with the Soviet invasion but a full six months beforehand when President Carter signed a directive to subvert the regime in Kabul. His national security advisor, Zbigniew Brzezinski, has bragged that he drafted a memo explaining that this covert operation would provoke Soviet intervention—and that this was in fact a desirable idea.[17] Second, the aid ended not when the Communist government collapsed but when the U.S. decided it was no longer necessary to punish the Soviets. In dollar terms, the entire operation cost American taxpayers an astounding $3 billion through the course of the 1980s. The extent of the "blowback" (when a covert operation or an intelligence asset turns against its initiator) first became evident not on September 11, but when Sheikh Omar Abdul-Rahman, the architect of the first World Trade Center bombing, entered the U.S. in 1990 on a visa obtained from an undercover CIA agent.[18]

The present Bush administration's war against terrorists, zealots, or those who are thought to be enemies of the United States combines several components from the past. Whereas before they were kept separate from the American population, under the new regime this is not thought to be necessary. Thus, covert operations during the Cold War were kept out of sight. Under the current Bush administration they are combined with military assistance and military police intervention. In fact, the activity is trumpeted. During the Cold War no administration cared to speak to the public as if American policies were predicated on wars without end. In the Bush administration they are articulated, applauded, and used as an instrument of manipulation of the public in order to obtain legitimacy and support from the populace.

Control of the public sphere

A second trait of the national security apparatus is that its managers seek to fill public space and undermine the autonomy and therefore the critical judgment of the independent citizen—especially where he might join together with other citizens. Mobilization of this nature was to be kept in the hands of governments, with the media playing a supporting role. The means of mobilizing the public for a stated threat of Soviet invasion, an imagined threat of domestic subversion, or an actual threat of terrorism are the same. The public can also be mobilized for passivity. This has been accomplished through the co-optation of labor unions, universities, and the media. Both strategies construct a false consensus and remain in use as tools for deceiving those on the outside and maintaining loyalty on the inside whether the threats are real or imagined.

Loyalty and security oaths are one form of mobilizing for passivity. Throughout American society during the Cold War, university professors, schoolteachers, union officials, and Boy Scouts were all required to sign a loyalty oath. Such oaths were enforced administratively and through the courts. These practices were inspired by and related to loyalty programs throughout the federal government that sought to fend off dissenting voices and keep public officials in line. "The concept of loyalty necessarily involved the notion of secrecy," writes Daniel Patrick Moynihan. "Disloyal employees revealed secrets; loyal employees would not. In such a setting apprehension rose, and so did the dimension of secrecy."[19] President Truman's Executive Order 9835 established the Federal Employee Loyalty Program in March 1947, creating a process and an organization for reviewing the "loyalty" of civil servants in all sectors of the government. In April 1953, President Eisenhower issued Executive Order 10450, detailing more elaborate security requirements for government employment, stating:

The head of each department and agency of the government shall be responsible for establishing and maintaining within his department or agency an effective program to insure that the employment and retention in employment of any civilian officer or employee within the department or agency is clearly consistent with the interest of national security.

As Senator Moynihan pointed out, this personnel security is basically still in place today and was extended under Clinton. And we argue in the chapter on Congress, oaths remain an important mechanism of control in Congress. Half a century after the McCarthy witch hunts, members fear both criminal punishments under national security laws and political isolation through ethics rules protective of secrecy.

A second form of mobilization occurs through the co-optation of key elements of civil society, such as universities and labor unions. Reinhold Niebuhr, the theologian of American engagement in the Cold War, claimed that a partnership between labor and capital was possible if labor had a role in the national security system. With millions of soldiers reentering the workforce and a subsequent series of strikes from 1945 to 1947, keeping this sector pacified was essential. According to Steve Schlossberg, the former general counsel for the United Auto Workers, unions cut a series of deals with the federal government in exchange for their unswerving criticism of communism and their support for, as well as junior associate decision power in, international activities.

Congress filled in the details of this compromise through several important pieces of legislation, starting with the Employment Act of 1946. This law that was first introduced as a full employment bill was changed to a "maximum employment" proposal. "In a word, the Employment Act was to be consistent with the needs of an economic system that required unemployment."[20] The real operators of the Employment Act can best be understood in the context of the Taft–Hartley Act of 1947, which had several important consequences. It placed explicit limits on organizing and collective bargaining. It prohibited communists from holding officer positions in unions, universities, or schools. It formalized the right of workers to not participate in union activity, outlawed the closed shop, and subjected the union shop to strict limitations. Finally, it prohibited various unfair labor practices, such as secondary strikes and jurisdictional boycotts. In return, unionized workers, for example in the electric, communications, steel, and machinist sectors, enjoyed financial stability in the military-industrial complex.

The unions' arrangement with the government lasted for some time, but in the war on terrorism the government has had the upper hand. After September 11, George W. Bush undermined labor as an element of civil society and to advance his own version of government interventionism in the economy. In the name of national security, Bush issued an executive order limiting the rights of Northwest Airline employees' rights to strike. In another action, United Airlines' mechanics were told that unless they agreed to the company's concessions—rather than launch the strike they had overwhelmingly voted for—the administration would withhold a $1.8 billion bailout. In another instance, union officials from the International Longshore and Warehouse Union (ILWU) claim that the Bush administration threatened to invoke the rarely used Taft–Hartley Act when the union was considering a strike in 2002; the action would have ordered the longshoremen back to work for 90 days. The administration even considered using Navy personnel to replace striking longshoremen.[21] In each case, any disruption to the economy, even if it served the interests of workers, was deemed a threat to national security. Control over the economy, foreign policy, and social control fused into one overarching notion of national security.

Strategies of legal and social control coincided with the use of lying and deception as an acceptable governing strategy. Then as now, the government proceeds in several stages. The first stage involves setting policy goals, which may or may not be related to the justification offered to the public, although it may serve the interests of a particular class. The second stage involves manufacturing a pretext for pursuing those goals. The pretext may be based on the reality of an external event or indeed may be totally falsified, or it may be somewhere in between. The final stage involves legitimation through the standard structures of constitutional government, which forms part of the appeal to the public for support. Beyond that mode of appeal is direct manipulation of the public through propaganda, predicated on the acceptance of government officials as superior authorities on matters of fact whose task is thought to be the common welfare of society. Such notions, internalized in people's understanding through ritual and propaganda, have rendered the process of declaring war irrelevant. The citizenry is taught that since there is a state of continuous war the executive does not require a declaration of war. It would be illogical.

The paradox of the system is the capacity for self-deception both within the bureaucracy and among the citizens. The process congeals into a conventional myth taught and retaught as the truth matters less and less. In the process Congress relinquishes power to the national security managers and the executive, allowing the bureaucracy to fight small wars for ambiguous reasons; the role of Congress becomes ornamental.

Limiting or undermining individual rights

A third common thread in the National Security State's practices is the subordination of civil liberties to state objectives. Through the NSS, the wishes of its managers have become routinized by the courts and formalized by Congress and administrative regulations. The war on immigrants today (in the name of fighting terrorism) resembles the war on communism. In the name of fighting communism, the federal government conducted dangerous experiments on human subjects, and intelligence agencies undertook extraordinary domestic spying programs on citizens engaged in First Amendment activities.

Domestic spying programs included surveillance of Vietnam War protesters, activists on Central American policy, key civil rights figures, and AIDS awareness leaders. During the Cold War, the CIA spied on the Vietnam antiwar movement with Operation CHAOS, the FBI sabotaged various political organizations with COINTEL-PRO, and the NSA indulged in Operation MINARET. Besides spying on U.S. citizens by the armed forces and local police departments, CHAOS alone produced files on over 300,000 individuals. More recent intelligence collection activities have been rooted in immigration laws permitting the use of secret evidence against detainees who are unable to fairly counter the charges against themselves. This is based on an expansion of "sources and methods" as a means of avoiding public examination of the facts. The ambiguous but seemingly hallowed phrase found in national security laws becomes a convenient dodge that masks how information is found, what is paid for the information, what information has to be given up, and how the source is to be repaid. Technical intelligence affords another problem and possibility, for it is reflective of the power of the National Security State to organize scientific and engineering elites to undertake closed studies of the earth.

Contrary to popular belief, the establishment of new oversight committees in Congress in the 1970s did little to curb domestic spying. In the 1980s the federal government continued to target organizations engaged in First Amendment activities, such as the Center for Defense Information, Medical Aid for El Salvador, Lawyers Committee on Human Rights, the Washington Office on Latin America, and numerous other organizations critical of President Reagan's policies in Latin America. The Committee in Solidarity With the People of El Salvador (CISPES) was one such target. CISPES's activities included "fund-raising and legislative campaigns, educational and outreach programs, and mass mobilizations." One declassified document issued in New Orleans declared: "It is imperative at this time to formulate some plan of attack against CISPES and specifically, against individuals . . . who defiantly display their contempt for the U.S. government by making speeches and propagandizing their cause."[22] Then in the early 1990s, the spying continued when the FBI opened an active file on the AIDS awareness organization ACT-UP. The bureau claimed it was concerned that the group would commit violent acts, even though it never had. Activists in the organization insist the FBI attempted to infiltrate the organization.[23]

Even before September 11 and the Patriot Act, the federal government sought an expansion of its powers, with the law often following enforcement practices already in use. The Communications Assistance for Law Enforcement Act of 1994 required telecommunications companies to keep their lines wiretap-friendly. This law allowed one out of every 100 phones in "high crime areas" to be monitored. The Intelligence Authorization Act for fiscal year 1999 enabled prosecutors to target persons instead of locations. The Immigration in the National Interest Act of 1995 generated nine entirely new categories of offenses for which electronic surveillance is permitted. Then even if the federal government did not obtain evidence legally, the so-called Antiterrorism and Effective Death Penalty Act of 1996 permitted illegally obtained evidence to be used in court in various circumstances. These and other capital punishment statues were signed into law by a Democratic president who had been elected with substantial support from the civil rights community.[24]

The Patriot Act set up a narrow framework for civil liberties and an infinitely expansive framework for security and when necessary the disappearance of civil liberties. Individuals invariably are held to be a nuisance compared to the needs of the state. The provisions of the Patriot Act, from presidential authority to use military tribunals against aliens and immigrants, holding detainees incommunicado without benefit of legal counsel, to wiretapping, secret judicial proceedings, freezing of corporate and nonprofit funds, increased surveillance on American citizens, encouragement of informing and spying on neighbors, and rifling through the records of student and faculty staffs without cause, is a recipe for a poisonous political stew that will be hard to swallow, but harder to pass from the body of our nation. It is important to reiterate that the predicate for the Patriot Act was laid before September 11. Now that the act is in place, its purposes are being mimicked in local regulations throughout the country: New York City loosened restrictions on surveillance of political groups, and peace activists in Denver and Washington, D.C., filed suits against police departments for spying on them. In response, the Justice Department advanced legislation that would support loosening restrictions on spying by local police.[25]

Electronic surveillance is even more prevalent and more difficult to detect. Federal surveillance of Internet traffic today is sweeping and was in place well before the attacks on the World Trade Center. This form of domestic spying poses one of the most significant threats to privacy and individual rights today. By installing surveillance tools such as Carnivore at Internet service providers, the FBI has broad access to subscriber e-mails, not just those who are the target of a particular criminal investigation. These activities were already routine even in the absence of guidelines under the Electronic Communications Privacy Act of 1986 and other statutes.

Between 1990 and 2000, the number of intercept applications increased 36 percent. The most common target was a portable electronic device, such as a cell phone. In the small minority of cases where the government encountered encryption, it was always able to circumvent it. A vast majority of these wiretaps were justified for drug-related investigations.[26] According to the U.S. Department of Justice and organizations such as the Electronic Privacy Information Center, there was a more than fourfold increase in Foreign Intelligence Surveillance Act Orders between 1979 and 1999. Most astounding is that for each federal or state electronic intercept, an average of 1,775 innocent conversations are overheard. A total of 2.2 million conversations were intercepted in 1996 alone. Hardly any of this eavesdropping is carried out to investigate acts of terrorism, bombings, or the categories of activities that are used to justify the expansion of wiretap and surveillance authority to the public. The expanding use of video spying further tears at the cloak of privacy.

The invasion on individual rights has also involved government scientists conducting radiation experiments on unwitting subjects in the name of nuclear technology. During the Cold War, citizens were used as involuntary guinea pigs for national security research. In a display of courage rare for a cabinet official, Secretary Hazel O'Leary instructed the Department of Energy's Office of Human Radiation Experiments to make public more than 300 experiments involving radiation testing on humans during the Cold War. Many of the experiments were not conducted in a clinical setting, and some deliberately released radioactive matter into the environment or the food chain. One experiment at Vanderbilt University, for example, injected eighty-six newborn babies with chromium-50 to measure the reaction of their blood to the radioactive material. For declining to play by the rules of the National Security State's game, Secretary O'Leary was marginalized by senior defense officials, and high-ranking career Department of Energy officials who shared her vision were stripped of their security clearances. "Those in the hierarchy looked down on people who deserved the truth," she said later. "I tried to change a culture that had become part of DOE." Eventually she was pushed out of the Clinton administration and investigated by Congress for overspending her travel budget. In the end, the special counselor appointed to the investigation exonerated her.

In 1994 Congressman Conyers chaired hearings that revealed that the radiation experiments disclosed by the Department of Energy were only half the story. The Army and Navy used blistering agents on sixty thousand subjects, the Naval Research Laboratory exposed three thousand subjects to mustard gas, and Army Chemical Corps tests with nerve agents and psychochemicals on 7,120 subjects continued in the 1970s. The Army carried out biological warfare tests with radioactive compounds on 239 American cities between 1949 and 1969; Conyers's hometown of Detroit had been doused with zinc cadmium sulfide by airplanes in 1958.[27]

The terrible illnesses suffered by Gulf War veterans point to continuing experimentation, albeit through the prosecution of war. The cause of terrible illnesses suffered by Gulf War veterans has yet to be determined, but it is now clear that depleted uranium and other dangerous substances whose hazards were unknown to tens of thousands of exposed American troops in Iraq in 1991 were used liberally. The most recent estimates indicate that more than a quarter of all of those who served in the Gulf War have been ill—a postwar illness ratio far in excess of the Vietnam War, the Korean War, or even World War II.[28]

Neither Congress nor the courts has been very successful in limiting encroachments on individual rights or holding the National Security State accountable.[29] By failing to curb the excesses of the National Security State, the courts revalidated an undemocratic judicial and executive architecture. This helped build a government obsessed with secrecy, and judges were fearful of holding government agencies to account because of national security and reasons of state. Courts have malfunctioned in key cases when misconduct was discovered. This occurred when Director of Central Intelligence Richard Helms was tried for perjury, and in the investigations into the Letelier-Moffitt assassination in Washington, D.C. The courts' use of secret proceedings in deportation cases and the Foreign Intelligence Surveillance Act (FISA) make a mockery of the adversarial process supposedly enshrined in our judicial system. After passage of the Patriot Act, the FBI gave false information to judges on dozens of occasions in order to obtain wiretap authority.[30] These constitutional perversions—recent by historical standards—raise an important question about whether the courts have engaged in the project of undercutting *Marbury v. Madison*, shortchanging their role in our legal system by allowing too many people and too many cases to slip out the national security window.

Concentration of authority

Many activities, including human experimentation and domestic spying programs, are possible because of a system of secrecy that is far more prevalent than people realize. The total of all classification actions reported for fiscal year 1999 increased by 10 percent, to 8,038,592—that is before September 11, when the Cold War had been over for a decade. The CIA accounted for 44 percent of all classification decisions but they were spread across other agencies: the Department of Defense accounted for 27 percent, the National Reconnaisance Office (NRO) 24 percent, the Department of Justice 2 percent, the Department of State 2 percent, and all others 1 percent.[31] This system of secrecy complements and makes possible decision-making procedures that tend to be centralized rather than shared. Resources for implementing these decisions are fenced off from scrutiny in secret budgets. As we have said, the American citizenry, which is constantly told that it is simultaneously victim and unbeatable warrior, may even require that immoral and illegal acts be kept from them. Indeed, congressional representatives often assiduously avoid finding out what the CIA and other intelligence agencies are doing. That is to say, they are prepared to vote secret budgets but not know what is in the budgets on the grounds that they might leak the secrets, have to exercise qualms on moral grounds, or fear thinking they might be in violation of the Nuremberg tribunal standards.

In the post–September 11 period it is taken for granted that the national security bureaucracies must intertwine themselves with the most nefarious elements as American administrations curry favor with violators of basic human rights. During the Cold War period, and especially as a result of President Carter's concern with human rights, the U.S. learned to lecture leaders of other nations about human rights. Such lectures did help some victims, but the net effect has been marginal. Why?

National security budgets were rationalized in terms of threats but actually had more to do with propping up corrupt dictators, buying off pro–American leaders through foreign aid, and military assistance. But why would the government bother executing such a foreign and national security policy? We find four reasons: Security and foreign policy activities have little scrutiny of the kind that shifts policy; bureaucracies replicate and expand on the basis of what the dominant trends are in the executive; foreign and security policy—if it were to be otherwise—would have to reflect different social forces than are now dominant; finally, the corrupt may be more reliable then the "virtuous government." These four reasons fit well with the interests of private corporations. For example, in the pursuit of oil in the Middle East there is a direct and continuing linkage between stable profits and what national security managers and politicians conclude is the national interest. The shroud of secrecy around these budgets keeps the public in the dark and encourages Congress to accept the premise that the executive branch knows best and no significant changes should occur in the purpose of the national security apparatus and its linkages to big business. The CIA established its own businesses (proprietaries) but also made available secret information to certain privileged corporations, especially in the energy industry.[32]

Secrecy also allows rogue bureaucrats at the middle level to operate in complex and contradictory ways. They may believe they are acting within an acceptable framework of policy. This was certainly the case in Iran–Contra. Regardless, secrecy facilitates the centralization of authority at high levels. As Peter Raven-Hansen shows in this book, much of the NSS's expanded authority comes from executive orders, presidential decision directives, and far-reaching administrative regulations instead of through public laws. These procedures build a bureaucracy protected from public and serious congressional supervision. Criminal behavior under the color of executive orders is increased domestically and abroad.

Equipped with this type of authority, national security managers can designate what constitutes a threat (a small Central American country of 2.5 million people, or perhaps an outbreak of disease in Africa) without much controversy. They also construct new forms of war that blur the distinction between acts of war and total war. Often this is accomplished by attaching an unequivocal sense of urgency to its actions, as was the case with the passage of the Helms–Burton Act in 1996 and the Patriot Act in 2001. "The bulk of Congress accepts the principle of 'emergency'," writes Raskin, "because its members have come to believe that they are constituted authority, holding legitimacy not through the people or an eighteenth-century Constitution, but through their identification with established institutions of which the president is the recognized leader and arbiter."[33] This was part of the strategy for laying out *post hoc* pretexts in Grenada in 1983, Panama in 1989, the Persian Gulf in 1990, and Sudan in 1998.

The concentration of authority works at odds with the basic principles of checks and balances, and this would not be possible without pretexts and propaganda that undermine Congress and other constitutional checks. The Gulf of Tonkin incident, the Gulf War of 1991, the Iraq War of 2003, and the bombing of Sudan in 1998 all illustrate how Congress has shortchanged its role on key constitutional questions. These events also show how the executive branch feels it is empowered to act on its own authority and is able to do so through deception. In such events (both before and after passage of the War Powers Act), the public sphere was not a place where the decision to go to war was debated. Instead, it was a space that government officials filled with propaganda in order to build support for grave decisions that had already been made and policies already being implemented.

The Gulf of Tonkin incident took place in 1964, when a U.S. Navy spy ship cruised into North Vietnamese waters shortly after a South Vietnamese raid on the North's shores on July 30 and 31. The first mission generated no response, but a second one provoked a torpedo attack on August 2. A report of the incident was prepared in Washington but it was released in Hawaii in order to give the impression of spontaneity.[34] During a massive storm, yet another patrol was sent into the Gulf and radioed back that it had been attacked on August 4. In the days that followed, President Johnson's team persuaded Congress to pass the Gulf of Tonkin Resolution, which mirrored language used to justify military adventures in Formosa in 1955, the Middle East in 1957, and Cuba in 1962. The resolution expressed support for the president to "take all necessary measures to repel any armed attack against the forces of the United States and to prevent further aggression." Metaphorically, this resolution was carried in President Johnson's back pocket for at least six months prior to the Tonkin events.

Congress was told not even half the story about U.S. incursions in Southeast Asia. As it had done in the early 1960s and later, the Pentagon had long been planning and carrying out covert actions involving

32

sabotage and psychological operations to provide "maximum pressure with minimum risk."[35] The July 30–31 raid by the South Vietnamese had really been part of a CIA directed "34A" destabilization campaign. Nor was Congress informed that the commander of the August 4 mission had cabled the Pentagon explaining that it was probably never attacked. Moreover, Senator William Fulbright, chair of the Foreign Relations Committee, was misled by Dean Rusk (and probably by the president himself) to believe that the president would not use the vast power implied in the resolution without consultation.[36] How the Senate did not think Johnson would have acted without consultation was a total misreading of Johnson as a leader. Furthermore, he was merely doing what previous presidents had done!

The ritual already established a generation earlier, it took little effort for the first Bush administration to drum up support in 1990 for war in the Persian Gulf. There was one irony. Saddam Hussein was supported by the U.S. against Iran for more than a decade. The new self-deception centered on convincing the American public that the military option was the only option, and persuading Saudi Arabia that it was threatened with invasion by Iraq. Saudi officials considered Secretary of Defense Dick Cheney's assessment of the threat to their country dubious but eventually agreed to let hundreds of thousands of U.S. troops set up camp. A Soviet satellite took high-resolution reconnaissance photos on September 11, 1990, but it wasn't until months later that military analysts admitted that the Pentagon exaggerated Iraq's numbers, a fact reconfirmed by later U.S. Landsat photos.[37] Americans were easily sold on the virtue of defending their client state, but pleas to defend the "American way of life" and the comparison of Saddam Hussein to Hitler were insufficient to mobilize them in support of an offensive war against Iraq.

A briefing organized by the Congressional Human Rights Caucus helped to escalate war hysteria by inviting witnesses who described Iraqis removing babies from incubators in hospitals in Kuwait. The media swarmed on the story, and President Bush repeated the horrors for the public six times in a period of five weeks. The story turned out to be entirely fabricated, but the lies went unpunished because the witnesses were not under oath and the media was too embarrassed; the *New York Times* did not retract the story until February 28, 1991, after the end of the Iraqi occupation. The witnesses included the daughter of the Kuwaiti ambassador and a vice president of the World Bank, who were coached by Hill & Knowlton, one of the top public relations firms.[38] It wasn't until the nuclear issue was put on the agenda (representing a retreat from Secretary of State Baker's inadvertently honest statement: "We seek a region . . . in which energy supplies flow freely") that the administration actually felt it had sufficient popular backing to proceed with the military option.[39]

Once the war was underway, the Bush administration churned out more fabulous stories in which every part of the national security apparatus was complicit. President Bush claimed the Patriot Missile had shot down 41 out of the 42 Scud missiles fired by Iraq, and television reporters were fed arcade game-style footage of bombs serving up direct hits on their targets. Congressional investigations after the war revealed the Patriot may not have accomplished more than one decisive interception. Further, the efficiency of high-tech bombers had been exaggerated as well. The F-117 Stealth fighter jet, for example, succeeded in only 40 percent of its missions—not the 80 percent claimed by the Department of Defense.[40] The deception about the troop buildup was needed to win Arab support, the fabrications about Iraqi atrocities helped mobilize Americans in favor of expanding the mission, and the disinformation on "smart weapons" reassured the country that technology was able to minimize the risk to American soldiers and the possibility of "collateral damage" to civilians.

The war against Iraq in 2003 rested on equally appalling deceptions and slender foundations of untruths that propped up preordained policy objectives. We know they were preordained because the president made the decision to go to war and directed the Pentagon to begin planning for it at about the same time—in the fall of 2002—that he conceded, "I don't have the evidence at this point" to attack Iraq.[41] George W. Bush claimed to have evidence of a clear link between al-Qaeda and Saddam Hussein. He insisted a centrifuge found by inspectors was part of a nuclear program—a claim that his own intelligence agencies were deeply divided over.[42] He also infamously informed the public during his State of the Union that Iraq had tried to obtain uranium from Niger even though a U.S. government inquiry led by Ambassador Joseph Wilson had previously concluded the evidence was phony. The administration in fact sought to conceal information about the 31 countries where Iraq's weapons of mass destruction had really come from. It sought redactions from Iraq's weapons inspection document submitted to the United Nations, which named 31 countries including the U.S. Secretary of Defense Rumsfeld claimed on CNN that he cautioned Saddam Hussein about chemical weapons during a meeting with him in 1983. State Department transcripts of the meeting and other declassified documents reveal, however, that he had never taken the moral high ground on Weapons of Mass Destruction in Iraq.[43] Finally, the American people had been reassured that troops would be welcomed by jubilant crowds, but after the invasion disgruntled Iraqis began waging a daily war of attrition against troops they deemed as an outside occupying force that addressed few of their daily needs and "installed" democracy far too slowly. Evidence later emerged challenging virtually all of the administration's justifications for going to war.

In both Iraq and Vietnam, the executive branch felt compelled to use propaganda and deception to mobilize public opinion after the decision to intervene had already been made. The narrow sets of military facts by themselves were insufficient to generate public support. A cycle of deception, self-deception, and very poor information resulted in a policy fog. In both cases, the executive branch attempted to validate its actions through a fig leaf of constitutional legitimacy with the cooperation of a passive Congress.

A particularly small fig leaf was used in the U.S. cruise missile strikes against Sudan on August 20, 1998, which hit the Shifa Pharmaceutical factory in Khartoum. Secretary of State Madeleine Albright and National Security Advisor Sandy Berger explained at a White House press conference that day that the attacks were ordered in retaliation for the bombing of U.S. embassies in Kenya and Tanzania, and to respond to "imminent" terrorist threats. "The United States will act unilaterally when we are doing something in the defense of our national interests," declared Albright, "and this was done in self-defense." Like the Iraq interventions, the attacks were justified to protect against weapons of mass destruction (in this case, chemical weapons).

The decision to attack was made by the "Principals Committee," a tightly knit group in the White House including Albright, Berger, Director of Central Intelligence George Tenet, Secretary of Defense Bill Cohen, Chairman of the Joint Chiefs of Staff Henry Shelton, the president and the vice president. "One of the things that was indispensable to this operation was secrecy," said Berger. The four top members of the congressional leadership (or in some cases their staff) were notified *after* the attack had been ordered, which the White House justified by noting that the president retained the logistical capacity to stop the reprisal attack for several hours. But once a reprisal, preventive war, or incursion is underway, few will challenge the executive decision and action.

Administration officials repeatedly claimed the Sudan facility was producing key precursor chemicals for VX nerve gas and described it as a secretive military-industrial site with close ties to Osama bin Laden, the wealthy Saudi exile who had yet to reach worldwide celebrity. "This facility is located within a secured chemical plant," said a fact sheet distributed to the House of Representatives by the White House. "Bin Laden has extensive ties to the Sudanese government and its industrial sector. And we are confident this Sudanese government-controlled facility is involved in the production of chemical weapons agents."

"Most of the intelligence people I have talked to in the last week," said Berger, "have indicated that they have never seen anything quite like this, in the sense of the amount of information that mutually corroborated itself and pointed in this direction." Shelton backed up this view in a press briefing at the Pentagon: "The intelligence community is confident that this facility is involved in the production of chemical weapons agents, including precursor chemicals for the deadly V-series of nerve agents like, for example, VX. We also know that bin Laden has extensive ties to the Sudanese government, which controls this facility."

In the weeks that followed the attack, the administration's key assertions about Shifa were contradicted. The director of central intelligence had been involved in the planning but apparently either discounted or ignored the findings of the CIA's own analysts, who had concluded that the alleged links between the Sudanese government and terrorism were fabricated by unreliable sources. The facility was not heavily guarded and was manufacturing a large share—perhaps as much as 50 percent—of Sudan's medicine, a fact the CIA failed to mention to senior Pentagon officials. The precursor chemical, EMPTA, cited as a justification for the attack, was even being manufactured and sold at the time by a company in Milwaukee.[44] The U.S. eventually had to cave in to a lawsuit, which was ironically brought by a former Clinton appointee, on behalf of the owner of the Shifa factory to unfreeze his assets and clear his name of any association with terrorists. Although the Clinton administration claimed the suit would jeopardize "sources and methods" of the intelligence agencies in court, attorneys refuted the government's key evidence, including the claim that soil samples near the factory showed residue of substances used in chemical weapons.[45] Sources and methods were used once again to avoid cross-examination and public discussion of evidence.

After the attack, Sudan's ambassador wrote to Congress: "To use an act of terrorism against unsuspecting and innocent people in the name of combating terrorism is highly contradictory. To precipitate sovereign action, moreover, military action, based on supposition or allegation, violates the most basic principles of American law, the United Nations treaties, and a humane sense of fairness."[46] The secretive and elitist nature of the decision-making process, concentrating authority in the Principals Committee, excluded officials better-informed about the quality of the evidence. But the important fact is that the mode of decision-making was permissible in the first place, encouraged by the National Security State's secrecy system and constrained only by the political judgments of those involved. In the Shifa attack, those judgments were influenced by two important factors. One was the propaganda against Sudan and Muslims in general that preceded the attacks, and the second was the ability of technology, as in the Gulf War, to mitigate the risk to U.S. troops. The first builds a domestic consensus and the other marginalizes the need for it, but both ensure that the democratic process is merely a footnote to war operations. (Whether Bill Clinton would have followed a different course had he not been overwhelmed with his impeachment problem is not clear.) The second factor was the bureaucratic impulse to use the military in combat or quasi-combat situations as a means of justifying their expense.

The Sudan episode, like the 2003 war on Iraq, suggests that American intelligence is very poor, since essential details about the Shifa plant and information about Osama bin Laden's links to it were apparently incorrect. Alternatively, intelligence agencies did have vital information correct but policy makers ignored it for their own purposes.

Either way, there is little reason to believe that expanding covert operations will improve with greatly increased budgets for covert operations, even if the U.S. cooperates more with the Israeli, British, or Pakistani intelligence agencies. And most importantly, such operations will do little in the end to prevent attacks like those of September 11, as the CIA itself conceded before the invasion of Iraq.[47]

The attack on September 11 meant that American policy makers and leaders faced a new and extraordinary challenge: no government, whatever its composition, could do "nothing." The attacks required a new answer, but the "natural" answer flowed from the assumptions of the National Security State. This meant organizing the foreign policy of the United States so that other nations will accept or join a new crusade, with the stirring call to arms of "either you are with us, or you are against us." This approach meant greatly increasing the defense and national security budget by 13 percent a year every year for the foreseeable future. The attack on the U.S. could have been presented as the work of madmen who must be captured. The war could thus have stayed in the legal category of the invasion of Panama, where one man, Noriega, was designated the enemy. However, the response to the September 11 attacks also meant identifying al-Qaeda and Afghanistan as horrific enemies who served a useful purpose in justifying the curtailment of civil liberties and increases in the national security budget. Paradoxically, the state did not declare war on Afghanistan. Indeed, it assiduously refused to bring such a declaration to Congress, for this would have meant having an enemy worthy of American antagonism and being bound by the rules of war rather than conveniently categorizing detainees as "unlawful enemy combatants."

If there is a parallel to be made, it is to the Oklahoma City bombing, where almost two hundred people were killed. However, the defendant was charged in the judicial system and war was not declared against the entire population of Oklahoma. This legal route, conforming to the most obvious standards of the rule of law, was never seriously discussed in the case of September 11. Whether or not it was discussed within the narrow confines of the national security apparatus is not presently known. The use of the UN as a legal instrument and authority would have required the U.S. to change its position vis-à-vis the international law of terror, given that the U.S. refused to accept definitions of terrorism that most of the world accepted.

The abridging of civil liberties, the absence of a declaration of war, and the circumvention of international judicial instruments has relegated the legislative branch to the sidelines. But these actions flow from a pattern long established in the National Security State. "When Congress itself is reduced to nothing but an applauding section of an executive that has already acted," writes Raskin, "then the entire process of separated powers and balanced government becomes farcical. In such a situation, the Congress is reduced to a bunch of lobbyists and cheerleaders begging for the executive's favors—and the citizen had better learn to fend for himself."

39

CONCLUSION

The pragmatist philosopher John Dewey argued that the reduction of intelligence to a private commodity or an individually exercised right is the status quo's principal means of defense. Writing only a few years before the outbreak of World War II, he pointed out that this organization of intelligence is linked to the habitualization of force in society by treating free inquiry as acceptable in science but not social organization. Ideas should be organized, but for the ends of human enrichment, cooperation, and social action. "Intelligence is a social asset and is clothed with a function as public as its origin, in the concrete, in social cooperation."[48] This is a different idea of citizenship, one unbound by an organization of knowledge predicated on ownership. It is also closer to a democracy rooted in the liberal tradition, one based on openness and participation rather than secret war-making bureaucratic structures operating according to their own rules.

At the dawn of a new century, democrats have a responsibility to construct a better framework for accountable public policy liberated from social pathologies and outdated institutions. "Lag in mental and moral patterns provides the bulwark of the older institutions," says Dewey. "In expressing the past they still express present beliefs, outlooks and purposes." It is time to inquire into how to make knowledge a cooperative endeavor that defines and approaches the common good. Then it will be possible to discover our past, and as painful as it may be, and identify the many problems that must now be understood and transcended if democracy is to be preserved.

NOTES

1 For information on these various proposals, see Marcus Raskin, *The Politics of National Security* (New Brunswick, NJ: Transaction Books, 1979) 34–38.

2 An assassination attempt was made on Palmer's life by anarchists.

3 Cited in David M. Kennedy, *Freedom from Fear: The American People in Depression and War, 1929–1945* (New York and Oxford: Oxford University Press, 1999).

4 Martin A. Lee, "The CIA's Worst-Kept Secret," Foreign Policy in Focus, Institute for Policy Studies/Inter-Hemispheric Resource Center. See also Christopher Simpson, *Blowback: America's Recruitment of Nazis and Its Effects on the Cold War* (New York: Collier, 1988).

5 Speech by John E. McLaughlin, deputy director of Central Intelligence, at Princeton University Conference on the CIA's Analysis of the Soviet Union, March 9, 2001.

6 Cited in Raskin, *The Politics of National Security* (New Brunswick: Transaction Books, 1979), 38.

7 This quote by Senator Lister Hill (D-AL) and the others that follow are from the *Congressional Record*, July 9 and July 7, 1947.

8 Demetrios Caraley, *The Politics of Military Unification* (New York and London: Columbia University Press, 1966).

9 Anna K. Nelson, "President Truman and the Evolution of the National Security Council," *The Journal of American History* 72, no. 2 (Sept. 1985), 360–378.

10 Morton Halperin, Jerry J. Berman, Robert Borosage, and Christine Marwick, *The Lawless State: The Crimes of the U.S. Intelligence Agencies* (New York: Penguin Books, 1976).

11 National Security Council, *National Security Strategy for a New Century*, May 1997. David Gordon, "The Global Infectious Disease Threat and Its Implications for the United States," (NIE 99-17D) National Intelligence Council, January 2000. "U.S. Treating AIDS as a Threat to Global Security," *U.S.A Today*, May 1, 2000, A11.

12 Gregory A. Bischak, "The Political Economy of an Alternative Security and Disarmament Policy for the United States," in *Towards a Peace Economy in the United States*, Gregory A. Bischak, ed. (New York: St. Martin's Press, 1991).

13 Allison Thomson, "Defense-Related Employment and Spending, 1996-2006," *Monthly Labor Review* (Bureau of Labor Statistics), July 1998.

14 See *Atomic audit: the costs and consequences of U.S. nuclear weapons since 1940*. Stephen I. Schwartz, ed. (Washington, DC: Brookings Institution, 1998).

15 Interview in *The Nation*, February 2/9, 1998.

16 Clark Clifford (with Richard Holbrooke), *Counsel to the President: A Memoir* (New York: Random House, 1999). Emphasis added.

17 Interview with Zbigniew Brzezinski, *Le Nouvel Observateur* (France), January 15–21, 1998, 76.

18 Mary Anne Weaver, "Blowback," *New Yorker*, May 1996.

19 *Secrecy: Report of the Commission on Protecting and Reducing Government Secrecy*. Appendix A by Daniel Patrick Moynihan, "Secrecy: A Brief Account of the American Experience," 1997.

20 Marcus Raskin, *Essays of a Citizen: From National Security State to Democracy* (Armonk, NY and London: M.E. Sharpe, 1991).

21 David Bacon, "In the Name of National Security: Bush Declares War on Unions." *The American Prospect* 13, no. 19, October 21, 2002.

22 Angus Mackenzie, *Secrets: The CIA's War at Home* (Berkeley: University of California Press, 1997). Hearing of the House Judiciary Subcommittee on Civil and Constitutional Rights, "CISPES and FBI Counter-terrorism Investigations," June 13 and September 16, 1988 (Serial No. 122).

23 "AIDS Groups Aware of FBI Spies," *Associated Press*, May 15, 1995. Thomas Pierre, "FBI Accused of Spying on AIDS Activists" *Washington Post*, May 16, 1995, A6.

24 See the dissenting views in the House Judiciary Committee's report on H.R. 729, the Effective Death Penalty Act of 1995 in House Report 104–23 (104th Congress), February 8, 1995.

25 "U.S. Police Surveillance Questioned." CBSNews.com, April 6, 2003.

26 Annual Wiretap Report for the Year 2000, issued by the Administrative Office of the U.S. Courts.

27 "Secret Cold War Experiments," hearing of the House Government Operations Subcommittee on Legislation and National Security, September 28, 1994.

28 Richard Leiby, "The Fallout of War," *Washington Post*, December 30, 2002, C1.

29 One important exception was the civil suit awarding nearly one million dollars to Americans and Canadians who were subjected to brainwashing experiments by the CIA. See James Turner and Joseph Rauh, "Anatomy of a Public Interest Case Against the CIA," *Hamline Journal of Public Law and Policy* (Fall 1990), 11, no. 2.

30 "The U.S.A PATRIOT Act in Practice: Shedding Light on the FISA Process," Senate Judiciary full committee hearing, September 10, 2002.

31 Information Security Oversight Office's 1999 Report to the President.

32 See "The Secret's Out: Covert E-Systems Inc. Covets Commercial Sales" by John Mintz, *Washington Post*, October 24, 1994, A1, and John Marks, "The CIA's Corporate Shell Game" in *Dirty Work: The CIA in Western Europe*, Philip Agee and Louis Wolf eds. (Secaucus, NJ: Lyle Stuart, 1978). For a discussion of how the CIA used journalists as spies see John M. Crewdson's three part series in *The New York Times*, December 25–27, 1977.

33 Marcus Raskin, *Notes on the Old System: To Transform American Politics* (New York: David McKay Company, 1974), 83.

34 Joseph A. Amter, *Vietnam Verdict: A Citizen's History* (New York: Continuum, 1982), 58.

35 Memorandum, "Vietnam Situation," from Secretary of Defense McNa-

41

mara to President Johnson, December 21, 1963, cited in *The Pentagon Papers* (New York: Bantam Books, 1971).

36 Robert S. McNamara, *In Retrospect: The Tragedy and Lessons of Vietnam* (New York: Random House, 1995).

37 Peter D. Zimmerman, "Experts Look Again at Wartime Satellite Photos," *St. Petersberg Times*, September 15, 1991, A1.

38 John R. MacArthur, *Second Front: Censorship and Propaganda in the Gulf War* (New York: Hill and Wang, 1992).

39 See Steve Niva, "The Battle is Joined," in *Beyond the Storm: A Gulf Crisis Reader*, Phyllis Bennis and Michel Moushabeck eds. (New York: Olive Branch Press, 1991).

40 Tim Weiner, "Smart Weapons Were Overrated, Study Concludes," *New York Times*, July 9, 1996, A1. See also the hearings held by the Government Operations Subcommittee on Legislation and National Security, U.S. House of Representatives.

41 See "On the West Wing," Anthony Lewis, *New York Review of Books*, February 13, 2003.

42 "Threats and Responses: Nuclear Technology; Agency Challenges Evidence Against Iraq Cited by Bush" Michael Gordon, *New York Times*, January 10, 2003, A10.

43 Elaine Sciolino, "Iraq Chemical Arms Condemned, but West Once Looked the Other Way," *New York Times*, February 13, 2003, A16. The CNN interview was on September 21, 2002. The National Security Archives deserve credit for documenting Rumsfeld's misstatement.

44 Editorial, "Dubious Decisions on the Sudan," *New York Times*, September 23, 1998. Tim Weiner and Steven Lee Myers, "Flaws in U.S. Account Raise Questions on Strike in Sudan," *New York Times*, August 29, 1998, A1. Steven Lee Myers and Tim Weiner, "Possible Benign Use is Seen for Chemical at Factory in Sudan," *New York Times*, August 27, 1998, A1.

45 Jerry Seper, "U.S. OKs Payout for Sudan Bombing 'Mistake'," *Washington Times*, May 5, 1999. The 9/11 Commission found that, "No independent evidence has emerged to corroborate the CIA's assessment" of the soil samples.

46 Letter from Mahdi Ibrahim Mohamed, ambassador of the Republic of Sudan, to Senator Trent Lott, Senator Tom Daschle, Congressman Newt Gingrich, and Congressman Richard Gephardt, September 8, 1998.

47 See Alison Mitchell and Carl Hulse, "CIA Warns that a U.S. Attack May Ignite Terror," *New York Times*, October 9, 2002.

48 John Dewey, "Socializing Intelligence" and "The Meaning of Office in Liberalism" in *Intelligence in the Modern World: John Dewey's Philosophy*, Joseph Ratner ed., (New York: The Modern Library, 1939).

2

THE CENTRALITY OF
THE ATOMIC BOMB

Gar Alperovitz and Kai Bird

The orthodox literature on the Cold War commonly avoids one of the most obvious and least understood changes the atomic bomb wrought on the U.S. policy; it literally revolutionized the U.S. approach to Germany.[1] There is very little dispute that throughout World War II the central postwar problem facing United States leaders was that of security—and above all, of how to control Germany. The obvious issue was how to insure that Germany would not start yet another world war in one century. "The German question," as Herbert Feis observed, boiled down to "what measures, acceptable to the conscience of our times, could eliminate the chance that they might rise from the rubble and strike out again?"[2] Put another way—as Assistant Secretary of War John J. McCloy noted in his diary—Germany was the "cockpit of our policy."[3]

Although the "German problem" was extremely important, the choices available were far more constrained than is commonly realized. The main difficulty was that no American president could count on the public allowing him to keep a significant number of troops in Europe for very long after the war. "Domestic political realities," as Stephen Ambrose has noted, simply "precluded the maintenance of a large conscripted, standing army in postwar Europe."[4] Indeed, as early as November 1943 at the Tehran Conference, Roosevelt had informed Stalin that American forces would be withdrawn from Europe within one to two years of victory over the Nazis.[5] Similarly, Roosevelt told Churchill in late 1944: "You know, of course, that after Germany's collapse I must bring American troops home as rapidly as transportation problems will permit."[6] A few months later, at Yalta, the president told both leaders "that he did not believe that American troops would stay in Europe much more than two years."[7] In fact, shortly after the war ended there were riots in Europe among American soldiers demanding immediate repatriation.[8]

In these circumstances, the question facing United States leaders was what—specifically—was there to guarantee American security against a revival of Germany? And, too, what answer to this question might a president give to the American people that could survive political challenge?[9] At the time of Roosevelt's death the only concrete strategy available to any president was the consolidation of an alliance with the other great power that had an equally strong interest in keeping Germany down—namely, the Soviet Union. "It is by now a commonplace," Willard Thorp, deputy to the assistant secretary of state for economic affairs, characteristically noted, "that Germany cannot commit another aggression, so long as the Big Three remain united."[10] The essence of U.S. preatomic security policy for Europe was just that—an agreement, sealed at Yalta, for joint control of Germany by the United States and the Soviet Union with the lesser great power, Britain, and with the then still lesser power, France, added as well. "It is our inflexible purpose," Roosevelt, Stalin, and Churchill proclaimed, "to destroy German militarism and Nazism and to ensure that Germany will never again be able to disturb the peace of the world."[11]

Given his domestic political constraints, Roosevelt needed some rough agreement with the other dominant military power—the Soviet Union—to control Germany *directly*; and he needed some concrete way (beyond rhetoric) to weaken Germany's underlying military potential. Exaggerated discussions of "pastoralization" apart, the fact is Roosevelt's strategy centered on the notion of "industrial disarmament." The goal was to weaken Germany's "military-industrial complex" and simultaneously cement American-Soviet cooperation. Reductions in German industry could be used to provide the short-term reparations Stalin sought to help rebuild the war-torn Soviet Union.[12]

Since the Soviet Union desperately needed help in rebuilding its devastated society, it was agreed at Yalta that "to the greatest extent possible" there would be large-scale reparations taken out of the German economy, in the neighborhood of $20 billion, half to go to the Soviet Union.[13] In fact, the Yalta protocol stated that it was "to be carried chiefly for the purpose of destroying the war potential of Germany."

Related to this, of course, were implications for Roosevelt's de facto acceptance of a Soviet sphere of influence in Eastern Europe.[14] To the extent there was certainty that Germany would not rise again, at least in theory, Soviet policy could be more relaxed in Eastern Europe.[15] The overall understanding was embodied in the Yalta agreement: great power control of Germany, large-scale reparations, and an extremely vague declaration on Eastern Europe.

What is often overlooked is that from the American point of view, the advent of nuclear weapons gave Washington an alternative to constructing a European peace in cooperation with the Soviet Union. At Yalta, Washington had essentially agreed to a neutralized Germany. With the bomb, however, U.S. policy-makers realized that they could afford the risks of acting unilaterally. The western portion of Germany could safely be reconstructed economically and, later, integrated into a West European military alliance. The atomic monopoly—and it alone—permitted this with little fear of German resurgence and without regard to Soviet interests. At Potsdam (July 17 to August 2, 1945), once the bomb was successfully tested, the basic Rooseveltian posture toward Germany at Yalta was abandoned. As Melvyn Leffler has observed, not only did American officials "distance themselves from the position on reparations taken by Roosevelt at Yalta," they also thereby committed an "overt violation of the meaning and spirit of the Yalta compromise."[16]

How and when this decision was made is crucial to an understanding of the bomb's role. There was no major shift in the stated position of the United States on the reparations security issues during May and June. Despite the fact that numerous State and War Department officials ardently wished for a stronger German economy (and therefore less reparations), and even though there was concern about Russian machinery removals from Eastern Germany, the U.S. did not officially

45

break with the Yalta reparations understanding throughout the summer.[17] Indeed, on July 2, Joseph Grew went so far as to cable Edwin W. Pauley, Truman's reparations negotiator at Potsdam, that

> The [State] Department is not opposed to the discussion of an amount of reparations. While it is felt that a figure of twenty billion dollars is too high and that one approaching twelve or fourteen billion dollars would be more appropriate, the twenty billion dollar figure may be adopted as a starting point for exploration and discussion.[18]

46

American policy began to take on new and tougher dimensions in Eastern Europe once President Truman departed for Potsdam, and it similarly began to shift in connection with Germany. At Potsdam, the actual reparations negotiation focused around two quite specific questions: first, whether to set any fixed target for reparations; and second, if a target were set, what would it be? If a target were set—and if the figure was large—the essence of Roosevelt's policy would be continued. If no target were set—or if a small figure were set—a very different approach would be implemented.

These questions first received serious consideration at lower levels on July 18. For three difficult days the economic subcommittee skirmished over such issues as the American insistence that "the necessary means must be provided for payment of imports . . . *before reparation deliveries are made* (i.e., there ought to be a 'prior change' on the German economy to pay for imports *before* calculating reparations)."[19] The U.S.S.R., for its part, attempted to justify seizures of material in Eastern Germany as "war booty" (as opposed to "reparations") so that no charge against its ultimate claims would occur.[20]

Only minimal progress had been made by the evening of July 21. At this point, however, things began to happen at quite a different level: sometime during the thirty-six hours between the evening of July 21 and the morning of July 23 the official position of the United States delegation became clear. A post-Potsdam report to the president provides this cool summary:

> . . . The U.S. delegation to the Allied Commission on Reparations came to the conclusion that an "overall percentage" allocation of shares as between the Big Three was no longer feasible. The division of

reparations . . . would have to be abandoned for some less controversial method of dividing what would be removed as reparations.[21]

Put boldly, the Yalta agreement—with its stipulation of 50 percent of a fixed sum in the range of twenty billion dollars to go to the Soviets—was simply abandoned. The United States now suggested that reparations essentially be taken from each zone by each occupying power rather than collectively from Germany as a whole. Since the Russians occupied predominantly agricultural areas while the West had the lion's share of industry, the implications were obvious. The new stance was far tougher than anything that had previously been proposed. Not only would there be no "fixed target," even the idea of "percentages" was now gone. As Carolyn Eisenberg has noted, the decision was "an open break with Yalta,"[22] and, as many others have observed, the idea that each side would simply focus on its own zone also inevitably implied that four-power control of a unified German economy was essentially, if implicitly, laid to rest.

Subsequently, the State Department produced a variety of "reasons" for the American reversal. The fact is, however, reparation issues had not even been discussed at the foreign minister's level when the new position was put forth. Secretary of State Byrnes was quite explicit about the source of his new confidence in private discussion with Joseph Davies: "Details as to the success of the Atomic Bomb . . . have him confident that the Soviets would agree as to these difficulties.[23] Much more fundamentally, he also was no longer worried about the security problem: "In the last analysis, it [the atomic bomb] would control."[24] We should note that several United States policy-makers (especially Benjamin V. Cohen) believed that international control of the Ruhr industrial heartland might be the key to a compromise approach.[25] In principle, this could achieve security without necessarily weakening the German economic reconstruction effort. But again, shortly after the report of the successful nuclear test, Byrnes rejected this proposal as well.

A brief review of the timetable at Potsdam helps illuminate some of the specific steps and relationships:

- July 21, 1945, 11:35 a.m.—General Groves's dramatic report of the Alamogordo test arrives.[26]

47

- July 22, 1945, 11:10 a.m.—Following disagreement in the economic subcommittee, the reparations question is referred to the foreign ministers and put on the next day's agenda by Byrnes.[27]
- July 23, 1945, 10:00 a.m.—Byrnes telephones Secretary of War Stimson and asks for further information "as to the timing of the S-1 program."[28]
- July 23, 1945, 10:00 a.m.—Byrnes meets with Molotov and informally indicates the new U.S. reparations position. ("Under the circumstances he wondered whether it would not be better to give consideration to the possibility of each country taking reparations from its own zone").[29]
- July 23, 1945, 11:00 a.m.—at the foreign ministers' meeting Byrnes declares: "The American position is clear. It is the position of the United States that there will be no reparations until imports in the American zone are paid for. There can be no discussion of this matter."[30]

From this time forward there were no real negotiations. Truman made it clear that he was leaving Potsdam as soon as possible, with or without an agreement. Even the proposal that each side satisfy its reparations requirements from its own zone (with a certain modest percentage to be transferred to the Soviet zone from the West) was to be "conditional upon agreement on two other proposals . . . " relating to the treatment of Italy and the satellite nations and the Polish western border.[31] As Byrnes later recalled, he was blunt: "I told him [Molotov] we would agree to all three or none and that the president and I would leave for the United States the next day."[32]

Nor, again, is the source of such confidence in doubt. Using the same characteristically poker imagery he had used in connection with the atomic bomb earlier in the summer, Truman wrote his wife Bess on July 31: "He (Stalin) doesn't know it but I have an ace in the hole and another one showing—so unless he has threes or two pair (and I know he has not) we are sitting all right."[33] The tough stance worked—probably because the Russians had little alternative—and in the end Byrnes's "package deal" became one of the very few substantive agreements reached at Potsdam. As John Lewis Gaddis has dryly commented: "News of the secret explosion in the New Mexican desert . . . greatly cheered Truman and his advisors, contributing to their firm stand on German reparations. . . ."[34] Stalin accepted the West's de facto abandonment of the Yalta reparations accord[35] (and, too, some minor alterations in connection with the Balkans); and the United States and Britain accepted the Oder-Neisse Polish border understanding (with the proviso that "the final delimitation of the western frontier of Poland should await the peace settlement").[36]

The atomic bomb also helped reduce the other truly fundamental difficulty facing the United States in Europe, economic chaos. Abandoning Roosevelt's Yalta reparations stand and reducing the amount of reparations extracted from Germany was part and parcel of an effort to strengthen Germany's contribution to continental economic stability—and, as we have just seen, the bomb was pivotal in this connection. Throughout the spring and summer of 1945, leaders had been deeply worried about the European economy in general, and about social and political unrest in particular. After visiting Germany in April, John J. McCloy had brought back reports of "near anarchy" and utter devastation—"something that is worse than anything probably that ever happened in the world."[37] "The problem which presents itself," Stimson wrote just before details of the atomic test arrived, "is how to render Germany harmless as a potential aggressor, and at the same time enable her to play her part in the necessary rehabilitation of Europe."[38] Within hours of his statement, however, the problem had been resolved at Alamogordo. Although Truman continued to endorse "industrial disarmament" as a way to achieve European security, the issue took on a distinctly secondary importance after the successful atomic test.

Further evidence on this point can be found in two August 22 1945, meetings with General de Gaulle. Here President Truman and Secretary Byrnes together urged that "the German danger should not be exaggerated." De Gaulle, however, continued to emphasize French fears—and, like Roosevelt's advisors and the Russians, urged *direct* security measures to manage the longer-term German threat (including international control of the Ruhr and severing the West bank of the Rhine). Finally, Truman and Byrnes, responding specifically to de Gaulle's continued concern about Germany, became blunt: " . . . the atomic bomb will give pause to countries which might [be] tempted to commit aggression."[39] Although American policy-makers continued to worry about the potential power of a united German state

49

for a substantial period, Germany no longer presented a *fundamental* military threat.[40]

The problem was obviously not quite the same from the point of view of the Soviet Union. In the first place, the new weapon itself was now a threat. "Before the atom bomb was used, I would have said, yes, we could keep the peace with Russia," a worried Eisenhower observed in an August 1945 visit to Moscow. "Now I don't know . . . People are frightened and disturbed all over. Everyone feels insecure again."[41] But generalized fear engendered by the new weapon was only one aspect of the problem. In the fall of 1945 and spring of 1946, partly as a result of French obstruction on the Allied Control Council, partly out of understandable fear of economic chaos and political disorder, and partly—but not at the outset[42]—out of frustration with Soviet policy, American policy shifted from industrial disarmament to the rebuilding of German economic power. A major turning point was probably the decision to stop reparation shipments in May 1946, followed and dramatized by Byrnes' tough Stuttgart speech in September.[43]

This shift occurred at the same time that policy-makers began to dramatize the bomb as a strategic factor. The United States stockpile of assembled weapons was actually quite small, but the potential of the nuclear monopoly was also obviously extraordinary—as was advertised by the spectacular atomic tests in June 1946 at the Bikini Atoll in the Pacific.[44] Code-named "Operation Crossroads," the tests took place at the same time Byrnes and Molotov were again trying to reach agreement over Germany. *Pravda* took note of the mushroom cloud over Bikini and accused Washington of plotting an atomic war.[45] And as the arsenal grew (by 1948 there were fifty weapons ready for use) the Truman administration steadily found the courage to act more forcefully—and unilaterally—in Germany.

Reams have been written about the extreme Russian security fears concerning the German threat. Stalin, in Khrushchev's judgment, "lived in terror of an enemy attack." The Soviet premier observed in April 1945 that Germany "will recover, and very quickly"—but apparently he believed "quickly" meant ten to fifteen years.[46] Sometime at the end of 1947 (as Michael McGwire observes in a recent study), "Stalin shifted focus . . . to the more immediate threat of war within five to six years against a capitalist coalition led by the Anglo-Saxon power."[47]

Declassified Soviet documents offer additional insight. For instance, the Soviet ambassador to Washington, Nikolai Novikov, painted a deeply disturbing picture of American intentions toward the Soviet Union in 1946. Citing the American "establishment of a system of naval and air bases stretching far beyond the boundaries of the United States," and the "creation of ever newer types of weapons," Novikov believed that Washington was preparing for war. In the heart of Europe, he stressed, the United States was taking "completely inadequate measures for the demilitarization of Germany." Instead, "the United States is considering the possibility of terminating the Allied cooperation of German territory before the main tasks of the occupation—the demilitarization and democratization of Germany—have been implemented. This would create the prerequisites for the revival of an imperialist Germany, which the United States plans to use in a future war on its side."[48]

Russian fears of Germany were fully understood by U.S. leaders. Ambassador Averell Harriman, for instance, later recalled:

> Stalin was afraid of Germany, Krushchev was afraid of Germany, the present people [Brezhnev] are afraid of Germany—and I am afraid of Germany . . . They [the Soviets] have a feeling that the Germans can arouse a situation which will involve us and that will lead to a disaster . . . And this is something very important for us to consider.[49]

Obviously the critical turning point came with the decision to partition Germany and rearm West Germany. American leaders recognized that even the restoration of significant German economic power would be viewed as a threat to the Soviet Union—and that this would have quite specific repercussions. At a cabinet meeting in early 1947, Secretary of State George C. Marshall predicted that because of what the U.S. was doing in Germany, the Soviet Union would have to "clamp down completely" on Czechoslovakia. And that when they did, it would be a "purely defensive move."[50]

Was Marshall's basic insight into a critical, dynamic feature of the early Cold War correct—that Soviet policy in Central and Eastern Europe was primarily defensive and a reaction to American policy toward Germany? It is impossible to know, of course, but others also recognized the central point early on. In his columns at the time,

51

Walter Lippmann, for instance, regularly pointed out the obvious connection between what happened in Germany and what happened in Eastern Europe.[51] Unless the German problem were settled *first*, he urged, the Russians were unlikely ever to relax their hold on Eastern Europe. Lippmann believed that Byrnes's strategy of pressing forward on Eastern Europe without simultaneously promoting a reasonable settlement of the German issue was demanding too much. American policy thereby made the best enemy of the good.[52] "We must not set up a German government in the two or three Western zones," Lippmann urged John Foster Dulles in 1947. "We must not make a separate peace with it."[53] A steadily expanding body of research and archival evidence suggests that Marshall's fundamental insight and Lippmann's early judgment offer the most plausible explanation for what came to be one of the most dramatic and painful features of the Cold War—Stalin's "clamp-down" not only in Czechoslovakia, but throughout Eastern Europe.

The Soviet archives have yet to divulge anything truly definitive about Stalin's intentions at the end of World War II. However, even Harriman, who is usually portrayed as a hard-liner in early postwar dealings with Moscow, thought the Soviet dictator had no firm plan at the outset. "I had a feeling," Harriman observed, "that they were considering and weighing the pros and cons of cooperating with us in the postwar world and getting the benefit of our cooperation in the reconstruction." In the spring of 1945, John J. McCloy confided to his diary that it was "little wonder" that these "two greatest powers" should "walk stiff-legged around the ring a bit. It is a natural human process which is going on and will go on in a much more acute form in . . . Germany before we emerge on a sound working basis."[54]

★

Modern scholarship has in fact uncovered far more indications of ambivalence—and indeed, great caution and cooperation—in Soviet policy during 1945 and 1946 than is commonly recognized.

Soviet doctrine in 1946, as enunciated in Stalin's famous, much-debated "election" speech of Feb. 9, 1946, held that the United States and Great Britain could coexist with the Soviet system, which was ready to accord "special attention" to "expanding the production of consumer goods." If, according to Leninist doctrine, war was inevitable, Stalin suggested it more probable that it would occur between rival capitalist states. The Soviet Union would be spared.[55]

Here is a short list of developments that helped produce judgments like Harriman's:

- General elections in Hungary in the fall of 1945 held under Soviet supervision resulted in the defeat of communist-supported groups.
- In September 1945, Moscow unilaterally withdrew troops from Norway, despite its long-standing claims on Bear Island and Spitzbergen.
- In the wake of the December 1945 Moscow agreements, the government in Romania was enlarged to include noncommunists, and both the U.S. and Britain recognized it.
- The Soviet military also withdrew from Czechoslovakia at this time, and free elections produced a noncommunist, coalition government.
- In the spring of 1946 troop withdrawals were also carried out from the Danish island of Barnhol.
- In accord with his "percentage agreement" with Churchill, Stalin abandoned the Greek communists at a critical juncture in their civil war, leaving Greece within the Western sphere of influence.
- In Austria, the Soviet army supervised free elections in its occupation zone and, of course, withdrew after the signing of the Austrian Peace Treaty in 1955.
- Stalin warned the French communist leader, Maurice Thorez, against attempting "to seize power by force since to do so would probably precipitate an international conflict from which the Soviet Union could hardly emerge victorious." (U.S. intelligence obtained a report on this conversation in November 1946.)[56]
- Despite a short delay, Soviet troops were *in fact* withdrawn from Iran—a country bordering on the Soviet Union—after a brief and, in retrospect, rather modest international dispute.
- Perhaps most revealingly, former Soviet officials who had defected to the West documented the fact that important railway lines running from the Soviet Union through Eastern Europe were pulled up in the very early postwar period. The working

assumption was that since there would be only a short occupation, Soviet forces should remove as much useful material as possible as fast as possible.

- Neither was Stalin pursuing an aggressive policy in the Far East during these early years. Indeed, for a good period of time Stalin was supporting Chiang Kai-shek—much to the lasting chagrin of Chinese communist leaders; and Red Army troops were withdrawn from Manchuria in May 1946.

Finland and Austria—neutral but free-standing states—serve as alternative models for border-area nations that might plausibly have been acceptable to the Soviet Union had a different dynamic been established after World War II.

★

Of course, Soviet policy in Eastern Europe was to shift—and shift dramatically—especially after 1947 and 1948. Along with the announcement of the Truman Doctrine, the Marshall Plan also appears to have been far more threatening to Stalin than was previously understood. It suggested the creation of a powerful "economic magnet" to draw Eastern Europe into the Western orbit.[57] However, once it was clear that Germany was to be rearmed, the "clamp-down" in Eastern Europe took on an irrevocable quality.

This brings us back to our central thesis. To begin with, we believe it difficult to disagree with the judgment that the U.S. decision to rearm West Germany was made possible—*and only made possible* —by the atomic bomb.

Modern writers often forget the degree of concern about the former Nazi state that existed throughout the top American foreign policy establishment in the early postwar years. Even after the outbreak of the Korean War—and even *with* the atomic bomb—Truman's high commissioner in Germany, John J. McCloy, for instance, expressed opposition to the creation of a German national army.[58] So, too, did his successor, James B. Conant. And when they changed their minds, both men had to deal with the unrelenting opposition of the French. As late as August 1950, the State Department declared it had "opposed, and still strongly opposes, the creation of German national forces."[59]

Furthermore, President Truman himself was deeply worried about the Germans—again, *even with the bomb*. Here is only one of many indications, a memo to Secretary of State Acheson in June 1950:

> We certainly don't want to make the same mistake that was made after World War I when Germany was authorized to train one hundred thousand soldiers, principally for maintaining order locally in Germany. As you know, that hundred thousand was used for the basis of training the greatest war machine that ever came forth in European history.[60]

Truman was also well aware of the fact that he faced very powerful domestic political opposition to rearming a nation that had so recently caused the deaths of so many American boys. "From today's perspective, the rearmament of Germany seems natural and almost inevitable," Frank Ninkovich writes in an important study. "To achieve it, however, American policy-makers had to clear a long series of hurdles, including self-doubts, widespread European reluctance, and Soviet obstructionism . . . The amazing thing, then, is not that rearmament took place with such enormous difficulty, but that it happened at all."[61]

Amazing indeed! All but unimaginable, we believe, in the absence of nuclear weapons—and for a second reason directly related to Roosevelt's fundamental judgment. In the early postwar era, Roosevelt's assumption that the American people were not likely to support the creation of a major conventional military force was verified. There was an overwhelming demand for rapid demobilization after the war. In June 1945, the United States had more than twelve million men and women under arms. One year later the figure was less than three million, and by June of 1947 demobilization had left *all* the armed services with no more than one and a half million personnel.[62] Furthermore, Congress twice defeated universal military training (in 1947 and 1948), and defense spending in general declined rapidly during the first postwar years.

★

Very few would disagree with the proposition that the Korean War was itself a second fulcrum upon which the Cold War pivoted. To cite just

55

a few particulars: National Secirty Council 68, most scholars accept, was a document going nowhere in early 1950; the defense budget was being cut, not raised.[63] The political drama surrounding the Korean War permitted both escalation in Cold War hysteria—and an extraordinary overall escalation in military spending *in general*. Before Korea such spending was in the 4 percent of GNP range; during the war it peaked at nearly 14 percent. After Korea it stabilized for the decade of the 1950s at roughly 10 percent of GNP—unimaginable levels of expenditure prior to this time. (And this, in turn, of course, established a structure of forces and political attitudes without which the subsequent intervention in Vietnam is difficult to imagine.) Most importantly, the rearming of Germany almost certainly became possible only in the domestic political atmosphere that accompanied the chaotic Korean conflict and the qualitative political shift in Cold War tensions that accompanied the war.

However, as General Omar Bradley put it, Korea was ". . . the wrong war, at the wrong place, at the wrong time, and . . . the wrong enemy." The fact is a major commitment of forces in Korea would probably have been all but impossible had the United States not been able to protect its global flank in Europe with the implicit threat of nuclear weapons.[64] But if, as is widely acknowledged, the rearming of Germany *and* the reconstruction of a major military capacity both flowed politically from the Korean War decision, then we suggest the entire scenario must also be understood to have depended ultimately upon the odd coincidence of historical timing that put nuclear weapons in U.S. hands at a particular moment in the twentieth century.

The point to grasp is that these domestic political realities left policy makers empty-handed. They did not have what was required in the way of conventional forces to hold down the Germans. Given such realities—and considering the extraordinary difficulties of achieving German rearmament even with American possession of the atomic bomb—we suggest that it is all but impossible to imagine the early rearmament of the former Nazi enemy had there been no atomic bomb. Put another way, had the scientific-technical track of development, which produced the knowledge prerequisite to making an atomic weapon not in the U.S. postwar diplomatic arsenal would not have existed.[65]

THE CENTRALITY OF THE ATOMIC BOMB

The full-scale Cold War that followed on these critical early developments cannot (and need not) be reanalyzed in this space. To be quite clear, however, we do not contend that the American-Soviet relationship would have been a tranquil sea of cooperation. We are suggesting that subsequent years of unusual and dangerous militarization of foreign policy are a very special historical construct that needs to be explained on its own terms—and that the particular coincidence of timing that linked particular developments in nuclear physics with particular developments in world affairs had particular consequences.

NOTES

1 Though this point was stressed in Alperovitz's 1965 edition of *Atomic Diplomacy* few critics have focused on the implications of the bomb on Truman's policy toward Germany. See also the new introduction to *Atomic Diplomacy* (New York: Penguin Books, 1985), 56–57. Recently, German scholar Bernd Greiner has undertaken important research on this and related problems. See, for instance, his "*Zwischen Demontage und Atombombe*," *Die Zeit*, Nr. 34–24 August 1990 Seite 17. See also Greiner's *Die Marganthan-Legende: zur Geschichte enies umstritten Plans* (Hamburg: Hamburger Edition, 1995).

2 Herbert Feis, *Churchill, Roosevelt, and Stalin: The War They Waged and the Peace They Sought* (Princeton, NJ: Princeton University Press), 530.

3 McCloy Diary, April 30, 1945. Box 1/3, McCloy Papers, Amherst College.

4 Ambrose, Stephen. *Rise to Globalism* (Viking Press, 1975), 70.

5 Richard Barnet, *The Rocket's Red Glare: When America Goes to War—the Presidents and the People* (New York: Simon and Schuster, 1990), 251.

6 *Foreign Relations of the United States* herein cited as FRUS, Malta and Yalta, 286.

7 FRUS, Malta and Yalta, 617.

8 In January of 1946, four thousand GI demonstrators in Frankfurt were stopped at bayonet point as they descended on the Supreme Commander, General Joseph T. McNarney, screaming, "We want to go home!" (Barnet, *The Rocket's Red Glare* 249).

9 In October 1945, a Gallup Poll reported that less than 8 percent of the American people thought foreign policy issues "most vital." The Truman administration was unable to resist overwhelming popular sentiment to demobilize the 12.3 million men and women in uniform. By the spring of 1945 there were less than 1.5 million soldiers in the army, and Congress was in no mood to back legislation for universal military training. [See Barnet, *The Rocket's Red Glare* 249–251.]

10 FRUS, Pots. 504

11 FRUS, Malta and Yalta, 970.

12 Roosevelt's plans for Germany were eventually formalized in Joint Chiefs of Staff 1067, which at its core was basically a watered-down version of the Morgenthau Plan. See Jean Edward Smith, *Lucius D. Clay: An American Life* (New York: Henry Holt Co., 1990), p. 202; Melvyn P. Leffler, *A Preponderance of Power* (Stanford, CA: Stanford University Press, 1991). For an important reassessment of Roosevelt's policies in general see: Warren F. Kimball, *The Juggler: Franklin Roosevelt as a Wartime Statesman* (Princeton, NJ: Princeton University Press, 1991), 159. See also Michael McGwire, "Perestroika and Soviet National Security" (Washington, DC: Brookings, 1991).

13 FRUS, Malta and Yalta, 971.

14 Melvyn P. Leffler, "Adherence to Agreements: Yalta and the Experience of the Early Cold War," *International Security* (Summer 1986), 88–123; Albert Resis, "Stalin, the Politburo, and the Onset of the Cold War, 1945–1946," Carl Beck Papers, No. 701, April 1988, University of Pittsburgh Center for Russian and East European Studies; Kimball, *The Juggler* 159.

15 For a statement of this general logic in the more modern period, see Brzezinski, Zbigniew, "The Future of Yalta," *Foreign Affairs* (Winter 1984–85).

16 Leffler, "Adherence to Agreements: Yalta and the Experiences of the Early Cold War," 105–106. Again, detailed studies based on recent documentary evidence have confirmed earlier general assessments. And, again, the complexities of the reparations discussion have been reviewed elsewhere and need not be reproduced here. [See, for example, Bruce Kuklick, *American Policy and the Division of Germany: The Clash with Russia Over Reparations* (Ithaca: Cornell University Press); Philip A. Baggaley, "Reparations, Security and the Industrial Disarmament of Germany: Origins of the Potsdam Decisions," Ph.D. thesis, Yale University, 1980.]

17 Baggaley, "Reparations, Security and the Industrial Disarmament of Germany," 419.

18 FRUS, Pots. I, 519

19 FRUS, Pots. II, 845; FRUS, Pots. I, 547–548.

20 FRUS, Pots. II, 942–943.

21 FRUS, Pots. II, 943.

22 Eisenberg, *Drawing the Line*, p. 149 of manuscript.

23 "Journal," July 28, 1945 (2-1-51), "Chrono File," Box 19, Davies Papers, Library of Congress, herein referred to as LC.

24 "Diary," July 29, 1948 ("Potsdam Diary"), "Chron. File," Box 19, LC.

25 See Walter Brown Diary ["WB's Book"], July 17, 1945. Folder 602; Byrnes Papers, Clemson University Library.

26 FRUS, Pots. II, 1361.

27 FRUS, Pots. II, 232.

28 Stimson Diary, July 23, 1945.

29 FRUS, Pots. II, 274–75.

THE CENTRALITY OF THE ATOMIC BOMB

30 FRUS, Pots. II, 279.

31 FRUS, Pots. II, 484–485.

32 Byrnes, *Speaking Frankly*, 85.

33 Truman Ferrell, ed., *Dear Bess*, 522

34 Gaddis, *The United States and the Origins of the Cold War*, p. 244.

35 FRUS, Pots. II, pp. 1485–1487.

36 FRUS, Pots. II, 1941–1942

37 Stimson Diary, April 10, 1945.

38 FRUS, Pots. II, p. 756

39 "Memorandum of Conversations at the White House on August 22, 1945 between the president and General De Gaulle," President's Secretary File, Truman Library, courtesy of Melvyn P. Leffler.

40 Recent scholarship has also demonstrated how early and how determined the U.S. was to develop West Germany and integrate it into a Western Alliance. Carolyn Eisenberg, in her recently published book, *Drawing the Line: The American Decision to Divide Germany, 1944–1949*, dates the decision to early 1946, by which time the New Dealers in the Truman Administration had "lost control of America's German policy." (Eisenberg manuscript, p. 15.)

German unification, even as part of an overall European settlement, was to be avoided at all cost. A neutral Germany was anathema to Washington's policy makers. See Kai Bird, *The Chairman: John J. McCloy / The Making of the American Establishment* (New York: Simon & Schuster, 1992), Wolfram F. Hanrieder, *Germany, America, Europe: Forty Years of German Foreign Policy* (New Haven: Yale University Press, 1989). Thomas Alan Schwartz, in his book, *America's Germany: John J. McCloy and the Federal Republic of Germany* (Cambridge: Harvard University Press, 1991), disagrees about the timing of the decision to divide Germany. Schwartz argues that Truman, Acheson, and McCloy "did not accept that Germany would be divided and rearmed by our side until after the outbreak of the Korean War." Schwartz points out that McCloy argued that even after the outbreak of hostilities in Korea that it would be a mistake to create a "German national army now or in the foreseeable future." (Schwartz, p. 130.) But we would suggest that McCloy's short-lived opposition—he changed his mind within weeks—was due to his perspective as a High Commissioner whose top internal priority in West Germany was "democratization." Dean Acheson's marching orders for McCloy in the spring of 1949 were clear: he was to "go ahead with the establishment of a Western government [in West Germany] come hell or high water." Bird, *The Chairman*, 311.)

41 Peter Lyon, *Eisenhower: Portrait of the Hero* (Boston: Little, Brown & Co,. 1974), 377. Edgar Snow, *Journey to the Beginning* (New York: Random House, 1958), 360–361.

42 In the early postwar period General Lucius Clay judged that "the entire record of the Control Council showed that the USSR was willing to cooperate with the other powers in operating Germany as a single political and economic unit." [Jean Edward Smith, *Lucius D. Clay: An American Life*

(New York: Henry Holt & Co., 1990), 283.]

43 Daniel Yergin, *Shattered Peace: The Origins of the Cold War and the National Security State* (Boston: Houghton Mifflin, 1978), 319. Michael McGwire, op. cit., p. 27. McGwire also dates the shift in American policy to the spring of 1946, when the U.S. unilaterally decided to renege on the Potsdam decision to treat Germany as a single economic unit. Instead, the American objective became to integrate "a rehabilitated Western Germany into the capitalist economic system." At Stuttgart, Byrnes delivered a ringing endorsement for the rebuilding of a united Germany in which the German people would be "the primary responsibility for running their own affairs." Jean Edward Smith has recently argued that Clay and Secretary of State James F. Byrnes nonetheless still advocated a "policy of tolerance, patience, and respect" for the Soviet Union. Clay was dismayed by Byrnes' abrupt replacement in early 1947 with Gen. Marshall, when, Smith writes, "American policy, both toward the Soviet Union and in Germany, changed abruptly." It is important to note that even at this late date Clay still believed an agreement on Germany with the Soviets was possible. [Smith, *Lucius D. Clay: An American Life*, 386–390, 414–415.] Many others, including, for instance, John Lewis Gaddis, mark the turning point in U.S. policy as Feb.–March 1976. [John Lewis Gaddis, *The United States and the Origins of the Cold War, 1941–47* (New York, Columbia University Press, 1972), 284, 304–306, 312–315. See also Deborah Welch Larson, *Origins of Containment: A Psychological Explanation* (Princeton University Press, 1985), 259.

44 David Alan Rosenberg, "U.S. Nuclear Stockpile, 1945 to 1950," *The Bulletin of the Atomic Scientists*, May 1982; James L. Gormly, *From Potsdam to the Cold War* (Wilmington, DE: Scholarly Resources, 1990), 168.

45 Ibid., 168. By the summer of 1947 the Joint Chiefs of Staff had prepared their first operationally oriented atomic target list. [David Alan Rosenberg, "The origins of Overkill: Nuclear Weapons and American Strategy, 1945–60" *International Security* (Spring, 1983), 12.]

46 William Taubman, *Stalin's American Policy: From Entente to Détente to Cold War* (New York: W. W. Norton, 1982), 134; Nikita Khrushchev, *Khrushchev Remembers* (Boston, Little Brown, 1970), 393. See also Andrei Gromyko, *Memoirs* (New York: W. W. Norton, 1989).

47 Michael McGwire, op. cit., 33.

48 Amb. Nikolai Novikov "Long Telegram" to Foreign Minister Viacheslav Molotov, Sept. 27, 1946 (provided initially through the courtesy of Professor Gaddis Smith). Novikov also observed, "The ascendance to power of President Truman, a politically unstable person but with certain conservative tendencies, and the subsequent appointment of [James] Byrnes as Secretary of State meant *a strengthening of the influence on U.S. foreign policy of the most reactionary circles of the Democratic Party.*" For an in-depth analysis of the Novikov cable, see Melvyn Leffler's unpublished essay, "On Novikov's Telegram," and Kenneth M. Jensen, ed., *Origins of the Cold War: The Novikov, Kennan and Roberts "Long Telegrams" of 1946* (Washington,

DC: United States Institute of Peace, 1991). For other actions taken by Washington that Stalin perceived as hostile, see: Thomas G. Paterson, *Soviet-American Confrontation Postwar Reconstruction and the Origins of the Cold War* (Baltimore: John Hopkins University Press, 1973), 258. See also John Gimbel, *The American Occupation of Germany: Politics and the Military, 1945–1949* (Stanford, CA: Stanford University Press, 1968).

49 "Off the Record Discussion of the Origins of the Cold War," Oral History conducted by Arthur Schlesinger, May 31, 1967, Harriman Papers, LC.

50 Kai Bird, *The Chairman* (New York: Simon and Schuster, 1992), 308.

51 Walter Lippmann, *U.S. Foreign Policy: Shield of the Republic* (Boston: Little Brown & Co., 1943), 152. By the end of the war, Lippmann judged that even neutralization was too much to expect in Eastern Europe, a region that realistically would fall within a Soviet sphere of influence. An independent Poland, he wrote in 1944, could survive "only if it is allied with Russia." [Ronald Steel, *Walter Lippmann and the American Century* (Boston: Little Brown Co., 1980), pp. 409, 415.] See also Martin Herz, *Beginnings of the Cold War* (Bloomington: University of Indiana Press, 1966); William Appleman Williams, *American-Russian Relations, 1891–1947* (New York: Octagon Books, 1952, 1971); James P. Warburg, *Germany: Key to Peace* (Cambridge: Harvard University Press, 1953).

52 Barnet, *The Rocket's Red Glare*, 260, 269. In 1943, Lippmann warned that a peaceful accommodation with the Soviets after the defeat of Nazi Germany depended solely on whether the East European border states adopted a policy of neutralization and whether Russia could accept neutralization: "The best interests of the United States would be served by such a solution. It would not bring us or the members of the Atlantic community into conflict with Russia. It would give Poland the Danubian states, and the Balkans the only form of security we are able to offer them, and it would give Russia security resting on the fact that the nations of Central and Eastern Europe, after Germany has been disarmed, could not become the spearheads of a western coalition." [Walter Lippmann, *U.S. Foreign Policy*, 152.] See also Richard Barnet article manuscript, "Lippmann, Kennan, and the Cold War," October 1990, 9.

53 Cited by Steel, *Walter Lippmann and the American Century*, 449.

54 "Off the Record Discussions on the Origins of the Cold War," Oral History conducted by Schlesinger, May 31, 1967, 11–12, Harriman Papers, LC; John J. McCloy diary, April 30, 1945.

55 Albert Resis, op. cit., "Stalin, the Politburo, and the onset of the Cold War," p. 16.

56 William Taubman, *Stalin's American Policy*, op. cit. pp. 134–135.

57 Vladislav M. Zubok, lecture presented at Institute for Policy Studies seminar on the Cold War, March 28, 1991. Zubok argues that Stalin perceived the Marshall plan as an "attempt at encirclement." Zubok further suggests that Stalin in 1946 did not expect imminent war, and that he was not surprised by the Truman doctrine. See also James L. Gormly's argument that in the wake of the Marshall Plan, "Stalin stopped his efforts to restore life

to the Grand Alliance," and his report that one Russian official at the time complained, "The imperialists will not let go . . . They wish to encircle the Soviet Union . . . No hand, not even one armed with the atomic bomb, will succeed." [James L. Gormly, *From Potsdam to the Cold War* (Wilmington, Del.: SR Books, 1990), 214.]

58 Bird, *The Chairman*, 332, 340.

59 Department of State memo, 16. August 1950; FRUS 1950, 3:213.

60 *Foreign Relations of the United States*, 1950, Vol. IV, 688.

61 Frank Ninkovich, *Germany and the United States: The Transformation of the German Question Since 1945* (Boston: Twayne Publishers, 1988), 80–83.

62 Gaddis, *The United States and the Origins of the Cold War, 1941–47*, p. 261.

63 James G. Hershberg, "Explosion in the Offing: German Rearmament and American Diplomacy, 1953–1955," *Diplomatic History* (Fall 1992), 531.

64 Melcyn P. Leffler, *A Preponderance of Power: National Security, the Truman Administration, and the Cold War* (Stanford, CA: Stanford University Press, 1992), 369–370.

65 Omar Bradley, *A General's Life: An Autobiography by the General of the Army* (New York: Simon & Schuster, 1983). Bradley indicates clearly why the Army was extremely reluctant to get involved in any war in Asia. See especially 558. Bruce Cumings, *The Origins of the Korean War*, Vol. II (Princeton University Press, 1990). Kathryn Weathersby, *Soviet Aims in Korea and the Origins of the Korean War, 1945–1950: New Evidence from the Russian Archives*, Working Paper No. 8, Cold War History Project, The Woodrow Wilson Center, November 1993, 24, 32.

3

THE COLD WAR AND THE FATE OF DEMOCRATIC CULTURE

Norman Birnbaum

The Cold War had economic, geopolitical, and ideological origins—and consequences. It formed our societies, in each of the contending camps and even in the ostensibly neutral nations. It began not at the end of World War II but during it, with the civil war in Greece and the imposition of a pro-Soviet regime in Poland—as well as obvious ruptures in the alliance between Communists and nationalists in China. By the time the Western public realized that the Cold War had replaced the wartime alliance (at the latest in 1948 with the Communist coup d'etat in Czechoslovakia and then the Soviet blockade of West Berlin) the beliefs and constraints that made ending it impossible were already in place.

The initial center of geopolitical confrontation was Europe. Destruction and impoverishment made life miserable for millions for whom the end of armed conflict brought relief but no surcease from brute problems of existence itself. The Soviet Union and the Western alliance divided Germany into occupation zones but could not agree on its future. Each suspected the other of intending to incorporate a revived Germany in its bloc and then using it to dominate the continent. The U.S.S.R. declared that it would accept a united but neutralized Germany, but the Western nations rejected the project to begin early planning for the remilitarization of their parts of Germany. In East Germany, in central and East Europe, the U.S.S.R. imposed its model of state and society. The division of Europe was a modern version of the initial political settlement after the Protestant Reformation: the ruler determined the identity of the church. The imposition of capitalist democracy in Western Europe was made possible by a bargain with the social Catholics and social democrats. They obtained a welfare state, in return for breaking (in France and Italy) their resistance alliances with the communists.

64   Meanwhile, the legacies of empire had to be dealt with. France reclaimed Vietnam and initiated a war, which led to its defeat in 1954 and that of the U.S. in 1975. France remained in North Africa, where the Algerian revolution erupted just as France was driven from Vietnam. The Labour government freed India, but the United Kingdom fought independence movements elsewhere in Asia and Africa, not least in Egypt. The United States voiced an anti-imperial ideology, but its relations with the Third World were determined by concern lest nations like India and Indonesia be lost to Communism. Authoritarian Pakistan became a client state as a counterweight to democratic India. The Indonesian communists were exterminated by the military as hundreds of thousands were slaughtered. What was lost was a state originally conceived as an American protectorate, China. Despite the obvious continuity between Sun Yat-sen's national revolution and Mao's, China's fate was ascribed to "communism." Its dangers were also found in Latin America, where Castro's revolution induced the U.S. to conspire in the destruction of democracy in Argentina, Brazil, and Chile.

The geopolitics of the Cold War—briefly—were global. What rendered geopolitical confrontation especially fearsome was not only its omnipresence. It was the possession, the initial American and British monopoly having ended, of nuclear weapons by both sides. Fear of war became fear of the extirpation of human continuity, of human existence itself. Ordinary humans grasped this as well as, if not better than, their leaders. A nuclear arms race having begun, it was exceedingly difficult to regulate it, even to slow it, much less end it. Robert McNamara in retirement declared that he had advised Presidents Kennedy and Johnson never to initiate the use of nuclear weapons, but that it was impossible to say this publicly since it would disturb NATO allies who relied on the U.S. threat to do just that. The same allies, of course, had one fear worse than anxiety lest the U.S. renege on its threat to use nuclear weapons, the possibility that the U.S. would one day keep its word. With the public excluded from discussion of humanity's life and death, its anxiety grew as powers of decision were concentrated in the hands of a very secular priesthood of bureaucrats, officers, and politicians. They were celebrants of a perpetual mass of death: the British historian and leader of protest movements Edward Thompson was right to describe their theology as "exterminism."

What impelled peoples to accept living with this threat? In the U.S.S.R. and communist China, they had no choice, since they had no rights of political participation. In the democracies, despite agitated and at times widespread opposition, publics acquiesced. Their acquiescence was not the result of helpless passivity. They accepted the ideology of the Cold War. That ideology used the obvious brutality and tyranny of the communist regimes to construct an image of a relentlessly aggressive political force, a military and political threat to the liberties and well-being of the democracies. Anticommunism had little use and less space for complexity and nuance, and none for the argument that on the very premises of Western democracy (that it was not only a higher but a more natural form of society) communism would eventually collapse. Orwell intended *1984* as a description of what could happen to modern Britain, but that was not emphasized in the culture of the Cold War. Many who had once been communists or revolutionary socialists themselves contributed to a systematic anticommunism that combined two elements: the depiction of communism as a Western heresy, a bastard offspring of the Enlightenment, and the judgment that it was irreversible.

Communism in its Maoist and Stalinist versions, for all of its common traits, was implanted in very different historical settings. In Poland, for instance, from 1956 onward the communists accepted coexistence with an authoritarian Roman Catholic Church, and the communists in the German Democratic Republic allowed the Protestant Church to form a (policed) counter society. Russian nationalism permeated Stalinism, and Maoism had a component of anti-imperial national revival. Anticommunism was partly universal and partly particular. Our millennialism encouraged Americans to believe that we had a unique responsibility to defend the world against evil. In Western Europe, Christians, liberals, and social democrats brought their own perspectives (and conflicts with their own communist movements) to it. In Germany, Italy, and elsewhere, those who could very truthfully say that they had been strenuously anticommunist for a very long time—since they had been active fascists or Nazis—welcomed the Cold War as a belated vindication.

The polyvalence of anticommunism allowed it to be joined to the basic project of the Cold War, the development of a consensual social order in the Western democracies, intended to achieve stability and welfare domestically and hegemony internationally. With Western Europe and Japan in no position immediately after the war to negotiate terms for aid and protection, American domination of the alliance struck many (especially our own citizens and our imperial ideologues and managers) as a fact of nature. It was, however, a fact of history. After the defeat in Vietnam and the devaluation of the dollar, deviation and dissent proliferated in the alliance. There were parallel processes, beginning earlier, in the communist bloc: the revolts in the German Democratic Republic (1953) and Hungary (1956), preceded by the Yugoslav schism (1948). Well before *Solidarnosc*, Poland struck out on its own and, without the benefits of Polish pluralism, so did the repellent regime in Romania. The key event was Khrushchev's 1954 speech on Stalin's crimes and his initiation of reforms. Why did this not convince the Western alliance to negotiate an end, or a serious truce, in the Cold War with Stalin's successors, which Churchill as prime minister urged on Eisenhower in 1953 after Stalin's death?

The answer may be that the Cold War had become an integrating factor in the domestic politics of the Western alliance, so much so that its end was literally inconceivable to elites and publics alike. I recall witnessing the West German election campaign of 1953. The Protestant anti-Nazi, Gustav Heinemann, had quit the Adenauer government to protest the decision to rearm Germany and join the Western alliance. He formed his own party and campaigned for discussion with the wartime allies on the basis of Stalin's 1952 proposal for a unified and neutral Germany and got 1.5 percent of the vote. Adenauer campaigned with the slogan "No experiments!" and won a majority. Memories of the early horrors of the Soviet occupation of East

Germany, the expulsion of Germans from Czechoslovakia and Poland with Soviet approval, and the grimness of life in communist Germany contributed to the result. However, by this time the West Germans had something to lose: the substantial beginnings of what was termed the social market economy, a welfare state. Throughout Western Europe, in fact, class compromises prevailed, and social democratic or social Christian parties joined in extending the prewar welfare states. The strongest proponents of the American alliance in Europe were the leaders of British Labour, in office until 1951 and then in opposition until 1964—despite the scant help and frequent opposition they experienced from the U.S. elite for their program of redistribution and improved general living standards. Their attitude to the Western alliance was a model for its later acceptance by the German Social Democrats. In both cases, that acceptance was a precondition of a domestic consensus on political alternation. The Italian Communist Party, already very much an integrating factor in Italian society, was allowed to join a governmental majority after accepting Italian membership in NATO.

The class compromise in Europe was influenced by the American New Deal. New Dealers in the early Cold War managed the Marshall Plan for economic reconstruction in Europe, and the reforms imposed in the first phase of the occupation of Japan. The U.S., to be sure, blocked the British Labour government's plans for socialization of German industry in the Ruhr. The American trade unions supported the Marshall Plan; its expenditures for capital goods were in the U.S. itself and were a factor (before the economic stimulus of the Korean War) in the expansion of the U.S. economy. The Marshall Plan sought more productivity in Europe, exactly the strategy adopted by the trade unions in the U.S. when early postwar projects of participation in management, or national health insurance, were thwarted.

The role of the American trade unions in the Cold War was hardly a matter of political economy alone. The Cold War was a continuation of an imperial project articulated earlier by Theodore Roosevelt: the integration of immigrants, and of the nation generally, in a larger mission. What is interesting about that larger mission is its ambiguity. Much of that concerns the revolutionary status of the United States. Is it the result of an achieved revolution (in which case we are "the greatest nation on earth" and entitled to pain and rage when others do not accept the idea), or is the revolutionary aspiration still open, and we can seek to implement Franklin Roosevelt's four freedoms at home and then abroad, and are obliged to pay attention lest we fall to the sin of pride. In the Cold War, pride certainly united Dean Acheson and his bitter enemy, Senator McCarthy. The patrician and the plebian contended for the right to set the terms by which the Cold War would be conducted. The Anglican bishop's son from Connecticut and Yale (who was also a New Dealer and wanted fairness for the American working class) believed that it should be entrusted to those at the summit of society who knew the value of discretion but had the habit of command. The alcoholic Catholic from Wisconsin sought to purge the nation's intellectual and social betters, liable to doubt and therefore disloyalty. Anticipating the contemporary Republican argument that the Democrats are culturally elitist, McCarthy led a revolt of ordinary citizens so enraged at the suggestion that they were inferior that they were easily manipulated by both McCarthy and the more established figures (like Senator Taft) who at first encouraged him. By the time the elite removed McCarthy, after humiliating him, there was little need for his persecutory tactics. A consensus as to the necessity to pursue the Cold War and as to the superiority of our institutions enraged the thinkers of the 1950s (Dwight Macdonald, C. Wright Mills, and William Appleman Williams) but exiled them to the margins of national politics. Their younger readers, in the 1960s, took adequate revenge.

They had to contend, however, with an entire set of institutions formed by or even original to the Cold War. A greatly enlarged bureaucracy managed our imperial project, providing rewards for the academics, bankers, businessmen, and lawyers, who moved in and out of its middle and top ranks. Much of American culture and large segments of society were militarized, and the nation's historical position and moral purposes were described in the language of perpetual warfare. The media and the universities were induced to collaborate actively in the mobilization of opinion. The Central Intelligence Agency's surreptitious purchase of intellectuals and journalists is not, in retrospect, made more honorable by the suggestion that those who were bought, in most cases, would have served without compensation. Their most substantial profit was intangible: the conviction of being at one with power. These thinkers were often eloquent critics of those

who sided with revolutionary movements because they were historically inevitable. A far greater paradox, however, was the assumption of
leadership in the Cold War by American conservatives who cast aside
habits of political thought like attention to complexity and the weighing of alternatives. George Kennan was appalled as his project of containment of the Soviet Union was converted into one for its
destruction. True, in one of the most dramatic moments of U.S. history, the senior leaders of the American foreign policy establishment
advised Lyndon Johnson that the war in Vietnam was a losing proposition and instructed him to end it. It was they, however, who had propelled him into it in the first place with notions like the need to
defend the nation's "credibility," whose shelf life seems eternal.

69

The European conservatives were (and are) made of different stuff.
De Gaulle took France out of the NATO military structure in 1966,
in the words of his letter to Johnson, to regain its sovereignty. A year
later, he warned the U.S. (in a speech in Pnom-Penh) of the disaster
it was incurring in Vietnam. Well before that, however, the Vatican (led
by Pope John XXIII and Cardinal Casaroli) had initiated its own version of coexistence. Recall, as well, that the major European allies of
the U.S. had diplomatic and other relations with communist China and
refused to send troops to Vietnam. It was Margaret Thatcher as well
as Helmut Kohl who insisted to Reagan and the elder Bush that Gor-
bachev and his projects for reform and coexistence should be taken
seriously. It is true that a large segment of the German right opposed
Brandt's policy of rapprochement with the U.S.S.R., the Eastern
European nations, and recognition of the communist German state.
That contributed to the electoral defeats of the Christian Democrats
and their Bavarian ally in 1972, 1976, and 1980—just as public doubt
as to the conservatives' capacity to withstand American pressure led to
their defeat in 2002. When the German right did form a government
again in 1982, it accepted the stationing of U.S. missiles on German
soil—and adamantly refused to take the process further, while actively
seeking new forms of coexistence with the U.S.S.R.

It was not simply the cautious realism of the European conservatives
that led them to refuse a crusade against the U.S.S.R. It was what they
shared with the European left; the memory of two devastating wars, of
the trauma of decolonization, and the wish to develop a model of society that, they thought, in the end would exert far more influence in the

Soviet bloc states than rhetorical celebrations of "freedom." The Vietnam War carried a message for Europe, although not the one intended by our imperial managers: in the event of military confrontation in Europe, the Western Europeans would neither be consulted or spared devastation and death. The European protests against the stationing of nuclear weapons in Europe began before the U.S. intervention in Vietnam; perhaps the memory of Hiroshima sufficed.

It was more than memory that was shared by those in Europe of differing degrees of enthusiasm about the alliance with the United States. They shared political space and—certainly at least until the end of the Cold War—an agreement on the indispensability of a welfare state for domestic social cohesion. They also agreed on the necessity of closer and deeper European cooperation if the sovereignty of the separate nations was to be maintained in the face of the two superpowers. Above all, with much higher rates of electoral participation than our own, with artists, writers, and scholars possessed of a pedagogic mission, with public television chains enjoying large degrees of political independence, they understood politics not only as the search for consensus but as a legitimate exercise in conflict. In West Berlin, the Iron Curtain was a stop on the subway. Yet it was in West Berlin that some of the most original thinking about ending the Cold War took place. In a very different cultural and political language, that was also true of Catholic Rome.

Why, by contrast, did the Cold War have the consequence of immobilizing so much of our politics? At its beginning it involved a state that combined warfare and welfare. The Marshall Plan, the Korean War rearmament boom, and a permanent war economy provided a good deal of investment. Some absurdities can be dismissed. One did not need to invent a new missile nose cone to obtain a more heat-resistant frying pan. Nonetheless, technological innovation did spread from arms production to the rest of the economy. Suppose the vast resources put into arms procurement were used to improve our educational, environmental, and health standards. Suppose, too, that the sums characterized as "foreign aid," which supplied arms to a variety of regimes—not all of them impeccably democratic or committed to human rights—were redirected to projects of economic and social development in the impoverished nations. These questions were indeed asked by a critical and vocal minority. They found occasional resonance in the Congress but little in the major media and were with time categorized as evidence only for the querulous utopianism of the questioners.

One answer is that the U.S. role in the Cold War, far from representing a break in an isolationist or self-contained national history, was entirely compatible with our expansionist and imperial past. The collapse not only of Germany, Italy, and Japan, but the death throes of the British and French empires after the war, allowed the U.S. to exert hegemony while proclaiming our supreme generosity. We experimented, in several parts of the earth, with indirect forms of domination and influence, which proved all the more effective for their indirectness. That also allowed the domestic depiction of our new imperial project as an expression of the concerns of ordinary citizens, who wished for prosperity and security and the good opinions of humankind—and who were glad to belong to "the greatest nation on earth."

The contrast with Europe is instructive. Relatively powerless after the war, the Western European nations used the alliance with the U.S. to achieve some part of their recovery. They accepted subordination to the U.S. for a period and became restive when its risks appeared too great and their own possibilities of autonomy were enlarged. In particular, the unification of Europe—however contradictory its progress—struck them as the *via regis* toward independence. The Cold War they and their peoples fought was, in brief, "not ours." Sometime in 2003, I heard Helmut Schmidt speaking in Washington on why he thought the German officers who declared that they would not use their nuclear weapons were right.

Vietnam ended the American Cold War consensus in two ways. It produced a body of experience and reflection that remains critical of attempts (as in Iraq) to repeat the enormous overestimation of American power that it entailed. Its economic cost coincided with the relative decline in U.S. economic power that has continued since. That in turn has increased domestic social tensions by intensifying class conflict—principally conducted, recently, from above. The connection between the propagation of a model of society organized as a market, with entire areas of culture and life commodified and the ascription to the U.S. of the right to dominate the world, is total. With welfare no longer possible, and warfare permanent, our elites have had to return to Rome for instruction: panem et circensis are once more on the historical agenda. Their difficulty, and ours, is that no society can function primarily as a market—especially if it claims to be a nation. There is an equal difficulty: the world will not accept American domination. A repetition of the Cold War, with "terror" substituting (poorly) for "communism," is impossible. The difference between the elections of 1972 and 2004 make that clear. Even with a candidate ambivalent about the war, the groups opposed to the Iraq War were part of a coalition that obtained 48 percent of the votes. The Cold War undermined American democracy. Opposition to its continuation may renew it.

72

The prediction is uncertain. The Cold War could have been ended decades before it actually ceased. Events like Watergate showed how much of our public life it corrupted. Watergate was the invasion of domestic politics by the techniques of the Cold War, just as McCarthyism was the extension to foreign policy of the primitiveness of much of American politics. Whether the war on "terror" can be stopped from defining all of our politics depends upon a reflective citizenry's engaging in critical scrutiny of the past century.

4

THE NUCLEAR CRUCIBLE
THE MORAL AND INTERNATIONAL LAW IMPLICATIONS
OF WEAPONS OF MASS DESTRUCTION

Terrence Edward Paupp, J.D.

The advent of the nuclear age has virtually erased the moral bound-aries that have acted as a constraint on decisions to make and wage war. The rise of a rational, technological society has elevated the place of "technique" as the guiding force for both technology and political discourse in the atomic age. Technology has been trans-formed into the new theology with autonomy of its own, and theology and moral argument have been subsumed under the umbrella of tech-nological discourse. Moral judgment is made in technical terms; the new faith is rationality. Throughout the Cold War, this divorce of moral constraint from decisions concerning nuclear technology led to the negation of our common humanity. This new theology of tech-nology is what I call "the nuclear crucible."

Moral and legal discourse leads us to remake and revise a world that lives within the shadow of weapons of mass destruction. The nature of moral discourse, in this context, means that "to see reality is to be wholly present at the crucifixion of the world; to live reality is to enter into that crucifixion, but to do so, in the phrase of Albert Camus, as neither victim nor executioner" (Douglas 1966, 3). Yet the processes of exclusionary governance, which gave birth to the nuclear state and

guide it to new levels of maturation, has created a world of both exe-
cutioners and victims. In this process, exclusionary states and establishments have been willing to offer up the sacrifice of both humanity
and the entire earth in this process. This reality constitutes the verti-
cal link of the nuclear crucible where morality, ethics, and the fate of
humanity are placed in the balance, in a revolt against an insanity and
injustice spawned by the doctrine of mutually assured destruction.
Such a situation demands opposition and revolt against its injustice.
This is necessarily the case insofar as "to revolt against injustice is at
the same time to revolt for life, life in the world and life in oneself"
(Ibid., 9). If the life of the world itself is to be preserved, the sanctity
of its life needs to be acknowledged as the transcendent value. The life
of the world and its future should not be subordinated in any nation's
national security establishment, individually or collectively. Yet we continue to live in an age in which the moral discourse and moral demand
for global peace and nuclear abolition are submerged discourses. The
dominant or hegemonic discourse of the age continues to reside in
delusions of Orwellian proportions and double-speak. In short, as C.
Wright Mills wrote, "It is this mindlessness of the powerful that is the
true higher immorality of our time; for with it, there is associated the
organized irresponsibility that is today the most important characteristic of the American system of corporate power" (Mills 1956, 342).

Mills, Jacques Ellul, Robert Jay Lifton, and Robert Michels all
have written of the dangers of irrationality and moral irresponsibility
under the auspices of a power elite governed by the law of expediency,
reinforced by propaganda, and caught in the matrix of the "iron law of
oligarchy." Mills cautioned that "laws without supporting moral conventions invite crime, but much more importantly, they spur the
growth of an expedient, amoral attitude" and that, as a consequence,
"a society that is merely expedient does not produce men of conscience" (Mills 1956, 347). In turn, the reliance upon expediency
exposes the increased reliance upon propaganda and the reintroduc-
tion of Hitler's "big lie" technique as a means of obfuscating the
demands of moral discourse and opens the gates for amoral accom-
modations. In this regard, the moral implications of propaganda in the
nuclear age are enormous. Ellul has suggested that the propagandist
has the capacity to mobilize man for action that is not in accord with
his previous convictions because "modern psychologists are well aware

that there is not necessarily any continuity between conviction and action and no intrinsic rationality in opinions or acts. Into these gaps in continuity propaganda inserts its lever. It does not seek to create wise or reasonable men, but proselytes and militants" (Ellul 1965, 28).

Additionally, Lifton has written of a kind of "nuclear fundamentalism" that leads to vicious circles of nuclear entrapment" (Lifton and Falk 1982, 80). The net result of this nuclear fundamentalism is that "bomb-induced futurelessness becomes a psychological breeding ground for further nuclear illusion, which in turn perpetuates and expands current arrangements." (Ibid., 80). And, in the expansion of current arrangements, political parties play their supporting roles.

From the perspective of a concern with a more democratic and egalitarian society, Robert Michels's book, *Political Parties*, is a pessimistic one. First published in 1911, Michels's famous "iron law of oligarchy" was set out with the observation that "it is organization which gives birth to the domination of the elected over the electors, of the mandataries over the mandators, of the delegates over the delegators. Who says organization says oligarchy" (Michels 1999, 15). In this statement, Michels laid down what would come to be the major political argument against Rousseau's optimistic concept of popular democracy that underlies most traditional democratic and socialist theory. In this book he analyzes the tendencies that oppose the realization of democracy and claims that these tendencies can be classified in three ways: dependence upon the nature of the individual; dependence upon the nature of the political structure; and dependence upon the nature of organization. These three classifications demand and deserve greater attention and explication in reference to the threat to humankind posed by weapons of mass destruction.

THE NATURE OF THE INDIVIDUAL AND THE POTENTIAL FOR NUCLEAR HOLOCAUST

In this bomb-induced matrix without a future for humanity, there are many possible reactions, including the embrace of all-or-none idea systems and institutional structures, which Lifton calls "ideological totalism" in which "there is a collective effort to reassert the endless life of a group (the 'Thousand-Year Reich,' for instance)" (Lifton 82). Such a collective effort, however, may cross the boundary line into the practice of genocide. The masters of the Nazi Holocaust have had their crimes replicated to greater and lesser degrees elsewhere, from the killing fields of Cambodia in the 1970s to Bosnia and Rwanda in the 1990s. The distinguished legal scholar Raphael Lemkin fought hard to establish the importance of the concept of genocide, as defined by the United Nations General Assembly in 1946, as "a denial of the right to existence of entire human groups" (Paupp 2000, 72). In view of this history, Lifton and sociologist Eric Markusen wrote in their book, *The Genocidal Mentality: Nazi Holocaust and Nuclear Threat*, that: "We believe that our efforts here to explore common patterns in Nazi genocide and potential nuclear genocide are in the spirit of Lemkin's work . . . Both Nazi and nuclear narrative are crucially sustained by certain psychological mechanisms that protect people from inwardly experiencing the harmful effects, immediate or potential, of their own actions on others" (Lifton and Markusen 1990, 12–13).

The nuclear crucible continues to sacrifice both the individual and the well-being of collective humanity vis-à-vis a Nazi/nuclear narrative, which induces a psychological sense of denial and inoculates those who adopt it against feeling the full weight of personal moral responsibility for a potential nuclear holocaust. The psychological surrender is tantamount to a surrender of moral responsibility. The effect of this process is twofold: on the one hand, it frees the individual from making choices and decisions that are then abdicated to the guardians of the nuclear arsenals and, on the other hand, it empowers the guardians of the nuclear arsenals to effectively ignore democratic demands for disarmament and nuclear abolition, thereby ensuring the maintenance of patterns of exclusionary governance through an exclusionary state (Paupp 2000, 51–112).

As an alternative, inclusionary governance seeks to de-emphasize limited and self-limiting concepts of national security (which emphasize threats to the nation-state) and reconceptualize security as something that is both common and comprehensive. As the Independent Commission on Disarmament and Security (the Palme Commission) concluded in 1989, the very destructiveness of modern war, even in its conventional forms and derivations, has become so terrible that it has lost its meaning as an instrument of national policy. Further, it leaves the root causes of conflict unresolved. Hence, the need for replacing traditional notions of security with notions of "inclusionary security" and "common security" is more apt to address the root causes of conflict and serve to obviate reliance on force or weapons (Ibid 2000, 87). In the absence of new notions such as inclusionary security and a common security framework to support it, I believe, as Michels suggests, that democracy will fail to be realized in the decision-making processes that will determine the ultimate fate of weapons of mass destruction.

THE NATURE OF THE POLITICAL STRUCTURE AND THE POTENTIAL FOR NUCLEAR HOLOCAUST

These forces converge on the organizational center of the national security state. The national security bureaucracy since the days of President Truman is testimony to this phenomenon. The blending of bureaucracy with technology has been transubstantiated in "technocracy." Its effect upon the political structure is antidemocratic insofar as the nature of technocracy leads to a culture of "apocalyptic concealment." The culture underlies not only the armaments culture but lies at the center of the nuclear state, the embodiment of the most deadly form of an exclusionary states. Its exclusionary nature corrupts the political process, as well as the media, which reports on it. In place of a sense of anguish there is a deterioration of public discourse (Ibid., 72).

With the deterioration of public discourse, democratic discourse has become a casualty of the National Security State. Franz Neumann's critique of law within the context of the oppressive totalitarian state may be applied with equal force to a critique of the nuclear monopoly of terror and the political structure that supports, funds, and maintains it. Neumann asserts that "the technological progress (the *conditio sine qua non* of cultural progress) is used today largely for armaments." The problem arises when there is no set timetable for ending the union between technology and arms production. On this matter, Neumann wrote that "no threat to the political system of democracy can arise if the fruits of advancing technology are diverted from normal use for a relatively short time. But our historical experience tends to show that a long-range postponement of expectations is possible only in a wholly repressive system" (Neumann 1953, reprinted in *The Rule of Law Under Seige: Selected Essays of Franz L. Neumann and Otto Kirchheimer* 1996, 222). Between 1945 and 2001, the United States government produced a repressive system in the name of "national security," not unlike Latin American versions of *"La Patria,"* which have justified the suspension of constitutional norms, the imposition of a "state of siege," and the imposition of antidemocratic initiatives (Paupp, 95). The concentration of authority in the American nuclear establishment is highly exclusionary, for with the adoption of barriers between government and citizenry in the policy area most critical to national and global survival "this characteristic nonaccountability and noncontroversiality of nuclear weapons policy naturally inclines policy in directions favored by the militarist cast of mind, which enjoys a permanent presence in the bureaucratic structure" (Falk 1982, 205).

78

The legacy of the National Security State is, in the final analysis, the denouement of freedom in a democratic society. As Karl Jaspers observed in his book, *The Atom Bomb And The Future Of Man,* "Whoever thinks that life may be worth living in a world that has been turned into a concentration camp must consider that confidence in man is justified only insofar as scope remains for freedom. This scope is the premise of man's potential. Mere life as such, under consummate total rule, would not be the life of animals in the abundance of nature; it would be an artificial horror of being totally consumed by man's own technological genius" (Jaspers 1961, 167). Such an outcome can and does have the potential to place church and state at odds.

From a moral perspective, man's technological genius, as exemplified in the creation of weapons of mass destruction, has betrayed the moral imperative of the Barmen Declaration of 1934, which juxtaposes the person and message of Jesus Christ and his church with the claims of loyalty made by the state upon citizens to subordinate their individual and collective conscience to the dictates of the National Security State.

In regard to opposition to the maintenance and deployment of weapons of mass destruction, and the state and technology supportive of it, the task that remains for the Christian in the most powerful of nations is to negate a politics of violence and of negation. As Jurgen Moltmann, professor of systematic theology at the University of Tubingen, Germany wrote in, *The Crucified God,* "The theology of the cross had to be worked out not merely for the reform of the church but as social criticism, in association with practical actions to set free both the wretched and their rulers" (Moltmann 1973, 73). In the absence of a theology of the cross that unites the mission of the church with social criticism, Moltmann warns that "men who have not found their free-dom in the humanity of God but, for whatever reason, feel anxiety at this God and the freedom that is expected of them, cling to the law of repressions . . . They hope for the absolute from relative values and eternal joy from transitory happiness. Instead of resolving conflicts, they construct aggressive images of enmity and make their enemies into demons in order to kill them spiritually. But because man knows at heart that in so doing he is making excessive demands of things, other men and himself, his anxiety remains" (Ibid., 301). Reliance on violence, through reliance on weapons of mass destruction, constitutes an idolatrous loyalty to the nation state. This conclusion is necessar-ily the case insofar as loyalty to the nuclear weapons state constitutes a betrayal of Christ and his church.

THE NATURE OF ORGANIZATION AND THE POTENTIAL FOR NUCLEAR HOLOCAUST

The impairment of any genuine democratic response and opposition to the growing and unresolved threat of weapons of mass destruction constitutes a serious moral, political, and legal crisis. To recognize this crisis of democratic impairment reveals that there is too little func-tional democracy in the United States, not too much. In fact, the organizational and bureaucratic walls that surround the Pentagon, the Department of Defense, the CIA, and the private corporations that contract for greater investments in a national missile defense must be confronted so that moral and legal claims can also be extended to dem-ocratic protests against the conventional trade in arms. In other words, the interjection of moral accountability is required with respect to "defense expenditures" so that such expenditures may be critiqued and evaluated from perspectives that are not driven by either profit or power, but are informed and judged by a higher standard—the dignity and value of life on this planet. In this respect, William Hartung has noted that "whether any president will have the political courage and the staying power to take on the permanent arms sales establishment that has shaped U.S. policy for the past twenty-five years will depend in large measure on how much pressure he or she gets from the Amer-ican people" (Hartung 1994, 298). Part of the difficulty in raising

79

levels of political pressure on these policies is associated with an established creed based on force.

Today's political parties at best play a supporting role in a "politics dominated by an intense mosaic of political elites engaged in carefully targeted strategic activation . . . Meanwhile, government remains a complex bureaucratic web of policies, each policy the concern of a particular set of candidates, bureaucrats, and elected officials . . . Popular control of government is less sure as a result" (Schier 2000, 87–88). This is especially the case with respect to the decision-making process within government as to the use of nuclear weapons to bring about a particular policy result (Krieger, March/April 2001, 8–11; Schell, January 2000, 41–56). In the case of the Vietnam war, it has been noted that "the critical disagreement between the Joint Chiefs of Staff and the civilians related not to the pace of American military action against the North but to how far it would go, and specifically to whether it would eventually include the use of nuclear weapons, if necessary, to compel Hanoi to give up. In the end . . . that question was never completely clarified" (Kaiser 2000, 371).

In 1961, the first year of the Kennedy administration, the Joint Chiefs of Staff made their own recommendations to the president regarding SEATO Plan 5, which contemplated their preferred option to ensure the defense of Southeast Asia as a whole. While the Kennedy administration expanded American ground forces, at least the Joint Chiefs of Staff had abandoned Admiral Arthur Radford's 1956 plans to defend South Vietnam with a few regimental combat teams armed with tactical nuclear weapons. Contemplating potential Chinese intervention, the issue of the authorization to use nuclear weapons was back on the table, as far as the Joint Chiefs of Staff were concerned. They answered Robert Kennedy's query at the meeting of August 9, 1961, regarding what would be necessary in response to Chinese escalation and they "confirmed Kennedy's suspicion that the war would become massive and perhaps nuclear. The president remained unlikely to accept such plans, but one service had also produced a smaller-scale plan tailored to fit the situation in South Vietnam" (Kaiser 2000, 97). Two years into his term, President Kennedy was still trying to implement his own ideas regarding certain critical Cold War issues. Among them, while ruling out nuclear war as a realistic option, he still felt that the United States needed a limited military option that would enable

Washington to reply to Soviet actions in Berlin or elsewhere (Ibid., 199). Kennedy's views on this matter were consistent ever since taking office, when he was immediately at odds with the Joint Chiefs of Staff over Cold War strategy insofar as "the Chiefs had thoroughly absorbed the Eisenhower–Dulles doctrine of treating nuclear weapons as conventional weapons, but the president was apparently appalled" (Ibid., 43).

After the events of November 22, 1963, however, presidential restraint was removed in contemplating the use of nuclear weapons as an instrument of both war and foreign policy. In 1968 and in 1972, the Johnson and Nixon administrations did just that. Both of these administrations "threatened the use of nuclear weapons to varying degrees, and both may seriously have discussed it at one time or another, but such an option was not politically feasible either domestically or internationally" (Ibid., 378). With respect to nuclear weapons, the policies and perspectives of the Johnson and Nixon period contrast sharply with Kennedy's views. For example, in 1961, Kennedy shied away from war in Laos when he realized that the United States "would be outnumbered on the ground and that the military would count on nuclear weapons to redress the balance" (Ibid., 378). Additionally, he avoided war in the 1962 Cuban missile crisis largely because of fear of nuclear escalation (Pious, Spring 2001, 81–105). In fact, "Whatever else the Cuban missile crisis might have been, it was certainly not an example of successful crisis management" (Ibid., 92). Insofar as "crisis management and game playing require effective control over the pieces on the board," the fact is that, given the number of near misses in the crisis involving these pieces, any one of these near misses "might have caused a cascading set of events to result in a nuclear holocaust" (Ibid., 93). Therefore, the "secret deal" to remove IRBM Jupiter missiles in Turkey was the true source of resolution in the Cuban missile crisis of 1962, a resolution born of diplomacy and politics. Therefore, "if we can learn anything useful from Kennedy's performance, it is that the art and science of politics and diplomacy, not gamesmanship and the methods of crisis management, are the keys to successful resolution of nuclear crises" (Ibid., 105).

The tragedy of Vietnam, in part, is that Johnson, McNamara, Bundy, and Rusk "tried to ignore the pitfalls of the policies and strategies the Eisenhower administration had left behind: that the

81

United States had undertaken to defend many areas on the assumption that nuclear weapons would be used as necessary and that nuclear weapons could be effective. The Joint Chiefs seemed to assume that these policies remained in force" (Kaiser 2000, 378–379). Within the matrix of this nuclear crucible, the civilians "who wanted to preserve a nuclear option even if in practice they might never authorize it, failed to see, as Kennedy had in 1961, that the only alternatives to the use of nuclear weapons were an unpopular and indecisive conventional war on the one hand, or an immediate political solution on the other" (Ibid., 379).

82

A media hostile to democratic discourse through inclusion and active engagement in a comprehensive and serious debate leaves the challenge of creating a more inclusive politics even more elusive. In the case of 1962, "Kennedy's failure in the Cuban missile crisis involved his abdication of the moral responsibility to educate the American people and rid them of their delusions of how the world works . . . He was willing, for political advantage, to leave the American people with the most dangerous illusion of all: the White House could 'manage' a superpower nuclear crisis and with sufficient military force could resolve it on terms favorable to the United States" (Pious 2001, 104). At least by June of 1963, in his American University address, Kennedy advocated the signing of a weak nuclear test ban treaty. In so doing, he had developed and was matured by the crisis, which suggests that "Kennedy's insight into the pathology of the Cold War had sharpened with experience" (Oliver 1998, 187). Therefore, in viewing Kennedy's commitment to and signing of the Nuclear Test Ban of 1963, it is difficult to "disassociate Kennedy's eloquent and determined exposition of this concern from his growing comfort with the responsibilities and duties of presidential leadership" (Ibid., 187). Kennedy privately expressed the view that nuclear weapons made a secure and rational world impossible and that it was important to find a means to get rid of nuclear weapons (Twigge and Scott 2000, 315).

In the year 2001, however, the lack of will and vision in American leadership capable of taking the nuclear issue in a more enlightened direction indicates that it is captive of an ancient cabal of the power elite. Therefore, the question that begs to be answered is: "Can a movement based on hope, confidence in the concerted powers of human beings, and faith in the human future be as great as one based on terror?" (Schell 1998, 17). Part of the answer to the question is the moral one. The other part of the answer is from the international law perspective. It is to the issue of the legality versus illegality of weapons of mass destruction that I now turn.

THE LEGAL CRUCIBLE

International law intersects with moral issues with regard to weapons of mass destruction. It is this intersection that creates the nuclear crucible that characterizes the post–1945 context in which the world finds itself. The role of international law as a force in the context of international relations has traditionally relied on enforcing restraints in the laws of land warfare by treaty, but such restraints are not limited to treaties. Long ago, the famous Martens Clause of the Preamble to the Fourth Hague Convention of 1907, concerning the laws and customs of war on land, introduced a very broad legal yardstick that was intended precisely for those situations in which no specific international law convention existed to prohibit a particular type of weapon or tactic. In part, it states:

> Until a more suitable code of the laws of war can be drawn up, the high contracting parties deem it expedient to declare that, in cases not covered by the rules adopted by them, the inhabitants and belligerents remain under the protection and governance of the general law principles of the law of nations, derived from the usages established among civilized peoples', from the laws of humanity, and from the dictates of the public conscience ("Convention Respecting the Laws and Customs of War on Land [1907]," L. Friedman, editor, *The Law of War: A Documentary History*, Random House, Vol. I, 1972, 309).

In the present day and age, the Eurocentric notion of legal usages "established among civilized people" varies across a wide spectrum, from differing visions of human rights to NATO's barbarism in its "humanitarian" war in the Balkans in the late 1990s and the invasion of Iraq in 2003. Further, the "laws of humanity" do not necessarily include the views of Third World states and are, therefore, filled with omissions as to critical concerns that neocolonialism, neoimperialism, and neoliberalism have conveniently overlooked and intentionally ignored. Finally, the "dictates of public conscience," in an age of propaganda and a media-saturated monopoly plagued by censorship, are left without the means to attain the velocity of moral outrage, political comprehension, or legal sensibility. Therefore, while the Hague Convention of 1907 is an important starting point in assessing the international law implications of weapons of mass destruction, its primary value in the twenty-first century is the explicit recognition of the legal perspective that the law of war is not only to be found in treaties. In fact, the Nuremberg Tribunal in 1945 was confronted with a similar problem in charging the Nazi leadership for war crimes in World War II in the absence of prior definitions of crimes against humanity or crimes against peace. In response to this situation, the Nuremberg judgment concluded that:

> The law of war is to be found not only in treaties, but in customs and practices of states, which gradually obtained universal recognition, and from the general principles of justice applied by jurists and practiced by military courts. The law is not static, but by continued adoption follows the needs of a changing world . . . (*Trial of the Major War Criminals*, Vol. 22, 1950, 445).

At the dawn of the twenty-first century, the relevance of the combined force of the Hague Convention of 1907 and the holding of the Nuremberg judgment is that "the legality of nuclear weapons cannot be judged simply by the existence or lack of a treaty rule specifically prohibiting or restricting their use. Instead, the legality of nuclear weapons must be judged in light of the various sources of international law, i.e., international treaties and conventions which limit the use of force in war; the fundamental distinctions between combatant and noncombatant and between military and nonmilitary targets, which provide the main foundation upon which the laws of war have been built; and the principles of humanity, including a prohibition against weapons and tactics that are cruel in their effects and cause unnecessary suffering" (Falk et al. 1980, 559).

It is important to outline the substantive prohibitions found in the Nuremberg Charter, which paid attention not only to the malign conduct of belligerents in war, but also to the crimes of conspiracy, planning, and threatening to commit the crimes of murder and other inhumane acts. The following table outlines the key prohibitions of the Nuremberg Charter, which have direct bearing upon the production, deployment, and potential use of weapons of mass destruction.

SUBSTANTIVE PROHIBITIONS FOUND IN THE NUREMBERG CHARTER

The following are crimes falling within the jurisdiction of the tribunal for which there shall be individual responsibility.

(a) **Crimes against peace**: namely, planning, preparation, initiation, or waging a war of aggression, or a war in violation of international treaties, agreements, or assurances, or participation in a common plan or conspiracy for the accomplishment of any of the foregoing.

(b) **War crimes**: namely, violations of the laws or customs of war. Such violations shall include, but not be limited to, murder, ill-treatment, or deportation to slave labor or for any other purpose of civilian population of or in occupied territory; murder or ill-treatment of prisoners of war or persons on the high seas; killing of hostages; plunder of public or private property, wanton destruction of cities, towns, or villages, or devastation not justified by military necessity.

(c) **Crimes against humanity**: namely, murder, extermination, enslavement, deportation, and other inhumane acts committed against any civilian population, before or during war; or prosecutions on political, racial, or religious grounds in execution of or in connection with any crime within the jurisdiction of the tribunal, whether or not in violation of the domestic law of the country where perpetrated.

SOURCE: A. Roberts and R. Guelff, *Documents on the Law of War,* Oxford: Clarendon Press, 1982.

In point of fact, by 1996, the International Court of Justice (ICJ), with its issuance of an advisory opinion, became—for the first time in human history—an international tribunal that had directly addressed the nuclear weapons issue as an unresolved threat to humanity. In its opinion, the ICJ had engaged in "forging a consensus that lends strong, yet partial and somewhat ambiguous, support to the view that nuclear weapons are of dubious legality" (International Court of

Justice Statute, Article 5592, and Paupp 2000, 66–70; Nanda and Krieger, 1998). Nuclear weapons are still primarily the product of and in the decisional domain of the nation states that possess them. As such, nuclear weapons serve to maintain an inherently exclusionary global hierarchy. Similarly, Falk has stressed the point that "the morality of the state system is built around the primacy of state interests as conceived by governmental leaders" and that the "use, development, and role of nuclear arms have been almost entirely determined by considerations of state power." This leads to the inevitable conclusion that "there is little reason to suppose that such considerations will not prevail in the future, as they have in the past, in determining whether additional governments will decide to develop, deploy, and use nuclear arms. Government leaders may pursue self-destructive policies based on the narrow interests of their ruling groups and may, further, be entrapped within horizons of time and security which are far too short from even the perspective of national well-being" (Falk 1984, 466).

86

In response to this situation, I have maintained the necessity for a different approach to national and global governance. "Insofar as the history of the international law system has been an exclusionary, hierarchical war system, the mandate provided by international law to move toward inclusionary governance restores to human beings the freedom to transform exclusionary states into inclusionary states. Greater degrees of inclusion have the capacity to transform governance by deepening democracy within and between nations" (Paupp 2000, 98). If nuclear issues have remained largely within the exclusive domain of governmental elites and bureaucratic systems that are inherently antidemocratic, it follows that the very notion of authority is what has to be understood and redefined from a moral and legal perspective. In other words, we must ask, "What and who is truly authoritative in this life-and-death context?"

In this regard, the juxtaposition of militarism and human rights law underscores the argument that a human rights agenda can only be comprehensively implemented within a framework of peace. In other words, there are two opposed sets of authoritative law that operate by contradictory criteria. If one rises, the other must of necessity fall. To recognize this dialectic as a global reality and not merely theory is to acknowledge that "militarism has neither created a world of peace and stability, nor protected the human right to physical security. Overemphasis on military superiority undermines the ability to build regimes of trust and harmony. The arsenals of the war system are symptoms of deep conflict" (Felice 1998, 35). Arsenals of weapons of mass destruction and associated proposals to keep them in play (i.e., a national missile defense advanced by the United States) can only paralyze the building of inclusionary forms of governance while, at the same time, strengthening existing systems of exclusionary governance that propagate the global war system. In this critical regard, "arms control and disarmament and the demobilization of armed forces are prerequisites to providing the institutional framework within which nations may pursue implementation of the corpus of international human rights law" (Ibid., 35).

The legal environment may be more precisely understood, as McDougal suggested, as one where "the rules commonly referred to as international law and national law are but perspectives of authority—perspectives about who should decide what, with respect to whom, for the promotion of what policies, by what methods—which are constantly being created, terminated, and re-created by established decision makers located at many different positions in the structures of authority of both states and international governmental organizations" (McDougal 1981, 487). The challenge presented to us at the dawn of the twenty-first century is to establish contending perspectives on authority—perspectives that would have the capacity to question the justifications and rationale of deterrence, which justifies investment in the weapons of mass destruction. The challenge is obviously not a new one in the history of military and legal discourse. In fact, "the outbreak of World War I in 1914 demonstrated how vulnerable international law was to the aggressive policies of a nation ready, willing, and able to employ military force" (Maguire 2000, 70). This vulnerability was clear in considering "war crimes."

The whole notion of "war crimes" first came into existence and was widely used during and after World War I. However, the employment of war crimes accusations were mainly used as a propaganda tool "to fuel the outrage necessary for modern war" and a significant "number of people in Britain and France began a movement that aimed to try the German Kaiser after World War I. The German government feared war crimes prosecution for a different reason. The ever practical

General-Staff believed that if common soldiers were encouraged to examine orders as international legal questions, military discipline would disintegrate" (Ibid., 71). Today, in the twenty-first century, the United States government is afraid that its own citizens, if exposed to the international legal questions surrounding weapons of mass destruction, may refuse to fund further investments in either the weapons themselves or in a national missile defense shield.

In remarks prepared for the twentieth anniversary of the Voice of America on February 26, 1962, President John F. Kennedy declared: "We are not afraid to entrust the American people with unpleasant facts, foreign ideas, alien philosophies, and competitive values. For a nation that is afraid to let its people judge the truth and falsehood in an open market is a nation that is afraid of its people" (Kennedy 1962, 163). A little more than forty years later, on June 21, 2001, Secretary of Defense Donald H. Rumsfeld was questioned by Senate Democrats about the high cost and unproven effectiveness of a national missile defense system, and they raised deep concerns about the administration's threats to withdraw from the 1972 Antiballistic Missile Treaty if the Russians refused to amend it (*New York Times*, June 22, 2001, A1 and A14).

Rumsfeld was greeted by a unified skepticism from liberal and centrist Democrats. Senator Carl Levin (D-MI), chairman of the Senate Armed Services Committee, asked Rumsfeld: "Would you agree it is possible, at least, that they could respond in a way to a unilateral withdrawal which would not be in our interest, that would make us less secure?" Rumsfeld responded that it was possible, but he added, "We're not hostile states. They are going to be reducing their weapons regardless of what we do. We're going to be reducing our nuclear weapons to some level, regardless of what they do" (Ibid., A14). Rumsfeld's nonresponsive answer highlights the crisis of exclusionary governance in the United States, the lack of fidelity that the United States has demonstrated to an existing treaty that, by the standards of international law, should not be subject to unilateral abrogation.

The indiscriminate effect of nuclear weapons on civilians and military targets alike conflicts with Article 6(c) of the Nuremberg Charter, which declares that the extermination of a civilian population, in whole or in part, is a "crime against humanity." Hence, "to recognize the legality of nuclear weapons, given their capacity and tendency to terrorize and destroy the civilian population, would virtually eliminate the entire effort to constrain combat, at least in large-scale warfare, through the laws of war" (Falk et al. 1980, 566). The Geneva Protocol in Article 51(2) states: "The civilian population as such, as well as individual civilians, shall not be the object of attack; acts or threats of violence the primary purpose of which is to spread terror among the civilian population are prohibited." Further, Article 51(4) states: "Indiscriminate attacks are prohibited." Article 51(4)(c) specifies indiscriminate attacks as "those which employ a method or means of combat the effects of which cannot be limited as required by this Protocol." Article 51 defines the essence of an indiscriminate attack as one that is "of a nature to strike military objectives and civilians and civilian objects without distinction."

89

By the time of the 1980 election and the ascendancy of Ronald Reagan to the presidency, missile-defense advocates around Reagan were simply purists of the Republican right. As such, "few of these people were technical or military experts; they simply believed that the U.S. should pursue the arms race in every area of military technology. For purists the whole arms-control process was a dangerous trap, and the ABM Treaty the worst of all agreements, precisely because it was the foundation of all the rest" (Fitzgerald 2000, 118–119). At its heart and center, the crusade to destroy the foundation of arms control was to create weapons which, "if they materialized, could contribute to an offense, as well as provide a defense for the United States" (Ibid., 499).

The creation of such an offensive capacity triggers the reality of the illegality of both the production and deployment of weapons of mass destruction as well as their placement in outer space. The reality of the illegality is more than a technical nuance. The illegality goes to the means through which dominance and domination are designed to occur vis-à-vis that technology. For with the ultimate purpose that of control and domination through terror, the employment of such a technology is truly beyond the limitations envisioned by the Geneva Protocol, the principles of the Nuremberg Charter, the various United Nations conventions and prohibitions against genocide, and the moral critique of the Barmen Declaration as well as the Catholic bishops "Pastoral Letter." Despite all of these prohibitions, between 1983 and the fall of 1999, the United States expended $60 billion on antimissile research, and "though technical progress had been made in a number of areas, there was still no capable interceptor on the horizon" (Fitzgerald 2000, 498). The irony is that should such a technology appear, its very appearance, its very existence, not to mention its production and deployment, would by definition become a violation of both legal and moral sanctions with respect to weapons of mass destruction. It would further wipe away any remaining technical boundary between annihilation and the constraints of the legal and moral aspects of the nuclear crucible. As such, even in the name of "self-defense," the laws of war would seem virtually meaningless insofar as "it would be a *fait accompli* that nuclear weapons abolished the weapons of war" (Falk et al. 1980, 568). It is the supreme irony at the dawn of the twenty-first century that the United States claimed that it needed to wage preventive war against Iraq, a nation shown not to have them, at a time when the U.S. lacks meaningful controls on its own weapons of mass destruction.

CONCLUSION

Since the end of 1945, the world has not been the same because of the introduction of weapons of mass destruction. These weapons defined the underlay, the great strategic games and confrontations of the Cold War—from Korea and the Cuban Missile Crisis of 1962, from the Vietnam War to investments in "Star Wars," revised calls for a national missile defense, and the symbolic destruction of the Berlin Wall. Now, along with the increased dangers of nuclear proliferation are the attendant social and economic dangers of undemocratic globalization. In the year of 2001, a new millennium brings in its wake the two dominant themes of the post–Cold War years—globalization and democratization. The research for and control of nuclear weapons are subject to the criteria of neither of these themes. Weapons of mass destruction reside both at the center and periphery of global consciousness, accountable to a power elite that remains exclusive and exclusionary in its policy-making and decision-making.

We must add the unaccountable and irresponsible drift of military and political policy-making with respect to weapons of mass destruction. Insofar as the state system has protected and maintained a monopoly on the production and use of weapons of terror in violation of major moral and international legal codes and mandates, it would seem that, in general terms, "to all those concerned about social justice and the creation of a humane global order, a democratic alternative to an ossified, state-centered system is becoming more compelling" (Falk and Strauss, January/February 2001, 220).

I seek to present such an alternative in this conclusion. I seek to identify the mutually reinforcing nature of the issues involved and their interrelationship to one another. In so doing, the following seven *"sustaining norms of nuclear restraint"* may be understood as emerging from the paths of what I am calling *"inclusionary governance"* (Paupp 2000, 84–112). The global processes associated with a deepening of democracy demand accountability and an end to imperial intentions, politics, and norms. I maintain that the violence in the current order of power and threats to research, produce, deploy, and use weapons of mass destruction are a global reflection of exclusionary states and exclusionary practices that have embraced militarization as a means of maintaining not only international hierarchy, but also the power that comes from the maintenance of class, ethnic, religious, and regional cleavages.

The Delhi Declaration of 1978 called for the entire world to be made into a nuclear weapons–free zone. The declaration proposes the immediate negotiation of a Nuclear Disarmament Treaty, outlining its principal features and insisting that serious negotiations to make it happen be held. Such an approach needs to be resurrected in the aftermath of the U.S. Senate's 1999 defeat of the Comprehensive Test Ban Treaty. To achieve this goal in the context of the nuclear crucible, seven conditions associated with the realization of inclusionary governance must be achieved:

(1) Structures and policies that allow for the continued investment in and expansion of both nuclear and nonnuclear assets shall be dismantled and replaced with peacekeeping and monitoring institutions. Actions not specifically mandated by Article 2 of the UN Charter must be clearly prohibited.

(2) In recognition of the fact that spending on nuclear and nonnuclear assets depletes First and Third World economies, it shall be the task of inclusionary governments and inclusionary regimes to embark upon the deepening of democratic norms,

practices, and policies so as to alter current spending priorities. These norms are not to be enforced by any one or coalition of nations without the support of the UN Security Council.

(3) The necessity to embark upon a path toward inclusionary governance and demilitarization is supported by accumulated scientific evidence, which provides sufficient proof that the exchange and/or detonation of just a few nuclear bombs will have the capacity to create a global condition known as "nuclear winter" that could lead to climatic catastrophe, agricultural collapse, and world famine.

(4) The history and evolution of international law is moving in the direction of disarmament and has the capacity to build a global institutional structure that supports an alternative security system.

(5) The historical and recent experience of war and conflict has proven that a failure to recognize the influence of preexisting beliefs has implications for decision-making and that, therefore, the process of decision-making must become more inclusionary so as to overcome a history and practice of concealment, secrecy, and distortion through propaganda as well as bureaucratic and media manipulation.

(6) Genuine security and a peaceful world order cannot be premised upon notions of "deterrence" and "balance of power" because a spiral of violence is created by these concepts so that the exercise of power becomes self-defeating.

(7) The recognized need for a global security policy that places emphasis upon nonmilitary incentives to channel government's behavior empowers the international system to give added support to an expanded role for international organizations or security regimes to facilitate cooperation and to regulate intergroup conflict. (Paupp 2000, 84–104).

Insofar as these seven principles represent a recognition of the need to build a new consciousness within human beings for the future of humanity and the earth itself, these principles emerge from an inclusionary consciousness that seeks peace and an end to further waste in the investments of nations for war and dubious conceptions of what actually constructs genuine security and peace. To emerge from the shadows of the nuclear crucible, therefore, it is necessary to realize that "action can no longer be done simply out of even the most profound attachment to humankind," as Harvey says. "Action must be done from an even deeper source, an even deeper passion—the passion for the Divine. Action for humankind will be inevitably soured by disappointment and tragedy, darkened by the endless defeats that anyone fighting for peace or justice, or love in this world is bound to suffer as we confront the stupidity of the politicians and the greed of the bankers and the death-merchants. As we confront the infinite lust for blood that rages in the heart of humanity, we will know disappointment, tragedy, disillusion, the 'Bosnia-zation' of the world as neighbor attacks neighbor, and the collapse of all values . . . Action truly, deeply, and most effectively springs from an absolute passion for the Divine, not just for humankind itself; an absolute passion to be a pure mirror for the Divine, and a claim and absolute passion to be the channel through which divine justice, divine purity, and divine love flow" (Harvey 1994, 198).

REFERENCES

Douglas, James W. *The Non-Violent Cross: A Theology of Revolution and Peace*. New York: Macmillan, 1966.

Ellul, Jacques. 1964. *The Technological Society*. Trans. John Wilkinson. New York: Vintage.

Ellul, Jacques. 1973. *Propaganda: The Formation of Men's Attitudes*. New York: Vintage.

Ellul, Jacques. 1990. *The Technological Bluff*. Trans. Geoffrey W. Bromiley. Grand Rapids, Michigan: William B. Eerdman.

Ellul, Jacques. 2000. Ideas of Technology: The Technological Order–*New Perspective Quarterly*, Vol. 17, No. 73.

Falk, Richard. 1981. *Human Rights and State Sovereignty*, New York: Holmes & Meier.

———. 1984. "Nuclear Policy and World Order: Why Denuclearization? *Toward Nuclear Disarmament and Global Security: A Search for Alternatives*. Ed. Burns H. Weston. Boulder: Westview Press.

——— and Robert Jay Lifton. 1982. *Indefensible Weapons: The Political and Psychological Case Against Nuclearism*. New York: Basic.

——— and Lee Meyrowitz and Jack Sanderson, 1980. Nuclear Weapons and International Law, *Indian Journal of International Law*, Vol. 20.

——— and Andrew Strauss. 2001. Toward Global Parliament. *Foreign Affairs*, Jan./Feb.

Felice, William. 1998. "Militarism and Human Rights. *International Affairs* 74, no. 1.

Fitzgerald, Frances. 2000. *Way Out There in the Blue: Reagan, Star Wars, and the End of the Cold War*. New York: Simon & Schuster.

Friedman, L. Ed. 1972. *The Law of War: A Documentary History, Vol. 1.* New York: Random House.

Hartung, William D. 1994. *And Weapons for All: How America's Multibillion-Dollar Arms Trade Warps Our Foreign Policy and Subverts Democracy at Home*. New York: Harper Perennial.

Harvey, Andrew. 1994. *The Way Of Passion: A Celebration of Rumi*, Berkeley: Frog.

Jaspers, Karl. 1961. *The Future Of Mankind*. Trans. E. B. Ashton. Chicago: University of Chicago Press.

———. 1961. *The Atom Bomb and the Future of Man*. Trans. E. B. Ashton. Chicago: University of Chicago Press.

Kaiser, David. 2000. *American Tragedy: Kennedy, Johnson, and the Origins of the Vietnam War*. Cambridge: Belknap Press.

Kauzlarich, David and Ronald C. Kramer. 1998. *Crimes of the American Nuclear State—At Home and Abroad*. Boston: Northeastern University Press.

Kennedy, Edward M. 1969. Introduction, *ABM: An Evaluation of the Decision to Deploy an Antiballistic Missile System*. Ed. Jerome B. Wiesner, et al. New York: Signet.

Kennedy, John F. 1963. Remarks on the Twentieth Anniversary of the Voice of America. *Public Papers of the Presidents of the United States—John F. Kennedy—Containing the Public Messages, Speeches, and Statements of the President, January 1 to December 31, 1962*. Washington: United States Government Printing Office.

Krieger, David. 2001. "Stopping the New Nuclear Arms Race. *The Humanist*, March/April.

Lifton, Robert Jay, and Richard Falk. 1982. *Indefensible Weapons: The Political and Psychological Case Against Nuclearism*. New York.

McDougal, Myres S. 1981. "The Impact of International Law Upon National Law: A Policy-Oriented Perspective. *International Law Essays: A Supplement to International Law in Contemporary Perspective*, by Myres S. McDougal and W. Michael Reisman, New York: The Foundation Press, Inc., 1981.

McNamara, Robert S. and James G. Blight. 2001. *Wilson's Ghost: Reducing the Risk of Conflict, Killing, and Catastrophe in the Twenty-first Century*. Washington: Public Affairs.

Maguire, Peter. 2000. *Law and War: An American Story*. New York: Columbia University Press.

Michels, Robert. 1999. *Political Parties: A Sociological Study of the Oligarchical Tendencies of Modern Democracy*. New Brunswick, NJ: Transaction.

Mills, C. Wright. 1956. *The Power Elite*. New York: Oxford University Press.

Moltmann, Jurgen. 1973. *The Crucified God: The Cross of Christ as the Foundation and Criticism of Christian Theology*. New York: Harper & Row.

Nanda, Ved P. and David Krieger. 1998. *Nuclear Weapons and the World Court*. New York: Transnational.

New York Times. June 15, 2001, A30. Editorial, "Misrepresenting the ABM Treaty."

New York Times. June 22, 2001, A-1 and A-14. "Skeptical Senators Question Rumsfeld On Missile Defense."

Oliver, Kendrick. 1998. *Kennedy, Macmillan, and the Nuclear Test-Ban Debate, 1961–63*. New York: St. Martin's.

Paupp, Terrence Edward. 2000. *Achieving Inclusionary Governance: Advancing Peace and Development in First and Third World Nations*. New York: Transnational.

Pious, Richard M. 2001. The Cuban Missile Crisis and the Limits of Crisis Management. *Political Science Quarterly: The Journal of Public and International Affairs*. Vol. 116, No. 1.

Schell, Jonathan. 1982. *The Fate of the Earth*. New York: Avon.

———. 1998. *The Gift of Time: The Case for Abolishing Nuclear Weapons Now*. New York: Metropolitan.

———. 2000. The Unfinished Twentieth Century: What We Have Forgotten About Nuclear Weapons. *Harper's Magazine*.

———. 2001. "The New Nuclear Danger. *The Nation*.

Schier, Steven E. 2000. *By Invitation Only: The Rise of Exclusive Politics in the United States*. Pittsburgh: University of Pittsburgh Press.

Singh, Nagendra and Edward McWhinney. *Nuclear Weapons and Contemporary International Law*. Kluwer, 1989.

95

FINDING OUR RECENT AND PRESENT PAST

5

THE NUCLEAR LEGACY OF THE COLD WAR

John Steinbruner and Jeffrey Lewis

On May 24, 2002, at a summit meeting in Moscow, Russian President Vladimir Putin and United States President George W. Bush signed a treaty and issued a declaration of political accommodation promising, in Bush's words, to "liquidate the legacy of the Cold War." That is, of course, an appealing phrase and an aspiration every reasonable person will endorse. But it is certainly not an imminent accomplishment—not yet even the predominant trend.

The underlying reality is that U.S. military forces are being prepared for extended confrontation, not political accommodation. Their projected capabilities are inherently provocative not only to Russia, but to China as well. They are also vulnerable to Russian and Chinese reactions, particularly in space, where some of the most critical assets are based. Soothing rhetoric cannot indefinitely obscure the ominous implications. It is time for everyone to pay attention.

The treaty negotiated in Moscow limits the number of strategic nuclear warheads that are to be operationally deployed by their respective military establishments on December 31, 2012—on which day the treaty expires. At first glance, that appears to establish the principle of legal restraint for both nuclear forces. But the treaty sets *no* significant limit on destructive capabilities. The imposed ceiling of 2,200 operationally deployed nuclear warheads permits the United States, for instance, a sufficient number of immediately available nuclear weapons to destroy much of the Russian nuclear arsenal in a first strike, while simultaneously devastating Russia's conventional forces, political leadership, and industrial base. Moreover, the treaty covers only those weapons that are present at the operational bases of intercontinental range forces, allowing both signatories to retain "reserve" inventories greatly in excess of the 2,200-warhead ceiling. Reserve warheads could be "uploaded" onto delivery vehicles and returned to immediately available status in a short period of time.

So, for the foreseeable future, both nations will retain nuclear weapons far in excess of the number needed for any conceivable purpose—and there are no supplementary restraints. As a result, compliance with the treaty will not meaningfully diminish the lethal potential of either nation's nuclear force. Nor will the treaty establish an equitable or stable strategic balance, since Russia does not have the resources to safely maintain its nuclear forces at the size and alert rates envisioned by the United States. Over time, a deteriorating Russian arsenal will become increasingly vulnerable to preemptive attack, particularly as the United States undertakes planned modernization of nuclear forces and the deployment of missile defenses.

If this agreement were seriously expected to carry any burden whatsoever, it would not pass even the most rudimentary scrutiny. Despite the treaty's glaring inadequacies, Congress ratified the treaty with very little debate.

It is tempting, of course, to believe that the spirit of accommodation rhetorically proclaimed in Moscow might gradually dissolve the operational confrontation of the two nuclear forces that has prevailed continuously since the 1950s. To achieve that result, all weapons would have to be consigned to secure storage; none could be held available for immediate use; and preparations for massive, rapidly enacted retaliation would have to be decisively terminated. If all that were to occur, managerial control of each arsenal would be assured at a much higher standard than currently prevails, and the practical significance of residual disparities between them would be substantially diminished. That would come much closer to liquidating dangerous legacies.

Unfortunately, the Bush administration appears to have no interest in altering either the Cold War configuration of the U.S. nuclear arsenal or the Cold War mindset that underlies it.

Under the current planning guidance issued for U.S. nuclear forces, thousands of nuclear weapons are to be maintained indefinitely on continuous alert status. Those forces will continue to retain the capacity to devastate any foe on a few-minutes' notice. As at the height of the Cold War, their massively destructive firepower will be directed primarily against Russia and China, even if that fact is not announced as bluntly as it once was. Moreover, the American nuclear arsenal will be coupled with increasingly capable conventional forces, able to undertake increasingly intrusive operations on a global scale. The traditional emphasis on responding to aggression is being overlaid with a new stress on *initiating* attacks against terrorist networks and "evil" states suspected of seeking weapons of mass destruction. The forces instructed to develop and preserve this array of capabilities are supported by a U.S. defense budget larger than combined defense expenditures of the next twenty-five countries.

These forces, moreover, are being directed by increasingly nationalistic security policies. The Bush administration has conducted an assault on the major elements of the multilateral legal framework that had been developed to regulate security policies and force deployments. The United States abrogated the Anti-Ballistic Missile Treaty, which stood for thirty years as a widely acknowledged pillar of restraint. The U.S. forced termination of efforts to negotiate a compliance protocol for the Biological Weapons Convention. It has repeatedly denigrated and refused to ratify the Comprehensive Test Ban Treaty, despite international consensus on the necessity of such a ban. Some senior Bush officials have even publicly questioned the negative security assurances that previous administrations issued in support of the Nuclear Nonproliferation Treaty.

These policies are a sharp departure from past administrations of both parties and do not reflect majority sentiment as measured in opinion polls. The American political system has nevertheless not responded to this dramatic shift in policy and approach; for the moment, the political system appears to be far more interested in wielding effective force than in promoting global reassurance.

There is good reason to expect that a more balanced attitude will eventually emerge. Globalization, particularly the attendant process of economic engagement, creates a strong incentive to pursue seriously the political accommodation declared at the Moscow summit. The impulse for assertive superiority emanating from the American military planning system is not realistic and does not reflect the broader interests of the United States. A democratic process worthy of the name will eventually have to represent those interests, and in doing so will have to pursue equitable accommodation not just with Russia, but with China and all of the other major societies currently outside of our alliance system.

There are serious questions, however, as to how gracefully the necessary adjustments might occur. There could be some painful lessons along the way.

One implication of the Moscow summit is that Russia will pursue incremental accommodation over some period of time. In the initial stages, that effort will require Russia to accept both the inequitable force balances that will result from the Moscow treaty and significant institutional discrimination imposed by the NATO–Russia Council Agreement announced in Rome shortly after the Moscow summit. That implicit strategy reflects an impressively prudent judgment in the face of what Russian leaders in earlier times would undoubtedly have treated as hostile provocation. By tolerating some immediate indignity, the Russians have gained time to try to induce the United States and its allies to be more forthcoming than they currently are. Meanwhile, there is no specific situation likely to generate a sudden confrontation with the United States, and the stark disparities in military investment will not become urgently dangerous to Russia for another decade or so.

In the long run, however, if the strategy of incremental accommodation does not produce solid results, future Russian leaders are likely to devise a more forceful reaction. They cannot advertise that possibility without undermining the effort to achieve meaningful accommodation, but the logic they are likely to use is already visible in China.

In recent years, China has pursued economic accommodation with all the industrial democracies much more assertively and effectively than has Russia. That effort was consolidated with China's entry into the World Trade Organization. China's attempts to establish corresponding security arrangements have not been successful, however.

...o treaties regulating its security relationship with the ..., and China considers the most relevant political document—a 1982 communiqué intended to limit arms sales to Taiwan—to have been violated by the United States. Many Chinese officials view U.S. military planning projections with growing alarm and have concluded that China is now the principal target for the advanced capabilities the United States is developing. These officials worry that the U.S. ballistic-missile defense program is a direct threat to the minimal nuclear deterrent force that China has chosen to maintain.

Unlike the Russians, who have the option of playing for time, the Chinese are confronted with the prospect of near-term confrontation over the status of Taiwan—a reasonable assessment in light of the identification of a conflict over Taiwan as one of a handful of "immediate contingencies" in the U.S. Nuclear Posture Review. The Chinese are especially concerned that increasingly sophisticated American capabilities for preemptive attack might be used to support Taiwanese independence.

Although it is common in the United States to depict China as a rising power bent on regional domination, the security assessments provided by Chinese leaders are much more circumspect. Their central planning documents identify internal economic development as the overriding national priority and frankly admit the constraint this imposes on military development. After allowing defense expenditures to decline for the first fifteen years of its economic reform program, China began to increase its defense effort in the 1990s. Still, China's military investment remains substantially below that of the United States, certainly in absolute terms and probably as a percentage of overall defense spending as well.

The maintenance of a large U.S. nuclear arsenal, coupled with advanced space systems including missile defenses, creates concern in Beijing about the survivability of the Chinese nuclear deterrent. In the necessarily pessimistic assessment of the weaker party, China's leaders are compelled to consider whether the deployment of missile defense systems might allow the much stronger United States, perhaps during a crisis over Taiwan, to become confident that it could conduct a disarming first strike against China's two dozen intercontinental ballistic missiles (ICBMs). The Chinese worry that the United States might believe that missile defenses would be able to intercept in flight any

103

Chinese missiles that were not destroyed on the ground. The United States could also use space-based surveillance, reconnaissance, and precision strike assets to find and destroy the mobile ICBMs that China hopes to deploy in the next eight to ten years, in order to increase the survivability of its deterrent.

The Chinese were particularly alarmed by a 1998 long-range planning document released by the then–United States Space Command (USSPACECOM). That document outlined a concept called "global engagement"—a combination of global surveillance, missile defense, and space-based strike capabilities that would enable the United States to undertake effective preemption anywhere in the world and would deny similar capability to any other country.

USSPACECOM was frank about the controversial nature of such a proposal. "At present," the authors wrote, "the notion of weapons in space is not consistent with U.S. national policy. Planning for the possibility [of weapons in space] is a purpose of this plan should our civilian leadership decide that the application of force from space is in our national interest."

Most recently, prominent civilian officials have endorsed the change of policy that would be required to pursue the USSPACECOM vision. The Congressionally mandated Commission to Assess United States National Security Space Management and Organization warned of a "Pearl Harbor in space" unless the United States developed the capability to "project power in, through, and from space." Secretary of Defense Donald Rumsfeld, who chaired the commission before his nomination, identified outer space as one of a small number of key goals for defense transformation and implemented the organizational recommendations contained in the Space Commission report. The chairman of the Joint Chiefs of Staff, Air Force General Richard Myers, is the former commander in chief of USSPACECOM and a strong proponent of *global engagement*. Under Rumsfeld and Myers, the Defense Department has imposed changes in doctrine, organization, and budgets in support of a "global engagement" capability. The Defense Department drafted a new Nuclear Posture Review, which reportedly advocates the use of space-based assets to enhance conventional and nuclear strike missions; combined USSPACECOM with United States Strategic Command, which maintains operational control of U.S. nuclear forces, to create a single entity responsible for early warning, missile defense, and long-range strikes. Furthermore, in 2004 DoD announced plans for a "space-based test bed" by 2012 that would comprise 3–6 staellites capable of intercepting ballistic missiles in space.

As a practical matter, China has no real hope of matching the military capabilities currently being developed by the United States. China's leaders clearly understand that fact—but they have no intention of submitting to intimidation, either.

They are therefore exploring the feasibility of what U.S. officials term an "asymmetric" military response. They have identified U.S. assets in space as the prime target for such a response, and that is indeed the best available strategic choice. Space assets are exceedingly valuable—and exceedingly vulnerable. They can be successfully attacked at a small fraction of the cost and effort required to develop, protect, or replace them. Acts of interference or direct destruction would entail no immediate human casualties but could be monumentally disruptive to military and commercial support services. The mere prospect of discreet "asymmetric" acts of that sort can be expected to induce a more inclusive and more penetrating discussion of national interests within the American political system. If Chinese leaders are skillful enough to present that possibility as a legitimate reaction to provocation, they could expect to attract very substantial support from an international community increasingly interested in commercial space activities.

There is some risk, of course; an asymmetric strategy of this sort might backfire in the United States. Advocates of expanding U.S. military activities in outer space might successfully use threats of interference to confirm the aggressive intentions they have been projecting to justify their efforts. In that event, China would have to develop sufficient capacity for interference—against dedicated resistance—to be able to blunt U.S. preemptive operations. The feasibility of that project remains to be demonstrated, but it is certainly a plausible aspiration.

The earliest stages of a confrontation between the United States and China are already occurring at the United Nations Conference on Disarmament (CD) in Geneva. That is a forum that does not attract general public attention or directly affect the main channels of diplomacy. It therefore provides a means of issuing official warnings that can readily be retracted.

In recent years, the Chinese delegate to the CD has repeatedly stated that the plans for the military use of outer space projected by USSPACECOM are not consistent with the 1967 Outer Space Treaty. The preamble of this treaty provides legal protection for existing space assets, provided they are peaceful in character. The introduction of weapons for offensive purposes would violate that provision, China's delegates have contended, and would therefore remove legal protection for any asset that could contribute to military operations, a formulation that potentially includes commercial assets as well. Denial of legal protection is the first step in a strategy of legitimized interference.

China's delegates have also repeatedly asked for a formal mandate for the CD to negotiate a supplemental treaty, specifically to prohibit the placement of weapons in space, and to define more explicitly the acceptable terms of military support activities. Such a display of benign intent would be the second step in a Chinese strategy to win international support. The U.S. delegate has helped to validate both steps by repeatedly rejecting any effort to negotiate a new treaty.

This dispute has deadlocked the CD, which operates on the basis of consensus, leaving it without a plan of work since 1998. The intransigence displayed by the United States appears to be alienating many allies who worry about the impact of U.S. missile defense deployments on international stability. Just days after the Moscow summit, the Russian delegate joined his Chinese counterpart in presenting a draft working paper that outlined tentative suggestions on a treaty to prohibit the placement of weapons and use of force in outer space. The coincidence of timing was undoubtedly not an accident, as the Russians are fond of saying.

The development of rules to regulate activity in space in the emerging global security situation is admittedly a complex matter. There are reasonable disagreements about how best to proceed. It should be obvious, however, that equitable accommodation is overwhelmingly in the general interest and that the incipient confrontation now in its earliest stages is a preventable calamity. If there is to be a reasonable outcome, then the most insidious of the Cold War legacies—the apparent commitment of the United States to active military confrontation for decisive national advantage—will have to be adjusted in reality, not merely in words.

6

THE IRAQ WAR AND THE FUTURE OF INTERNATIONAL LAW

Richard Falk

The Iraq War, more than any foreign policy concern since Vietnam, has raised crucial issues about whether the United States government is prepared to comply with the core rules of international law governing the use of force. The failures of the policy are evident in the human and material costs of the operation as well as in the depth of resistance encountered in Iraq, despite the removal from power of a hated tyrant. Such obstacles raise further questions about whether the national interest, much less the human interest, is served by American political leaders claiming for themselves discretion to wage "wars of choice," that is, wars that are neither validated by the right of self-defense (as delimited by the UN Charter) nor by a mandate from the UN Security Council. The Iraq War outraged world public opinion, which viewed it as a flagrant instance of aggressive war against a sovereign state, and disturbed the leadership of most governments traditionally aligned with the United States on vital global policy issues. For all the dissent in the United States during the Vietnam War, it was only Cold War adversaries and neutral Sweden that explicitly opposed the war. In contrast, the United States was unable to win support in the UN Security Council for the war despite a determined diplomatic effort. Then, on February 15, 2003, an unprecedented outpouring of opposition to the impending war against Iraq resulted in demonstrations involving as many as eleven million persons, in more than 60 countries, and some 800 cities. As we know, despite this resounding "no" uttered by global civil society, the invasion of Iraq proceeded on schedule a few weeks later, exhibiting American unilateral defiance of this concerted expression of global public opinion, which was itself expressive of support for the prohibition on aggressive war. By American insistence, this prohibition was written into the UN Charter in Article 2(4), and served as the basis for indicting German and Japanese leaders after World War II as war criminals.

The main American pretext for war was the contention that Iraq possessed weapons of mass destruction (WMD) in violation of earlier Security Council resolutions requiring the elimination of all such weaponry from Iraqi stockpiles, and that Iraq posed a threat to neighbors and the United States that was intolerable in the aftermath of September 11. As we now know, these claims turned out to be false, although we do not yet know whether American leaders were at the time themselves fooled by faulty intelligence or engaged in deliberate deception so as to carry out their war plans. There are strong circumstantial reasons to be suspicious. There was much neoconservative advocacy of a regime-changing war against Iraq *prior* to September 11, leading many commentators to assume that the war was undertaken in pursuit of preexisting strategic goals involving oil, and of establishing military bases in the region, goals that were at best only tangentially related to either the presence of WMD or to the secondary claim of antiterrorism.[1]

A major concern here is with the relationship between how controversial foreign policy decisions are made and the vitality of constitutional democracy, specifically whether there is sufficient disclosure and assurances of integrity to allow Congress and the citizenry to play their proper roles of restraint and vigilance with respect to recourse to war. The unrestricted use of secrecy as a shield that precludes scrutiny further erodes any prospect of democratic accountability before, during, and after wars are launched. The manipulative presentation of the case for the Iraq War to the American people and to Congress by the Bush administration amply justifies a sense that the quality of democratic governance is once again being seriously eroded in the name of national security. This dynamic recalls the presence of similar worries throughout the course of the Cold War.

It is here, also, that an interface exists between constitutionalism and international law. Article VI(2) of the Constitution makes ratified treaties "the supreme law of the land," and the UN Charter is such a treaty, arguably the most important instance. So considered, both the executive and legislative branches of government have a constitutional obligation to uphold these charter norms, especially those dealing with recourse to war. The pretension that such legal constraints are inapplicable should have produced a strong congressional reaction, but part of the wider crisis arises because of the complicity of Congress in the disregard of international law dimensions of foreign policy decisions.[2]

This imperial style of presidential leadership is, of course, not new. It was a major topic that surfaced during the Vietnam War and was confirmed by the higher degree of transparency, after the fact, achieved by the whistle-blowing publication of the Pentagon Papers and a belated awakening of Congress. The continuing impact of September 11 has been to encourage almost unconditional deference to presidential authority, a tendency reinforced by the rightward trends in domestic politics, producing the reelection of George W. Bush despite his record of domestic and foreign policy failure.

The experience in Iraq needs to be evaluated from these perspectives. The obstacles encountered have not led to a softening of the approach to the use of force as a foreign policy option. President Bush in the 2004 State of the Union address received bipartisan applause when he declared that this country would never seek "a permission slip" when national security was at stake. In effect, the United States was announcing to the world and its own population that it would not condition its policy with respect to recourse to war on either international law or on the authority of the United Nations. Such a posture has several detrimental implications: It rejects international law as a constraining framework in the setting of war and peace; it endorses the resolve of the United States to engage in preemptive wars at times and places of its own choosing; it provides other potential aggressor states with an enabling precedent that poses real dangers for the future of world order; and it suggests a dual structure of rights in the world, with some countries facing intervention if they do not uphold international obligations as these are interpreted in Washington, and others being treated as sovereign entities not subject to any external forms of accountability.

The Iraq War provides a concrete instance of this attempt by the president to reconstitute world order along imperial lines. Although the Iraqi resistance to the ongoing American occupation shows no signs of abating, the outcome of the war remains in doubt. What cannot be doubted is the damage done to international law and the authority of the United Nations, at least in the short run, by American unilateralism with respect to war making. This chapter will assess the overall impact of the Iraq War on international law by asking and responding to six questions:

(1) Should the Iraq War be treated as a defining moment for international law?

(2) Should the refusal to endorse the Iraq War be regarded as a triumphant moment for the United Nations, especially the Security Council?

(3) Can the Iraq War be interpreted as an illegal, but legitimate war of choice?

(4) Should the legal norm of nonintervention in the internal affairs of sovereign states be abandoned?

(5) Are the legal norms associated with international humanitarian law, as incorporated in the Geneva Conventions of 1949, outmoded or "quaint"?

(6) Does the Iraq War provide an occasion for incorporating new norms of international law that expand the discretion of states to make war?

My response to each of these questions is a resounding "no," and the remainder of this essay will give the essential reasoning behind the answer.

I. Should the Iraq War be treated as *a defining moment* for international law? No.

Proponents of the war contend that the Iraq War was a defining moment for international law and for the authority of the United Nations. The argument made is that the Iraq War has vindicated the doctrine of preemptive war, thereby making nondefensive wars of choice an option for states in shaping their security policy, and that the failure of the UN Security Council to back the invasion has made the organization, as President Bush warned before the war in his speech to the General Assembly of September 12, 2002, "irrelevant." But this effort to rewrite the most significant parts of the UN Charter and of modern international law has proved to be totally unconvincing outside the annals of neoconservative partisan renderings of international law.

Recourse to war against Iraq in March 2003 on the facts and allegations that existed at the time is regarded around the world as flagrantly at odds with international law and the UN Charter. The war against Iraq is widely viewed as an instance of illegal or aggressive war. The clarity of this consensus among respected international law specialists and public opinion deprives the Iraq undertaking of any stature as a *legal* precedent.[3] Of course, it may still be invoked by future governments as a *political* precedent, as a claim and enactment by a state that could be imitated by other states, but without the effect of establishing new, less restrictive legal constraints on recourse to war.

The American invasion of Iraq is best understood as a prominent instance of a violation of the core obligation of the UN Charter, as embodied in Article 2(4), and as such qualifies as a potential crime against peace in the Nuremberg sense. It provides an occasion to reaffirm the fundamentally sound idea embodied in international law that force can only legally be used under conditions of palpable *defensive necessity* (or possibly on the basis of an explicit mandate from the Security Council). Note that defensive necessity is broader than "self-defense" and does take realistic account of the extent to which the stability of the prohibition on force needs to be adapted to post–September 11 circumstances by potentially giving greater latitude to the meaning of "self-defense" than is suggested by the textual language of Article 51 of the UN Charter. In this regard, it is imaginable that preemptive uses of force against imminent or menacing credible threats of major attacks might be treated as "lawful" under such exceptional conditions, although the burden of persuasion would be upon the claimant state. The Afghanistan War might qualify under such legal reasoning as a valid claim of defensive necessity even in the absence of a demonstration of imminence. The legal argument, never clearly made by the Bush administration, would have been that the al-Qaeda threat was of such a character that any state that failed to control its territorial operations was complicit in the planning, preparations, and execution of megaterrorism, and subject to attack on grounds of defensive necessity.[4]

It is worth noting that several of the staunchest supporters of the Iraq War as a matter of strategic and moral necessity, such as British Prime Minister Tony Blair and the influential American neoconservative Richard Perle, have acknowledged that respect for international law was unwarranted to the extent that it would have precluded the Iraq War. In effect, the most articulate advocates of the Iraq War concede, either implicitly or explicitly, that it was "illegal." Or, that if "regime change" to overthrow a tyrant by force was precluded, then it was "bad law," and should not be respected. It is notable in this regard that the Bush administration made only the most minimal effort to provide a *legal* rationale for the Iraq War and based its public justifications on a confusing and shifting mixture of security and humanitarian rationales. And as for the irrelevance of the UN, the difficulties of the occupation have increasingly led even the Bush administration to seek UN help in bringing stability to Iraq. The U.S. government's initial plans to control the entire reconstruction of Iraq have been abandoned, and American officials have pleaded with the United Nations to assume greater responsibilities. This has been evident in identifying the personnel for the so-called interim Iraqi government and in establishing conditions that might enable the election of an Iraqi legislature to go forward in early 2005.

Shifting ground, I would insist that even if the Iraq War had turned out to be an entirely successful political project, it would not have altered the legal status of the invasion. It is possible that if the occupying forces had been generally and genuinely greeted as liberators, and had not generated widespread resistance, the intervention might have been influentially viewed as an instance of humanitarian intervention and a contribution to the Iraqi right of self-determination, enjoying a status somewhat analogous to the Kosovo intervention of 1999. That status has been described as illegal, yet legitimate.[5] But there is nothing about this dynamic of stretching international law to address changing norms of humanitarian and defensive necessity that in any way justifies the overall abandonment of the international law of war on the grounds that it has become obsolete for various reasons. Indeed, making such an argument in the setting of the Kosovo debate contributed to an atmosphere of legal nihilism exhibited a few years later by a legally inexcusable recourse to war against Iraq, followed by the grossly irresponsible language of announcing that the United States will never seek a permission slip from a global institution for its wars.[6]

What might have been the case if the Iraq invasion had been the cakewalk promised by its most vocal advocates is that the preemptive claim would produce a defining moment for American foreign policy and for the future character of world order. It could have become a precedent for American unilateralism within the context of recourse to war and for regime-changing interventions. If this pattern were to be established it would produce what might be called a *geopolitical norm*, that is, a use of power by a hegemonic state in a predictable pattern to achieve specified goals. The main feature of such a norm would be a repudiation of the authority of international law and the UN Charter by state practice that violates an abiding consensus that joins the views of the majority of states and world public opinion.

At present, the U.S. government seems to be claiming for itself the role of being the legislative agency for the creation of geopolitical norms, reinforced by ad hoc coalitions of the willing, in at least two areas impinging on the legal norms governing the use of force: intervention in sovereign states to achieve regime change, and selective, coercive pressure and threats of war and intervention to promote counterproliferation goals beyond the legal mandate of the nonproliferation treaty regime. To the extent that these geopolitical norms are acted upon, it represents a fundamental shift from world order based on the principles of territorial sovereignty to a world order based on hegemonic edict and superpower managerial authority. Such a world is best denominated as an *imperial* world order, and would almost certainly be challenged in various ways by statist and nonstatist forms of armed resistance, as well as by diplomatic efforts to form countervailing alliances. Indeed, the European refusal to go along with the Iraq War was based to a significant degree on the importance of respecting international law.[7]

II. Should the refusal to endorse the Iraq War by the United Nations, especially the Security Council, be viewed as a *triumphant moment*? No.

Many opponents of the Iraq War have praised the UN Security Council for remaining steadfast in the face of formidable U.S. pressure to provide a formal mandate for the initiation of a regime-changing war against Iraq. I agree that the Security Council deserves some credit for this result, but I would argue that it did only about 25 percent of the job entrusted to it by the UN Charter. If the American-led claims against Iraq were evaluated from the perspective of international law or by reference to the war prevention goals of the charter, then the UN performance was still 75 percent or so deficient.

There are several dimensions of this deficiency: The UN imposed on Iraq a punitive peace via Security Council Resolution 687 (April 3, 1991) comparable in the setting of the Gulf War to the discredited Versailles approach to Germany after World War I; the UN lent its authority to twelve-plus years of punitive sanctions against Iraq despite evidence of indiscriminate, massive harm to the Iraqi civilian population; the UN did not censure the United States or the United Kingdom for repeated, unauthorized threats and uses of force that intruded upon the sovereign rights of Iraq in this same period and inflicted damage and casualties; Security Council Resolution 1441 (November 8, 2002) adopted the main premises of American geopolitical norms relating to counterproliferation and regime change, seemingly suggesting that if Washington had been more patient or Baghdad more recalcitrant the endorsement of recourse to war would likely have been forthcoming from the Security Council.

In the background of the UN role with respect to the Iraq War are some important issues of an admittedly hypothetical character. Suppose that the UN Security Council had authorized the Iraq War. Would that have made it "legal"? Is the UN legally entitled to endorse and cleanse what would otherwise be considered a war of aggression without such an endorsement? Who is authorized to make such a determination if there is no judicial review of Security Council decisions, as seems to be the implication of the World Court judgment in *Lockerbie*? It seems reasonable to assume that only the General Assembly has some sort of residual responsibility to assess whether the Security Council has acted beyond the constitutional limits imposed by the UN Charter, but it lacks the power of decision, and its judgment would be only an expression of opinion that would not have much legal weight.

III. Can the Iraq War be interpreted as an *illegal, but legitimate* war of choice? No.

In my view, as suggested, the illegality of recourse to war against Iraq in 2003 was clear. It was also clear before and after the war that there was no reasonable basis for invoking the "illegal but legitimate" formula developed by the Independent International Commission for Kosovo to deal with an exceptional circumstance of *humanitarian emergency*. With respect to Iraq, the worst humanitarian abuses were associated with the campaign carried out against the Kurds in the late 1980s, and against the Kurds in northern Iraq and the Shia in southern Iraq immediately following the Gulf War in 1991. Perhaps a case for humanitarian intervention could have been credibly made in these earlier settings. But the Kosovo exception was based on the *imminence* of danger associated with the feared ethnic cleansing of the Albanian population, made credible by Serb behavior in Bosnia just a few years earlier, by the rising tide of Serb atrocities in Kosovo in the months preceding recourse to war under the NATO umbrella, and by the massive exodus of Albanian Kosovars. In these circumstances, the absence of a Security Council mandate posed a legal obstacle, but the opposing political and moral urgencies, as well as the regional backing of the intervention, seemed of sufficient magnitude to justify the use of force.

115

Given the failure to find weapons of mass destruction of any variety in Iraq, and considering the intense resistance to the occupation, there is also no way to maintain convincingly that either a condition of defensive necessity or humanitarian emergency, existed in Iraq as of 2003. If there was such an emergency it was not attributable to the Baghdad regime, however dictatorial its record, but at that point in time was primarily a result of UN sanctions and numerous uses of force against Iraq.

IV. Should the legal norm of nonintervention in internal affairs of sovereign states be abandoned? No.

The Iraq War, along with other experiences of interventionary diplomacy, suggests that respect for the norm of nonintervention,

along with accompanying respect for territorial sovereignty, continues
to represent a prudent guideline for statecraft. If the U.S. government
had adhered to such a guideline over the course of the last several
decades it would have avoided its two worst foreign policy disasters: the
Vietnam War and the Iraq War. Additionally, if it had refrained from
regime-changing covert interventions in Iran (1953) and Guatemala
(1954), it might have avoided the Iranian Revolution and not had
blood on its hands due to the years of atrocity and brutality in
Guatemala.

116

The Iraq War confirms the wisdom of avoiding interventionary
diplomacy unless genuine conditions of defensive necessity or humanitarian emergency exist, and even then extreme caution is appropriate.
As the Iraqi resistance confirms, interventionary wars are primarily
"political" phenomena, not "military," and are decided by the play of
nationalist, ethnic, and religious passions. In the absence of a genocidal spiral or severe widespread crimes against humanity, it is best to
await the dynamics of self-determination to achieve transformative
changes in dictatorial states. The experience with Eastern Europe, the
Soviet Union, and South Africa is both instructive and encouraging.

V. Are the humanitarian laws of war outmoded and "quaint"? No.

Members of the Bush administration's legal team rendered advice
that made it permissible to use violence and humiliation as part of
interrogation techniques. Prisoners were classified as "enemy combatants" and were on some occasions transferred for interrogation to
countries known to practice torture in order to extract information
from them. The legal arguments put forward questioned both the
applicability of the humanitarian law of war (the Geneva Conventions)
because of the nature of the jihadist enemy, and regarded the legal edi-
fice as "quaint" due to the character of conflict in the post–September
11 world. Such a loosening of legal bonds has produced the repre-
hensible practices reported to have occurred in American military
prisons, involving sexual abuse and shameless humiliation of Iraqi
and other detainees at Abu Ghraib and elsewhere. The recording of
this behavior on the digital cameras of the soldiers is indicative of the
effects of suspending the operation of law in combat contexts. It is true
that some of the immediate perpetrators are being court-martialed for
this behavior, but as yet procedures of accountability have not been

extended to those at levels of military command or political authority. What has become clear is that compliance with international humanitarian law is more important now than ever before, precisely because of the character of the conflict and its tendency to give rise to patterns of ethnic hatred and religious hostility.

VI. Does the Iraq War suggest the need for adapting international law to the new conditions of international conflict in the aftermath of September 11? No.

From the argument made above, the simple conclusion here is that the Iraq War is an occasion for reaffirming the continuing viability and validity of the legal prohibition on nondefensive uses of force that is contained in the UN Charter. At the same time, the grave threats posed by the sort of megaterrorist attacks of September 11 do justify stretching the right of self-defense to validate uses of force, as necessary, to remove threats associated with nonstate actors in the event that the territorial government is unable or unwilling to address the situation decisively and with due urgency. The Afghanistan War, with qualifications, arguably fits within such an expanded conception of self-defense, but, as noted, to act on this legally plausible claim was probably imprudent, especially given the American unwillingness to carry out the mission effectively by encircling the area known to be held by al-Qaeda and to provide the necessary countrywide security and reconstruction aid to create a normally functioning state that operates according to constitutional guidelines. The decision to implicate "the axis of evil" countries, followed by recourse to the Iraq War, doomed the reconstruction of Afghanistan, and has certainly made the country a major source of drugs and a scene of turmoil and civil violence. The point here is that not every legally permissible war is politically beneficial.

A CONCLUDING NOTE

The Iraq War showcases the consequences of abandoning a law-oriented approach to foreign policy and world order. It represents for the United States a complete inversion of its earlier role in the aftermath of World War II as champion of the Nuremberg approach to international accountability for those who act on behalf of sovereign states and of the unconditional repudiation of aggressive war. The experience in Iraq would tend to confirm the *practical* wisdom of these earlier *normative* views as to the limits of legal discretion given to states with respect to recourse to war. The United States, the world, and the future would all benefit from the voluntary acceptance of the constraints of international law as the foundation of a global security system. Such a generalized assertion loses none of its persuasiveness due to the September 11 attacks or the persistence of international jihadism, but it should also be understood that law evolves in response to changing values and defensive imperatives. International law is not a legalistic prison that requires states to expose themselves and their populations to imminent and palpable threats. There exists ample flexibility within international law to deal with legitimate claims of self-defense, but with respect to illegitimate claims, such as Iraq, there is no occasion for innovative evasions of international law.

118

NOTES

1 This was enunciated by the notorious report of Project for a New American Century, "Repairing America's Defenses," Washington, D.C., September 2000, as well as extensively documented in Robert Woodward, *Plan of Attack* (New York: Simon and Schuster, 2004).

2 The crisis is wider and deeper. The complicity of the media represents a serious aspect of the overall situation, including the most trusted and responsible organs of opinion. See Howard Friel and Richard Falk, *The Record of the Paper: How the* New York Times *Misreports U.S. Foreign Policy.* New York: Verso, 2004.

3 This consensus was probably most authoritatively expressed by the World Court in a case repudiating the American role of support for the Contras in their efforts to overthrow the legally constituted government of Nicaragua. See *Nicaragua v. United States of America*, International Court of Justice Reports, 1986.

4 I made an argument along these lines in *The Great Terror War* (Northampton, MA: Olive Branch Press, 2003), although I now believe that it was a serious mistake of policy to have adopted a "war" mode of response to September 11 as distinct from fashioning a robust "law enforcement" mode. At the same time, from the perspective of legality, it still seems that the U.S. recourse to war was a justifiable extension of the right of self-defense, and did establish a *legal* precedent. For an account of the manner by which "incidents" or claims based on state practice lead under certain circumstances to the reconfiguration of norms see W. Michael Reisman and Andrew Willard, eds., *International Incidents: The Law That Counts in World*

Politics (Princeton, NJ: Princeton University Press, 1988). For a more extensive consideration of how the law governing force evolves see Myres S. McDougal and Florentino P. Feliciano, *Law and Minimum World Public Order* (New Haven, CT: Yale University Press, 1962).

5 This distinction will be discussed below. It was first used to lend moral and political support to the Kosovo War, while acknowledging its dubious legal character. See *Kosovo Report: Conflict, International Response, Lessons Learned*, Report of the Independent International Commission on Kosovo (Oxford, UK: Oxford University Press, 2000, 163–200).

6 The most intelligent version of such a nihilist position is that argued by Michael J. Glennon, *Limits of Law, Prerogatives of Power: Interventionism After Kosovo* (New York: Palgrave, 2001).

7 This refusal has been given a neocon spin that consigns "law" to the weak, and claims "force" for the strong in Robert Kagan, *Of Paradise and Power* (New York: Knopf, 2003).

7

WEAPONS OF MASS DESTRUCTION AND HUMAN RIGHTS

Peter Weiss and John Burroughs

You can't trade your freedom for security, because if you do you're going to lose both.

—Braydon Mayfield[1]

With a few exceptions those who think, write, and speak about Weapons of Mass Destruction (WMD) live in a different world from those who think, write, and speak about human rights.[2] WMD experts in the field of arms control consider such problems as how to abolish these weapons or at least reduce the risk of their being used, how to prevent their proliferation, what damage they cause to humans and other living things, etc. Human rights specialists contemplate which human rights are "real," what should be their order of priority, how best to enforce them, and whether a culture of human rights can be introduced to society. Rarely do these two communities consider the overlapping issues of their respective fields.

And yet linkages between WMD and human rights are manifold, including the following:

- The incompatibility of the right to peace and the right to life with the existence of WMD;
- The vanishing line between the humanitarian law aspects of WMD and the human rights aspects in the strict sense;

- The fear engendered by the thought of WMD "in the wrong hands," which has been used by governments as a justification for curtailing or suspending human rights; and
- The effect of WMD on the perpetuation of the war system and the resulting drain on resources that would otherwise be available for the implementation of economic and social human rights.

As this article will explore, the linkages have become more complex since the September 11, 2001, terrorist attacks and the invasion of Iraq. To be sure, much has not changed. The risk of nuclear war with which the world has lived since World War II remains. Shockingly, the United States and the Russian Federation, despite their apparent partnership, are still locked in a nuclear stand-off in which each side maintains many hundreds of warheads ready for launch at a moment's notice. India and Pakistan have more than once teetered on the brink of a major war that could go nuclear. Other scenarios for use of nuclear arms cannot be ruled out, for example on the Korean Peninsula or in a China-United States conflict over Taiwan. But the world now faces new consequences of states' reliance on WMD. The specter of its spread to additional states has become a stated rationale for war. And the fear of its acquisition by Al Qaeda-like groups has given powerful impetus to the worldwide efforts to suppress terrorism.

While the category of WMD encompasses chemical, biological, and nuclear weapons, it must be remembered that, while chemical and biological weapons have the capacity to cause great and indiscriminate harm, their overall effect is infinitesimal compared with that of today's strategic nuclear weapons, some of which have a destruction capacity thirty times or more that of the bombs the United States dropped on Hiroshima and Nagasaki in 1945.[3] In this article, the emphasis will be on nuclear weapons.

WMD AND THE RIGHT TO PEACE

While the UN Charter excludes a commitment to peace as its principal objective—from the first sentence of the Preamble, "We the Peoples of the United Nations determined to save succeeding generations from the scourge of war," to the prohibition of aggression in Article 2(4) and the mandate for peaceful resolution of conflicts in

Article 33—the right to peace as such is not found in the Universal Declaration of Human Rights, nor in any of the conventions that have evolved from it. The closest the Universal Declaration comes is Article 28, which provides that "[e]veryone is entitled to a social and international order in which the rights and freedoms set forth in this Declaration can be fully realized." However, this omission was cured by General Assembly resolution 39/11, adopted on November 12, 1984, the "Declaration on the Right of Peoples to Peace." It "[s]olemnly proclaims that the peoples of our planet have a sacred right to peace" and declares that "the promotion of its implementation constitute[s] a fundamental obligation of each State."[4]

123

But the right to peace has fallen on hard times and WMD have played a central role in its demise. A section containing contributions on the legal aspects of the Iraq war in the July 2003 issue of the *American Journal of International Law* begins with the following words from the editors: "The military actions against Iraq in Spring 2003 is one of the few events of the UN Charter period holding the potential for fundamental transformation, *or possibly even destruction*, of the system of law governing the use of force that had evolved during the twentieth century."[5] These are strong words, to be sure, but justifiably so when seen in the context of the new doctrine of preemptive war propagated by the United States and accepted by a number of other countries, a doctrine that should more accurately be called preventive war and that bears a close connection to WMD.

In order to examine this connection we must first review briefly the principles that have governed the legality of going to war since the UN Charter came into force in 1945. The first is Article 2(4) of the Charter, which states that "[a]ll members shall refrain in their international relations from the threat or use of force against the territorial integrity or political independence of any state, or in any manner inconsistent with the purposes of the United Nations."

Only two exceptions are allowed to this prohibition against the threat or use of force by one nation against another. Article 42 permits the Security Council to "take such actions by air, sea, or land forces as may be necessary to maintain or restore international peace and security" once it has determined that a threat to the peace, breach of the peace, or act of aggression has occurred and that the measures not involving the use of force would be or have proved to be inadequate to maintain or restore international peace and security. Article 51 states that "[n]othing in the present Charter shall impair the inherent right of individual or collective self-defence if an armed attack occurs against a member of the UN, until the Security Council has taken measures necessary to maintain international peace and security." This article is the codification of the definition of self-defense as it has existed in customary law since at least the famous *Caroline Incident* of 1837, when Daniel Webster, then the American Secretary of State, defined justifiable self-defense as requiring that it be "instant, overwhelming and leaving no choice of means, and no moment for deliberation."[6]

How far from the mandate of the Charter the new policy of preventive war digresses is made plain by President Bush's introduction to the *National Security Strategy* of September 17, 2002,[7] in which he states: "As a matter of common sense and self-defense, American will act against such emerging threats before they are fully formed."

What are these emerging threats that, according to some, call for the scrapping of the fundamental structure of the UN Charter insofar as it relates to the use of force? We find the answer in the following comments by defenders of the legality of the Iraq war:

- According to William Howard Taft IV and Todd F. Buchwald, the legal advisor and assistant legal advisor of the United States Department of State: "A central consideration, at least from the U.S. point of view, was the risk embodied in allowing the Iraqi regime to defy the international community by pursuing weapons of mass destruction."[8]
- Professor John Yoo of the University of California states: "In addition to the probability of the threat, the threatened magnitude of harm must be relevant. The advent of nuclear and other sophisticated weapons has dramatically increased the degree of potential harm, and the importance of the temporal factor has diminished. Weapons of mass destruction threaten devastating and indiscriminate long-term damage to large segments of the civilian population and environment."[9]
- Professor Ruth Wedgwood of Johns Hopkins University uses President Kennedy's handling of the Cuban missile crisis as a precedent for President Bush's decision to invade Iraq: "The introduction of nuclear weapons into Cuba," she writes, "reducing Soviet launch time to seven minutes, would have destroyed any adequate interval for the assessment of nuclear

warnings," thus justifying the United States imposing a defensive quarantine.[10]

What about this new doctrine of preemptive/preventive war has made it palatable to so many people, despite the fact that it undermines the very essence of the United Nations Charter? Apparently it is the *magnitude* of the armed attack that the preemptor sees coming from the presumed attacker, as well as the impossibility of determining just when the attack will occur. It has been argued that the September 11, 2001 attacks on the United States radically altered interpretations of international law. It is doubtful that the United States would have felt justified invading and occupying Afghanistan *before* the tragic events of 2001, simply on the speculation that a devastating terrorist attack might occur someday.

Thus, the characteristics of WMD, and of nuclear weapons in particular, provide both the magnitude and condensed launch time that expand the concept of self-defense from a reaction to actual or imminent aggression to a preventive strike against aggression that may occur at any time in the future, be it weeks, months, or years from now. What makes this front attack on the Charter's regime of *ius ad bellum* particularly invidious is that it leaves each state the sole judge of when preventive war is justified, even when, as in the case of Iraq, the "emerging threat" proves eventually to have been based on faulty or deliberately misconstrued intelligence.[11]

The mere invocation of the threat of nuclear weapons, whether delivered by plane, by missile, or by suitcase, the rhetorical projection of a mushroom cloud over Manhattan—or London, Mumbai, or any other city—tends to cut off rational discussion. It is likely, therefore, that the preemptive/preventive war doctrine will spread as long as the spectre of nuclear weapons in the arsenal of a state or in the hands of a nonstate actor can be summed up. It is worth noting in this connection that, according to United States Deputy Secretary of Defense Paul Wolfowitz, when justification for going to war with Iraq was being discussed at the highest levels of the American government, "For bureaucratic reasons, we settled on one issue, weapons of mass destruction, because it was the one reason everyone could agree on."[12]

According to Mohamed El Baradei, the director-general of the International Atomic Energy Agency (IAEA), in addition to the known nuclear-weapons powers, "there are an increasing number of countries with the technological capability of making . . . nuclear weapons."[13] This makes it imperative that the world community find a way to end, once and for all, the chimera of nuclear weapons as a deterrent and address in a serious way the mandate of the International Court of Justice "to pursue in good faith and bring to a conclusion negotiations leading to nuclear disarmament in all its aspects under strict and effective international control."[14]

WMD AND THE RIGHT TO LIFE

In the contest for primacy among the variety of human rights, the right to life arguably occupies the highest rank. As provided by Article 6(1) of the International Covenant on Civil and Political Rights, "Every human being has the inherent right to life. This right shall be protected by law. *No one shall be arbitrarily deprived of his life.*"[15]

While there is clearly an overlap between the right to peace and the right to life, they are not coextensive. In the armed conflicts of today, increasing numbers of civilians are being deprived simultaneously of the right to peace and the right to life. However, the right to life survives in wartime, if only because of the humanitarian law prohibition of weapons and tactics that fail to discriminate between combatants and noncombatants.

Although we are witnessing a strong trend toward the convergence and integration of human rights law and humanitarian law, it was not always so. The 1948 Universal Declaration of Human Rights and the 1949 Geneva Conventions were negotiated by separate bodies, the first in the UN General Assembly in New York, and the second in a diplomatic conference in Geneva with the assistance of the International Committee of the Red Cross, and mostly by different diplomats. There was little recognition of commonalities despite the fact that the Third and Fourth Geneva Conventions manifestly seek to safeguard the human rights of prisoners of war and of civilians in occupied territories.[16] The initial division of the branches of international law arose from the newness of *international* human rights law and a desire in the wake of a disastrous war to focus on the maintenance of peace through the UN Charter and on respect for human rights during peacetime. The two branches also have differing approaches: one focuses upon the articulation of *rights* held by individuals vis-à-vis states; the other imposes *duties* upon states and their personnel in inner-state conflicts as well as in internal conflicts with organized armed forces.[17]

As human rights law grew in prominence, and as the necessity was recognized of limiting the ravages of war, especially internal conflicts, that persisted around the world during the Cold War, it became impossible to ignore the core idea shared by the two branches: the protection of the human person. In the case of humanitarian law, the idea is exemplified by the principle of civilian immunity—that civilians are never to be the target of attack and are additionally to be protected against the effects of warfare to the maximum extent possible consistent with military necessity.

In 1968, a resolution entitled "Human Rights in Armed Conflicts" was adopted by the Teheran International Conference on Human Rights.[18] The resolution began by observing that "peace is the underlying condition for the full observance of human rights and war is their negation" but that agreements "to ensure the better protection of civilians, prisoners and combatants in all armed conflicts," as well as the "prohibition and limitation of the use of certain methods and means of warfare." By 1977, a comprehensive codification of humanitarian law protecting civilians against the effects of warfare had been negotiated, Protocal I to the Geneva Conventions. Agreements providing the prohibition and elimination of weapons that inflict mass or indiscriminate destruction also were created, initially the 1972 Biological Weapons Convention, and later the 1993 Chemical Weapons Convention and the 1997 Mine Ban Convention.[19]

In the years following the Teheran conference, while the formal division between human rights law and humanitarian law remained, there was widespread recognition of their interdependence and common elements. This was spurred by the fact that in situations of internal strife, the distinction between the two branches becomes hard to maintain, as it is not always possible to determine whether or not violence has reached the level of intensity and organization qualifying as "armed conflict" to which humanitarian law applies.[20] The close relationship is well illustrated by the fact that NGOs specializing in human rights, notably Human Rights Watch, have undertaken in-depth monitoring of compliance with humanitarian law requirements.[21]

In 1985, the UN Human Rights Committee, the body charged with overseeing implementation of the Covenant on Civil and Political

127

Rights, strongly asserted the relevance of human rights law to the consequences of reliance on nuclear weapons, both in the context of war, traditionally the province of humanitarian law, and of international relations more generally. The committee commented that:

> It is evident that the designing, testing, manufacture, possession and deployment of nuclear weapons are among the greatest threats to the right to life which confront mankind today. This threat is compounded by the danger that the actual use of such weapons may be brought about, not only in the event of war, but even through human or mechanical error or failure.
>
> Furthermore, the very existence and gravity of this threat generate a climate of suspicion and fear between States, which is itself antagonistic to the promotion of universal respect for and observance of human rights and fundamental freedoms in accordance with the Charter of the United Nations and the International Covenants on Human Rights.[22]

In 1994, overcoming the determined opposition of the nuclear-weapons states, nonnuclear weapons countries mustered a majority in the UN General Assembly for a resolution requesting the International Court of Justice to render an advisory opinion on the following question: "Is the threat or use of nuclear weapons in any circumstance permitted under international law?" In vivid and extensive written and oral argumentation by more than forty states, the focus was mostly on the UN Charter, the requirements of necessity and proportionality for the lawful exercise of self-defense, and humanitarian law governing the conduct of warfare. But human rights arguments also had their part, with many states referring to the right to life, and some advancing comprehensive and sophisticated analyses encompassing economic and social rights.

Thus the Solomon Islands linked the right to life with the right to health and with international law requiring global protection of human health and the environment, arguing that a nuclear explosion—with effects well beyond the target state—would violate the human rights of persons in neutral as well as target states.[23] As the Solomon Islands noted, Article 12(1) of the International Covenant on Economic, Social, and Cultural Rights recognizes "the right of everyone to the enjoyment of the highest attainable standard of physical and mental health," and mandates in Article 12(2)(b) that states take steps to accomplish "the improvement of all aspects of environmental and industrial hygiene." Article 25 of the Universal Declaration of Human Rights provides that "[e]veryone has the right to a standard of living adequate for the health and well-being of himself and his family." A right to a clean and healthy environment has been implied from these provisions and other instruments of international law and policy.

Professor Philippe Sands commented regarding the counter-arguments of the nuclear-weapon states France, Britain, the Russian Federation, and the United States:

> [T]hese same States which pride themselves—with some justification—on their role in promulgating the rule of law, promoting human rights, and preserving the environment. Yet when it comes to those very weapons of mass destruction which pose a greater threat to human rights and the environment than anything else imaginable, these States ask you to set aside that body of principles and rules so carefully put in place over the past 50 years. They ask you, in effect, to re-situate yourself in 1945, to ignore all subsequent developments and to follow Balzac's dubious proposition, "that laws are spider webs through which the big flies pass and the little ones get caught."[24]

Arguing for Costa Rica, human rights specialist Carlos Vargas-Pizarro invoked a still larger frame, stating that "nuclear threat or use cannot coexist with the achievement of a global order embodying common security that realizes the purposes of the United Nations and provides fundamental human rights for all persons. . . ."[25]

In its 1996 opinion, the International Court of Justice primarily addressed the human rights arguments under the rubric of the right to life. The Court held that, contrary to the position advanced by some states, this fundamental human right applies in time of war as well as in time of peace, subject to the following qualification:

> The test of what is an arbitrary deprivation, however, then falls to be determined by the applicable *lex specialis*, namely, the law applicable in armed conflict which is designed to regulate the conduct of hostilities. Thus, whether a particular loss of life, through the use of a certain

weapon in warfare, is to be considered an arbitrary deprivation of life contrary to Article 6 of he Covenant [on Civil and Political Rights], can only be decided by reference to the law applicable in armed conflict and not deduced from the terms of the Covenant itself.[26]

In other words, the interpretation of the human right to life in wartime depends on applicable principles of humanitarian law. Citing particularly the humanitarian law principles forbidding the infliction of indiscriminate harm and unnecessary suffering, the Court held the threat or use of nuclear weapons to be generally contrary to international law. It follows that use of nuclear weapons would necessarily entail a massive violation of the most basic of human rights, the right to life.[27]

The human rights arguments also seem to have influenced the Court's strong discussion of the relevance of environmental law. The Court stated that the "use of nuclear weapons could constitute a catastrophe for the environment" and observed that the environment "represents the living space, the quality of life and the very health of human beings, including generations unborn."[28] Further, in explaining the principles of humanitarian law upon which it primarily relied, the Court stated that there is broad adherence to the Hague and Geneva Conventions because "a great many rules of humanitarian law applicable in armed conflict are so fundamental to the *respect of the human person* and '*elementary considerations of humanity*'."[29]

Why is it important to insist on respect for the human person and elementary considerations of humanity—on fundamental human rights—even during the chaos and intentional violence of war? The international lawyer Henri Meyrowitz answers:

> The true foundation of civilian immunity . . . resides . . . in what one could call the necessity of the long run, the necessity of beyond-war. . . . [It] represents an indispensable barrier, which, due to its nature as a *recognizable threshold*, constitutes the unique means preparing civilization to survive in resisting the destructiveness, potentially unlimited, of modern war.[30]

The political philosopher John Rawls, articulating a modern Kantian view, similarly holds: "The aim of war is a just peace, and therefore the means employed must not destroy the possibility of peace and encourage a contempt for human life that puts the safety of ourselves and of mankind in jeopardy."[31]

The essential fact about nuclear weapons is that they inherently surpass the boundaries of warfare and make impossible the resumption of civilized, peaceful life. That is why human rights law and humanitarian law join hands to condemn them; that is why, as the International Criminal Court of Justice unanimously affirmed, the world must create mechanisms for their elimination as has already been done in the conventions on chemical and biological weapons; that is why, ultimately, war must be abolished and the right to peace secured. As Kant presciently wrote, "a war of extermination . . . would allow perpetual peace only on the vast graveyard of the human race. A war of this kind and the employment of all means which might bring it about must thus be absolutely prohibited."[32]

WMD AND CIVIL AND POLITICAL RIGHTS

Since 2001, in many parts of the world the fear of terrorist attacks has combined with the fear of chemical, biological, and nuclear weapons to produce a climate in which governments are increasingly prone to enact "emergency measures" that infringe civil liberties and that citizens find increasingly difficult to undo. Terrorist acts of the past— assassinations, train derailments, arson—are as nothing compared with the technologically sophisticated and militarily coordinated mass assaults of al-Qaeda and its imitators.

Every time one of these dreadful incidents occurs, the natural reaction is to think "What if?" What if it had been a nuclear device? What if the still-unidentified anthrax terrorist had managed to more widely distribute the substance? What if Aum Shinrikyo had succeeded in spreading sarin throughout the Tokyo subway system? It is a line of thinking to which only hyperboles can do justice. Thus, former United States Defense Secretary William Cohen, testifying on March 23, 2004, before the National Commission on Terrorist Attacks Upon the United States, stated that terrorism, combined with WMD, "is likely to pose an existential threat to the world."[33]

It is also a line of thinking that leads people like Daniel J. Popeo, chairman of the conservative Washington Legal Foundation, to run an advertisement on the Op-Ed page of the *New York Times* entitled "'Civil Liberties' for Terrorists?" and to conclude with the following rhetorical flourish: "So it's time we got our priorities straight. Do we defer to the ideologues' rigid agenda of absolute 'civil liberties' for all, including our enemies, or do we trust government officials and our military to use their powers wisely and protect us from the horror terrorists can unleash?"[34]

When "civil liberties" gets bracketed in quotations marks to indicate a concept dear to ideologues but alien to right-thinking lawyers, when citizens used to holding their leaders accountable for their actions are asked to put blind trust in government officials and the military, something serious has happened to the culture of human rights. Poorly conceived counterterrorism efforts are encouraging this trend around the world.

Needless to say, there would be tension between security and human rights even if there were no WMD. However, as in the case of security and war, a whole new dimension is given to the security/human rights equation when WMD are factored in. In order to appreciate just how serious this phenomenon is, it is necessary to take a closer look at the impact on the observance of certain fundamental civil and political rights since September 11, 2001. These impacts have taken a variety of forms, from torture and degrading treatment of prisoners and detainees to privacy issues. A few are briefly mentioned here.

Article 7 of the International Covenant on Civil and Political Rights explicitly prohibits torture: "No one shall be subjected to torture or to cruel, inhuman or degrading treatment or punishment." A similar set of prohibitions is contained in the Convention Against Torture and Other Cruel, Inhuman or Degrading Treatment or Punishment to which 136 states were parties as of June 2004. Various investigations currently underway will reveal about the level of command and authorization from which the culture of "aggressive" interrogation and pre-interrogation measure of prisoners of war and other detainees by the American military in Afghanistan, Guantanamo, and Iraq have emanated. What is already clear is that somewhere along the line the notion of fighting fire with fire, or terror with terror, replaced the notion of intransgressible norms of behavior mandated by the Geneva Conventions and the above-mentioned treaties.[35] Thus, Alan Dershowitz, the well-known Harvard law professor, has publicly taken the position that torture is justified when undertaken to prevent a terrorist nuclear attack.[36]

A report issued on June 2, 2003, by the Inspector General of the United States Department of Justice confirmed that the treatment of large numbers of mostly illegal immigrants arrested in the United States since the 2001 attacks clearly exceeded the bounds of applicable legal and moral norms.[37] Additionally, the "rendering" of prisoners to other countries known to practice torture, such as Jordan, Egypt, and Morocco, is a particularly disturbing trend.[38]

The instances above also involve violations of Art. 10(1) of the Covenant on Civil and Political Rights, which provides that "[a]ll persons deprived of their liberty shall be treated with humanity and with respect for the inherent dignity of the human person."

Article 9(1) of the Covenant also states that "[n]o one shall be subjected to arbitrary arrest or detention," while Article 16 guarantees that "[e]veryone shall have the right to recognition everywhere as a person before the law." These articles are violated by the Kafkaesque rationale developed by some governments for holding large numbers of persons for long periods without charging them with a crime or other offense.

Much antiterrorist legislation has been passed in many countries since 2001.[39] Some of these laws and regulations, like those aimed at drying up sources of terrorist funding or improved exchanges of information between various intelligence agencies, serve a useful and legitimate purpose. Others, however, are of doubtful international legal validity and may be tested in the courts for years to come.

WMD AND SOCIAL AND ECONOMIC RIGHTS

In 1998, Stephen I. Schwartz and nine other nuclear experts produced a book containing the results of an extensive study of the cost of the American nuclear weapons program up to that year.[40] The figure they arrived at was 5.5 trillion U.S. dollars. Imagine if one were to include the amounts spent on nuclear weapons programs by other countries and the amounts spent by all countries on other WMD. It requires no particular proficiency in the art of economics to appreciate what this amount could have produced if used instead on providing millions of people with their right to health, housing, education, culture, social security, and all the other desiderata guaranteed to them—on paper—by the International Covenant on Economic, Social and Cultural Rights.

The eighteen targets for implementation of the right to development to which the world community committed itself in the Millenium Declaration,[41] including eradication of extreme poverty, full primary education, gender equality, and empowerment of women, reduction of child mortality, combating HIV/AIDS, and ensuring environmental stability, among others, still seem far out of reach, especially in the poorest countries. Yet billions of dollars go into the maintenance of nuclear arsenals, research into modified or new nuclear weapons, and measures to prevent or mitigate WMD attacks like research on vaccines. The G-8 meetings, originally intended to develop a common plan for meeting these goals, now seem increasingly concerned with questions of nonproliferation and counterterrorism, at the expense of economic progress and human rights. As one nongovernmental leader put it following the latest G-8 meetings in Sea Land, Georgia, in June 2004:

> Bold action at this year's summit could have taken the issues of AIDS, debt-relief and peacekeeping off the table and offered new hope for those with so little. Instead, the people on the run from militias in the Sudan or those dying from AIDS from lack of medicine will have to see whether they can stay alive until next year's summit.[42]

CONCLUSION

There can be no doubt that a world rife with weapons of mass destruction is less safe a place than a world without them, a point only reinforced by the rise of catastrophic terrorism.

The elimination of WMD is a matter of political will. It can be achieved through full implementation of the Chemical Weapons Convention and the Biological Weapons Convention and the negotiation of measures to eliminate nuclear arms within the overarching framework of a convention. The nuclear-weapons states are pledged to negotiate in good faith toward this end, but so far have refused to honor their pledge. When they do, they will also be acting to uphold the human rights to life and peace.

The elimination of terrorism may be a more difficult goal to reach. When leaders speak of waging the war against terrorism to its final victory, one can only wince and wonder what they have in mind. What war? Where fought? Against whom? With what weapons?

The last question is probably the crucial one. Yes, competent intelligence and brute force can reduce the danger of terrorist attacks. But if there is one lesson that history teaches it is that social, economic, ethnic, and religious differences can translate into feelings of powerlessness and give rise to violence—that the powerless call the search for justice and those at whom the violence is directed call terrorism.

This is where human rights come in. There may never be a world without terrorism. But it is reasonable to expect that the closer the world comes to realizing the full panoply of human rights enshrined in the Universal Declaration and the International Covenants, the closer it will be to freedom from terrorism, not least WMD terrorism. It is a goal worth striving for.

NOTES

1 S. Kershaw and E. Lichtblue, 2004, Bomb Case Against Lawyer is Rejected, *New York Times*, 25 May, p. A16. Mr. Mayfield is an Oregon lawyer who was arrested and released after two weeks' detention by order of a federal judge after the Federal Bureau of Investigation admitted that it had erroneously associated his fingerprints with those of another person found at the site of the Madrid train bombing.

2 One such exception is Douglas Roche, former Canadian Ambassador for Disarmament, author of *Bread Not Bombs* (University of Alabama Press, 1999).

3 475 kiloton warheads are deployed on American submarine-based missiles. See NRDC Nuclear Notebook, US Nuclear Forces, *Bulletin of the Atomic Scientists*, May/June 2004, at www.thebulletin.org/issues/nukenotes/ mj04nukenote.html. The Hiroshima and Nagasaki bombs had yields of 12-15 kilotons. In his recent book *Disarming Iraq*, Hans Blix says that "[w]hile nuclear weapons are routinely lumped together with biological and chemical in the omnibus expression 'weapons of mass destruction,' it is obvious that they are in a class by themselves. The outside world's concerns about Iraq's weapons would never have been a very big issue if it had not been for Iraqi initiatives to acquire nuclear weapons capacity." H. Blix, 2004, *Disarming Iraq*, Pantheon Books, p. 260.

4 See www.unhchr.ch/html/menu3/b/73.htm; J. Fried, 1994, *Toward a Right to Peace: Selected Papers of John H. E. Fried*, Aletheia Press, pp. 81–88.

5 L. F. Damrosch and B. H. Oxman, 2003, Agora: Future Implications of the Iraq Conflict, Editors' Introduction, *American Journal of International Law* vol. 97, no. 3, p. 553 (emphasis supplied).

6 Letter from Daniel Webster to Lord Ashburton, 6 August 1842. See R.Y. Jennings, 1938, The Caroline and McLeod Cases, *American Journal of International Law*, vol. 32, pp. 82–99.

7 See www.whitehouse.gov/nsc/nss.pdf.

8 W. Taft and T. Buchwald, 2003, Preemption, Iraq, and International Law, *American Journal of International Law*, vol. 97, no. 3, p. 563.

9 J. Yoo, 2003, International Law and the War in Iraq, *American Journal of International Law*, vol. 97, no. 3, p. 572.

10 R. Wedgwood, 2003, The Fall of Saddam Hussein: Security Council Mandates and Preemptive Self-Defense, *American Journal of International Law*, vol. 97, no. 3, p. 584

11 See "The Deceptions Exposed" in B. Burrough et al., 2004, "The Path to War," *Vanity Fair*, May 2004, pp. 286–287.

12 *Associated Press*, "Wolfowitz's comments revive doubts over Iraq's WMD," June 1, 2003, quoting from *Vanity Fair* interview.

13 Interview in *Der Spiegel*, "America's sense of timing is different," September 2003.

14 International Court of Justice, Advisory Opinion, *Legality of the Threat or Use of Nuclear Weapons*, issued July 8, 1996 (hereafter cited as "ICJ Opinion"), para. 105(2)F.

15 Emphasis supplied. Similar language is found in the American Bill of Rights: "No person . . . shall be . . . deprived of life . . . without due process of law." United States Constitution, Amendment V.

16 R. Kolb, 1998, The relationship between international humanitarian law and human rights law: A brief history of the 1948 Universal Declaration of Human Rights and the 1949 Geneva Conventions, *International Review of the Red Cross*, no. 324, pp. 409–18.

17 See generally L. Doswald-Beck and S. Vite, 1994, International Humanitarian Law and Human Rights Law, *International Review of the Red Cross*, no. 293, p. 99.

18 Resolution XXIII of May 12, 1968. Adopted as United Nations General Assembly resolution 2444 (XXIII) of December 19, 1968.

19 See N. Deller, A. Makhijani, and J. Burroughs (eds.), 2003, *Rule of Power or Rule of Law? An Assessment of U.S. Policies and Actions Regarding Security-Related Treaties*, Apex Press.

20 See K. Watkin, 2004, Controlling the Use of Force: A Role for Human Rights Norms in Contemporary Armed Conflict, *American Journal of International Law*, vol. 98, no. 1, pp. 1–34.

21 See, for example, Human Rights Watch, 2003, *Off-Target: The Conduct of the War and Civilian Casualties in Iraq*, Washington, DC, at www.hrw.org/reports/2003/usa1203/.

22 *Report of the Human Rights Committee*, Official Records of the General Assembly, 40th Session, Suppl., no. 40, document A/40/40 of 1985.

23 Verbatim Record, hearing before ICJ, November 14, 1995, 10h00, pp. 66–67 (Professor Philippe Sands); Solomon Islands' Written Observations regarding World Health Organization question on the legality of use of nuclear weapons in armed conflict (considered together with the question posed by the General Assembly that yielded the opinion on the merits), paras. 4.1–4.46, pp. 76–95, esp. 86–87.

24 Verbatim Record, hearing before the ICJ, November 14, 1995, 10h00, p. 66.

25 Verbatim Record, hearing before the ICJ, November 14, 1995, 15h00, p. 31.

26 ICJ Opinion, *op. cit*, paras. 24, 25. Regarding the opinion generally, see L. Boisson de Chazournes and P. Sands (eds.), 1999, *International Law, the International Court of Justice, and Nuclear Weapons*, Cambridge University Press; J. Burroughs, 1997, *The Legality of Threat or Use of Nuclear Weapons: A Guide to the Historic Opinion of the International Court of Justice*, Lit Verlag; V. Nanda and D. Krieger, 1998, *Nuclear Weapons and the World Court*, Transnational Publishers; P. Weiss, 2000, Book Review, *American Journal of International Law*, vol. 94, no. 4, pp. 815–18.

27 Except perhaps in the scenario that some WMD experts have dubbed "The case of the mininuke in the Gobi Desert," i.e., a hypothetical scenario in which a low-yield and fallout-free nuclear weapon is used in an area free of civilian population for a great distance.

28 ICJ Opinion, *op. cit*, para. 29.

29 *Ibid.*, para. 79 (emphasis supplied).

30 H. Meyrowitz, 1981, Le bombardement strategique d'appres le Protocole additionnel I aux Conventions de Geneve, *Zeitschrift Fur Auslandisches Offentliches Recht Und Vokkerrecht*, vol. 41, p. 26 (translation by J. Burroughs).

31 J. Rawls, 1971, *A Theory of Justice*, Belknap Press of Harvard University Press, pp. 378–79.

32 Immanuel Kant, *Perpetual Peace: A Philosophical Sketch*, in H. Reiss (ed.), 1970, *Kant's Political Writings* (trans. H. B. Nisbet), Cambridge University Press, p. 96.

33 See cnnstudentnews.nn.com/TRANSCRIPTS/0403/23/se.05.html

34 As printed in the *New York Times*, March 22, 2004, edition, p. A23. Full text available at www.wlf.org/upload/3-22-04civilliberties.pdf.

35 See the articles by S. Hersh in *The New Yorker*, editions of May 10, 17, and 24, 2004, available at www.newyorker.com/archive/previous/?040614frprsp_previous1.

36 D. Glenn, 2002, A Civil Libertarian Wants Professors to Talk About Morality and Tactics, *The Chronicle of Higher Education*, September 6.

37 See United States Department of Justice, Office of the Inspector General, 2003, *The September 11 Detainees: A Review of the Treatment of Aliens Held on Immigration Charges in Connection with the Investigation of the September 11*

137

Attacks, June, Office of the Inspector General, at www.usdoj.gov/oig/special/0306/index.htm

38 D. Priest and B. Gellman, 2002, U.S. Turns to Torture to Crack Prisoners of War, *Washington Post*, December 27, available at www.smh.com.au/articles/2002/12/26/1040511135568.html?oneclick=true.

39 For a country-by-country overview of measures to combat terrorism taken since September 11, 2001, see the reports submitted by states to the UN Counter-Terrorism Committee at www.un.org/docs/sc/committees/1373/submitted_reports.html.

40 S.I. Schwartz (ed.), 1998, *Atomic Audit: The Costs and Consequences of U.S. Nuclear Weapons since 1940*, Brookings Institution Press, Washington, D.C.

41 United Nations Millenium Declaration, General Assembly resolution A/55/PV.8 of September 8, 2000. See www.un.org/millenium/declaration/ares522e.htm.

42 D. Gartner, G-8 Summit: World Leaders Missed Good Opportunities on Several Issues, *Miami Herald*, 17 June. Gartner is policy director of the Global AIDS Alliance.

8

COLD WAR CONTINUUM

William Blum

istorians of the Cold War have conventionally referred to the post–World War II period as one of "containment." The keynote address of this convention was famously delivered by George Kennan in his 1947 essay in *Foreign Affairs*, in which he called for a "long-term, patient, but firm and vigilant containment of Russian expansive tendencies."

However, as a description of what United States foreign policy was actually doing in that period and afterward, the containment paradigm is seriously misleading. For in real, nonpropagandistic terms, American interventions throughout the world, in the decades following the war, time and again had but the most precarious or only imagined connection to the Soviet Union and its alleged expansionism.

The CIA's most chronicled "success" story, the overthrow of the government of Guatemala in 1954, was, in the words of the American ambassador, carried out because "we cannot permit a Soviet Republic to be established between Texas and the Panama Canal."[1]

The Soviet Union could have been excused if it was somewhat bewildered by such rhetoric, for the Russians had scant interest in Guatemala, did not provide the country with any kind of military assistance, did not even maintain diplomatic relations with it, and thus did not have the normally indispensable embassy from which to conduct such a nefarious scheme.

In 1960, Patrice Lumumba, prime minister of the newly independent Congo, was overthrown and then killed with deep United States involvement after CIA director Allen Dulles warned of a "communist takeover of the Congo with disastrous consequences."[2] Not long afterward, Dulles—now the ex–CIA director, thanks to the Bay of Pigs—declared that the U.S. had "overstated the danger" of Soviet involvement. "It looked as though they were going to make a serious attempt at takeover in the Belgian Congo; well, it did not work out that way at all."[3]

Similar "anti-Soviet" operations were executed by the United States in Iran, the Philippines, Korea, Indonesia, British Guiana, Syria, Italy, Indochina, El Salvador, and numerous other Third World countries right up to the very end of the Soviet Union, virtually every one accompanied by swollen rhetoric about the international communist conspiracy, each one likewise marked by very minimal, innocuous, or nonexistent Soviet involvement.[4] Did not the U.S. diplomatic and intelligence communities know they were fighting a phantom in these interventions? Was it all a cover?

Other interventions can be cited that had at least a superficial connection to the Soviets, such as CIA covert activities throughout Eastern Europe. But the point here is that similar interventions and covert activities were being carried out by the United States in every corner of the world, *whether the Soviet Union or one of its alleged proxies were a factor or not.*

The key determinant in American foreign policy decisions—the *sine qua non*—was clearly not the Soviet role, but rather whether a government was in power, or a movement was threatening to come to power, which did not promise to be a pliable client state of Washington. In addition to any other factor, it was believed that if such a government or movement were allowed to get away with such independence, there was a danger that this might inspire like-minded political entities.

If further proof were needed that the international communist conspiracy—a mythical creature in any event—was not the real motivating force behind U.S. interventions into other countries, the end of the Cold War should have dispelled any lingering illusions.

The evidence presented itself almost immediately. Just weeks after the fall of the Berlin Wall in 1989, the United States bombed and invaded Panama. The American forces stormed the country, pillaging, kidnapping, and killing at will, with nary a Russian or Russian proxy in sight. Communism wasn't even mentioned. Panamanian leader Manuel Noriega, formerly a valuable American liaison in Central America, had done several things to fall out of Washington's grace before he was ever accused of being involved in the drug trade; his loyalty and usefulness to the American empire was in doubt. This, combined with Washington's likely desire to send a clear message to the people of Nicaragua—who had an election scheduled in two months that would decide the fate of the Sandinista government, which was even further removed from grace than Noriega—was enough to send in the Marines to Panama.

Soon afterward the Warsaw Pact dissolved itself. NATO was not inspired to follow suit, though for decades it had counterpoised itself to the Warsaw Pact, justifying its own existence principally on the need to establish a bulwark against this eastern monolith of the Soviet Union.

Then the Soviet Union itself folded up its tent and walked off into history. Surely this would have written *finis* to NATO's *raison d'etre*. Not at all. NATO today is stronger and more far-reaching than ever, looking to incorporate virtually all of Europe, East and West, under its wings.

This life after logical death enjoyed by NATO was not the only slap in the face to the peace dividend Americans and others of the world had long been led to believe would be theirs once the Cold War came to an end and the "Evil Empire" had been vanquished. As if nothing had changed, the United States maintains its extraordinarily bloated military spending, even increasing it. President Reagan's discredited missile defense system is fervently pursued in the complete absence of any "enemy" with both a capable missile system threat and an irresistible desire to commit national suicide. Many hundreds of U.S. military installations, serving a vast panoply of specialized war-making needs, still dot the global map, including Guantanamo Bay in Cuba, and for the first time in Albania, Macedonia, Hungary, Bosnia, Croatia, Kosovo, and elsewhere in the new client states of Eastern Europe. Camp Bondsteel in Kosovo, one of the largest U.S. Army bases in the world, was built from scratch in 1999 in the wake of the NATO bombing. "Nothing about it," said the *Washington Post*, "seems temporary."[5] Even as you read this, American armed forces and special operations forces, such as the Green Berets, are being deployed in more than 100 countries in every part of the world. Washington is supplying many of these countries with sizeable amounts of highly lethal military equipment and training their armed forces and police in the brutal arts, regardless of how brutal they already are. American nuclear bombs are still stored in seven European countries, if not elsewhere. And American officials retain their unshakeable belief that they have a god-given right to do whatever they want, for as long as they want, to whomever they want, wherever they want.

142 Washington's remarkable record of interventions into the affairs of sovereign nations continued post–Cold War with actions such as the following:

- Left-leaning governments in Bulgaria and Albania were destabilized from 1990–92.
- For more than two years, the progressive priest, Father Jean-Bertrand Aristide, who had been ousted in a 1991 coup, was kept from returning as Haiti's president until it was no longer politically feasible for the U.S. to block him from doing so. Then he was returned weighed down with enormous restrictions imposed on his ability to make economic changes, only to be deposed again a few years later.
- Iraq was bombed back to a preindustrial age in 1991.
- Many missile and strafing attacks were carried out upon the people of Somalia in 1993 in an attempt to rearrange the country's political map.
- Peru and Colombia were provided with an unending stream of military equipment, advisors, trainers, surveillance flights, radar stations, communications intercepts—whatever was needed to suppress leftist rebel movements, all in behalf of often corrupt and brutal regimes, militaries, paramilitaries, and/or police, under the cover of the war on drugs.
- In similar fashion, aid was provided to suppress the Zapatista movement in Mexico beginning in 1994.[6]

Impoverished Indians in Ecuador rose up in desperation in the year 2000 and were joined by sympathetic junior military officers; together they took over the congress and supreme court buildings, ousted the president, and announced a new government. At this point, Washington and the American embassy in Quito exerted considerable pressure upon the rebels, warning of a cutoff in aid and other support and that "Ecuador will find itself isolated." Sandy Berger, President Clinton's national security advisor, phoned the Ecuadorian chief of staff to tell him that the U.S. would never recognize the new government and there would be no peace in Ecuador unless the military backed the vice president, who must continue to pursue neoliberal "reforms." Within hours, the heads of the Ecuadorian army, navy, and air force declared their support for the vice president. The leaders of the uprising fled underground.[7]

For years, up to the present day, anticommunist Vietnamese, Cambodians, and Laotians living in the United States have been financing and instigating their countrymen abroad in attacks on their governments, at times traveling from the U.S. to those countries to carry out attacks themselves—all this with the tacit approval of the American government, which turns a blind eye to the Neutrality Act that prohibits American citizens or residents from using force to overthrow a foreign government.[8]

In 2001, the U.S. publicly announced millions of dollars in support for opposition forces in Iraq and the Sudan, while in Nicaragua, U.S. Ambassador Oliver Garza and U.S. Acting Assistant Secretary of State for Western Hemispheric Affairs Lino Gutierrez each issued warnings of serious economic and military repercussions if Sandinista leader Daniel Ortega, who the polls suggested would win the upcoming presidential election, was returned to power. They also exerted relentless pressure on the Conservative Party and succeeded in making it withdraw from the election so as to avoid splitting the conservative vote against the Sandinistas.[9]

A few months later, the U.S. embassy in San Salvador tried its best to torpedo a meeting—the First International Conference for Solidarity and Peace in Colombia and Latin America—by successfully pressuring the National University to not allow its premises to be used, and the embassy's political affairs officer called up one of the conference's organizers, the *Frente Farabundo Martí para la Liberación Nacioal* (FMLN), to exert further pressure.[10]

The FMLN, like the Sandinistas, had been an ODE (Officially Designated Enemy) of Washington during the Cold War; as had, of course, the communists of Laos, Vietnam, and Cambodia.

143

What are we to make of all this? Is the Cold War—by whatever name—not over? Or was the Cold War not what we were told it was?

It would appear that whatever the diplomats and policymakers at the time *thought* they were doing, the Cold War skeptics have been vindicated—it was not about containing an evil, expansionist Soviet communism after all; it was about American imperialism, with com-munist" merely the name given to those who stood in its way. This imperialism continues, more brazen and unrestricted than ever, with its victims no longer able to turn to the Soviet Union for moral or material support or to play off one superpower against the other. The question that often vexed the CIA—would the Russians intervene or escalate their aid if the U.S. intervened in a particular country?—troubles no more.

Imagine that NATO had gone out of business at the same time as the Warsaw Pact. Imagine that the world was exactly the way it is right now, but that there was no NATO. What argument could anyone give for the creation of such a body? To defend against a Soviet invasion of the West? To carry out humanitarian interventions? The latter ration-alization is as contrived as the former was.

NATO still exists and expands principally to serve the American empire, to be the army of the New World Order. (The decision to go to war in Iraq in 1991 was, said President George H. W. Bush at the time, "an opportunity to forge for ourselves and for future generations a new world order.)[11] NATO—over which Washington has much more control than it does over the United Nations, which is ignored when feasible—stands ready to squelch any government that is not a true believer in the World Bank, the International Monetary Fund, the World Trade Organization, and its sundry trade agreements, and/or NATO itself; any nation that will not easily tolerate the scorched-earth policy inflicted upon the country's social services and standard of living by these august bodies; that does not look upon the free market or the privatization of the world as the *summum bonum*; that will not rearrange its laws to favor foreign investment; that will not be uncon-cerned about the effects of foreign investment upon the welfare of its own people; that will not produce primarily for export; or that will not welcome an American or NATO military installation upon its soil.

Yugoslavia was such a nation. Unlike the rest of Eastern Europe, it did not plead to join NATO and the European Union, nor did it show proper reverence for joining the club of globalized American allies *cum* obedient junior partners. Instead, President Slobodan Milosevic was part of a burgeoning plan in 1997 to form a union of Southeastern European nations.[12] This could not have endeared him to the Western powers. Moreover, most of Yugoslavia's industry and financial institutions were still state owned; "worker control" was commonplace; and the Serbs had not even banned the word "socialism" from polite conversation yet. Mad raving dinosaurs they were! All in all, an ideal humanitarian bombing target.

The fact that Milosevic could be dictatorial was of no strategic significance, except for propaganda value. As Noam Chomsky has written, "The criterion that distinguishes friend from enemy is obedience, not crime."

To be sure, the International Tribunal has documented gross human rights violations. But the claim that the NATO bombing (more precisely, a scenario instigated and staged by Washington from start to finish) was carried out to save the Kosovars from "ethnic cleansing" was no more than a highly successful piece of propaganda.

In actuality, the systematic, forced deportation of large numbers of people did not begin until a few days *after* the bombing began and was clearly a reaction to it, born of extreme anger and powerlessness. This is easily verified by looking at a daily newspaper for the few days before the bombing began the night of March 23–24, 1999, and the few days after. Or simply look at page one of the *New York Times* of March 26, which reads:

> With the NATO bombing already begun, a deepening sense of fear took hold in Pristina [the main city of Kosovo] that the Serbs would *now* vent their rage against ethnic Albanian civilians in retaliation[emphasis added].

On March 27, we find the first reference to a "forced march" or anything of that sort.

After destroying the Serbian infrastructure, ending the lives of thousands, bringing the economy to its knees, and pouring in multiple king's ransoms in support of political-party, media, and nongovernmental organization (NGO) opposition to defeat Milosevic in the 2000 elections,[13] the United States was free to do in Yugoslavia what it's been doing since the end of the Cold War all over the former Soviet Union and Eastern Europe, indeed throughout the world.

Teams of specialists are sent in from U.S. government agencies, such as the National Endowment for Democracy (NED), or from NGOs funded by American corporations and foundations, as well as religious, academic, and labor groups. They go in disbursing free cars, computers, faxes, cell phones, and the like. They hold conferences and seminars and hand out tons of papers and manuals and CD-ROMs and—not least of all—money, to establish think tanks and other enterprises, to educate government employees and other selected sectors of the population, including students, on the advantages and the joys of privatizing the economy. They create a new class of managers to manage a new market economy, enlightening them on how to remake the country so it's appealing to foreign investors.

The NED, its affiliates, and other American organizations engaged in this process maintain that they're engaged in "democracy building," "opposition building," or "encouraging pluralism." "We support people who otherwise do not have a voice in their political system," said a NED program officer in 1997.[14] But this American traveling show hasn't bestowed any of its largesse on progressive opposition groups in Central America or Eastern Europe—or, for that matter, in the United States—even though these groups are hard-pressed for funds and the means to make themselves heard. Cuban dissident groups and media are heavily supported, however, as was the opposition in Nicaragua in the 1980s, when the U.S. was endeavoring to overthrow the Sandinista-led government.

NED's reports carry on endlessly about "democracy," but at best it's a modest measure of mechanical electoral democracy they have in mind, not economic democracy—nothing that aims to threaten the powers that be or the way things are, unless of course it's in a place like Cuba.

And, often the consequence of these policies is that the mass of the population is left in misery, struggling to attain even the basics, decidedly worse off than they were under communism in the case of the former Soviet republics and satellites. But a wealthy elite class is created as privatized state assets are sold at bargain prices and the country is thrown open to foreign investment and the control that attaches to ownership. Often the factories that are bought are closed down, with many jobs lost, so as not to compete with those of the foreign purchaser.

By April 2001, we could read in the *Financial Times* of London: "Serbia is preparing to launch a comprehensive privatization programme as part of economic reforms introduced following the overthrow of former president Slobodan Milosevic . . . [There will be a] sale of some 4,500 companies by tender and auction to strategic investors. Controlling stakes of up to 70 percent of a company's equity will be on offer to Serb and foreign investors."[15]

The Western powers like to call this this "reintegration of Yugoslavia into the European family."

Serbia's enterprises were not all that the United States and its NATO allies wanted. They also wanted Milosevic himself. A so-called "donors conference" organized by the European Union and the World Bank was scheduled for June 29, 2001, reportedly to consider payment of $1.2 billion to Belgrade, though it was actually as much a "creditors conference" to exact debt payments. The United States made it clear that the degree of its financial outlay, and even its attendance at the conference, depended on Belgrade's turning Milosevic over to the International Criminal Tribunal for Yugoslavia (which had been created in 1993, with the U.S. as the father, the UN Security Council as the mother, and Madeleine Albright as the midwife).

Serbian Prime Minister Zoran Djindjic needed very little encouragement to comply, being one of a class of Eastern Europeans with stars in their eyes when they look Westward, the type of individual selected by the NED and other "democracy builders" to carry the torch for globalization, with suitable rewards built in for the selectees. Three days before the conference, Djindjic phoned U.S. Secretary of State Colin Powell to reassure him that he would perform as expected. Powell then reassured Djindjic that the United States would attend the conference.[16] Two days later, Milosevic was kidnapped (there's no better word for it) by Djindjic and his cohorts.

Slobodan Milosevic had to be very publicly tried for all manner of crimes, whether real or simply alleged, in order that—as Milosevic himself declared to the court—the seventy-eight–day bombing of Yugoslavia by NATO could be justified before the world and before those who charged NATO leaders with being the real war criminals.

The United States had played a crucial role in the breakup of the six republics of the former Yugoslavia; it had sufficiently maneuvered the

147

electoral process in Serbia, as well as other former republics, to insure victory for its preferred political actors; it had undertaken a radical reeducation of these children of communism; it had snatched much of the countries' wealth at fire-sale prices; it had successfully demonized Milosevic. Then Washington declared: "Send us the head of Slobodan Milosevic." And a plane from NATO's vast armada promptly flew the head to be paraded before the court in The Hague.

It was the kind of power that any emperor of the past would have deeply envied.

It was not the kind of post–Cold War world that critics and victims of American foreign policy had hoped for.

American leaders like to say things like "world peace through world trade." But what they actually practice is "perpetual commerce through perpetual war."

NOTES

1 *Time* magazine, January 11, 1954.
2 *Interim Report: Alleged Assassination Plots Involving Foreign Leaders*. The Select Committee to Study Governmental Operations with Respect to Intelligence Activities (U.S. Senate, the "Church committee"), November 20, 1975, 15.
3 CBS Reports. April 26, 1962, The Hot and Cold Wars of Allen Dulles.
4 For details, see Blum, William, *Killing Hope: U.S. Military and CIA Interventions Since World War II* (Monroe, Me:, Common Courage Press, 1995).
5 *Washington Post*. July 25, 2001.
6 Ibid., series, July 12–14, 1998.
7 Hahnel, Robin, *Z Magazine*. February 2001, 36–7. Also *Washington Post*. January 23, 2000, A1.
8 *Washington Post*, July 30, 2001, A1.
9 Associated Press. August 18, 2001. Also reports from organizations active on Nicaraguan issues, such as the Nicaragua–United States Friendship Office and Nicaragua Network, both based in Washington, DC.
10 The conference, organized by the Network Against Plan Colombia, of Washington, DC, began on July 19, 2001, at a different location in San Salvador. The U.S. embassy officer was Julia Chester.
11 *Los Angeles Times*. January 18, 1991.
12 From Conversation with Milosevic: "Our Crime was Independence." To be published at: http://emperors-clothes.com/milo/indep.htm.
13 *New York Times*. September 20, 2000, A3.
14 Ibid., March 31, 1997, A11.
15 *Financial Times*. April 10, 2001.
16 *Los Angeles Times*. June 28, 2001, A4.

NATIONAL SECURITY SUBSTRUCTURES

9

A REPORT ON NAFTA AND THE STATE OF THE MAQUILAS

Saul Landau

With the passage of The North American Free Trade Agreement in 1993 investment in Mexican maquilas became the United States' most intimate experience with economic globalization. U.S. Customs adjusted its rules to permit the rapid entrance of trucks into the United States carrying goods made by U.S.-owned companies across the border. After September 11, however, security concerns began to conflict with the rationality norms of free trade. The large corporate and banking interests and those of the newly empowered security elite came into conflict: inspecting the cargos of incoming trucks meant costly delays and reduced profits.

In addition, September 11 and the corresponding U.S. economic dip revived xenophobic movements whose leaders began to press Congress for increased restrictions on "illegal" Mexican immigration. As 2004 ended, the maquila remained for Mexico as a sector that could provide jobs and attract larger-scale foreign investment. The maquila also functioned as a tension reliever, a place that absorbed more than a million people from the rural areas who might well have developed into a major "problem." For the United States as well, the maquila helped deflect "illegal immigration" by providing a Mexican safety net of jobs.[1]

On both sides of the border, residents understand globalization as a result of living the experience. In the last four decades, tens of millions of Mexicans have moved from the impoverished countryside to the overcrowded cities, where they could find work in or around the maquilas, the foreign-owned factories that export parts or finished goods. From the building of the first export factory in Ciudad Juarez in 1965 to the present, this low-wage and relatively productive workforce has attracted foreign investment. In 1993, the U.S. Congress endorsed NAFTA, and investors received an extra incentive: the equivalent of the U.S. government's Good Housekeeping Seal of Approval. A decade after NAFTA became law the maquila economy merits an assessment.

152

The contemporary maquilas symbolize yet another industrial revolution. Instead of reading about Manchester or Leeds in the 1840s, visit Tijuana or Juarez today. The modern equivalent of a Dickensian cultural saga centers around the maquila as the setting. The country folk, forced to move to cities for jobs, play out their human dramas against this ugly, anarchically landscaped, industrial backdrop.

Police authorities in Juarez, for example, claim that in the last ten years they have found the remains of more than three hundred women—all raped and mutilated. Almost all of them were under thirty and worked in maquilas. Police have arrested more than a dozen people, but the slaughter continues.[2]

When families moved from tradition-bound rural communities to the noncommunity urban life—where each person must suspect his neighbor—they also became actors in a new stage of Mexican and third world history. This historical process of movement from countryside to city parallels earlier population transfers in preindustrial Europe.

Ciudad Juarez, across the Rio Grande—once mighty but now reduced to a trickle—has grown cancerously. From barren, sandy hills have sprouted unplanned *colonias* (euphemism for hideous slums). Rural families leave land that no longer supports them. They find jobs in the export factories, patch together what they hope are only temporary homes from pieces of wood, metal, and plastic, and find ways to tap into the power line. (Some get electrocuted.) They wait for the circulating water and gas trucks blasting "La Cucaracha" on their speakers to bring the needed material for life and cooking. The families often store the drinking and washing water in old metal chemical barrels. The air, once just dusty during the high wind season, now reeks of emissions from factories and the stench of unmuffled auto exhaust. Since September 11, the United States has tightened border security,[3] which means that the cars sit two to three times longer on the bridges connecting Juarez with neighboring El Paso. The residents suck in the fumes.

In *colonias* like Anapra and Lago Poniente, the rural folks rapidly acquire urban ways. They try to raise their kids to become academic achievers or send them into the maquilas in their midteens to contribute to scarce family income. Alarming numbers of young people turn to drugs, prostitution, and gang delinquency. Some of the young men play soccer after work and on Sunday on a pebble-strewn, dusty field. The city government has not built parks or athletic fields, but it has catered to every conceivable need a potential maquila investor might have. It emphasizes how well built are the factories of Juarez and how the local authorities will provide security over potentially rebellious workers. (They might want genuine unions.) In contrast, visit the shacks in the *colonias*, which face unpaved streets where mangy dogs drop their loads and little kids run barefoot through the summer dust and excrement. Ana Maria, mother of three, and Catalina, mother of seven, agreed that for all the horrors of slummy urban life, at least Juarez meant certainty of employment. That was then, in 2000, when most of the maquilas boasted "help wanted" signs and ran three shifts a day. Employment neared 100 percent. An unhappy worker in factory A could quit and find work at factory B across the street, where the wages were five centavos an hour more, or the cafeteria had better food. That workplace mobility slowed down with the onset of recession in the United States.

The economic downturn, followed by the al-Qaeda attacks in New York and Washington, meant recession for the maquila industry as well. Between mid-2000 and mid-2003, more than four hundred thousand factory workers lost their jobs in Mexico. Ironically, some of the very factories that moved from the United States in the 1980s and 1990s to take advantage of "cheap labor" now find compelling reasons to lower wages even further. They have begun to shift operations to Asia.[4]

Catalina and Ana Maria, with their many children to support, have recently received pink slips. The once buzzing factories where they worked have transmogrified into misshapen tombstones; industrial parks have turned into industrial cemeteries. Creeping weeds and blowing plastic and paper now litter a once buzzing parking lot in front of Quality Industrial Services. A lone security guard shares the space with a scruffy cat and an elusive bird. "It's difficult," the guard told me, "to see maquilas shutting down, moving to China, or wherever." He blamed last year's U.S. economic downturn for putting Mexicans out of work. "But, that's the way it goes," he concluded with a sigh.

"On the surface," says Chihuahua sociologist Victor Quintana, "the job losses come from the U.S. recession and the post–September 11 shocks, but in reality that's a smoke screen for deeper causes. The U.S. recession was hardly a cold, while we in Mexico developed full pneumonia ... The maquila model," Quintana predicts, "has exhausted its potential. Mexico cannot compete with China."[5]

The maquilas still account for about half of Mexico's $150 billion in annual exports. But efficient as Mexican labor has proven to be in global competition, it falls far short of Chinese workers for the low-wage labor champion. Quintana sees further erosion in the maquila sector as Asian nations offer equivalent productivity for one-fourth the wages of Mexican workers.

But the model has done its damage. Two years ago, he says, "Chihuahua led Mexico in high employment; today, Chihuahua leads in unemployment." Thanks to layoffs from factory closures, factories moving, or reduction of shifts, Chihuahua has lost more than 100,000 jobs.[6]

According to a June 20, 2002, *Washington Post* story,[7] over two years more than five hundred foreign-owned assembly-line factories in Mexico moved to China. The company accountants at the home offices concluded that the wage differential between the two Third World countries more than outweighs the increased costs of shipping and the inconveniences of distance. Before the U.S. recession hit, maquila developers promoted a bullish sentiment to foreign investors and Mexican officials. In 1999, Federico de la Vega, one of Juarez's leading developers of maquila parks, predicted that maquilas "would be the cornerstone of the Juarez economy for the next fifty years."[8]

In a Juarez maquila, where the cost of living runs about 75 to 80 percent of El Paso's across the river, a beginning machine operator earns less than $8 a day, whereas his counterpart in China makes only a quarter of that pathetic wage.

Victor Quintana doesn't mourn what he believes is the end of the maquila era. He thinks that NAFTA and the whole free-trade model launched the equivalent of a cultural offensive against the majority of the world's poor. Quintana insists that the maquila represents a form of terrorism, which leads people to ways of avoiding life; booze, crack, and cult religions arise from maquila work.

The maquila, asserts Quintana, has its own discourse, "one that mocks traditional values like cooperation and solidarity. Its only values are individualism and competition." Quintana has little patience with the rich and powerful, including President Vicente Fox himself, "who wring their hands about our 'losing our traditional values' while they eagerly bring the value-destroying maquilas into the country for economic growth."

Maquilas offer growth rates but also crime rates. "Those who preach that we should respect nature bring in the maquilas. They destroy nature, people, and their natural bonding."[9]

Leticia Ortiz exemplifies Quintana's point. She came to Juarez from the countryside nineteen years ago and worked her way up the ladder in a large maquila to become head of personnel. Then, without warning, in 2000, she received her unceremonious dismissal. The CEOs located in some First World city—she wasn't sure which one—had decided to move their Mexico-based plants to China, where they would pay significantly lower wages while productivity would remain equally high. Bitter?

"No, just disappointed," she said. "After working my way up for all those years I guess I foolishly developed a sense of loyalty to the company, a sense that was not reciprocated. They didn't even pay me what they owed me for severance according to the law. But it would take too long and it would be too expensive to fight it, so I accepted their less than generous offer."

After receiving her pink slip, Leticia said she went home and cried for hours. Then, she said, "I basically slept for the next six months. I guess you could call it depression."

She smiled. "I don't think I smiled for an entire year," she said. "My self-esteem seemed to drain from my body. Each day I would tell myself it will get better,' but it didn't. Maybe now [in the summer of 2002] I'm starting to regain some of my equilibrium."[10]

THE HISTORY OF MAQUILAS IN JUAREZ

Juarez opened its first maquilas in 1965. For decades, Mexicans had crossed legally into the United States under the Bracero Program to work in the Texas cotton fields. By 1964, however, these workers found themselves replaced by a newly designed machine that picked cotton faster and cheaper than people could. Faced with this laid-off labor force of hundreds of thousands of migrant workers, Mexican leaders adjusted their laws to allow foreign capital to enter.

U.S. investors quickly learned of the lucrative possibilities for investment on Mexico's northern border. And Mexican developers, working hand in glove with government officials in Chihuahua, offered low wages, no unions, productive workforce, low taxes, and no environmental regulation or costs related to OSHA-like agencies—features that made Mexico attractive.

But, gradually, a few independent labor organizations, backed by some AFL-CIO unions, began to move into the border cities. Add to their organizing efforts a steadily rising cost of living, and the employers felt an impact on wages. Although the maquilas offered no drastic pay raises, some maquila owners did feel the social pressure to improve working conditions.

Despite these factors, investment in Mexican maquilas continued to rise, until 2002. In 1994, NAFTA had provided formal U.S.-government backing for wary investors. The rate of maquila growth had reached double digits. NAFTA provided tax-free incentives for maquila owners and facilitated plans for efficient corporate integration.

U.S. companies ship raw materials to Mexico and then import finished parts or assembled products tax-free: electronics, electrical goods, automobiles and trucks and trailers or their parts, wood and plastic products, and textiles.

When the maquila experiment began in 1965, Juarez attracted only a handful of factories. But now almost 4,000 of these mostly foreign-owned export-production plants dot the landscapes of border cities like Juarez, Tijuana, Mexicali, Nogales, Matamoros, Piedras Negras, and other border towns. Indeed, many maquilas have moved further into the interior of the country as well.

Some Juarez plant owners, anticipating labor problems, built automated, even robotized factories. An Italian-owned factory manufactures TVs and computer chassis made in a mold and extracted by a robot. The plant uses comparatively few workers. Pasquale Galizzi, an Italian plant manager, said it made strategic sense to open a plant in Juarez, given its proximity to the U.S. border. "The wages we pay here are about one-fourth of what we would have to pay in Milan," he explained.[11]

Just as the multinational corporation found it necessary "to globalize or die," in Galizzi's words, so too did rural Mexicans come to Juarez out of necessity. No longer able to eke out a subsistence livelihood on the land, they came to the place where the maquilas promised permanent, albeit low-level, job security.

What happens now that some of these people have become unemployed? According to Quintana, a few return to the villages they were forced to leave to find gainful employment. Some still try to traverse the difficult obstacles of the U.S. border. Near El Paso, however, since September 11, the Immigration and Naturalization Service (INS) reports far fewer attempts to cross the border. U.S. technology and vigilant patrols act as a virulent form of deterrence. Certain sectors of the U.S. public have traditionally responded to economic downturn by resorting to xenophobic actions.

Further west, in the hottest and remotest sections of the Arizona desert, where summer temperatures top 115 degrees, the "coyotes" lead their human prey. These dealers in human flesh offer their "crossing-the-border services" for a price to those desperately wanting to reach U.S. territory. The coyotes assure their clients of plentiful water but often abandon their charges just at the point when the water runs out and the temperature becomes inhospitable for human life. Through mid-June 2003, more than twenty Mexicans, including an eleven-year-old girl, had died trying this route. Stories regularly appear in the media about speeding vans carrying undocumented workers crashing and killing the occupants in attempts to elude border patrol chasers.[12]

Since October 2003, more than fifty Mexicans have fallen trying to make it to the Tucson area. "U.S. immigration laws are death laws," said one Mexican border resident. Thanks to the newly militarized border patrol, the traditional flow of Mexicans into the United States has noticeably decreased. The usual zones have too many patrols, so the perilous desert has become the choice of the truly desperate and adventurous.

As a result of this crackdown on *braceros* or *mojados*, most of the newly unemployed will remain in Juarez. "The population here may have reached three million," speculates Juarez environmentalist Felix Perez. No one has counted. Each day hundreds, maybe thousands, arrive at the bus station, looking for work in the maquilas.

"I'm staying in Juarez," Ana Maria said. "It's rough here, but it's impossible in the countryside where I came from." Some of the newly arrived women and men send parts of their wages back to their families in the rural areas. Indeed, many families that cling to their non-productive land as the source of identity and history depend on the Juarez or Tijuana factory worker to provide the meager monthly subsidy that keeps the bank or the money lender from seizing the traditional family plot. This pressure acts as a disciplinary factor on the maquila worker. He or she knows that the family's survival depends on those remittances.

Maquila missionaries use this example when they preach to potential investors about the reliability of Mexico's workforce. Thanks to such cultural force, they argue, Mexico can still compete for low wages and high productivity with other Third World countries. That's global competition: which country can offer its people for the lowest wages, can promise polluting industries the least environmental regulation, the lowest taxes, the least workplace monitoring for health and safety, and the least prospect for unionization! This is the free market.

To keep it healthy, if you listen to President Bush or President Fox, we need more of the same. President Bush makes no reference to the labor, environmental, and social horrors that have developed alongside what has become known euphemistically as "free trade." Indeed, he expanded his free trade authority, called Fast Track, meaning that Congress will not have a chance to debate the details.[13]

THE ENVIRONMENT AND THE MAQUILAS

Like the advocates of the current national security system, the maquila system promoters also make claims of rationality, meaning efficiency. But both systems suffer from the inability of their managers to make reasonable judgments about the impact of such "rationality." For example, the global production network needs good water, air, and land to continue to make the products it pushes relentlessly on all prospective buyers. Yet in order to make these commodities competitively, it systematically ruins the earth's water, air, and soil and destroys prematurely the essence of the very people who must work in its factories. In short, it defies the wisdom of the old Arab saying: "Don't foul the plate you eat from."

Ciudad Juarez provides an immediate illustration. In late June 2002, I stood on the south bank of a twenty-foot-wide canal with sewer water (*aguas negras*) running through it. Our video camera pointed at Osvaldo Aguinaba, an elderly farmer, on the other side. I tried not to let the stench rising from the rapidly moving stream interfere with my own stream of thought.

"So," I shouted across the fetid tributary, "has this stinky water always run through here?"

"Yes, but it used to be pure sewage. You know, from human beings." Osvaldo, dressed in white work clothes, nodded his head and pointed at the putrid watercourse. "But now it's mixed with the chemical wastes from the factories. Yes, those factories make most of this crap. It's ruining the countryside."

Another elderly farmer in blue jeans, a red shirt, and a baseball hat joined the one in white. He shook his head sadly. "The government is allowing agriculture to die," he said, pointing at the *aguas negras*.

From the farmers' side of the canal, standing on a ladder, you can see Texas, about half a mile away. On the Mexico side of the border, some twenty-five miles southeast of Juarez, alfalfa, sorghum, and other cattle feed grow alongside cotton. "They don't let us use the water to irrigate the fruit trees anymore," he told me regretfully. ("Thank God," I muttered to myself. But I wondered how much enforcement exists in rural Chihuahua.)

Osvaldo claimed that he still grew some wheat. I shuddered. "Yes, the *aguas negras* drain into the fields. What can we do? There's been a long draught here. We have to eat. The animals have to eat. We have to grow our crops and sell them with whatever water we can find."

People presumably eat the meat and milk from the cows after they eat grains irrigated with this toxic river. A few miles further south a plant converts the solid waste into sludge bars that farmers then use as fertilizer.

"The worst contaminators are the dangerous metals used in metal processing," says Federico de la Vega, who studied chemical engineering at MIT and went home to Juarez to run a beer and soda pop distribution business and lease industrial parks to foreign maquilas. "Cleaning metals for locks and other industrial products involves the use of chlorine, bromine, and other truly toxic elements, and I know that some of the maquila managers don't dispose of these poisonous residues properly. I worry especially about the health of pregnant women who come into contact with these dangerous compounds."[14]

Even Jaime Bermudez, the father and foremost promoter of Juarez industrial parks, admitted that environmental problems are serious. "But these are problems we can solve," he insists. "The maquilas bring jobs and without jobs we have nothing."[15]

It reminded me of the mantra of some U.S. labor unions some decades ago when their members demanded they confront chemical, nuclear, and other workplace hazards. What's more important: a little poison in the air and water, or a chance to earn a good living for your family? Be a tough working man. Environmental concerns are for sissies.

In border cities like Juarez, pollution hits you in the eyes, ears, nose, throat, and lungs. Take a deep breath, even if you're not standing next to one of the putrid streams. "First, we have the ancient buses," says Felix Perez, a local environmental activist. "These very used vehicles are the city's basic means of transportation. Not only are they extremely uncomfortable, they emit immense amounts of noxious exhaust."

Perez points to the old U.S. school buses, which load workers going to and from the *colonias* where they live and the factories where they work. Some buses have little or no shock absorbers as they bounce along the rutted, unpaved streets, lined with ramshackle huts— the housing for some of those who produce home furnishings, parts for fancy trailers, and new auto and computer accessories. The average ride from the *colonia* to the factory takes an hour and a half.

"The fact is," Perez says, "that we have no environmentally good transportation system. Add to that the contamination produced by the post–September 11 security measures taken by the U.S. border agencies, and you have truly nonbreathable air."

Perez refers to the extra time now required to cross the three bridges that link Juarez to El Paso. The delay has at least doubled the waiting time, so Juarez and El Paso residents suck double the emissions from the idling autos and trucks as they wait their turn to get cleared for entry by U.S. Customs. Needless to say, the Mexican vehicles have not passed emissions inspection.

Then there's the scarce water issue, Perez continues. The once mighty Rio Grande has been reduced to a trickle in parts of Juarez. Juarez has five years of water remaining, he proclaims. In the future, the city officials have found a water source in the desert some miles from here, but it's located in a nuclear graveyard, where they buried, among other things, radioactive cobalt. So it may well have leaked into the water.

No one knew for sure whether the water will be safe to drink. But industrial planning in Third World countries doesn't take into account the human health factor. The rich will of course buy bottled water, and the supply of cheap labor in places like Mexico will be abundant for decades to come. Indeed, companies shun older workers in favor of teenagers, most of whose health and energy will prove sufficient for production needs over the next five years. In their forties, the cancers, lung diseases, and syndromes associated with repetitive motion emerge.

The border area has become an environmental nightmare. Raw sewage without treatment plants! Toxic material unleashed into soil, water, and air! President Clinton allocated $20 billion for border environmental cleanup. By the time he left office in January 2001, less than $100 million had been spent—and most of this on administrative costs.

So the balloon of high employment that attracted millions of people to frontier industrial cities lost a lot of its air. In July 2002, Scientific-Atlanta, the second-largest U.S. maker of television set-top boxes, announced that it had eliminated 1,300 jobs in Mexico because of declining demand. Scientific-Atlanta had moved its manufacturing operations from Atlanta to Juarez in July 2001 and after one year it had to downsize. A company spokesman, Paul Sims, warned that more job cuts lie ahead.

The new residents of Juarez, lured by announcements of certain jobs, now face unemployment without any safety net and a physical environment that appears unsustainable. Why, I ask rhetorically, couldn't the brilliant people who developed the idea of maquilas as an economic base have thought about some worst-case scenarios? Their insight into business efficiency has propelled into place a production system that has caused, and will continue to cause, catastrophic results for people and the entire human environment.

In the next decade, the demands of anti-immigration groups and the expanding security bureaucracy may come into sharper conflict with the needs of the corporate globalizers, whose insatiable demand for low-wage labor will grow stronger.

NOTES

1 Clinton said that NAFTA had created hundreds of thousands of new jobs in the United States. Bush echoes this line. True! Thousands of skilled Michigan auto workers, for example, lost their $25–30 an hour jobs to Mexican workers who earned $8 a day. But that former welder, let's say, did get another job checking groceries at $8–9 an hour. And so did his wife, who previously stayed home and cared for the children. The two now earn around $17 an hour and have created a third job: someone to care for their small children, at less than minimum wage.

In Mexico, NAFTA has also created jobs related both to the immediate manufacturing process and the work that naturally derives from setting up factories. After spending time in the El Paso–Juarez area in 2002–3, I can report that NAFTA works fabulously if you're a speculator—investor—or a multinational corporate CEO, and your Juarez branch plant was able to survive the U.S. recession and the September 11 aftershocks and still remained open.

A few Mexican "developers" who lease land for industrial parks and those who feed off contracts to the export factories have also fared well. The maquilas also offered work for architects, plumbers, electricians, construction crews, landscapers, food caterers, and a variety of other "services" required to maintain the plant and the workforce.

For the vast army of "contractors and subcontractors" and the more than two million Mexicans working inside the maquilas, those who have not lost their jobs recently, well, they've survived, which they could not have done had they remained on the unproductive land of their origin.

2 According to the June 4, 2004, *El Paso Times* (Louie Gilot, "Juarez Slayings Report Finds Police Abuses"), "Maria Lopez Urbina, the special federal prosecutor appointed by Mexico President Vicente Fox, listed 81 Juarez police officers, including 17 detectives, who might have committed criminal or administrative violations."

3 According to the March 22, 2002, *BBC News* (Rob Watson, "U.S. Tightens Mexico Border,") in March 2002, President Bush announced new high-tech security measures including the use of "X-ray machines to

examine the contents of lorries crossing the border . . . to stop potential terrorists entering the U.S. along its long border with Mexico."

4 Mary Jordan, "Mexican Workers Pay for Success: With Labor Costs Rising, Factories Depart for Asia," *Washington Post*, June 20, 2002.

5 Personal interview, 2000.

6 Chihuahua, Mexico's largest state, is located at the northern end of Mexico,
on the northwest central plain. It borders the U.S. to the north, the state
of Sonora to the west, Sinaloa to the southwest, and Coahuila to the east.

7 Jordan, "Mexican Workers Pay for Success: With Labor Costs Rising,
Factories Depart for Asia."

8 Personal interview.

9 Personal interviews, 1998–2000.

10 Personal interview, June 2002.

11 Personal interview, 1999.

12 According to the June 4, 2003, *Washington Post* ("U.S., Mexico Discuss Trying to Cut Migrant Deaths"), a joint effort by U.S. federal officials and the
Mexican government called Operation Desert Safeguard, formed in
response to the escalating deaths of migrants attempting to cross the border, "will add 150 Border Patrol agents along the southern Arizona border,
west of Nogales. Two additional surveillance aircraft have also been
assigned to look for migrants. Twenty search-and-rescue beacons also are
being placed across the desert, allowing migrants in distress to press a but-
ton that will summon Border Patrol agents."

In the 2004 election, both candidates called for military participation in
an effort to exert greater control of the border. In their "control the border" rhetoric, neither candidate evinced concern for civil liberties.

13 On December 6, 2001, Congress narrowly passed the Trade Promotion
Authority Bill, also known as Fast Track.

14 Personal interview, June 2002.

15 Personal interview, 1999.

163

10

COURTS AND UNIVERSITIES AS INSTITUTIONS IN THE NATIONAL SECURITY STATE

Anabel L. Dwyer and David J. Dwyer

1. INTRODUCTION

We focus on the impacts that the American National Security State (NSS) has on the institutions of higher education and the judiciary. We characterize the NSS as a type of capitalist imperialism called "militarism" that is premised both on the ideology that peace and security can only be achieved through the threat and use of greater force and on the presumption of a constant threat against which we must be ever vigilant to preserve the ideal state. This vigilance typically calls for the adoption of antidemocratic steps such as the suspension of basic rights and the resort to secrecy to preserve the democratic state. This is also why the NSS requires the allocation of large amounts of the nation's resources to weapons and why we find ourselves in a state of perpetual war. Further, we argue that the NSS exemplifies the institutional pathology in which a subordinate segment of society hijacks the governmental apparatus and undermines its capacity to meet its responsibilities to its citizenry. In this context, member institutions like higher education and the judiciary can, knowingly or not, succumb to the influence of the NSS and participate in its goals.

1.1 What is the Ideal State?

We recognize the legitimate function of the democratic state apparatus, consisting of a collection of governmental institutions, as one of serving and protecting its citizens equally and fairly. In practice, few states ever live up to all these expectations. However, all practical democratic states use a "legitimating discourse" to appeal to this ideal characterization to legitimize their existence.

Leman-Langlois (2002: 81) states that

> *Legitimating discourse* refers to the institution's internal logic or rationale, where its goals, methods and principles are articulated in harmony with prevalent norms and may be presented as "right" (or lesser evils) or "good" (or the best possible) to the concerned social groups. It serves to justify to its members and others who are expected to support the institution's existence and activities. Legitimations appeal to a variety of justifications: moral (this institution is good . . .); theological (this institution is ordained by god); practical (this institution is the best, fairest way to govern); etc. Without this understanding, that is, the consent of society, the institution has no social imperative.

Central to this statement is the normal functioning of institutions through the voluntary—and unforced—participation of its members. Thus, the threat and the use of violence to maintain institutional discipline characterize an abnormal situation, as in the case of the NSS.

The disconnect between practices and legitimations is a characteristic of abnormal institutions, and when this happens, as Leman-Langlois suggests, the institution loses its social imperative and requires corrective measures. Such measures include adjusting its institutional practices to make them consistent with their legitimations, suppressing awareness of the gap (secrecy and lying), changing the legitimation (to fighting terrorism) and resorting to physical force (the police state). Democratic states need to build into their institutions procedures and mechanisms to prevent slippage and to provide remediation when necessary.

Changing the legitimation introduces the concept of an insincere legitimation (propaganda). Sincere legitimations derive from principles of fairness and equal treatment, whereas insincere legitimations contain a privileging ideological component (see section 2.4) as in the use of a constant threat to justify the antidemocratic practices of the NSS. Insincere legitimations attempt to associate themselves with sincere ones. For example, University of California administrator, Bolton (1968) suggested that the CIA legitimize its status by claiming that the "agency is really a university without students and not a training school for spies," something the CIA now takes for granted. Not all insincere legitimations are this transparent, for people can honestly offer—as they can honestly accept—insincere legitimations. Insincere legitimations are proffered to justify an institutional practice whose real purpose may be otherwise unappealing to participants. This is why, when the inconsistency between legitimation and practice becomes apparent, proponents of the practice offer a new legitimation in its place. For example, when the insincere claim that Iraq had Weapons of Mass Destruction (WMDs) (to justify a war) failed, the need to depose a tyrant quickly replaced it.

167

The legitimacy of a democratic government depends on three important concepts. First, the government is accountable to its citizens for its actions. Second, mechanisms (the capacity to select and change practices and principles, or laws, of government and its governmental agents) exist for citizens to redress governmental actions they find at odds with their expectations. Third, its citizens are capable, both intellectually and physically, of making such decisions. Here we stress the fundamental importance of the institutions of the law (to ensure the principle of accountability and the capacity to redress) and education (to ensure that citizens are intellectually capable of making such decisions).

1.2 Pathologies of the State

Democracies vary in their success in achieving these desired practices. Any failure of this sort constitutes a coup. In an overt coup, the perpetrators make no pretense of maintaining democracy in their seizure of the governmental apparatus, even though they may attempt insincerely to legitimize the coup by claiming that the termination of democratic processes is in the best interest of the citizenry and perhaps promising that when order is restored, democracy will return.

The covert coup rests on the pretense that the institutions are still living up to their legitimating discourse despite the erosion of governmental responsibilities. This type of coup is much less obvious, for the government continues to proclaim its legitimacy as a democracy and, in fact, many of the operations of the democracy do continue, including an appearance of accountability and lawful procedures. Such coups typically involve the commandeering of aspects of the governmental apparatus by the commercial sector through such practices as of campaign financing (thereby selecting candidates), lobbying, or influencing the society's commonsense understanding of the world. In addition, we find the inclusion of normally subordinate governmental institutions, such as the military, in the decision-making process through membership on government (national security) councils, and the development of secret societies (the CIA) and the control of information (secrecy). Crucial to the covert coup is the degree to which individuals—be they judges or professors—who are not really part of the inside group willingly participate in the process of maintaining the NSS.

1.3 The National Security State

Clearly, the U.S. NSS exemplifies a covert coup in a "democratic," capitalist society in which the institutions of the military (with an annual commitment of over $400 billion—half of the planetary military expenditure) and the associated defense industry have come to dominate the governmental apparatus and have diverted national resources to privileging selected members of those institutions. Other states, though on a smaller scale (e.g., Indonesia), possess many of the same characteristics of the U.S. NSS, namely the manufactured threat of enemies to justify a large military. A comparative study of such NSSs would be instructive both in understanding the workings of our own and in understanding its influence on other such states.

The NSS arose with the establishment of a persistent threat that justifies a high level of military preparedness and expenditure, beginning with the cold war threat of nuclear attack. Following the collapse of the U.S.S.R., and with it the Cold War, terrorism and other weapons and tactics of mass destruction (re)joined nuclear weapons as perpetual threats. Both WMDs and terrorists are aptly suited to the NSS for, in addition to legitimizing the necessity for force, they instill fear in the general public, thus encouraging them to "voluntarily" support high levels of military expenditure. Ironically, September 11 demonstrated that our massive military might fails to provide any practical security. Yet, the U.S. has used this incident to move beyond a state of permanent threat to a state of permanent war and, with it, the suspension of constitutional rights and treaty obligations.

However, the threat must be such that it can be addressed with military force—through the threat or use of violence. For this reason, ecological threats like global warming and toxic waste, including nuclear waste fail, while the "War on Drugs" succeeds. In fact, because of the NSS's dependency on oil, environmental threats like global warming are antithetical to its interests and helps to explain why "in mid-June [2003], the Bush administration edited out passages in an E.P.A. report that described scientific concerns about the potential risks from global warming (Thompson 2003). It also illustrates the NSS's selective use and control of knowledge to benefit its own agenda and its opposition to open scientific research. This has also led to using the budget to marginalize academic research other than that benefiting the military, and has, Thompson argues, increasingly alienated the scientific community.

Frequently associated with the NSS—and certainly true of the U.S. NSS because of the huge military expenditures—is the complicity of the commercial sector, a "syndical fascist system, . . . a series of partnerships between business, labor, the university, the military, . . . [which is] an attempt to replace the social contract in terms of a corporative system of agreements between leaderships" (Raskin 1971:168), or "the military/industrial complex" of Eisenhower.

1.4 The institution

Anthropologists (e.g., Bourdieu 1977) increasingly advocate an institutional analysis that views any society as a collection of interconnected institutions, particularly with respect to the study of large-scale societies. Key elements include: *legitimations*; *a playing field* with players or assigned *roles*; *goals*; resources or *capital* to accomplish them; and prescribed and proscribed role assignments and procedures. We consider, following Fairclough (1989), *orders of discourse* to be a part of institutional practices, consisting of what can (and can't) be said, how it is to be said and what knowledge is needed to say it. The learning of any order of discourse (e.g., academic or legal) empowers the members to act, but at the same time constrains what and how members may act and speak. This power, the capacity to enable and constrain, may be either legitimate or illegitimate, characterized by Foucault (1994b) as "domination." In his view, power is inseparable from knowledge because the control of knowledge, including secrecy and the classification of documents is empowering. Given that different representations of the same situation have the capacity to privilege some at the expense of others, access to and control of knowledge is also a form of power. This is why the analysis of legitimations, especially separating sincere and insincere legitimations, is so important. Also, as we show in section 2.4, background knowledge, essential the acquisition of new knowledge, is a form of power.

170

Institutional practices, especially proscribed elements, often reflect impositions from the interests of other institutions that may not be consistent with existing role assignments and can lead to role conflicts that can in turn lead to new practices. The analysis of interinstitutional linkages can help to explain why institutional practices deviate from their legitimations.

Praxis and the Individual. In addition to examining institutions as social structures, Bourdieu (1977) and others propose that we look at social events from the perspective of the individual agent. From this perspective, institutional structures appear as resources. Bourdieu also notes that institutional structures arise and are reproduced by the activities of these individual agents who may not fully comprehend the functions of the institution. This suggests the possibility that no one is in charge, for it is possible with everyone operating within assigned roles and under the guidance of the *habitus* that no one has a sense of what the institution is actually doing. Thus, an institution can end up performing unintended and unwanted practices. This possibility raises the important need for institutional members to be aware of the actual functions of their institution and to possess and exercise social responsibility.

Habitus. Bourdieu and Foucault ask us to look at the individual, not as fully autonomous and freethinking, but as someone whose orientation has been shaped by his/her culture (or rather the collection of institutions). Bourdieu uses the term *habitus* to describe this orientation, not as a set of mastered rules or structures, but rather as an inculcated set of dispositions that incline the individual to respond to events in certain ways. This should not be taken to mean that the individual is not free to act according to his/her own will, but rather that the individual will be inclined to operate within the parameters of one's roles. Habitus is important to our argument because it imposes a form of control including self-discipline or censorship.

2. HIGHER EDUCATION[1] AND THE NATIONAL SECURITY STATE

Today we recognize the responsibility for both practical (preparing an individual for securing a livelihood) and general (or liberal) educational (GenEd) goals (preparing the individual for life and especially the preparation of the individual for political participation in society). Yet, historically, universal education arose because of its potential to provide discipline, cultural uniformity, and loyalty to the state (Ramirez and Boli 1987). Rudolph (1977) notes a counterrationale for founding universities in this country—providing moral guidance for the future ruling elites. While initially, this morality was equated with biblical teaching, today it has broadened into what we now call GenEd.

2.1 The Relationship between Education and the State

The institution of education appears to be insulated from external influence, being the financial and political responsibility of state and local government. Yet, this institution has been colonized by external forces, including various institutions of the NSS through mandates and incentives. Many mandates require these institutions to meet their civic responsibilities (instruction in civics and history; insuring equal opportunity; and access to low interest student loans). One such mandate, whose origin can be traced back to Nuremberg, requires Institutional Review Boards (IRBs) at research institutions to protect the rights of human research subjects. Other mandates like the Patriot and Homeland Security acts require universities to report changes in foreign student status. Institutions failing to comply become ineligible for federal funding.

The federal government provides about 10% of the budget for education at all levels 6% of which (2.9% of the federal budget) funds the U.S. Department of Education (U.S.ED) whose mission is "to ensure equal access to education and to promote educational excellence throughout the Nation" (U.S.ED 2003b). In 1999, according to the National Science Foundation, the U.S. government spent slightly over $40 billion on research and development of which a little over half was characterized as defense-related and of which $1.8 billion went to universities. Of this amount, 40% goes to 10 universities with Johns Hopkins receiving 15% of the total. Way down the list, Michigan State University (MSU)[2] received $2.5 million from the Department of Defense, approximately 0.2% of MSU's total budget. Sciences and technology receive substantially more funding, with the engineering disciplines receiving 42% of their funding from the DOD (U.S. Government 2003). In addition, some of the 2003 Department of Homeland Security (U.S. DHS 2003) research and development's $1 billion budget will find its way to the universities in the form of graduate and undergraduate fellowships.

The social sciences accept defense grants at a much lower level. The National Defense Education Act, now known as the Title VI of the National Education Act, calls for the funding ($27 million dollars in 2002) of 118 university-based National Resource Centers for language and world area studies (U.S.DE 2003a). The original legitimation of this act had been to develop expertise in the languages and cultures of the world in the event of war. Subsequent legitimations involve developing an awareness of the world in which we live, by training teachers for and offering area studies and language courses. Other academic global studies units arose from defense-related activities. Columbia University's School of International Affairs, the nation's first international center, grew out of its wartime Naval School of Military Government and Administration (Horowitz 1969).

The limits to what sort of defense-related research a university may accept are at best inexplicit, though most consider MSU to have crossed the line in 1954 when it became involved in a project to train and install a government in Vietnam. This program, which began as a seemingly innocent training program, turned into a military operation supplying guns and ammunition to the U.S.–supported Diem puppet regime and, in the words of its coordinator, Stanley Sheinbaum (1966), "our Project had become a CIA front." Soon, MSU found itself supporting an undemocratic regime with serious human rights abuses. Yet, Sheinbaum notes, the faculty and university administrators were generally "untroubled" by the project until exposed later. Were this an isolated event then, perhaps, we could understand it as the result of an overzealous college president wanting to put his university on the map, but there are too many similar examples at other universities to justify this interpretation.

2.2 Extra Institutional Influences on the University

The public often questions the "ivory tower" autonomy of the university without realizing how essential this is to the university's GenEd mission and that this autonomy has been substantially compromised by external influences.

The Political Filter. The university and the academic disciplines have developed a set of orthodox practices that insulate them from extramural criticism such as steering clear of partisan viewpoints, while professing at the same time that the academy is a place where such discussion should take place freely and openly. In popular terms, this practice means avoiding "political" positions and discourse. This use of the term "political" departs from its literal sense of "discourse pertaining to how decisions are made in society" but refers to discourse that challenges the prevailing orthodoxy.

Since the 1960s, universities have increasingly depended on tuition, grants, and gifts to supplement state support. In this context, the cost to the university of being "political" is estrangement from these sources. Consequently, these potential costs often lead to self-censorship and the avoidance of "political" discourse in the classrooms, political research, and public service. Joas (2003:1), citing Bahrdt, observed "that a scrutiny of school textbooks on social studies or introductions to sociology must give the impression that the societies we live in have neither armed forces nor police." Wolf (1982) noted the skewed subject matter of the social sciences (in the U.S.) and that they rarely address the needs of the working people, with political science being preoccupied with orthodox policy, and economics focusing on the needs of corporations.

Ravitch (2003) reports that "bias panels," such as the National Assessment Government Board censor controversial (political) words and topics from the nation's textbooks thus lessening student exposure to anything but the orthodox. Bias panels legitimatize this practice by citing the need to avoid stereotypes and situations not common to all so that tests will be fairer to all. Such legitimations pose a danger to the state for they legitimate the avoidance and the examination of controversial issues so necessary to the democratic state.

The avoidance of political topics that might jeopardize either the individual or the institution narrows the academic discourse and helps to explain why academics find it difficult to teach and write about problems associated with the NSS. The result is that the NSS gains legitimacy from the absence of this critical circumspection.

174

The Research Filter. In 2002, universities received research and development contracts for over $37 billion (AAAS 2001). Because today only 40% of MSU's annual expenditure of $1.4 billion in 2001–2 comes from the state-supplied general fund, increased emphasis has been placed on research revenue that has risen to 20% of the operating budget (MSU 2003). In contrast to the U.S. system, Dutch faculty obtain internal (rather than external) funding for research projects, by submitting their proposals to a university committee, much in the same way individuals are reviewed for tenure in U.S. universities. In the U.S., most grants come from outside funding agencies, be they government (MSU=47% federal, 15% state), foundation (MSU=2.4%) or industry (MSU=3.5%). Given that these funding agencies also evaluate each proposal with respect to their own agenda, they help to define the domain of legitimate research in a way far different from the Dutch example.

Because some disciplines (agriculture, engineering, business, medicine, the "hard" sciences and economics) receive more support than others, they are more influenced externally. Furthermore, the ability to garner grants is now understood as a means of acquiring academic capital, almost on a par with publication. Thus, faculty in the more heavily endowed areas find it easier to obtain academic capital than those in other areas like literature, languages, history, and philosophy. This availability of specific types of research money helps to explain the skewing of the social science research agenda, described by Wolf above, and the skewing of the level of prestige of members of different disciplines. This effect also reaches into the curriculum and the classroom, for professors teach what they know and what they know comes from their research. This practice contrasts sharply with the legitimation of the university as a free and open place to investigate and explore ideas.

2.4 Internal Influences on the University

The educational process involves socialization, discipline, and the acquisition of orthodox knowledge. Students quickly learn the consequences of compliance and noncompliance. Good grades depend as much on following procedures as they do on mastering knowledge. Faculty undergo several filtering processes, first, as students at the primary, secondary, and collegiate level, then as graduate students (and apprentice teachers), the job interview and the tenure process.

The Scholarship Role. Above all, faculty are expected to be reliable scholars by conducting research, publishing its results in journals using appropriate scholarly discourse and behaving in a dignified, scholarly manner. The *Faculty Handbook* (MSU 2003) describes both faculty rights and responsibilities.

> *MSU endorses academic freedom and responsibility as essential to attainment of the University's goal of the unfettered search for knowledge and its free exposition. Academic freedom and responsibility are fundamental characteristics of the University environment.*

Responsibilities:
- pursue excellence and intellectual honesty in teaching, research . . . and public service activities; and in publishing;
- encourage students and colleagues to engage in free discussion and inquiry; . . . evaluate student and colleague performance on a scholarly basis;
- work in a collegial manner . . . encourage the free search for knowledge;
- refrain from introducing matters which are not consistent with their teaching duties and professional competence;
- differentiate carefully their official activities as faculty members from their personal activities as citizens.

Rights:
- seek changes in institutional policy through established University procedures and by lawful and peaceful means;
- discuss in the classroom any material which has a significant relationship to the subject matter as defined in the approved course description;
- determine course content, grading and classroom procedures in the courses they teach;
- conduct research and to engage in creative endeavors . . . publish or present research findings and creative works . . . engage in public service activities.

The *Handbook* shows a concern for the rights of the students as well, but, at the same time, it protects the university from legal challenges. It also contains considerable vagueness: "pursue excellence"; "in a collegial manner"; "in a professional manner." This is quite typical of documents that also serve as institutional legitimations, allowing for multiple interpretations with the advantage that more people can subscribe to them and the disadvantage that nobody knows what they really mean (Rappaport 1979). This vagueness also makes it difficult to test whether our legitimations actually match our practices and facilitates the opportunistic hijacking of these terms by the NSS for its own purposes. For example, Bolton (1968) suggested that the term "academic freedom" could be used to justify the participation of scholars in CIA projects.

The importance accorded scholarship derives in part from its ability to legitimatize the institution. But absent from this discourse are questions of the relationship of the university to the state such as will the subject matter of this scholarship be beneficial to citizens? Also absent from this discourse is a discussion of whether our students are rewarded for scholarship or for obedience.

The Tenure Filter. Originally conceived to protect the academic freedom, tenure has become a major instrument of academic control. The university argues that tenure enables academic units to maintain—and improve—their faculty. To achieve tenure, new faculty have to perform at a high level, especially in the areas of grant getting and publication. These requirements impose heavy burdens on individual faculty including twelve-hour days and missing out on social and family life, even postponing the decision to have children. Young faculty also need to watch what they say. Several years ago, a friend of ours at another university, distributed a factual leaflet concerning the similarity in practices by the apartheid government of South Africa and the state of Israel. He received a "friendly" warning to postpone such activities until after tenure, which he did not receive.

This redefinition of tenure also illustrates that institutions are viewed and used by its users as resources that can be put to their own uses. This example exposes the tenure process as an important mechanism for controlling deviance. It renders the faculty more cautious, less "political" and less likely to take on issues such as the NSS in their teaching, research, and in conducting university business. Tenure illustrates the potential of the institution to change its practices and purpose, thus distancing itself from its original legitimation.

The Knowledge Filter. An acute sense of orthodoxy concerning what constitutes permissible knowledge pervades the academic field. This sense of orthodoxy often takes the form of self-discipline (even habitus) as in the avoidance of unorthodox and political positions, despite the institution of tenure and academic freedom. It derives in part from the awareness of what might happen were one to go against the prevailing orthodoxy. One of the most celebrated examples of this comes from the field of geography. Not so long ago, the concept, then called "continental drift," but now theorized as "plate tectonics," was considered as wrong as Lamarkianism is today. Alfred Wegener (1880–1930) espoused the concept of continental drift and was so shunned that the only academic job he could find was teaching high school. As faculty, we learn the limits of acceptable knowledge and undertake extreme caution whenever we venture outside its bounds, academic freedom not withstanding. This helps to explain why the academy does not embrace research into "political" areas such as militarism and popular economics.

2.5 General Education and its Role in a Democratic Society

Very few books show up in a library search using "General Education" as a key word. At the university, we give little attention and discussion to what it is and how to achieve it. We unanimously accept the capacity for critical thought as the cornerstone of education and a democratic state, even though we rarely make an effort to explain what this means. Ironically, we honor Socrates for his ability to teach critical thinking, but we often forget that his success proved fatal. Critical thinking has come to mean something "smart" people avoid, i.e., "political." This situation is symptomatic of overlooking the disconnect between our legitimations and our practices.

Eco (2001) speaks of the importance of the "intellectual function" that he considers as "theoretical" as opposed to "moral." It "consists of identifying critically what one considers a satisfactory approximation of truth" and involves "delving for ambiguities and bringing them to light." Furthermore, "the first duty of the intellectual is to criticize his own traveling companions ('to think' means to play the voice of conscience)." But the intellectual function differs from and must be kept separate from "the moral function" of the citizen, which "requires the elimination of nuances and ambiguities." Finally, the intellectual function is not limited to intellectuals. We see the intellectual and moral functions operating dialectically for all citizens in the sense that each informs the other. The task of deciding when to use either poses an important challenge to all.

For us, "critical" entails the ability to identify the workings of ideology. Following Fairclough (1989), we take ideology to be the use of knowledge, regardless of its truth-value, in the service of inequality. Ideology is not always overt as in a statement like "The poor will always be with us"—a statement that suggests that no matter how hard we work to eradicate poverty, we have to accept the fact that this inequality will always remain. Covert ideology exists in the form of background knowledge, something we draw on to interpret overt texts. For example, the statement that "we must be ever vigilant against terrorism" requires that we know the meaning of terrorism. In popular usage, terrorism is something used by our enemies and not by us. This background knowledge causes us to interpret the text to mean that we must be vigilant against others who wish us ill and not against members of our own society who might perpetrate violence to maintain the NSS.

Ideological knowledge often exists as part of our commonsense understanding of the world—it is so ubiquitous and natural that we do not even notice of it. For example, we understand the word "security" as having to do with ways of making us safe; yet, the meaning of the word has narrowed to issues of law enforcement and the military. In the NSS, "health" is not a security issue and the term "food security" does not mean preventing hunger, but rather the need to insure that there is enough food in time of war. This narrowing excludes from discourse crucial topics pertaining to the security of the nation. Homeland security, for example has nothing to do with social security. Uncovering ideological knowledge requires exposure to a wide variety of opinions on the same topic, especially those that are "political" so that they challenge standard or orthodox understanding, for it is here that clash of background assumptions can come to the fore and hence lead to critical analysis.

The academy itself is not immune from such ideology. Both Giroux (1987) and Bourdieu (1982) point out that academy maintains and legitimates as standard English, a genre that privileges academics and the university-trained at the expense of the (relatively) uneducated. Critical thinking requires self-reflection and critical examination of one's own practices, especially with respect to one's own legitimations. In this matter, Fairclough (1995) calls for the teaching of critical language awareness—the teaching about the role of language in creating inequality.

2.6 Towards a More Socially Responsible Educational Institution

Contrary to the expectations of the enlightenment, many postmodernists argue the concept of an enlightened electorate is impossible and consequently that democracies in the postmodern era are destined to fail as in the case of the current NSS. In contrast, we believe education can produce an enlightened electorate and can assist in providing remedial measures for restoring our democracy to its legitimacy. However, this requires that we respond to the calls of Freire (1987) and Giroux (1987) that we take a more critical view of how we are preparing our children as citizens in a legitimate democracy.

External influences severely compromise the university's ability to fulfill its civic mission and the effects of political and research filters increase with the loss of financial and political autonomy so that universities find it more difficult to carry out the academic function. We need to find a way for the university to be politically and financially autonomous, perhaps like the Dutch example, while at the same time be responsible to its mission (legitimation) especially in the area of GenEd. This depoliticizing of the university poses a challenge to the state governments, for there are political forces that are likely to oppose this solution.

We also need to address the task of distinguishing between legitimate and illegitimate research. In retrospect, the illegitimacy of the Vietnam Project is clear, but no one at the time questioned it. Furthermore, without constraints, the university is free to do the bidding of the NSS, thus being a contributor to its strength rather than a source of democratic renewal.

Existing Mechanisms. MSU's publicly elected Board of Trustees is responsible for the running of the university, approving budgets, selecting the president and senior administrative officers and granting faculty tenure and promotions, though in practice they delegate the actual activities to their appointees, except when problems arise. For example, in the 1970s, the Board chose to divest its holdings of stocks in corporations doing business in apartheid South Africa, because they concluded that MSU should not profit from a system based on inequality. However, this *ad hoc* decision never moved beyond the South African question to the broader question of how it should invest its holdings, or of the limits of university's involvement in the outside world with regard to research. Furthermore, the trustees would not have decided to divest had not the community inside and outside the university energetically and persuasively brought it to their attention.

MSU's *Faculty Handbook* (2003) recognizes that the university's responsibility to provide "a research environment for free and unfettered pursuit of knowledge" is "clearly essential to the protection of individuals and the public at large" and that "there exist federal or state laws, regulations and guidelines in several areas which are designed for this purpose." It delegates responsibility to the university's "advisory committees and academic governance bodies to insure that individual research and scholarly projects incorporate appropriate safeguards." Accordingly, before submission to a granting agency the proposal undergoes several screenings, at the departmental and administrative level. Each unit reviews the project and examines it with respect to its purview and interests including the treatment of human subjects (see 1.1), protecting the researchers' right of first publication and with classified research.

The advisory committee to MSU's Dean of International Studies and Programs (ISP), consisting of scholars representing each of the university's colleges, advises the dean on a variety of topics including the appropriateness of international projects. Had this committee existed at the time it would probably have concluded that the Vietnam Project was not in the best interests of the university. Another safeguard is the proviso that "the university should retain for its scholars the right of first publication." This imposition impedes secrecy in favor of openness and public discussion. However, it is doubtful that this important proviso would have prevented the Vietnam project, nor would it prevent NSS projects in which secrecy is not involved and rights of first publication remain with the researcher.

Even more problematic are projects like National Security Educational Program (NSEP), enacted in 1991 and currently funded through the Department of Defense. NSEP (2003) calls for the strengthening of "national security" through training in international studies and language and requires its fellowship recipients to subsequently work for government agencies (mainly associated with the NSS) following their studies. Several academic organizations, including the African Studies Association, the African National Resource Centers, and the Association of African Studies Programs have criticized this program, because of its connection to the NSS and its advocacy of secrecy and clandestine activity and runs counter to a commitment to open research. A more appropriate way, critics of NSEP argue, would be to transfer the money to the Department of Education as an incentive program to increase area and language studies without the service requirement.

Within MSU, the faculties of MSU African Studies Center and the Center for the Study of Latin America and the Caribbean have also opposed the NSEP fellowship program because of its potential to interfere with research. After reviewing this program, MSU's ISP Advisory Committee resolved to write a letter to students interested in an NSEP fellowship stating the centers' concerns. These actions have aroused the ire of NSS sympathizers like Stanley Kurtz (2003) of the

Hoover Institute who suggests "Congress needs to pass an amendment that would take funding out of the hands of any Title VI center that engages in or abets a boycott of national security related scholarships." In addition, MSU president Peter McPherson, who in 2003 went to Iraq to "reconstruct" its economic system, has publicly criticized the opposition to NSEP awards, seeing nothing wrong with accepting funds from institutions advocating violence and secrecy. And this is why the *Handbook*'s (2003) caveat that "exigencies of national defense may at times make exceptions to this policy on publication necessary" is so troubling, for the university can invoke "national defense" to justify the acceptance of NSS funding.

182

The university's research guidelines also suggest that research projects must be consistent with a discipline's principles and practices. For example, the American Anthropological Association's (AAA) statement of ethics (AAA 1998) suggests further guidance on the appropriateness of research (see Web site for full text):

- The anthropologists' paramount responsibility is to those they study.
- In relation with their own government and with host governments, research anthropologists should be honest and candid.
- They should demand assurance that they will not be required to compromise their professional responsibilities and ethics as a condition of their permission to pursue research.
- Specifically, they should not agree to any secret research, secret reports or debriefings of any kind.
- Anthropologists must retain the right to make all ethical decisions in their research.

The more explicit and more demanding nature of these guidelines appear to be sufficient to challenge, if not prevent, something like the Vietnam project though they probably would not prevent the university or individuals from participating in programs like NSEP.

These *Handbook* guidelines did not arise without struggle. Nothing of the sort was in place to protect Franz Boas of Columbia University, from censure in 1919 by the Governing Council of the AAA, an organization Boas founded. Stocking's (1968) account of this somewhat complicated event states that Boas was censured in large part because he wrote a letter to *The Nation* publicly condemning four individuals who used their position as scholars to spy for the U.S. government during WWI.

Neither the university guidelines nor those of the AAA appear to be sufficient to resist the colonization of the university by the NSS through the medium of research. What is missing is a condemnation of the use of violence and force, something antithetical to the institution of education and indeed to normal institutions as a whole. We suggest that universities and professional organizations add to their research guidelines a proviso to exclude the acceptance of any funding from institutions that espouse secrecy and/or violence. We are aware that what constitutes violence will inspire a good deal of healthy "political" discussion and welcome the debate as essential for a healthy university and society. No doubt, this debate will address abortion and gun rights. It will also draw in the nature of the NSS and the question of the legitimacy of violence as a procedure to resolve problems.

The *Handbook* (2003) also states "no publication, statement, or activity, either on behalf of the University or by an individual in their official capacity, shall endorse any commercial product, or advocate any specific commercial method or device, either directly or by implication." This proviso requires reexamination both in the athletic arena, where it is shamelessly overlooked, and in the acceptance of grants and gifts. Isn't the acceptance of a grant from a major corporation an endorsement of some sort? Were this proviso taken seriously, it could serve as a means of insulating the university from undesirable outside interests.

Internal Considerations. We also need to review the practices of the institution to make sure that they are consistent with its legitimations and especially the teaching of critical thought and providing an atmosphere of openness. This should not, writes Leman-Langlois (2001) following Foucault, "entail the eradication of any competing discourse . . . Rather, it is sufficient that a context arise where a critical mass of individuals (1) perceive a discrepancy between current practices and the dominant conceptualization of the social context and (2) adopt a sufficiently unified way to define the 'problem' and the new solution it appears to demand." Umberto Eco (2001) argues for much the same approach, that the university be a place of openness and exploration and not a position of advocacy, a challenge for an institution constantly assaulted by the NSS. This position of openness is essential not only to the critical exploration of ideas, but for the protection of the institution, for academics (rightly or wrongly) are being accused of a closedness and bias (Kurtz 2003), as opposed to the openness advocated here. Importantly, we propose, not the political filter described above, but a discipline that enables critical thought or as Leman-Langlois puts it, "an adjustment of the intellectual tools we use to understand reality, in order to repair the broken consistency between the world and our actions."

Placing the university in a nonadvocacy position raises the question of where resistance to the NSS and progressive change is to arise.
184 Again, Leman-Langlois (2002), following (Foucault 1984, 388) suggests that the process of "problematization" may be instigated by social, economic, or political processes that make the conventional at odds with new empirical realities—and the abandonment of apartheid is certainly an extreme example of such change.

In addition to critical thought, we need to establish a new perspective more appropriate for the global community in which we live. For example, Nussbaum (2000) calls for developing

> the ability to think of oneself as what Stoic philosophers called a citizen of the world, . . . [to explore] issues from agriculture to human rights to the relief of famine [to] require our minds to venture beyond local affiliations and consider the reality of distant lives. To attain this ability, however, students need to learn a great deal more than students in previous generations typically did about the history and culture of non-Western people, and of ethnic and racial minorities within their own culture; about the achievements and experience of women; and about the variety of human sexuality.

We see the tremendous potential that the actual experience of living abroad through overseas study and volunteering offers to individuals. The vast majority of those with an international experience report a new perspective in which they no longer see the world exclusively through American eyes. Nussbaum also calls for the development "of a *narrative imagination*"; the ability to try to understand what it might be like to experience life from a position other than one's own, to be an intelligent reader of other life stories—and also to understand how difficult it is to be an intelligent reader.

Each of these suggestions deserves much deeper exploration and discussion than we are able to offer here. We offer them with the understanding that institutions are not static but evolve and the understanding that we can help them evolve, but only if we take education seriously and that means insisting that our practices live up to our legitimations.

3. THE LEGAL COMMUNITY AND THE U.S. NATIONAL SECURITY STATE (NSS)

3.1 Nuclear Weapons and International Legal Discourse

By signing the United Nations Charter (6/26/1945) and the London Charter (8/8/1945) the U.S. recognized that the customary rules and principles of humanitarian law were universally binding and that legal processes could end "the scourge of war." Conversely, by the atomic bombings of Hiroshima and Nagasaki (8/6 and 9/1945), the U.S. asserted war powers unlimited by law. We continue to struggle with these two views of reality, whether international law premised on nonviolent resolutions and agreements or imperial law based on greater threat or use of force provides for security.

Nuclear weapons as a key component of the NSS. The development of nuclear weapons marked the emergence of the U.S. NSS. The secrecy and the massive scale of the Manhattan Project institutionalized policies of constant threat of use and proliferation. These were justified as deterrence (Schell 2003) and glorification of things nuclear, both military (the bombings of Hiroshima and Nagasaki "saved lives" and "ended the war") and civilian ("atoms for peace" and "power too cheap to meter") and required denial of the deadly short and long-term effects of the nuclear system: the mining, refining, production, testing, and use of nuclear weapons. With the Manhattan Project and "the black budget," Congress abdicated its public fiduciary responsibility and both Congress and the Executive ignored positive customary and conventional international laws of war. Unchecked concentration of power permitted the Truman, Groves, and Stimson decision to drop the bombs without debate and despite the opposition of 80% of the Manhattan Project scientists (Lanouette in Bird and Lipschultz 1998:109).

Nuclear Weapons as Antithetical to the Rule of Law. The legality and use-fulness of nuclear weapons has been challenged over the past 60 years both formally or directly (the ICJ Opinion ICJ-OP, UNGA Resolutions, the Shimoda case, resistance cases, compensation claims, etc.) and informally (through demonstrations and protests). The antiwar movement has long understood that "the new empirical realities" (Leman-Langlois 2002:81) were at odds with the conventional wisdom that the nuclear system or war could provide security or freedom. Eco, for example, concludes "the discovery of atomic energy, television, air transport, and the birth of various forms of multinational capitalism have resulted in some conditions that make war impossible" (Eco 2001:7). Together, the civil rights, human rights, women's rights, anti-war, antinuclear, environmental, and economic justice/corporate responsibility movements all address pieces of "the problem and the new solution it appears to demand" (Leman-Langlois 2002:81). While by 1970, the U.S. formally recognized that nuclear disarmament and general and complete disarmament were essential (Nuclear Non-Proliferation Treaty, Art. VI), the U.S. NSS practices, including development and deployment of nuclear weapons, continued unabated.

3.2 The 1996 International Court of Justice (ICJ) Opinion

These two views of reality, that complete nuclear disarmament is a universal obligation for legal, moral, and practical reasons versus the view that U.S. deterrence provides security, are articulated in the dissenting opinions of ICJ Judges Weeramantry and Schwebel, regarding the United Nations General Assembly advisory opinion question, "Is the threat or use of nuclear weapons in any circumstance permitted under international law?" (ICJ-OP 1996)

In that remarkable case in which nuclear weapons went "on trial" before the most authoritative court in the world, thirty-two states participated with written and/or oral submissions including the U.S. and all other permanent members of the Security Council except China. The ICJ held unanimously that "a threat or use of force by means of nuclear weapons that is contrary to Article 2.4 of the United Nations Charter and fails to meet all the requirements of Article 51 is unlawful" (ICJ-OP 1996: §105[2]D); and that "a threat or use of nuclear weapons should (ICJ-OP 1996:§ 42, "must") also be compatible with the requirements of the international law applicable in armed conflict, particularly those of the (ICJ-OP1996:§79, "intransgressible," "fundamental") principles and rules of international humanitarian law as well as with specific obligations under treaties and other undertakings which expressly deal with nuclear weapons" (ICJ-OP 1996: §105[2]E).

Importantly, the unanimous court also concluded that, "There exists an obligation to pursue in good faith and bring to a conclusion negotiations leading to nuclear disarmament in all its aspects under strict and effective international control" (ICJ-OP 1996: §105[2] F). But, having found general illegality of any threat or use, the ICJ hedged, saying, " . . . the court cannot conclude definitively whether the threat or use of nuclear weapons would be lawful or unlawful in an extreme circumstance of self-defense, in which the very survival of a State would be at stake" (ICJ-OP 105[2]) to avoid direct challenge to the bald mischaracterizations made by the U.S. and UK, that "modern nuclear weapon delivery systems are indeed capable of precisely engaging discrete military objectives" (ICJ-Verbatim Record/CR05/ 35/15Nov1995:88) and are "an essential element of national security" (Ibid., 84).

Delusions of grandeur pervade Judge Schwebel's dissent from the ICJ's general finding of illegality. Judge Schwebel, consistent with NSS practice, justifies deterrence or threat to nuclear weapons: "There is on the record remarkable evidence indicating that an aggressor [Iraq] was or may have been deterred from using outlawed weapons of mass destruction . . . by what the aggressor perceived to be a threat to use nuclear weapons against it [by the U.S. James Baker to Tariq Aziz] should it first use weapons of mass destruction against it" (ICJ-OP 1996:88). The U.S.'s 2003 invasion of Iraq, in direct violation of the United Nations Charter, bursts the thin veneer of the "deterrence" justification and marks a fully ascendant NSS policy that openly encourages proliferation and claims an apotheosized right to strike any self-defined "tyrants" preemptively including with nuclear weapons.

Empirical realities by contrast are faced by Judge Weeramantry in his dissent that is, arguably, the most important and complete modern legal opinion on this topic. Judge Weeramantry challenges the ICJ's hedge by saying: "The use or threat of use of nuclear weapons is illegal in any circumstances whatsoever. It violates the fundamental principles of international law and represents the very negation of the humanitarian concerns which underlie the structure of humanitarian law" (ICJ-OP 1996:170). He reasoned further that, "All postulates of law presuppose that they contribute to and function within the premise of the continued existence of the community served by that law. Without the assumption of that continued existence, no rule of law and no legal system can have any claim to validity, however attractive the juristic reasoning on which it is based. The taint of invalidity affects not merely the particular rule. The legal system which accommodates that rule, itself collapses upon its foundations, for legal systems are postulated upon the continued existence of society" (ICJ-OP 1996: 237). This is because the *de jure* undergirding of the international legal system, sovereign equality of states, cannot tolerate *de facto* inequality in which some country's "security" depends on threat or use of nuclear weapons or other weapons or tactics of mass destruction. "A legal rule would be inconceivable that some nations alone have the right to use chemical or bacteriological weapons in self defense and others do not. The principle involved, in the claim of some nations to be able to use nuclear weapons in self-defense, rests on no different juristic basis" (ICJ-OP 1996:242).

These dissents reflect the contrasting views on the legality of nuclear weapons: Weeramantry argued that they are fundamentally antithetical to the rule of law; and Schwebel, that they can be accommodated. And while the ICJ-Opinion certainly establishes a strong presumption of illegality, these dissents are informative because the ICJ's hedge leaves the question of illegality of a particular threat or use to be decided and implemented by courts in countries relying on nuclear weapons and war for "security" as, for example, in resistance cases.

3.3 Sacred Earth and Space Plowshares II, 2002 (SESPII)[3]

The Plowshares Movement, led by Philip and Daniel Berrigan and Elizabeth McAlister, combines Isiah 2:4, "they shall turn their swords into plowshares . . . and study war no more" with what Foucault calls "that great conquest of Greek democracy, that right to bear witness, . . . that right to set a powerless truth against a truthless power" (Foucault

1994:33) and to fairly, equitably and independently seek truth through exercise of a nonviolent "relation of struggle, domination, servitude and settlement" (Foucault 1994:9). Acts of nonviolent resistance to illegal and criminal threat or use of a particular nuclear weapon complement acts of civil disobedience that protest unjust laws. From 1983–2003, there were more than 55,000 arrests in the U.S. and Canada for anti-nuclear acts of civil resistance and civil disobedience (*Nuclear Resister* 2001, 2003).

Plowshares resisters refuse complicity with the NSS and its violence and instead insist on legitimate, open, accountable and nonviolent mechanisms for problem resolution and agreement. The Plowshares movement's emphases on prison-witness and noncooperation with illegitimate courts are undertaken in solidarity with those (the Hibakusha[4], African-Americans, Native-Americans and the poor) involuntarily subjected to the clear civil, political, economic and social injustices of the NSS. These two groups, the oppressed and the resisters and disobedients, or as Marcus Raskin puts it, those "with a surplus of pain and surplus of consciousness," acting in solidarity, expose empirical realities and participate in solutions framed by a good-faith rule of law view of normalcy.

This struggle between human (nonviolent) and inhuman (violent) responses to nuclear weapons also plays itself out in conflicting translations of the inscription on the cenotaph at the Hiroshima Peace Memorial. The English translation reads variously, "May their souls rest in peace. May the *mistake* or *evil* never be repeated." The Japanese word translated as "evil" implies something natural and unchangeable. But the accurate translation, "mistake/error" connotes a common human problem that, however serious, can be resolved. As a child at the Hiroshima Peace Memorial Ceremony in 1999 put it, "Men made the bomb. Men can unmake it." Or, as Foucault (1994:7) says, "knowledge was invented . . . it has no origin." Accordingly, "we must never lose sight of the extraordinary humanity of the people of Hiroshima" (Oe 1998:413), who despite experiencing the unspeakable horrors of the atomic bombs, have concluded that nuclear weapons have made retribution unthinkable and unjustifiable and that security and justice can only be practically achieved through negotiation for complete nonviolent disarmament.

189

Critical analysis of the SESPII case reveals the depth of the problem. In that case, three elderly Dominican Sisters resolved to illustrate that the illegal and criminal threat and use of weapons and tactics of mass destruction can be ended by nonviolent declaration, inspection, and disarmament of each of the thousands of nuclear weapons one at a time. Calling themselves "Sacred Earth and Space Plowshares 2002," Ardeth Platte, 67, Carol Gilbert, 55, and Jackie Hudson, 68, donned hazardous materials suits with "Disarmament Specialists" on the front and CWIT (Citizens Weapons Inspection Team) on the back. In the early morning of October 6, 2002, the first anniversary of the U.S. bombing of Afghanistan, they cut one link in two chains to inspect a Minuteman III, N-8 (MM III) nuclear missile silo site in northern Colorado. They found, as their research had indicated, a 335-kiloton, first-strike intercontinental ballistic missile on high alert, ready to unleash within 15 minutes uncontrollable heat and radiation twenty times greater than the Hiroshima bomb. They placed on the silo cover slab a copy of Francis A. Boyle's *The Criminality of Nuclear Deterrence* (2002) and other evidence of their understanding of the law that prohibits any threat or use of this weapon. In an act of symbolic disarmament, they poured their own blood in the form of six crosses on the silo cover and tracks. They then carefully lowered thirty-two feet of perimeter fence to symbolically expose the egregious threats to commit war crimes. They prayed and sang until some very young and heavily armed Air Force personnel arrived, arrested them, and took them to jail.

A court beholden to or subservient to the NSS loses its independence and competence and subverts constitutional guarantees of fair trials. When faced with open, good-faith, nonviolent and symbolic resistance to the ongoing threat of use of one nuclear weapon, the trial court awkwardly justified the legality of nuclear weapons and used the essentially non-violent arena of the courtroom to ratify its violent view of order and security.

The court acted in cahoots with overzealous prosecutors backed by heavily armed guards. In the SESPII case, the prosecutor brought two felony charges against the nuns: one from the Sabotage chapter entitled "Destruction of national defense materials, national defense premises or national defense utilities" (Count I 18-U.S.C-2155) and the other "Depredation of Property" over $1000 (18-U.S.C-1361). The prosecution and the court, in tandem, used two strategies. First, they excluded any discussion of the effects of the Minuteman III and of international and domestic law concerning the illegality of the Minuteman III. The trial court and prosecutor together held fast to NSS justifications so that the nuns' speaking ill of "our" nuclear weapons was felonious. The laws of war, directly relevant to all elements of the crimes charged, were dispensed with. Second, the court relieved the prosecutor of his burden to prove each and every element beyond reasonable doubt by eliminating elements of the crimes charged and prohibiting any defense evidence or argument. The result was that both crimes became strict liability destruction of any property crimes. Both strategies ignore well-understood foundations for a fair trial.

Pretrial Motions. The Sisters began their defense with several motions to dismiss, arguing that the government lacked discovery to prove beyond a reasonable doubt each and every element of the offenses charged and that the government failed to apply or misapplied the intransgressible laws of war directly relevant to all elements of the crimes charged. The prosecutor countered with a motion *in limine* to prohibit all defenses. At the Motions hearing international law Professors Francis Boyle and Ved Nanda testified that the binding law applied to uncontested facts positively prohibits any threat or use of even the one Minuteman III at issue and that under current law the nuns' measured, symbolic, public acts were reasonable especially in light of current new and expanded threats to use nuclear weapons (*Nuclear Posture Review*, 1/02, *National Security Strategy*, 9/02).

The legality of U.S. nuclear weapons, the court contended, had already been decided:

> "I find and conclude that in enacting 18 U.S.C 2155, Congress did not intend to require debate about the quintessential character of our weaponry in a criminal trial. To conclude otherwise, deconstructively, would create two unintended and untenable consequences: 1) inconsistent verdicts; and 2) unworkable national security policies . . . Twelve citizens acting as jurors, but without political responsibility and

accountability would have authority to determine which people could vandalize or destroy which weapons systems." (Judge Robert Blackburn, Pre-trial Orders in Limine (PTO 2003:25–26); "the will of the majority, legitimately expressed, had prevailed" (PTO 2003:13).

The trial court found that it was not competent to deal with this situation for judgments "regarding the course of action chosen by elected representatives, . . . are not the province of the judge (or jury) under the separation of powers established by the Constitution" (PTO 2003:13). With this conclusion, the court should have dismissed the criminal charges against the nuns. Instead, the court wrongly declared that all defense evidence was irrelevant.

Denial of the dangers of the Minuteman III. Having denied admission of all the nuns' proffered fact and law evidence regarding actual and intended effects and uses of the Minuteman III, Judge Blackburn indulged in unfounded speculation about nuclear weapons. The court found that deterrence is a "nebulous contingency plan" that involves "no credible threat of the imminent use of the Minuteman III" (PTO 2003:8) and that the Sisters were "seeing ghosts under every bed" (PTO 2003:9). Along the same lines, the prosecutor charged the nuns as saboteurs, while at the same time claiming that they engaged in a "typical protest" or "vandalism." We wonder why such wholly inaccurate glosses are considered necessary since a premise of the NSS is that the U.S. "national defense" has no legal limits. Surprisingly, the court found further that the Minuteman III poses no "imminent harm," not "a real emergency" and that the nuns were "devoid of fears of an immediate U.S. first strike" (PTO 2003:8). And in case some jury members might see through these justifications, the jury was instructed, under penalty of perjury, not to consider any of the nuns' testimony regarding the realities of the threat or use of the Minuteman III or any rules of law that apply.

The question of jurisdiction to consider the laws of war, ironically, echoed the attempted defenses offered by Germans judges at Nuremberg (cf. *The Justice Case*, Three Trials of War Criminals Before the Nuremberg Military Tribunals Under Control Council Law No. 10 [1951] at 1086). The court inverted its and the nuns' responsibilities by pronouncing that "an individual cannot assert a privilege to disregard domestic law in order to escape liability under international law unless domestic law forces (as opposed to authorizes) that person to violate international law" (PTO 2003:18). Furthermore, Blackburn ignored the positive limits to U.S. war powers as expressed in numerous treaties, the U.S. criminal code [war crimes, 18 U.S.C 2441; genocide, 18 U.S.C 1091–1093] and the intransgressible rules and principles of humanitarian law, finding that international law in general is "not grounded in the framework of positive domestic law" (PTO 2003:21).

This position left the court with the conclusion that while citizens have the right to decide to use nuclear weapons, they are not responsible for the consequences of their decision. "To hold that the criminal statutes here are supplanted by continually evolving customary international law would be to substitute the wisdom and judgment of democratic political branches of government for that of an independent academic community" (PTO 2003:21). This ignores basic rules of law and the principle of the separation of powers that any law passed by Congress or applied by the Executive is subject to review for constitutionality.

For the court to hold as it did that war crimes don't apply because they aren't *jus cogens* prohibitions like slavery, torture, or genocide, "none of which are implicated here" (PTO 2003:19), is not only factually and legally wrong, but delusional. Judge Blackburn claimed, based on faulty *stare decisis*, that "we will apply international law when it suits us" (PTO 2003:21) following incorrect federal appeals court holdings that the laws of war don't apply, because protection of property statutes are "wholly independent" (*U.S. v Allen*, 760 F 2d 447, 453 [1985] and "would be equally valid if there were no Trident [or Minuteman III] system" (*U.S. v May*, 622 F 2d 1000, 1009–10 [1980]).

Judge Blackburn further showed his incompetence by denying the relevance of the ICJ's findings and holding that "judgments of the ICJ do not fall within the definition of *jus cogens* or peremptory norms of international law" (PTO 2003:20). And, not having understood the sources and application of law as described in Article 38 of the Statute of the ICJ (an integral part of the UN Charter, a U.S. treaty), the court refused to hear expert testimony on the grounds that, "The ostensible jurisprudential puissance of the *Paquette Habana*, 175 U.S. 677 (1900) has evanesced" (PTO 2003:20).

As Judge Weeramantry predicted deductively, the trial court's holdings in the SESPII case demonstrate how a legal system that accommodates a rule of legality of weapons of mass extermination "collapses upon its [substantive] foundations." In addition to lack of both independence and competence related to the directly relevant laws of war, Judge Blackburn went further, denying the nuns numerous substantive and procedural constitutional guarantees essential for fair criminal trials.

Excluding the Elements of the Charge. Felony or depredation of property (18 U.S.C 1361) requires proof of damage of over $1000, which the prosecution could not substantiate. Consequently, the prosecution brought a sabotage charge as a "greater-included" felony that does not require the establishment of damage costs, only that defense materials, were damaged. But this method also required the court to eliminate necessary proof of "willful injury, damage or interference with the national defense," also elements of the sabotage charge. The "national defense" in 18 U.S.C 2155 became anything/everything or nothing through lifting out of context an unqualified and nonexistent "black letter rule" that "national defense" was merely "a generic concept of broad connotations, referring to the military and naval establishments and related activities of national preparedness" (*Gorin v U.S.*, 312 U.S. 19 [1941]. Thus, 32 feet of fence became the national defense.

Denial of 6th amendment right to be informed of nature and cause of the accusation was accomplished by the prosecutor's frequent refrain that 18 U.S.C 2155 was not sabotage. The indictment read "willful injuring, damage, interference with the national defense" but sabotage was "proved" as "injury to national defense materials" without more specific details. The court based its rulings on cases involving "trespass, vandalism and protest" (PTO 2003: 3, 7, 8, 9, 10, 11, 23). Astoundingly, the court found that this wasn't a criminal case at all for "the defendants lack standing to argue that the Minuteman III missile system was developed and deployed in violation of international law" (PTO 2003:14). The Sisters' exposure of the U.S.'s grossly illegal high alert threat to use a weapon of mass extermination was irrelevant because "they cannot skirt the standing requirement by factitiously creating circumstances to cast themselves as defendants rather than plaintiffs" (PTO 2003:15). This finding alone, of course, required the Court to dismiss the criminal charges brought.

Specific intent crimes were turned into strict liability crimes. The nuns were denied any evidence to show reasonable doubt that they had any intent to injure or interfere with the national defense no matter how broadly it may be defined. The MM III was presumed innocent and the nuns presumed guilty. The court denied the Sisters 6th Amendment right to a defense by holding the laws of war irrelevant and nonexistent and by reducing specific intent crimes to strict liability crimes. Again in flowery language, the trial court tried to cover its tracks, "I do not gainsay the right of criminal defendants to present defenses . . . but that does not include the right to present irrelevant evidence" (PTO 2003:28). In prohibiting even a good-faith defense the court resorted to *ad hominem* attacks against the nuns' expert witnesses (PTO 2003:22). No justification defenses were permitted because, the Court held the nuns had no reason to expect that they would be successful; "Defendants anticipation of effecting change in this country's or this administration's policies concerning nuclear weapons is pure conjecture" (PTO 2003:9). They could have sought other ways to address their concerns for legal alternatives are available by "the thousands" and "the fact that the defendants are unlikely to effect the changes they desire through legal alternatives does not mean, ipso facto, that those alternatives are nonexistent" (PTO 2003:11).

Outcome. The logic of the court, along with the predetermined guilty verdict, led the press and the public to label this a kangaroo court defined as "a mock court in which dominant prisoners tyrannize the defenseless, trying them on trivial or merely fanciful charges, as loitering with intent to breathe someone else's air" (Ciardi 1980: 216–17). The trial court's orders attempt to justify the trap as if we are all prisoners who can do nothing about the demonic doom of nuclear weapons. The court sentenced the nuns to 30, 33, and 41 months in prison and 3 years of supervised release so broad that it amounts to house arrest. While using the sabotage conviction as a sentencing base, the court departed downward because the nuns did not injure the national defense. The court held that if the nuns had "prevented an imminent nuclear launch by terrorists" their acts would have been an

195

excusable lesser harm. The thousands of letters that came to the judge in support of the nuns from people all over the world made it clear that terrorists include the U.S. that threatens to use a grotesque weapon of mass destruction like the Minuteman III and that the nuns inspired them to take action for nonviolent nuclear disarmament, the only legal kind possible.

3.4 How will change happen?

The African National Congress (ANC), the major organ of resistance to apartheid, accomplished elimination of apartheid without the commission of parallel *jus cogens* crimes, without the predicted retaliatory "blood bath." Following the end of apartheid, the South African Truth and Reconciliation Commission (TRC) examined the complicity of both individuals and institutions in the plainly illegal system of apartheid that had been "justified" as the "democratic" law of the land. The TRC examined the processes of colonization and the necessary presumptions and elements for transformation. We expect that the abolition and elimination of nuclear weapons and war will follow a similar process and have used the present tense to indicate points of problems and leverage. We both cite and rephrase the TRC's institutional analysis of the Legal Community under apartheid to reflect an institutional analysis of the U.S. legal community under the NSS TRC/CL:

1. Human rights are rights of all, not rights of Americans or a privileged few.
2. "Enormously principled and courageous action by a small minority of lawyers from all branches of the profession, assist in establishing a climate in which a constitutional and negotiated dispensation of the problem" of WMDs and war is possible. In addition to "resting on the twin foundations of a bill of rights and the power of judicial review," the Courts must take forthright cognizance of the primacy of treaties (U.S. Constitution Article 6) and of the fundamental rules and principles of humanitarian law.
3. Because Congress and Executive in the U.S. "represent" the military/industrial complex or the NSS, attempts by federal judges to act independently are discouraged. For example, judges' amelio-

ration of harsh effects of mandatory sentencing guidelines has resulted at best in further legislative steps "to curtail judicial independence and at worst to the overt subversion of the formal independence of the courts and the 'packing of the Bench.'"

4. The record of judicial impartiality and pursuit of justice in many U.S. state courts, with regard to cases of nonviolent civil resistance to nuclear weapons and war, is generally better than federal courts. But there is enormous variation and many courts' understanding of "certainty" in national defense or security matters leads courts to refuse to look at the reality of the effects of nuclear weapons, to find no legal limits to U.S. war powers and to give dangerous and unwarranted deference in "national security" matters. Such political views of the courts result in manifest injustice both substantively and procedurally. Since the NSS legitimations of nuclear weapons and unlimited war are thoroughly embedded in the federal judiciary, corrective recourse through the appeal process may be futile and may reinforce "bad law" of federal appeals courts cited by trial courts.

5. Legal education in the U.S. neglects or does not generally include study of human rights or humanitarian law and even the latest most distinguished U.S. Human Rights (Henkin, et al. 1999) omits any discussion of nuclear weapons or the seminal ICJ-Opinion.

6. "The administration of justice and a legal order must preserve impartiality and independence." The trial judge often acts as prosecutor and jury. Nonviolent resisters to nuclear weapons and others oppressed are stripped of basic rights in criminal cases including: notice of actual charges, presumption of innocence, right to bring witnesses in their defense directly relevant to elements of the offense(s) charged, holding the government to its burden to prove each and every element of a criminal offense charged beyond a reasonable doubt and the right to have a jury to decide relevant facts and be properly instructed on existing law. The courts abrogate, ignore, or misapply the fundamental rules and principles of humanitarian law and reverse and confuse issues of standing and relation of laws problems that prohibit use of domestic law to override these basic rules of law.

7. "All participants in the legal process" including judges, prosecutors, defense lawyers, juries as well as litigants or defendants
   such as nuclear resisters have "responsibilities to articulate, and
   argue in a truthful manner and with integrity."

Most importantly, the TRC concluded, "There needs to be substance to the notion of judicial independence, otherwise the courts
will be seen as the mere obedient servants of the other branches of
government . . . to preserve the basic equity and decency in a legal
system" (TRC/LC 1998:28). The NSS characterized in its current
extreme state by bankrupt policies of nuclear imperialism and con-
comitant economic and social injustices both at home and abroad is
bolstered by the legitimations of plainly illegitimate nuclearism. "It
is useful to government and legislatures pursuing obvious injustice
to have superficial and sanctimonious justifications by courts"
(TRC/LC 1998:28).

Abandonment of illegal and criminal threat or use of nuclear weapons. As
Mayor Takashi Hiraoka of Hiroshima said in his August 6, 1997,
Hiroshima Peace Declaration, "Nuclear weapons stand at the very
apex of all the violence that war represents." Thus, it is highly alarming that "counterproliferation" has replaced "nonproliferation" in the
current U.S. administration and that nonviolent disarmament, the
only real and possible solution, is off the table as an obligation of
the U.S. (Keller 2003). Already with Martin Luther King's assassination, the most coherent articulation of the problem and the new solution died too and the so-called "real politik" of perpetual violence
surged to an even uglier phase. The seeds of a coherent mass movement raising alternatives to war, militarism, and nuclearism are again
sprouting precisely because the divergence between justifications for
war and militarism are ever more plainly divorced from unjust economic, social, civil, and political realities. The central justification
for attack on Iraq, "Iraq's threat of use of weapons of mass destruction"
was an outright lie and, even had it not been a lie, use of threat of
weapons or tactics of mass destruction cannot stop the threat or use
of weapons or tactics of mass destruction. Nor can it make any such
threat or use legal. Required changes may derive from more massive
and concerted national and international grassroots nonviolent

198

resistance and protest actions such as those that hundreds of people engaged in at all 49 of the MM III sites in Colorado the days after the nuns' sentencing (2003) and appeal hearing (2004). Because the threat or use of "legal" nuclear weapons is thoroughly institutionalized, resolving the problems of their illegality and criminality requires full institutional analysis and systemic corrective measures beyond insisting on fair trials in resistance cases. The UN must again be persuaded to take a role. For example, the UNGA clearly has the responsibility to draft a Uniting for Peace Resolution reaffirming the rules and principles of the Charter, requiring U.S. withdrawal from Iraq and beginning, with or without the U.S., negotiations for "nuclear disarmament in all its aspects" according to a step-by-step process of declaration, de-alerting, disassembling, inspections, and disarmament. A Truth and Reconciliation Commission leading the way to nuclear disarmament and general and complete disarmament could be convened in the U.S. and demanded collectively by resolutions by Mayors for Peace, municipalities, counties, states, universities and NGOs.

The truth that nuclear weapons—and thus also war—must and can be abandoned will continue to come forth and the seeds of reconciliation of this central problem of our day plainly sprout when citizens and lawyers act nonviolently and consistently with the new formation of the problem of security and continuance requiring not ever greater use of force but care for each other and our common environment. These actions must result in consistent institutional and economic transformation.

4. CLOSING REMARKS

The NSS, due in part to its flimsy "foundation" in nuclear weapons, represents a very dangerous state, threatening both ordinary society and life itself. Yet, there is reason for hope, even though the NSS has colonized many crucial democratic institutions, including education and the judiciary, because the potential for institutional change depends on the awareness, commitment, energy, and knowledge of participants. We hail acts of nonviolent and symbolic civil resistance as essential for positive institutional change, for unveiling plainly illegitimate threat or use of nuclear weapons and urging nonviolent participation. We also recognize the need for those assigned institutional roles, charged with the protection of the democratic state, to fulfill their roles responsibly by endeavoring to safeguard the legitimate functions of their institutions, including guaranteeing an open space for the critical exploration of ideas and knowledge and the fair and equitable hearing of grievances including redress for *ultra vires* acts of state. But we also need 1) to understand the functioning and purpose of normal institutions as the foundation of human societies and especially the necessity for institutional practices to be consistent with their legitimations within an egalitarian society; and 2) to recognize the distinction between sincere and insincere legitimations (propaganda), and to emphasize the importance of internal and external protective and corrective mechanisms, to protect the state and its institutions from erosion of its democratic protections and against the hijacking of the state. Change, however daunting, is possible; the alternative is unworkable.

200

NOTES

1 We concentrate on higher education because of our greater familiarity with this area. This is where internal and extra institutional influences are most transparent, and much of what is said here also applies to K-12 education.
2 We chose MSU as an example because we are familiar with it (D. Dwyer teaches there) and not because it is at all exceptional in the example it provides.
3 *U.S. v Gilbert, Hudson and Platte*, U.S. District Court Colorado, Criminal No. 02-CR-509-RB. Now on appeal, In the U.S. Court of Appeals for the Tenth Circuit, Case Nos. 03-1351, 03-1345, 03-1347.
4 Victims of nuclear bombings (narrowly defined) or of the nuclear system (widely defined).

REFERENCES

American Anthropological Association (AAA). Code of Ethics of the American Anthropological Association. Approved June, 1998. http://www.aaanet.org/committees/ethics/ethcode.htm.

American Association for the Advancement of Sciences. 2001. Research and Development FY 2001. www.aaas.org/spp/rd/xxv.

Bird, Kai and Lawrence Lifschultz (Eds.). *Hiroshima's Shadows* 1998. Stony Creek, Connecticut: The Pamphleteer's Press.

Bolton, Earl Clinton. Memo on Agency-Academic Relations. August 5, 1968. http://www.cia-on-campus.org/foia/ac01.html.

Bourdieu, P. *Language and Symbolic Power*. 1982. Cambridge: Harvard U.

Bourdieu, Pierre. *Outline of a Theory of Praxis* (translated by Richard Nice). 1977. Cambridge: Cambridge Press. Original edition entitled: *Equisse d'une théorie de la pratique, precédé des trois etudes d'ethnologie kabyle*. Switzerland: Librairie Droz S. A.

Boyle, Francis A. *The Criminality of Nuclear Deterrence*, 2002. Atlanta, GA: Clarity Press.

Ciardi, John, *A Browser's Dictionary*, Harper & Row, 1980.

Eco, Umberto. 2001. "Reflections on War," *Five Moral Pieces*. 2001. New York: Harcourt, Brace.

Fairclough, Norman. *Critical Discourse Analysis*. 1995. London and New York: Longman.

Fairclough, Norman. *Language and Power*. 1989. London and New York: Longman.

Foucault, Michael. Polemics, Politics, and Problemenations: An Interview. In *The Foucault Reader*. Paul Rabinow (Ed.). 381–90. New York: Pantheon. 1984.

——— Truth and Power. In *Michael Foucault:* Power Volume III (James D. Faubion Ed.) New York: The New Press. 1994a: 111–133.

——— Truth and Juridical Forms. In *Michael Foucault: Power Volume III* (James D. Faubion Ed.) New York: The New Press. 1994b: 1–89.

Freire, Paulo and Donaldo Macedo. *Literacy: Reading The Word and The World* (foreword by Ann E. Berthoff; introduction by Henry A. Giroux). 1987. South Hadley, Mass.: Bergin & Garvey Publishers.

Giroux, Henry. Introduction to *Literacy*. In Freire and Macedo 1987.

Henkin, Louis. Gerald L. Neuman, Diane F. Orentlicher and David W. Leebron. *Human Rights*. New York: Foundation Press, 1999.

Hiraoka, Takashi. The Hiroshima Peace Declaration. August 6, 1998.

Horowitz, David. Sinews of Empire. *Ramparts*. October, 1969.

International Court of Justice, Advisory Opinion, *Legality of the Threat or Use of Nuclear Weapons* 8 July, 1996. General lists No. 95. United Nations General Assembly A/51/218/

Joas, Hans. The Dream of a Modernity without Violence by Hans Joas (ms. 2003) from *War and Modernity*. Oxford: Polity Press. 2003. ISBN: 0-7456-2645-9.

Judis. John B. and Spencer Ackerman. The Selling of the Iraq War: The First Casualty. *New Republic* June 30, 2003.

Keller, Bill. The Second Nuclear Age. *The New York Times Magazine*. May 4, 2003.

Kurtz, Stanley. Studying Title VI: Criticisms of Middle East studies get a congressional hearing. *The National Review*. 2003. http://www.national review.com/kurtz/kurtz061603.asp.

Leman-Langlois, Stéphane. Constructing a Common Language: The Function of Nuremburg in the Problematization of Postapartheid Justice. 2002. *Law and Social Inquiry*. 27.1:79–100.

Michigan State University (MSU). *The Faculty Handbook*. Office of the Provost. 2003a. http://www.msu.edu/unit/facrecds/FacHand/.

201

—— 2003b. Budget. Office of the Provost.

National Science Foundation (NSF). National Patterns of R and D Resources. 1999. http://www.nsf.gov/sbe/srs/nprdr/archive.htm.

National Security Education Program (NSEP). 2003. Originally at http://www.defenselink.mil/pubs/nsep/, but now at http://www.ndu.edu/nsep/.

Nussbaum, Martha C. Liberal Education in the United States: The Three Abilities. Forward to *Alive At The Core*: Exemplary Approaches to General Education in the Humanities, by Michael Nelson and Associates. 2000. San Francisco: Jossey-Bass Inc.

Oe, Kenzaburo. Hiroshima Notes. 1995. Translated by David L. Swain and Toshi Yonezawa. New York: Marion Boyars.

Ramirez, Francisco O. and John Boli. On the Union of States and Schools. *Institutional Structure: Constituting State, Society and the Individual* (Thomas, George, John Meyer, Francisco Ramirez and John Boli Eds.). 1987. Sage Publications, Newbury Park. Pp. 173–197.

Rappaport, Roy A. The Obvious Aspects of Ritual. In *Ecology, Meaning, and Religion*. 1979. Richmond, California: North Atlantic Books.

Raskin, Marcus. *Being And Doing*. 1971. New York, Random House.

Ravitch, Diane. *The Language Police: How Pressure Groups Restrict What Children Learn*. 2003. New York: Alfred A. Knopf.

Rudolph, Frederick. *Curriculum: a history of the American undergraduate course of study since 1636*. [Prepared for the Carnegie Council on Policy Studies in Higher Education]. 1977. San Francisco: Jossey-Bass Publishers.

Scheinbaum, Stanley K. Introduction to University on the Make. *Ramparts*, 1966. April.

Schell, Jonathan. "A Nuclear Education," *The Nation* 5/26/03.

Stocking, George W. The Scientific Reaction against Cultural Anthropology, 1917–1920. *Race, culture, and evolution; essays in the history of anthropology* 1968. New York: Free Press.

The International Court of Justice. 1996. (*Legality of the Threat or Use of Nuclear Weapons*, Advisory Opinion, International Court of Justice, 8 July 1996, Gen List No. 95 A/51/218)

The Nuclear Resister. 2003 POB 43383, Tucson, AZ 85733, No. 122 (2001), No. 132 & 133 (2003).

The South African Truth and Reconciliation Commission, Vol. Four Chapter Four, Institutional Hearing: The Legal Community, http://www.polity.org.za/govdocs/commissions/1998/trc/4chp4.htm.

Thompson, Nicholas. The growing—and dangerous—divide between scientists and the GOP. *Washington Monthly*, 2003 July/August http://www.washingtonmonthly.com/features/2003/0307.thompson.html

U.S. Department of Education. National Resource Centers. 2003a.

—— The Federal Role in Education. 2003b. http://www.ed.gov/offices/OPE/HEP/iegpslnrc.html.

U.S. Department of Homeland Security. 2003 (http://www.orau.gov/dhsed/.

202

U.S. Government. Fiscal Year 2004 Budget Summary and Background Information, February 3, 2003. http://www.ed.gov/offices/ous/Budget04/04summary/section2e.htm/#iefla.

U.S. Department Of Health And Human Services, National Institutes of Health. 2003. Office for Protection from Research Risks, Part 46, Protection of Human Subjects. Revised November 13, 2001, Effective December 13, 2001.

Wolf, Eric R. *Europe and the People without History*. 1982. Berkeley: University of California Press.

11

THE PENTAGON'S WELFARE BUDGET

Seymour Melman

The president of the United States cannot escape the implications of his role as top manager of the military economy. As the executive over that economy, the secretary of defense reports to him. A top manager, chief of a managerial hierarchy—civilian or military—does not willingly give up decision-power, for that would breach an inviolable code of the managerial occupation.

Accordingly, it is understandable that neither the president nor the secretary of defense, nor their subordinates who deal in policy alternatives, have ventured planning for conversion of the U.S. military economy to civilian work even following the acknowledged termination of the Cold War by 1991.

At this writing, the Department of Defense is committed to the completion of military hardware contracts whose aggregate program cost exceeds 1.3 trillion.[1]

Knowledgeable people in the Department of Defense have reckoned that during this period the actual cost and price of many of these weapons systems (like the F-22 and the Joint Strike Fighter) quadrupled.[2] In turn, this could induce fiscal crises hitherto unknown in the budgets of both the Department of Defense and of the entire United States government, more than half of whose "discretionary accounts" are now allotted to the military. No economist has ventured to assess the possible corrosive consequences of such developments for the value of the U.S. currency and, more critically, for the viability of the United States as a productive society.

The state/corporate partnership is notably active, as a direct sales organization for the U.S. munitions industry. A variety of possible arrangements has been institutionalized. A "Defense Export Loan Guarantee" program in its first year allows the Department of Defense to cover 100% of the principle and interest for as much as $15 billion if the recipient defaults. A recycled weapons program permits the U.S. to transfer billions of "surplus" weapons mostly for free. (During 1990–95 this included 4,000 tanks, 125 attack helicopters, 500 bombers and 200,000 pistols and rifles.) The Pentagon is also empowered to lease equipment at little or no cost. Under an "Excess Defense Articles" program, Pentagon stocks may be "drawn down" and given to governments in Latin America and the Caribbean to "fight narco-trafficking," and to African countries "to support participation in peacekeeping and other operations." All this is backed up by aggressive U.S. government participation in air and ground *matériel* weapons shows around the world.[3]

America's state/corporate managers pursue the militarization and extension of hegemonic controls on a worldwide scale. The array of easy-financing devices is applied to yield worldwide preeminence in the sale of weapons. U.S. weapons export shipments 1991–95 exceeded $70.5 billion, greater than the combined shipments from Russia, France, U.K., China, Germany, and Italy. The armed forces of numerous client states are thereby locked into dependence on the U.S. for continuing technical support of every sort. The five-page enumeration of "Deals in the Works—1996" (*Arms Sales Monitor* No. 33, Feb. 1997) is an eye-opening array of weapons—all classes—that will contribute mightily to the decision-power of U.S. military-political managers.

A further—and decisive—step in the power extension process is illustrated by the ongoing expansion of NATO membership. Thereby, the governments of Eastern Europe—and others—are gathered into an international network that is dominated by American state/corporate managers.

A MYTH OF STATE

Intended or not, all this is encouraged by the myth that the economic capability of the United States is, for all practical purposes, without limit. A choice between guns and butter need not be made.

Such a view of the matter was encouraged by the National Security Council's Memorandum Number 68 entitled "United States Objectives and Programs for National Security, April 14, 1950." This document, a strategic Cold War policy guide, was kept secret until May 1975 when it was published in full text in the Naval War College Review. An economic assessment given in that memorandum stated that

... One of the most significant lessons of our World War experience was that the American economy, when it operates at a level approaching full efficiency, can provide enormous resources for purposes other than civilian consumption while simultaneously providing a high standard of living. After allowing for price changes, personal consumption expenditures rose by about one-fifth between 1939 and 1944, even though the economy had in the meantime increased the amount of resources going into Government use by $60–$65 billion (in 1939 prices) . . . [4]

There was a major omission from that influential assessment. During World War II, there were major cutbacks on all manner of infrastructure expenditure—both in capital outlays and maintenance. These were postponed until after the war. And many are still deferred. The Guns and Butter optimism about the United States economy was a staple myth during the Kennedy and Johnson administrations, and thereafter was an undebated, tacitly accepted myth, part of the conventional wisdom.

Nevertheless, despite the acknowledged weight of conventional ideology, thoughtful people have wondered how something so huge could remain so hidden, especially from the consciousness of the Left, with their history of critiquing ideas that support the establishment. At this writing, the managers of America's military and civilian economy have joined in a grand political consensus to omit from public discussion—notably during major elections—all references to civilian infrastructure decay and the relation of all this to the prospect of the new $1,450 billion commitment toward new weaponry. (Thus, public announcement of the Pentagon's new Joint Service Fighter, with prospective outlays of $750 billion was withheld until after the November 1996 elections.)

What exactly is achieved by national leaders, as they succeed in preventing a public discussion of a large tradeoff and silencing the question: "What else could be bought for $750 billion?"

- To electrify U.S. mainline railroads is a $250 billion project that would replace America's decrepit railroads with modern (West European, Japanese) style 150–200 mph travel, while employing 500,000 people directly and indirectly.
- To provide decent housing for the 5.32 million U.S. families living in "worst case" housing would cost $369 billion and would engage about 1.5 million people, directly and indirectly.

The combined cost of these two transformative investments, over a period of twenty years, would be $619 billion—$308 billion less than what the American Commander-in-Chief plans to spend on new weapons to sustain the operation of his very own military-industry empire.

But modernizing American railroads and replacing substandard housing are only two items in a long agenda. Table 3 provides a list of infrastructure components that are being underfunded and are therefore deficient in performance.

Table 3. Underfunded Components of U.S. Infrastructure

AMERICAN SOCIETY OF CIVIL ENGINEERS
2003 Report Card for America's Infrastructure

SUBJECT	GRADE	COMMENTS
Roads	D+	The nation is failing to even maintain the substandard conditions we currently have, a dangerous trend that is affecting highway safety. The average rush hour also grew by over 18 minutes between 1997 and 2000.
Bridges	C	As of 2000, 27.5% of the nation's bridges were structurally deficient or functionally obsolete,

an improvement from 29% in 1998. It is estimated that it will cost $9.4 billion a year for 20 years to eliminate all bridge deficiencies.

Transit	C–	Transit ridership has increased 22% since 1998—the highest level in 40 years. Capital spending would have to double to maintain the system in its present condition.
Aviation	D	Airport capacity has increased only 1% from 1991 to 2001, while air traffic has increased 35% during that time. The FAA expects dramatic growth in aviation demand over the next decade. Congestion also jeopardizes safety—there were 429 runway incursions ("near misses") reported in 2000, up 25% from 1999.
Schools	D–	Due to either aging or outdated facilities, or severe overcrowding, 75% of our nation's school buildings are inadequate to meet the needs of schoolchildren. The average cost of capital investment needed is $3,800 per student, more than half the average cost to educate that student for one year. Since 1998, the total need has increased from $112 billion to $127 billion.
Drinking Water	D	The nation's 54,000 drinking water systems face an annual shortfall of $11 billion needed to replace facilities, that are nearing the end of their useful life and to comply with federal water regulations. Nonpoint source pollution remains the most significant threat to water quality.
Wastewater	D	The nation's 16,000 wastewater systems face enormous needs. Some sewer systems are 100 years old. Currently, there is a $12 billion annual shortfall in funding for infrastructure needs in this category; however, federal funding has remained flat for a decade. More than one-third of U.S. surface waters do not meet water quality standards.

Dams	D	The number of unsafe dams has risen by 23% to nearly 2,600. There were 21 reported dam failures in the past two years. The number of "high-hazard potential dams"—those whose failure would cause loss of life—increased from 9,921 in 2001 to 10,049 in 2003.
Solid Waste	C+	The amount of solid waste sent to landfills has declined 13% since 1990, while the amount of waste recovered through recycling has nearly doubled. Most states have ten years' worth of landfill capacity and waste-to-energy plants now manage 17% of the nation's trash.
Hazardous Waste	D+	Aided by the best clean-up technology in the world, the rate of Superfund clean-up has quickened—though not enough to keep pace with the numbers of new sites listed as the backlog of potential sites is assessed. Nearly 10,000 contaminated sites could end up in the program.
Navigable Waterways	D+	The U.S. Army Corps of Engineers has a backlog of $38 billion in active authorized projects. On the inland waterways system, 44% of all the lock chambers have already exceeded their 50-year design lives. Key deep-draft channels are inadequate for the mega-container ships, which are the world standard for international trade; and intermodal connectors to ports are in poor condition. Transportation demand on waterways is expected to double by 2020, and serious performance problems are likely if current levels of investment continue.
Energy	D+	Since 1990, actual capacity has increased only about 7,000 megawatts (MW) per year, an annual shortfall of 30%. More than 10,000 MW of capacity will have to be added each

year until 2008 to keep up with the 1.8% annual growth in demand. The U.S. energy transmission infrastructure relies on older technology, raising questions of long-term reliability.

A = Exceptional		Each category was evaluated on the basis of
B = Good		condition and performance, capacity vs.
C = Fair		need, and funding vs. need.
D = Poor		
F = Inadequate		

America's Infrastructure G.P .A. = D+
Total Investment Needs = $ 1.6 Trillion
(estimated 5-year need)

American Society of Civil Engineers, 1015 15th street, NW, Suite 600, Washington, DC 20005; 202/789-2200; www.asce.org/reportcard

All these are infrastructure components that are underfunded with resulting downward impacts on the economy and quality of life.

But the effect on our lives is "class-weighted." The wealthiest people can bypass the effects of almost all the infrastructure deficiencies that are listed here. The top corporate and government managers can apply money and/or privilege: to guarantee the quality of their drinking water, to use transportation that avoids bad roads, bridges, airports, etc.; to get superior medical care; to educate their children in schools with none of the big-city public school handicaps, etc.

By way of contrast, liberal and conservative members of Congress focused on funding cuts for multiple government programs:

FUNDING CUTS

Head Start (Proposed for 2006)	$177 million[5]
Vocational & Adult Education (Proposed for 2006)	$ 26 million
(316 million cut predicted for 2005)[6]	
Medicaid (Over 10-year span)	$92 Billion[7]
School-to-Work Opportunities	Eliminated
Summer Youth Employment and Training	Eliminated

Focus on these items in the name of reducing "government spending" shows how committed the U.S. Congress and executive are to the military arms of America's state capitalism. Similar reasoning explains why the U.S. government does not employ a single person with responsibility for planning moves toward demilitarization.

What is the background for continuing patterns of military excess after the end of the Cold War? Since 1940, the United States spent more than $4 trillion (in 1996 dollars) on nuclear weapons. This includes research, testing, and production, delivery systems, command, control and early warning networks, defenses against nuclear attack, and the management and disposition of nuclear waste. In that time, the government produced 70,000 nuclear explosives.

There is surely this real limit to military power: a person or community can be destroyed only once. We need reminding that Hiroshima was destroyed on August 5, 1945, by a single nuclear explosive with a power of 15,000 tons of TNT. (Visualize 15,000 tons of TNT as the contents of 750 railroad freight cars, each carrying 20 tons of TNT.) About 140,000 people were killed by that one explosion.

Consider, as purely hypothetical nuclear targets, the combined present populations of Russia and China: 1,351,000,000, equal to 9,650 Hiroshimas of 1945. Using the Hiroshima yardstick, warheads with the combined power of 144.7 million tons of TNT (9,650 X 15,000 tons) would be required to destroy these two countries. (Selection of warhead sizes and dispersion would have to take into account that blast effect does not increase proportionately with size.) Allowing for an additional 30% to account for possible launch and warhead failures, then 188.2 million tons of TNT would be needed. The U.S. currently deploys warheads with power of some 2.3 billion tons of TNT. That 188.2 million tons of TNT, enough to destroy both Russia and China, is merely 8% of the active U.S. nuclear arsenal's power. The rest, 92%, represents an outrageous excess of killing power and military spending overkill.

Let us assume $4 trillion as an understated cost of America's nuclear enterprise. Then the 92% overkill share is $3.7 trillion. *That sum is more than twice the net value of the plant and equipment in America's manufacturing industries.* What has been forgone (a partial national opportunity cost) is the possibility of applying the technical manpower and allied resources that were used up for the nuclear enterprise toward building and operating a superior manufacturing system far and away more sophisticated and "user friendly" than what is visible today. And we must remember that the incredible waste of the nuclear enterprise was not Cold War history. It continues annually in the weapons systems contracting of the Pentagon and the Department of Energy. (A full accounting of the cost of America's nuclear weapons enterprise was published in 1997 by the U.S. Nuclear Weapons Cost Study Project at the Brookings Institution.)

At this writing, there is no estimate of the cost of correcting the array of deficiencies noted as present in the infrastructure of American society. Such societal renewal is what has been sacrificed. It is the opportunity cost of using up so much of the nation's wealth on economically dead-end military extravaganzas. Slowing or reversing this process requires that we transform or rein in the state management and their corporate allies.

After World War II it was fashionable among many economists who were critical of capitalism to ascribe the failure of public investment in these areas to business opposition. The businessmen did not want government as a business competitor. Consider, however, the case of housing for families in poverty (35.9 million living below the poverty line in 2003).[8] There has been no house building by private business that caters to such families. Hence the political-conservative opposition to such government-financed housing is in the service of another agenda: to put down the poorest paid working people and to keep them down, the better to retain them as a "reserve army" of unemployed and hardly employed, competing for the poorest paid work and, by "domino effect," restraining the economic prospects of many others (e.g., the "workfare" program of the New York City government that replaces union labor with welfare recipients, and the 300 "workfare" participants in Alabama employed in a BMW plant).

Pentagon spending is often justified by jobs created. That is the oft-repeated mantra of legislators who push for defense contracting in their home states. In reality, $1 billion of military procurement generates 21,500 jobs directly and indirectly. The *same $1 billion* invested in industrial renewal, mass transit, housing, education and health care will produce, on average, 33,100 jobs. If job increases, not profits or power, were a primary goal of government policies, then money for infrastructure and industry renewal, and not overkill, would get central attention. Overkill spending in the Pentagon diverts enormous resources from domestic civilian use. That is why there is no money to employ millions of people to repair our housing, streets, schools, and environment, or to reverse the plague of shut-down industrial facilities that account for 3 million manufacturing jobs lost American working people and replaced by imports, notably imports of capital/durable goods.[9]

NOTES

1 Department of Defense, Selected Acquisition Report Summary Tables, August 13, 2004

2 Franklin Spinney, "Defense Time Bomb: F-22/JSF Case Study Hypothetical Escape Option," July–August 1996. Note: *The New York Times*, October 30, 2004.

3 Federation of American Scientists Fund, *Arms Sales Monitor.* No. 33, Feb 24, 1997.

4 "NSC-68, A Report to the National Security Council by the Executive Secretary on United States Objectives and Programs for National Security, April 14, 1950." Naval War College Review, May–June 1975. Note: U.S. National Security Strategy, The White House, September 2002.

5 http://zfacts.com/metaPage/lib/2006-proposed-fed-budget-cuts.pdf.

6 http://www.house.gov/budget_democrats/pres_budgets/back_to_school.pdf.

7 http://www.cbpp.org/3-12-03bud2-pr.htm. March 21, 2003.

8 http://www.census.gov/Press-Release/www/releases/archives/income_wealth/002484.html.

9 See Annette Fuentes, "Slaves of New York," *In These Times*, Dec. 23, 1996. Updated research by Diana E. Alonzo Nov. 30, 2004.

★ **PART** ★

4

ACCOUNTABILITY AND DEMOCRACY

12

SECURITY'S CONQUEST OF FEDERAL LAW ENFORCEMENT

Peter Raven-Hansen

Since 1986, presidents have taken international terrorism, drug-trafficking, and international organized crime out of the law enforcement closet of ordinary crimes and relabeled them as "national security threats." "Threats" must be prevented, not just detected and prosecuted like ordinary crimes. To prevent them, law enforcement must conduct the open-ended collection of intelligence, instead of just the more focused and close-ended assembly of criminal evidence. Furthermore, law enforcement cannot do it alone. Both the intelligence community and the military are therefore now tasked to participate, breaching the walls that society (and, some would have said, our Constitution) has traditionally maintained between civilian law enforcement and military or intelligence operations.

In short, under the twin banners of the wars on terrorism and international crime (including drug trafficking), federal *law enforcement* is metamorphosing into *security enforcement* in the New National Security State. In part I of this essay, I briefly outline the defining characteristics of traditional law enforcement. In part II, I survey national security initiatives that are transforming federal law enforcement within the United States.[1] In part III, I analyze some implications for democratic accountability.

I. THE TRADITIONAL MODEL OF LAW ENFORCEMENT

Traditionally, law enforcement has been primarily reactive. A crime is committed. The police or, at the federal level, the FBI, investigate, searching for the perpetrator and collecting criminal evidence with which he can be prosecuted. The completed or ongoing crime focuses and delimits the investigation. To conduct a search, the police or FBI must usually have probable cause to believe that evidence of the crime will be found; to arrest, they must have probable cause to believe that the suspect has committed or is committing the crime. Ordinary searches and seizures are limited in scope to historical evidence of the completed or ongoing crime and therefore close-ended, because their chief aim and endpoint is conviction of the perpetrator.

In this traditional reactive law enforcement model, due process bars preventive detention, except when, after charges have been brought and a speedy trial is to be held, the prosecutor can convince a judge in open court that the accused is a flight risk or danger to the community.[2] Nor does the traditional model tolerate lengthy investigatory detention (holding for questioning), except when the government can convince a judge in open court that it needs the testimony of a material witness who may not be available at trial.[3] Even in these exceptional cases, when the traditional system permits preventive and investigatory detention, the detainee has access to lawyers to help him defeat the government's burden of proving the required need for detention and thereby win his freedom.

Finally, of course, when the investigation and arrest lead to prosecution, the trial itself is conducted in the open, on the public record, with admissible evidence that is made known to the defendant and that he is given a full opportunity to test by cross-examination and confrontation. Secret justice is the antithesis of ordinary criminal justice. The open texture of criminal justice is an important check on the state.

A. Walling Off Intelligence Collection in the Traditional Model

This summary is oversimplified, however. In addition to its ordinary criminal investigation mission, the FBI has long been tasked both with counterintelligence and foreign intelligence collection in the

United States. Such intelligence is different from criminal evidence, as the Supreme Court has recognized. The focus of domestic surveillance may be less precise than that directed against more conventional types of crime.[4]

Therefore, although the Court found that the Fourth Amendment still required prior judicial approval for electronic domestic security surveillance, it decided that the Amendment did not necessarily require the same probable cause standard for such approval. Congress was thus freed to fashion reasonable standards more lenient than those in Title III [of the Omnibus Crime Control and Safe Streets Act of 1968, which governs wiretapping in ordinary criminal investigations].

219

In 1978 Congress fashioned such standards for *foreign* intelligence surveillance, but left domestic security surveillance subject to Title III. In the Foreign Intelligence Surveillance Act (FISA),[5] it authorized a Foreign Intelligence Surveillance Court of federal judges meeting in secret and ex parte with government lawyers to issue FISA orders approving electronic surveillance, and later, physical searches, in the United States (FISA does not govern purely extraterritorial searches). But because of the differences between intelligence collection and criminal evidence-gathering, the probable cause required for a FISA order is probable cause to believe that the target of the surveillance is a foreign power or an agent of a foreign power (defined to include members of international terrorist groups), not the more stringent traditional probable cause to believe that a crime has been or is being committed.

But if the rationale for relaxing the probable cause standard is that *foreign* intelligence is different, it follows that the government should only obtain FISA orders if it certifies that the target is a *foreign power* or *agent of a foreign power* and that "the purpose of the surveillance is to obtain *foreign intelligence* information."[6] Recognizing that information collection during foreign intelligence surveillances could often also support a criminal prosecution, the courts interpreted this requirement to mean that the "primary purpose" of the surveillance had to be collecting foreign intelligence.

Fear that a criminal prosecution motive would taint a FISA surveillance, as well as concern that sources and methods of foreign intelligence collection might be compromised by using such evidence in a criminal prosecution, also led the FBI and the Department of Justice to erect a "wall" between criminal investigators and prosecutors, on one hand, and foreign intelligence investigators, on the other. Information could be shared across the wall only in the presence of a "chaperone," in the form of the Office of Intelligence Policy Review in the Department of Justice. The wall discouraged information-sharing, but it also discouraged criminal investigators and prosecutors from doing an end run around the Fourth Amendment's traditional warrant requirement by using FISA to collect criminal evidence.

B. Excluding the CIA and the Military from Traditional Law Enforcement

220

This whirlwind tour of the landmarks of traditional law enforcement has not mentioned either the CIA or the military. The omission is not an oversight. When Congress authorized the CIA by the National Security Act of 1947, it ordered that "the Agency shall have no police, subpoena, or law enforcement powers or internal security functions"[7] out of fear of creating an American Gestapo. This boundary was not so much geographic as functional. The CIA was still authorized to perform counterintelligence and foreign intelligence functions inside the United States in coordination with the FBI (which had lead responsibility), but was not to involve itself in law enforcement or strictly internal security. When it strayed across this boundary in mounting Operation CHAOS during the Viet Nam War to spy on homegrown antiwar activities, it was sharply criticized by the Church Committee and Rockefeller Commission and sued for civil rights violations. These reactions suggested continued public support for fencing the CIA out of traditional law enforcement.

The military, too, had a boundary on its activities, this one imposed by the Posse Comitatus Act of 1878.[8] The act criminalizes use of any part of the Army or Air Force as "a *posse comitatus* or otherwise to execute the laws" except when expressly authorized by the Constitution or another statute. (Its proscription has been extended by regulation to the Navy.) The courts have therefore interpreted the act to prohibit the military from participating directly in coercive, compulsory, or regulatory actions against civilians, such as arrests, detentions, or custodial interrogation. Before Congress made exceptions for the wars on terrorism and drug-trafficking, the military could only provide logistical assistance or other indirect support to law enforcement authorities. Statutory exceptions to the act for military responses to riots and insurrections or conspiracies to obstruct the execution of federal laws, however, permitted the deployment of federal troops to deal with violent strikes, race riots, and official resistance to school integration. Still, calling in the troops after reading a mob the riot act is a far cry from using them to enforce ordinary criminal laws. Like the CIA, the military therefore had been fenced out of traditional law enforcement.

II. PROACTIVE SECURITY ENFORCEMENT AND THE "PREVENTION PARADIGM"

221

The traditional model of law enforcement began to erode even before September 11 and the war on terrorism. In 1986, the president first declared that terrorism and international drug-trafficking are threats to national security.[9] In 1995, President Clinton added international organized crime to the list.[10] Although the pertinent presidential directives were classified, we can discern the central thrust of the resulting new model from publicly disclosed strategy documents and official statements: "Our approach must be proactive where possible and reactive where necessary."[11] We have embraced what former Assistant Attorney General Viet Dinh calls the "prevention paradigm."[12]

A. Lowering the Wall

Proactive law enforcement means anticipating and preventing crime. This requires collecting intelligence, not just criminal evidence after the fact. Since "reactive" prosecution is still a backstop to prevention, the transformation of traditional law enforcement also required lowering, if not dismantling, the wall between intelligence collection and criminal evidence-gathering. Although the process got underway well before September 11, the pre-September 11 focus was primarily on the intra- and inter-agency cultural foundations of the wall—helping the FBI and CIA understand each others' culture in order to make their cooperation easier. After September 11, the administration struck at the wall's legal foundations by asking Congress to change the purpose requirement for FISA surveillance orders. The USA Patriot Act[13] changed the requirement that "*the* purpose" of a FISA order be the collection of foreign intelligence to "*a significant* purpose," effectively broadening the availability of FISA orders. It also author-ized the sharing of grand jury information.

Attorney General Ashcroft quickly took advantage of the change to order new "Intelligence Sharing Procedures," not only permitting communications between intelligence and law enforcement officials, but affirmatively authorizing the latter to advise about the "initiation, operation, continuation, and expansion" of FISA searches or surveil-lance. When the Foreign Intelligence Surveillance Court unanimously balked at this change and ordered the Justice Department to "ensure that law enforcement officials do not direct or control the use of FISA procedures to enhance criminal prosecution,"[14] the government suc-cessfully appealed to the Foreign Intelligence Surveillance Court of Appeals. Though admitting that the reasonableness of the Attorney General's rules under the Fourth Amendment had no "definitive jurisprudential answer," that court of appeals upheld them, deciding that no FISA search or surveillance violates FISA or the amendment, "[S]o long as the government entertains a realistic option of dealing with the . . . [target] other than through criminal prosecution . . . ."[15] Since that option is open at the initiation of *every* FISA search or sur-veillance, the caveat was illusory. If the court is right, the "wall" erected by FISA and the Fourth Amendment is rubble.

B. Unleashing the CIA

The wall erected around the CIA by the National Security Act of 1947 still stands, but it has been significantly lowered. As early as 1981, an executive order directed at the intelligence community authorized the CIA to "collect foreign intelligence or counterintelligence within the United States" in coordination with the FBI, though "without assuming or performing any internal security functions."[16] Five years later, the same directive that declared drug-trafficking a national secu-rity threat reportedly tasked the CIA with assisting law enforcement in combating it. In 1996, Congress effectively amended the 1947 CIA charter by authorizing law enforcement agencies for the first time to task the entire intelligence community to collect intelligence outside the United States about non-U.S. persons, "notwithstanding that the law enforcement agency intends to use the information collected for purposes of a law enforcement investigation or counterintelligence investigation."[17] None of these initiatives unleashed the CIA to conduct law enforcement or internal security activities inside the United States, but they invited a larger domestic role for it as more and more criminal activity could be traced to foreign roots or support.

C. Keeping Secrets By Expanding Secrecy

The increasing "fusion" of intelligence and law enforcement in investigations has also prompted changes in the prosecution phase of the traditional law enforcement model. When intelligence is used as evidence, the fear of compromising "sources and methods" of intelligence creates a hydraulic pressure for secret justice. Even before September 11, we observed some of this pressure at work in the immigration setting, when the government used secret evidence to remove selected terrorist suspects. Despite two lower court rulings that the use of secret evidence violated the due process rights of even immigrant suspects, after September 11 the chief judge of the immigration court ordered the blanket closure of such hearings in "special interest" cases—those involving immigrants suspected of having connections with or information about international terrorism.[18] Though at this writing no court has yet ruled that the blanket rule violates the due process rights of the immigrants, two courts have split on whether it violates the First Amendment rights of access by the press and the public.

These proceedings, however, were immigration proceedings conducted within the executive branch. Historically, the federal courts stood as a check against efforts to close judicial criminal proceedings in the same fashion or to prosecute on secret evidence never disclosed to the defendant.[19] Even that check may be eroding, however, in the prosecution of the so-called 20th hijacker, Zacarias Moussaoui. Moussaoui has invoked his Sixth Amendment right to confront witnesses against him and to access exculpatory evidence in the prosecution's control by demanding access to witnesses who are being interrogated by the United States abroad. The government has resisted, invoking military necessity to protect the psychological dynamics of ongoing interrogations.

Moreover, if this claim ultimately fails, the government reportedly may pull Moussaoui out of the federal court and prosecute him in a military tribunal, in which military officers selected by the president serve as both judge and jury. The president authorized such tribunals for alien terrorist suspects by "Military Order" shortly after September 11.[20] Though such tribunals could hold their proceedings in public, the Order and implementing regulations would allow them to try such suspects at least partly in secret or on secret evidence, as necessary to protect the interests of the United States.[21] If media reports are correct, the government's position amounts to this: either the federal court subordinates Moussaoui's constitutional rights to the government's claims of military necessity, or the government will try him in a military tribunal where those rules apply only so far as the government allows.

224

D. Detaining Preventively: "Operation Find and Hold the Muslims"

Proactive law enforcement has also expanded the use of preventive detention. After September 11, Attorney General Ashcroft ordered the FBI and INS to embark on what he conceded was "a deliberate campaign of arrest and detention to remove suspected terrorists who violate the law from our streets," resulting in the detention of some 1200 Arab or Muslim immigrants. As one commentator put it, "if [this campaign] had a code name fitting its focus, or lack thereof, it would have been called 'Operation Find and Hold the Muslims.'"[22] Some of those detained apparently *had* violated the laws, but they were laws against "spitting on the sidewalk"—in Ashcroft's borrowed phrase—not laws against terrorism. These detainees were arrested for minor nonviolent crimes, and the charges were pretexts for holding the arrestees preventively.

An even larger number were arrested for immigration violations, typically technical visa overstays, which also historically had resulted in bail or releases on personal recognizance pending immigration hearings. What was really at work here, however, was again the campaign to detain such immigrants for questioning, as an FBI affidavit in one case made startlingly clear. Emphasizing that "the business of counter terrorism intelligence gathering in the United States is akin to the construction of a mosaic," by way of explaining why it had no evidence that the immigrant had any knowledge of or involvement in terrorism, the FBI affiant concluded that "the FBI has been unable to rule out the possibility that respondent is somehow linked to, or possesses knowledge of, the terrorist attacks on the World Trade Center and the Pentagon."[23] Under the traditional law enforcement model, of course, the burden of justifying detention falls on the government to show probable cause, not on the detainee to "rule out the possibility" that he is "somehow" knowledgeable about or linked to a crime.

The Department of Justice's Inspector General (IG) later found that many of these immigrant detainees were held for weeks and even months under "extremely restrictive conditions of confinement" before being cleared.[24] In bending immigration law to secure preventive detention of mainly Muslim immigrants, the IG concluded, the government made little or no attempt to distinguish between aliens actually suspected of connections to terrorism and those who, while possibly guilty of violating immigration laws, were unconnected to terrorism.

E. Deploying the Military at Home

Civil preventive detention is not the government's only detention option in the war on terrorism. By a November 2001 "Military Order," President Bush authorized indefinite military detention of alien terrorist suspects without judicial review. The administration defended the Order in part with the argument that it applied, by its terms, only to aliens, and was to be applied, in any case, to aliens captured abroad in the Afghan battlefield. But less than a year later, two *U.S. citizens* were subjected to military detention in the United States on the same legal reasoning that the government had used to support the Military Order. One was reportedly captured on the Afghan battlefield, thus arguably falling within the category of persons who had historically been subjected to military detention. But the other was arrested at O'Hare Airport, based upon actions he had allegedly taken or planned to take in the United States.

At this writing, military detention of U.S. citizens and aliens with substantial connections to the United States is apparently still rare. But the rapid slide down the slippery slope from detaining aliens to detaining U.S. citizens makes the mere assertion of authority for military detention controversial. Military detention is intended to avoid issues of secrecy, media access, confrontation of witnesses, right to counsel, and probable cause; the only requirement, according to the government, is

225

that the president designate the detainee an "enemy combatant." If the courts have any role at all—a point which the government has been slow to concede—it is only to ascertain that the designation was made, or, at most, that it was made on "some evidence."

The wall between the military and law enforcement has also eroded in other ways in the wars on terrorism and drug-traffickers. The Posse Comitatus Act ban on use of the military in law enforcement was never absolute, as the express statutory exceptions for riot control illustrate. Within two years of President Reagan's directive identifying drug-trafficking as a national security threat, Congress enacted express statutory exceptions for the military to assist in drug interdiction.[25] Military assets were used not only for interdiction abroad, but also at our borders. Political scientists Peter Andreas and Richard Price report that U.S. soldiers conducted "more than *three thousand* drug and immigration control missions along the U.S.-Mexico border in the 1990s."[26] Military assets were also used to ferry Drug Enforcement Agency supplies in the United States, to support domestic police searches, and even to conduct a massive marijuana drug eradication program in northern California. Even military assistance in preparing for the Bureau of Alcohol, Tobacco, and Firearms raid on the Branch Davidian compound in Waco in 1993 was rationalized by reports of a suspected methamphetamine lab in the compound.[27] A 1994 statute prohibiting detailing of Department of Defense personnel "to implement the National Drug Control Strategy" unless the secretary of defense certified to Congress that the detail "is in the national security interest of the United States"[28] posed no practical obstacle to the trend. It was precisely because the president had designated drug-trafficking as a *national security* threat that such personnel were detailed to begin with.

More recently, an office of the Pentagon undertook a major research project on data-mining for counterterrorist purposes. The ensuing outcry over the choice, to head the project, of a retired admiral who had been convicted of destroying documents and lying to Congress tended to divert attention from a more interesting question: why was the Pentagon involved in designing data-mining engines for *civilian* U.S. databases in the first place? While the Supreme Court has approved Army surveillance of antiwar protesters in alleged preparation to quell possible disorders, it has also acknowledged the "traditional and strong resistance of Americans to any military intrusion in civilian affairs."[29]

III. IMPLICATIONS FOR DEMOCRATIC ACCOUNTABILITY AND THE RULE OF LAW

Security's conquest of federal law enforcement in the war against terrorism is not yet complete. Although federal antiterrorist law enforcement's self-transformation is well-advanced, the fusion of intelligence and military operations into law enforcement has barely begun. We are observing the early stages of a possible trend, not the end-points. Yet it may not be too early to draw some implications for democratic accountability and the rule of law from the emergence of security enforcement.

A. Centralizing Security Enforcement

Historically, U.S. law enforcement was decentralized, even at the federal level. The FBI was the chief among several federal law enforcement agencies concerned with antiterrorism, but the priority accorded the anti-terrorist effort was seemingly left to field offices by default. The FBI was answerable on the organization chart to the attorney general, but the FBI director enjoys a 10-year statutory term of office intended to give him substantial independence and having that effect. Military forces answer to their own rigidly hierarchical chains of command, formally running to the commander in chief, but effectively running to the Defense Department secretariat. The organization chart places the intelligence community under the director of Central Intelligence, but in reality he directed only the CIA, barely even coordinating with intelligence assets outside the Agency.

The transformation of antiterrorist law enforcement into security enforcement, however, has been top-down. Proactive law enforcement means more centralized law enforcement and a larger decision making role for political appointees as against career professionals, and therefore a smaller circle of executive officials making the decisions. After September 11, the attorney general ordered the FBI to give priority to an aggressively proactive anti-terrorist campaign, and the FBI followed orders. Power flowed from the field offices to headquarters, and from FBI headquarters to the attorney general's office.

The fusion of intelligence and law enforcement may also promote the centralization of security enforcement. Even before September 11, it was said that the intelligence community served a constituency of just a few hundred executive officials; "no other part of the government has so narrow an audience—or responds so enthusiastically to guidance from above."[30] Although the audience for raw intelligence work product has broadened after September 11 to include the FBI (if the planned fusion succeeds), the intelligence community now appears to be responding to guidance from an even smaller group of Cabinet level and White House officials.

Of course, to note such centralization of power is not necessarily to decry it. The threat of terrorism required better coordination of intelligence collection and distribution, which can arguably be achieved in part by subjecting the collectors and analysts to more centralized direction. Furthermore, any observable centralization of security enforcement power after September 11 may reflect only the personal predilections of members of the instant administration, rather than some inexorable institutional trend in security enforcement. Different political appointees might conceivably tolerate a more decentralized bureaucracy. Bureaucratic turf wars, too, might counter any centralizing tendencies and keep power dispersed. After all, FBI Director Hoover blocked the Huston Plan to protect the FBI's turf. Perhaps today Secretary of Defense Rumsfeld will offset any increase in the authority of the DCI or the CIA by developing a competitive in-house intelligence/special operations capability.[31]

But relying upon the personal predilections of our political leadership or the dysfunctions of bureaucracy to counter the centralization of power is not enough in a government which is to be ruled by laws, not men or women alone. We should not have to rely on individuals to protect us from excessively centralized security enforcement power.

B. Increasing Secrecy

The fusion of intelligence and law enforcement inevitably has infected the law enforcement process and related immigration proceedings with the intelligence community's obsession with secrecy. At first, the mantra of "sources and methods" was invoked in a few immigration proceedings, denying the respondent immigrants access to evidence against them. Then it lay behind the blanket closure of special interest immigration proceedings, denying the public and the press access.

But the infection cannot be contained in immigration proceedings alone. In the Moussaoui prosecution (at this writing), the government is effectively insisting on military secrecy to deny the defendant his constitutional right to exculpatory evidence. Although the trial court has rejected this claim, oral arguments on its very existence were conducted in secret behind the closed doors of the traditionally open federal appellate court.

Similarly, further relaxation of FISA's already lenient search standards has increased the number of surveillance orders issued by a secret court without notice at any time to targets of the orders. Although the Foreign Intelligence Surveillance Court unanimously rejected the government's interpretation of the new FISA requirements, its opinion was only made public months after its issuance and after the administration belatedly gave it—in secret—to congressional intelligence oversight committees. The government's subsequent appeal of the court's decision was argued in a secret, one-sided hearing which the senior appellate judge himself admitted was "strange," as reflected in the subsequently released transcript of oral argument.

If secrecy has infected even such traditionally public judicial and quasi-judicial proceedings, it should come as no surprise that it is a contagion in the executive branch. But there, an obsession with secrecy not only curtails what the public, and even the Congress, know about the decisions and actions of the executive in the war against terrorism, it also curtails what one part of the executive knows about another. Furthermore, secrecy magnifies the power of the few who are privy to the secrets and thereby reinforces the tendency toward centralization of power in a security enforcement system. Inevitably, the cumulative effect of such secrecy is to hide the transformation of law enforcement from the public. Thus, even before the post–September 11 changes, scholars wrote, "It is dismaying that this move to reinvent the relationship between spies and federal agents took place with virtually no meaningful public debate and little journalistic scrutiny."[32]

Rejecting the government's effort to deny the media access to special interest immigration hearings, the Sixth Circuit Court of Appeals worried that "[t]he Executive Branch seeks to uproot people's lives, outside the public eye, and behind a closed door. Democracies die behind closed doors."[33] Democracy is also threatened by closed doors elsewhere in the executive branch, especially when it is just a "single body" of decision makers who are meeting behind them. Acting on secret information, often without telling or hearing out others, such a body is even more likely to err, miscalculate, and fall victim to group-think and wishful thinking than it is intentionally to abuse its power.

C. Weakening Checks and Balances

The vagaries of national security and the terrorist threat often made it difficult for Congress to legislate with much specificity in this field or, therefore, to cabin the executive. Instead, even before September 11, Congress used *post hoc* legislative fixes, appropriations limitations, and oversight to perform its constitutionally assigned checking function reactively. The courts, too, sometimes played a reactive checking role in enforcing statutory standards, but even then often found that national security statutes were not specific enough to supply judicially enforceable standards.

If reactive law enforcement thus left room for reactive legislative and (sometimes) judicial checks, proactive law enforcement indisputably favors the executive. Congress *has* legislated (though many would say, indiscriminately) by enacting the omnibus USA Patriot Act, but it otherwise disappeared into the woodwork as the executive shaped post–September 11 security enforcement. Apart from the USA Patriot Act, the preventive paradigm described above is chiefly an executive project. The "laws" authorizing much of the transformation of law enforcement have taken the form of executive directives, many of them unpublished, including, presumably, secret national security directives. No legislative process attended their making; no political consensus was immediately required to put them into effect, as would have been required had they taken the form of legislation. In fact, Congress has fared little better than the press in learning their details, much less their effects. The executive has consistently resisted efforts to make public full information about its detention policy, its use of new USA Patriot Act surveillance authorities, and its own decision-making process.

D. Compensating with Internal Checks(?)

"Failure of checks and balances" would be an overstatement, however, not only because it may still be too early to tell, but also because it ignores the role of checks internal to the executive branch. The government's enviable won-lost record in the Foreign Intelligence Surveillance Court, for example, is not necessarily proof of the failure of FISA to check surveillance, because the prospect of judicial review of a FISA application disciplines the executive process for preparing one. Justice Department lawyers, in effect, substitute for judges in screening FISA applications, and the most problematical applications are intercepted by them before ever reaching the FISC. If this is true, FISA *does* check executive surveillance by prompting the executive to check itself.

231

The Justice Department IG's report on the September 11 immigration detentions provides additional illustrations of internal checks. The report is itself one (although it is debatable whether it should be classified as "internal" when it was the USA Patriot Act, in part, that directed the IG to review claims of civil rights or civil liberties violations by department employees): it reports the findings of a seemingly thorough, sometimes critical, and partly independent survey of the post–September 11 immigration detentions. But the report also describes another check. Its account of the rising tensions between immigration officials, especially lawyers for the Immigration and Naturalization Service, and the FBI, and the way these tensions caused changes in the detention policy to conform with immigration law, suggests that the professional ethics and acculturation of government lawyers to the rule of law make such lawyers themselves an important check on the law-bending or possibly lawless decisions of their political superiors.

The limits of internal checks are well-illustrated by the deputy attorney general's response to the OIG report. Citing the "imperative placed on these detentions by the department"—that is, the top-down orders for preventive detention—he stated that "I would not have expected [his Justice Department staff] to reconsider the detention policy in the absence of a clear warning that the law was being violated."[34] When the political leadership lays down an "imperative" of security enforcement, in other words, staff are expected to exploit every legal ambiguity and to resolve any in favor of the imperative instead of enforcing the rules of law as they best understand them.

E. Enforcing More Harshly

Preventive detention is a harsher tool of enforcement than judicially approved arrests on probable cause, both wider in scope and longer in duration. Its aim, after all, is neither to set up prosecution nor to punish after conviction; it is to capture and hold the enemy until they are all removed or killed.[35]

Intelligence-gathering has always "tolerate[d] a degree of intrusiveness, harshness, and deceit that Americans do not want applied against themselves," as Stewart Baker, former general counsel of the National Security Agency, has acknowledged.[36] If this is true, then the expansion of intelligence-collecting activities by the FBI in the United States may increase the tolerance for these aspects of collection. After September 11 many non Arab-Americans would not object to seeing "intrusiveness, harshness, and deceit" applied against Muslims and Arabs. But then they should not be surprised if, should present trends continue, they are turned against them, too.

Finally, the military is primarily and properly trained to use force to accomplish its missions. When it is given missions inside the United States, or law enforcement is militarized in its own missions, force may cease being a last resort, as it has been in traditional law enforcement. At the same time, traditional law enforcement's embrace of military equipment and technologies, apparently promoted heavily by equipment manufacturers,[37] inevitably increases law enforcers' willingness to use it. And even when force is not used, the mere prospect of military or military-style force "may . . . chill the exercise of fundamental rights, such as the rights to speak freely and to vote, and [may] create the atmosphere of fear and hostility which exists in territories occupied by enemy forces,"[38] as a federal appellate court recognized in a Posse Comitatus Act case.

★

The good news is that our military commanders and our intelligence officers are neither driving the metamorphosis of American law enforcement into security enforcement nor terribly enthusiastic about it. The military, steeped in subordination to civil authority and extraordinarily respectful of our constitutional scheme, have consistently resisted law enforcement assignments, partly out of fear of their mismatch with military training and of their competition for scarce military resources, and partly out of the intuition that carrying them out will sully the military's hard-won reputation with the public. Although some political scientists have asserted that "the CIA has embraced a new crime-fighting role" in order "[t]o reinvent itself after the Cold War,"[39] it may be more accurate to say that the intelligence community, too, at least at first resisted civilian law enforcement assignments out of fear of compromising its sources and methods as well as fear of competition for intelligence resources already strained abroad. The trends described above are to a significant degree coincident, the product of many independent decisions, not some master plan, despite their top-down origins.

233

The good news, however, is also the bad news. The military and intelligence communities follow orders (though sometimes at a lag). If the political leadership insists on enlisting them in security enforcement, they will obey. Then mission creep, target fixation, excessive secrecy, and bureaucratic turf-building may well accelerate the transformation of law enforcement and reinforce the adverse consequences for democratic accountability outlined above. It would therefore be a mistake to trust in the good intentions of our leaders and their security enforcement troops. Justice Brandeis warned us, "The greatest dangers to liberty lurk in insidious encroachment by men of zeal, well-meaning but without understanding."[40]

The September 11 attacks and the threat of worse have posed a challenge which may justify the adoption of preventive measures which will transform traditional law enforcement and rewrite the rules governing military and intelligence operations at home. But under the rule of law, that transformation should be effected only by laws publicly and deliberately made by our elected representatives on full and current information, checked by courts in appropriate cases, continuously overseen by the legislature, and, to the extent consistent with legitimately protecting sources and methods and the small amount of information which is truly properly classified, reported by the media. At this writing, the transformation of law enforcement to security enforcement is outpacing these essential checks and balances.

1 The transformation I am describing is not confined geographically to the United States, of course. For example, Andreas and Price depicted it more broadly in a thoughtful article as the blurring of traditional boundaries "between an internally oriented domestic police sphere and an externally oriented military sphere," Peter Andreas & Richard Price, "From War Fighting to Crime Fighting: Transforming the American National Security State," 3 *Int'l Studies Rev.* 31 (2001), while Luban focusses chiefly on the latter sphere when he describes it as "selectively combining elements of the war model and elements of the law model . . . to mobilize lethal force against terrorists while eliminating most traditional rights of a military adversary. . . ." David Luban, "The War on Terrorism and the End of Human Rights," 22 *Phil. & Pub. Pol'y Q.* 9, 10 (2002). My discussion, however, is focussed strictly on security enforcement within the United States, where our constitutional rights and liberties and the system of checks and balances apply with greatest force.

2 Bail Reform Act of 1984, 18 U.S.C. § 3142(e) (2000).

3 18 U.S.C. §3144 (2000).

4 *United States v. United States District Court*, 407 U.S. 297, 322 (1972).

5 50 U.S.C. §§ 1801–1811 (2000).

6 Pub. L. No. 95-511, §1566 (1978), formerly codified at 18 U.S.C. §1804(a)(7).

7 50 U.S.C. §403-3(d)(1) (2000).

8 18 U.S.C. § 1385 (2000).

9 NSDD 207 and NSDD 221 (1986) were both issued in 1986, but remain classified, their contents known only from unclassified fact sheets released by the administration. *See* Christopher Simpson, *National Security Directives of the Reagan & Bush Administrations* 632–34, 640–41 (1995). In 1995, President Clinton issued Presidential Decision Directive (PDD) 39, which stressed that "the United States regards . . . terrorism as a potential threat to national security as well as a criminal act. . . ." It, too, has not been completely declassified.

10 PDD 42 (Oct. 21, 1995) is also classified.

11 *International Crime Control Strategy* 6 (released by White House May 12, 1998).

12 Viet Dinh, remarks delivered at George Washington University Law School, spring 2003.

13 Pub. L. No. 107-56, §§ 218, 115 Stat. 291 (amending 50 U.S.C. §§ 1804(a)(7)(B) and 1823(a)(7)(B)), and 203(d)(1), 115 Stat. 281.

14 In re All Matters Submitted to Foreign Intelligence Court, 218 F. Supp. 2d 611, 675 (Foreign Intel. Surv. 2002), *rev'd sub nom.*, 310 F.3d 717 (Foreign Intel. Surv. Rev. 2002).

15 In re Sealed Case, 310 F.3d 717, 720 (Foreign Intell. Surv. Rev. 2002).

16 Exec. Order No. 12333 (1981), 46 Fed. Reg. 59,941 (1981). This order is still in effect, as the principal publicly disclosed executive charter for intelligence operations.

17 50 U.S.C. §403-5a(a) (2000).

18 Quoted in *Detroit Free Press v. Ashcroft*, 303 F.3d 681 (6th Cir. 2002), and *North Jersey Media Group, Inc. v. Ashcroft*, 308 F.3d 198, cert. denied, 123 S. Ct. 2215 (2003).

19 The Classified Information Procedures Act, 18 U.S.C. app. III §§1–16 (2000), does permit closed hearings, but chiefly for the purpose of deciding whether and how classified information will be used by the defendant at trial.

20 Military Order of November 13, 2001, Detention, Treatment and Trial of Certain Non-Citizens in the War Against Terrorism, 66 Fed. Reg. 57,833 (2001).

21 *Procedures for Trials by Military Commissions of Certain Non-United States Citizens in the War Against Terrorism*, 68 Fed. Reg. 39,373, 39,375, 39,377–78 (2003).

22 Steven Brill, *After: How America Confronted the September 12 Era* (New York: Simon and Schuster, 2003).

23 Affidavit of Michael E. Rolince, In re Osama Mohamed Bassiousny Elfar (A# 79016726, filed Oct. 4, 2001).

24 U.S. Department of Justice, Office of the Inspector General, *The September 11 Detainees: A Review of the Treatment of Aliens Held on Immigration Charges in Connection With the Investigation of the September 11 Attacks* (April 2003) (hereafter *OIG Report*).

25 *See* 10 U.S.C. §§124, 371–381 (2000).

26 Andreas & Price, *supra* note 1, at 43-44 (emphasis added), from H.G. Reza, "Military Silently Patrols U.S. Border," *L.A. Times*, June 29, 1997, at A3, A30.

27 Andreas & Price, *supra* note 1, at 44, *quoting* Kirk Spitzer, "Military Plays Large, Low-Key Role in Domestic Law Enforcement," Gannett News Serv., July 13, 1995.

28 Pub. L. No. 103-337, § 1011(c), 108 Stat. 2836 (1994).

29 *Laird v. Tatum*, 408 U.S.1, 15 (1972).

30 Stewart Baker, "Should Spies Be Cops?," 97 *Foreign Policy* 37, 40 (1994–95).

31 Thomas E. Ricks, "Rumsfeld Stands Tall After Iraq Victory," *Washington Post*, April 20, 2003, at A1, A24

32 Jim McGhee & Brian Duffy, *Main Justice: The Men and Women Who Enforce the Nation's Criminal Laws and Guard Its Liberties* 373–74 (New York: Simon and Schuster, 1996).

33 *Detroit Free Press v. Ashcroft*, 303 F.3d 681, 683 (6th Cir. 2002).

34 Letter from Larry D. Thompson (Deputy Attorney General) to Glenn A. Fine (Inspector General), April 4, 2003, *OIG Report, supra* note 24, Appen. K.

35 *Compare* David Luban, *supra* note 1, at 13 (because capitulation is not

possible, "the real aim of the war [on terrorism] is, quite simply, to kill or capture all of the terrorists—to keep on killing and killing, capturing and capturing, until they are all gone.").

36 Baker, *supra* note 31, at 40.

37 Andreas and Price, *supra* note 1, at 38–40.

38 *Bissonette v. Haig*, 776 F.2d 1384, 1387 (8th Cir. 1986) and *aff'd*, 800 F.2d 812 (8th Cir. 1986) (en banc), *aff'd*, 485 U.S. 264 (1988).

39 Andreas and Price, *supra* note 1, at 41.

40 *Olmstead v. United States*, 277 U.S. 438, 479 (Brandeis, J., dissenting).

13

THE SEEDS OF SECRECY, THEN AND NOW

Anna K. Nelson

This is war, announced President George W. Bush, as Americans sat traumatized before their TV screens watching replay after replay of the suicide bombers destroying two symbols of American power, the World Trade Center and the Pentagon. Few citizens would dispute the need to punish the perpetrators responsible for the death of approximately three thousand people. But the president's announcement also sent an unpleasant message to those who remembered the wars of the last fifty years.

All modern American wars shared certain attributes. A refigured national budget immediately transferred money from domestic agencies to the military, for example, and increased the power of the executive at the expense of the legislature. At the conclusion of the war, balance was restored between civil and military spending, and Congress began challenging the president's enhanced power.

The Cold War was no different, except that it brought into play a third and more pernicious attribute: a wall of secrecy that separated the government from its citizens. Based upon the need to keep national security information from its enemies abroad, this wall of secrecy also kept such information from the people at home. Moreover, secrecy did not disappear after the Cold War. After forty years, the habits of secrecy had bred such a deeply established protective culture within the White House and national security agencies that there was no turning back when the Cold War finally came to an end.

After the disintegration of the Soviet Union and throughout the 1990s, the wall of secrecy did contract slightly under the provisions of a new executive order opening national security records and a more lenient interpretation of the Freedom of Information Act (FOIA). But just as the national security state was never dismantled, neither was the secrecy attached to it. Thus it was the system perfected under the Cold War that was ready for use as President Bush declared that we were at war with terrorists.

The day after the World Trade Center was demolished and the Pentagon damaged on September 11, 2001, Secretary of Defense Donald Rumsfeld began to warn those who might wish to leak classified information. On October 17, Attorney General John Ashcroft turned his attention to the FOIA. He urged agencies to be cautious in releasing information, opening records only after "full and deliberate consideration." Implementation of the act, he continued, must be balanced by the need for national security and business protection. He further noted that the Justice Department would stand behind agencies that turn down FOIA requests. Under the cover of national security, November brought an executive order nullifying the intent of the Presidential Records Act by requiring the permission of the incumbent president as well as past presidents before the release of White House documents after twelve years. This new executive rule effectively allowed President George W. Bush to control information concerning President Reagan's and Vice President George Bush's papers. Ashcroft rounded out the year by moving beyond Rumsfeld's warning and announcing the creation of a task force to review sanctions against leakers.

Congress contributed to "homeland" security by quick approval of the U.S.A. Patriot Act. Under that act, the FBI and CIA were given additional domestic intelligence-gathering powers. Guidelines governing FBI domestic security and counterintelligence operations in effect since the Watergate scandal were modified to remove perceived handicaps to gathering information. Using his executive powers, President Bush announced that conversations between suspected terrorists and their lawyers would be monitored and some non-American suspected terrorists would be tried before secret military tribunals. Some members of Congress and civil libertarians protested the usurpation of power by the president, but polls indicated there was overwhelming public support for all these actions. The trauma of September 11 and the fear of unknown future attacks were no doubt responsible for this support. Yet for Americans who came to adulthood during the last fifty years, the secret agencies of the National Security State and its secret policies were an accepted part of life.

Nation-states, whether in the hands of kings, despots, or parliaments, have traditionally conducted their foreign policy behind closed doors. There was no demand for access to this secret information when wars were fought by mercenary armies and decisions made by officials responsible only to the ruling elite. Modern wars, however, were fought by citizen armies, and dangerous new technology threatened the lives of entire populations. As early as World War I, it was clear that secret diplomacy could no longer be ignored when unwieldy cannons pulled by horses were replaced by powerful motorized artillery, submarines skulked under the ocean, and airplanes could wipe out civilians and soldiers alike.

Similarly, for two centuries the conduct of foreign policy in the United States was of interest to Congress and the American public only when war was at hand. Congressional war hawks of 1812 and the jingoistic public of 1898 exemplify this point. But in the twentieth century two world wars brought into play an active Congress and an interested public. Congress began to investigate crucial decisions, such as President Woodrow Wilson's decision to go to war in Europe, the disaster at Pearl Harbor, and President Franklin D. Roosevelt's diplomacy during the wartime summits. Woodrow Wilson's "open covenants" notwithstanding, American officials followed their European counterparts by failing to inform their citizens.

The great awakening came after the unspeakable devastation of World War II, the rise of a new military power with a formidable ideology, and the detonation of a nuclear bomb. By 1950, foreign policy had gained a wide constituency in the United States. Political and diplomatic decisions required the support of citizens if liberal capitalism were to flourish, individual liberty preserved, and the world saved from nuclear destruction. That support depended upon knowledge, however.

239

Historians and other scholars, not content with information provided by those in charge, sought the documentation that explained those policies. A simple if unfair system was devised to allow privileged access to World War II documents. Basically, the State Department released old documents, kept recent ones closed to the public, and allowed selected researchers to see those in between. Under that provision, for example, William Langer and Everett Gleason wrote *The Challenge to Isolation: The World Crisis of 1937–1940*, a careful, if uncritical, study of those crucial years based upon original sources long before they were available to other researchers.[1]

240 The flow from hot war to Cold War irrevocably changed this system after 1947. *Ad hoc* access to foreign policy records disappeared behind a veil of secrecy. New factors were responsible for this change. First, foreign policy was no longer the monopoly of the State Department and the president but had silently morphed into National Security Policy. The military services and intelligence agencies now joined State in making policy. As a result, there were many more secrets to keep, since each agency had a separate set.

Second, President Harry Truman and his advisors were intent on assuring that the U.S. keep its atomic monopoly, while the Soviets, of course, were seeking information to destroy that monopoly. Secrecy designed to keep information from the Axis powers during the war continued into the postwar era, when the Soviet Union became the new enemy.

There really were spies, or at least had been spies. The fact that Klaus Fuchs and the Rosenbergs, et al., were prosecuted for passing nuclear information during World War II was lost in the accusations of espionage during the Cold War. In any case, there was agreement that the Soviets were eager to catch up and would resort to espionage in the U.S. and Britain whenever possible. Nuclear secrets, the most important government secrets, were added to the mix.

Third, U.S. policy-makers were convinced that they were dealing with an enemy willing to devote untold resources to undermine the governments of the Western nations. They pointed to the pervasive Soviet propaganda machine and the communist infiltration of labor unions. Meanwhile, they were fearful of Communist Party members who, they believed, constituted a ring of informers and spies ready to become a "fifth column."

A feeling of national inadequacy dominated the administration in Washington. How could a democracy compete with a ruthless dictatorship based upon a competing ideology?

In response to Soviet activities, the U.S. began meeting the Soviet challenge by matching it, fighting fire with fire. Psychological warfare, covert infiltration of political parties in Western Europe, and paramilitary operations behind the Iron Curtain became a part of U.S. policy as early as 1948. To effectively counter the Soviets, these actions had to be shrouded in secrecy, withheld from Congress (supposedly notorious leakers), the press, and the public. Another potent set of secrets were stirred into the expanding brew.

To understand the rising trend of secrecy, its duration and consequences, it is necessary to examine the rise of the National Security State, as they are merely two sides of the same coin.

The institutional apparatus for the National Security State was established in 1947 with the passage of the National Security Act. While primarily designed to unify the armed services, it also created the National Security Council (NSC), Central Intelligence Agency (CIA), and the short-lived National Security Resources Board. The creation of the NSC brought into the realm of foreign policy the military services and the intelligence agency as well as the State Department. The act did not fully unify the armed services but marked the culmination of attempts to organize a central agency for the gathering and disseminating of intelligence. The State Department had declined to assume responsibility for the nitty gritty of psychological warfare, since it would threaten the course of open diplomacy. However, within the Truman Administration, Secretaries of State Marshall and Acheson and their advisors, including George Kennan, not only supported the CIA, but were eager to exert control over the agency's work in order to put it into the context of foreign policy.

The NSC immediately turned its attention to psychological warfare, a murky concept that in 1947 generally meant the use of local media for spreading information and disinformation. An example was Radio Free Europe, funded by the CIA and beamed to countries in Eastern Europe. But by 1950, psychological warfare was a code word for covert action that encompassed many more intrusive methods for confronting the enemy.

241

Within four months of its first meeting, the NSC approved policy papers sanctioning the use of covert activities. A top secret paper (NSC 4) called for covert action, and an even more secret paper (NSC 4a) put the CIA in charge of these activities, even though there was some question as to whether the statute creating the agency provided for this kind of activity. As a result of NSC 4a, the CIA redefined and broadened psychological operations. The key to covert action was the concealment of the originating role of the U.S. government. Government deniability of covert action became deeply rooted in the national security system.

242   The immediate crisis that provoked these papers was the Italian election of 1948, which threatened to bring into power a coalition government including members of the Italian Communist Party. The 1948 Italian elections marked the first of a long line of interventions into the political affairs of other states. In this instance the Communists were defeated, and American intervention was regarded by the policy-makers as a great victory. Nevertheless, the effort was disorganized and the less than enthusiastic director of central intelligence (DCI) was reticent to follow psychological warfare to its logical conclusion. Plans were made to bypass him. The result was NSC 10, written from a draft by George Kennan.

Unlike its predecessor, NSC 4a, NSC 10 was quite explicit about the need for covert operations. It also reiterated the important tie between covert operations and "deniability." In addition, a new entity, the Office of Policy Coordination, was established, with a director appointed by the State Department, and while it was approved by the DCI, it was independent of the agency. Thus, NSC 10 placed the State Department squarely into the forefront of covert activities. Clandestine activities permeated U.S. foreign relations with its Western allies. Indeed, local currency (counterpart funds) earned under the Marshall Plan provided a secret cache of money for CIA operations. The State Department and the CIA now had large stakes in preserving secrecy.

By 1950, Western European countries were no longer threatened by communist subversion. Covert and overt attempts to defeat the Soviets were perceived as successful, even though the Iron Curtain proved impenetrable. Yet there was a continuing sense of unease among the national security establishment, especially in the State Department. The Russians had detonated an atomic bomb, China was "lost," Truman was proposing an inadequate budget, and there seemed to be no plans for the long haul.

Nineteen-fifty proved to be a decisive year in the history of the national security state and the secrecy that accompanied it. During that year, President Truman decided to proceed with the development of the hydrogen bomb, a bomb with no size limitations. Simultaneously, under the leadership of the State Department, the NSC approved a new document numbered 68. This was a terrifying document that proposed a battle plan against the communist monolith encompassing every government agency. Among the appendices to this consummate Cold War document is one setting the agenda for the CIA, in which its clandestine operations were confirmed and promoted. Although there was recognition that the budget to implement this plan would require public and congressional support, it was, like its predecessors, top secret with an extra warning to those who might be careless.[2]

Three months after Truman received NSC 68, the virtual war became a real war on the Korean peninsula. This war convinced Truman and his advisors that the Soviets, thwarted in Europe, had turned to Asia and would soon turn to other parts of the world.

The Korean War also created a new level of secrecy. It was a decisive event that turned the tide in the history of the National Security State. The military budget burgeoned, and military intelligence agencies once again began to flourish. A new agency, the National Security Agency, emerged to provide a sophisticated approach to eavesdropping on the enemy—and with it, more secrets.

In addition, the perceived need for a more active intelligence agency brought a new director to the CIA, General Walter Bedell Smith. Although the original legislation established the DCI as the coordinator of all government intelligence agencies, neither the military services nor the State Department would give up their individual domains. General Smith began the process of turning the agency into a more powerful, independent entity. Recognizing the futility of trying to coordinate agencies, he enhanced the scope of his own agency, absorbed the Office of Policy Coordination, and took control of covert actions. By 1952, the CIA was a formidable organization ready for its halcyon decade of covert activity.

The seeds of secrecy planted between 1947 and 1950, and fertilized by fears at home and fearful events abroad, bore unanticipated fruit. Secrecy covered covert activities of the CIA as it influenced elections abroad, sponsored paramilitary interventions, and practiced assassination skills. Secrecy also covered the activities of the FBI as it obsessively searched for communists and "fellow travelers." Secrecy overtook presidents and their national security advisors, whose actions would not always have withstood the test of public scrutiny.

Until the Soviet Union collapsed in 1989, the secret side of the National Security State was based upon the Cold War. In spite of a slight de-escalation in the 1950s and Kissinger and Nixon's attempt at *détente*, the nation was at war with the U.S.S.R. and its satellites. In the words of President Ronald Reagan, the Soviet Union was the "evil empire," and was still our enemy after forty-five years.

Each war the U.S. has fought since the middle of the twentieth century created more excessive forms of secrecy. Americans themselves were urged to watch their words during World War II. But the posters telling Americans that "loose lips sink ships" were quite different from the secrecy that followed. Throughout the Cold War, government grew experienced in managing the information it controlled. However, Congress and the press remained skeptical and the worst of the efforts were slightly curtailed. Passage of the FOIA and the information uncovered by the Church Committee were exemplary attempts at open information.

Once again we are at war, and once again it is a war without end. Our enemies are bands of terrorists and nation-states that form, in the words of President George W. Bush, an "axis of evil." A combination of new executive orders and legislation has spawned new restrictions on the release of government information. The opening of documents will be delayed, former presidents' papers will be withheld if the current president so desires, and many agencies have removed information from their Web pages. Why is the outcry against this administration's control of information so muted? Regrettably, Americans have simply grown accustomed to the national security state and its partner, secrecy. After fifty years, the seeds of secrecy are still bearing fruit.

NOTES

1 William Langer and Everett Gleason. *The Challenge to Isolation.* New York: Published for the Council on Foreign Relations by Harper, 1952, reprinted 1964.
2 NSC 68 was finally released in 1975.

14

THE NATIONAL SECURITY STATE, WAR, AND CONGRESS

Marcus G. Raskin and A. Carl LeVan

Governments that purport to be presidential democracies inherently face a division of power and authority between different branches of government. In the American system, the flow of real power between the branches, especially the executive and legislative, varies from issue to issue. On matters of national security, the political power of the people is reduced because the questions may appear too complicated, and many critical national issues seem beyond the reach of the average citizen, especially those who are not part of organized groups or who do not have access through wealth, celebrity, or perseverance. These inhibitors to participation have the added effect of giving citizens an often misplaced trust in government officials; citizens are told they don't have all the information, and knowing this, they come to believe they don't need to know.

While some policy debates may still occur with a modicum of balance between the Congress and the executive, this is no longer true in the area of making war and preparing for it. While in the latter case Congress is able to gain certain amounts of largesse for its particular constituencies in the form of defense contracts, the underlying reality is that the executive frames the issues, drives the purpose and does so through military and covert means, which leaves Congress with no prior notification, little oversight, and only sham investigations of actions that the national security establishment and any particular president may take. The public itself is the outsider, unaware or impotent to restrain the behavior of elected officials. Deprived of public intelligence, it is unable to make collectively shared judgments that are necessary to define and secure democracy. Justice Stewart, in the Pentagon Papers case, wrote: "The only effective restraint upon executive policy in the areas of national defense and international affairs may lie in an enlightened citizenry—in an informed and critical public opinion which alone can here protect the values of democratic government." Public participation in the absence of public knowledge makes democratic accountability impossible.

In this essay we are concerned with the nuts and bolts of congressional power either as informed body, participant, or representative of the people at least as a coequal branch. From one Congress to the next, Congress is confused about its role. There are many committees and subcommittees that attend to different aspects of security and intelligence. There are a plethora of explicit and implicit limitations on Congress though, manifest in laws and customs that reduce its—and the public's—ability to know what is going on. One set of these rules is manifest in "ethical" standards and oaths devised to enforce a code of secrecy. This includes the Select Intelligence Committee's role as conduit and sometimes enforcer of the "code." A second set of rules stems from limitations on oversight mechanisms such as inspectors general and the General Accounting Office. Oftentimes, national security bureaucracies enjoy exemptions from the watchful eye of these mechanisms. A third type of limitation on Congress is more nuanced but no less problematic for the balance of power. This occurs when members are duped (sometimes willingly) into authorizing programs that the National Security State has already set in motion, thus raising the cost of congressional criticism.

All of these rules, customs, and laws have the intended effect of handicapping Congress from performing its intended constitutional responsibilities as a coequal branch. In practice this means that Congress seeks to fit into the National Security State structure, becomes dependent on its information, and acts as a rationalizer for varieties of imperialism. It acts as a passive branch. The ultimate tool for restoring balance between the Congress and the executive is impeachment or the threat of impeachment. But this, too, has become a blunt constitutional tool, and Congress has failed to use it to regain a measure of authority on questions of war. The final section of this essay explores why Congress has failed in this area (reserving impeachment most recently for presidential pecadilloes rather than for errors of constitutional judgment), and argues that it may be a necessary last resort if Congress is to regain its proportionate constitutional authority. In the twenty-first century, if the United States is to have a constitutional democracy, Congress must return to "first principles," and this requires rethinking its relationship to an imperial executive who rides roughshod over law whether national or international.

247

ACCOUNTABILITY AND IMMUNITY

In much of the national security establishment, from the intelligence agencies that acquire and protect secrets to the Pentagon programs operating in dozens of countries overseas, barriers to accountability generate fundamental contradictions with American democracy. The National Security State has survived and thrived beyond the Cold War because of its *tertium quid* status with a democratic system of government. Its fabric of bureaucratic interdependencies, woven into vastly different bodies of law, extends well beyond the roughly $40 billion intelligence community consisting of 13 agencies and now a Department of Homeland Security. These interdependencies prevent the reduction of the National Security State to one identifiable entity.

The replacement of identifiable, compartmentalized bureaucracies with these coral reeflike interdependencies makes it extremely difficult to control, because they form a network insulated from accountability mechanisms assumed to apply universally across all democratic institutions. For example, CIA assets do not need to meet physical presence requirements for naturalization, and the CIA and the National Security Agency do not need to undergo systematic review of agency operations. They are exempt from laws ranging from the Endangered Species Act to personnel laws restricting the hiring of alcohol and drug abusers. Other anomalies in personnel laws protect the CIA, the Defense Intelligence Agency, the Federal Bureau of Investigation, and the National Security Agency from the Whistleblower Protection Act, designed to promote integrity in government.[1]

A second important internal accountability mechanism, the inspector general (IG), is also constrained by anomalies in the law. The secretary of defense is able to stop an IG investigation if it threatens "the national security interests of the United States"—a lower standard for interference than that for other agencies. And the CIA enjoys protection from a key provision of the Inspectors General Act of 1978, which states "nothing in this section . . . shall be construed to authorize or permit the withholding of information from the Congress."[2] Nor does it impair the CIA's ability to withhold information from the public. When John Deutch traveled to Los Angeles in November 1996 and promised the Inspector General would examine evidence of the CIA's role in drug smuggling. He promised "anyone in the public who has a wish to look at the report will be able to do so ... The results will be made public. And finally, if any wrongdoing is discovered, we will pursue it, and those responsible will be brought to justice." Although some wrongdoing was subsequently uncovered, no one was ever brought to justice.[3]

The problem is not merely the exemptions themselves but the climate of fear they cultivate. For example, many CIA employees who take their case to the IG (or to Congress) end up being reprimanded by their supervisors.[4] Or they may cultivate a culture of noncooperation, such as that faced by House Permanent Select Committee (HPSCI) when investigating the Ames espionage case, where the committee described "a lack of candor by CIA officials in answering questions of committee members about the losses of Soviet assets." This is true among national security managers themselves, and the November 30, 1994, committee report on the Ames case said even DCI Robert Gates claimed that he was not kept informed about the accumulating losses. Overcoming these exemptions requires the construction of an impossible political coalition altering laws in all of these agencies. It is difficult enough for Congress to curb military expenditures such as the C-17 military transport plane, whose manufacturer protected it by spreading its contracts for parts across more than 300 congressional districts. But the task is even further complicated when confronted with a network consisting of vested interests, both seen and unseen, embedded in many institutions that may or may not be defending the nation from danger.

Controlling the National Security State apparatus is therefore difficult due to institutional arrangements that reinforce shared loyalties to a secrecy system rather than promote a Madisonian system of checks and balances, where "ambition is made to counter ambition." The concentration of oversight responsibilities within the congressional committee system, the continuation and extension of exemptions for national security organizations, and provision information labeled as "intelligence product" to an expanding body of consumers have all served to exacerbate opportunities for co-optation and to undermine accountability.

INTELLIGENCE OVERSIGHT AND ITS LIMITS

In the early years of the Cold War, Congress willingly overlooked many intelligence and secret government activities, and did not have specialized designated mechanisms to oversee them. An unpublished CIA Staff study found that the appropriations and armed services committees were not briefed on covert operations at all in the early 1950s, and as late as 1968 there were only eight briefings in that year for these important committees. During this period, congressional oversight was nominally in the hands of the House and Senate Armed Services Committees and the defense subcommittees of the Appropriations Committees. The members of these committees who were assigned to liaise with the CIA even had their names kept secret from published lists of congressional committee membership.[5]

In 1956, when Senator Mike Mansfield (D-MT) sought to establish a joint oversight committee on intelligence, Senator Leverett Saltonstall (R-MA), advocating the ostrich's position, noted, "It is not a question of reluctance on the part of CIA officials to speak to us. Instead, it is a question of our reluctance, if you will, to seek information and knowledge on subjects which I personally, as a member of Congress and as a citizen, would rather not have" (cited in Snider *supra* 1997). Some of these habits have endured. For example, fewer than a dozen members of Congress utilized their right to examine the classified portion of the annual intelligence budget for the several years in which the authors checked in the 1990s.

The Watergate scandal showed that the intelligence agencies were willing to use their blank check to operate domestically to (illegally) interfere in partisan activities, and further revelations in the press exposed an extensive program of spying on Americans and other even more horrendous activities such as assassination missions. Congress responded with the Hughes-Ryan Amendment in 1974, which added language to the Foreign Assistance Act prohibiting "operations in foreign countries, other than activities intended solely for obtaining necessary intelligence unless and until the president finds that each such operation is important to the national security of the United States." It also required congressional notification "in a timely fashion," including a description of the operations. The appropriate committees for notification at the time included the committees on Armed Services, Foreign Relations and Foreign Affairs, and Appropriations.[6]

Following dramatic revelations by investigative committees headed by Senators Frank Church (D-ID) and Representative Otis Pike (D-NY), Congress established designated intelligence committees. The Senate Select Committee on Intelligence (SSCI) and the House Permanent Select Committee on Intelligence (HPSCI) were both assigned to keep the legislative branch "fully and currently informed" of intelligence and intelligence-related activities, and to assume the principal oversight responsibilities entailed in the Hughes-Ryan Amendment. Following the recommendation of the investigative committees, they also were to draft a separate annual intelligence authorization bill to be publicly debated, but whose appropriations would be concealed by distortions in the defense budget, and whose overall figure remains officially secret.

REINING IN COVERT OPERATIONS?

In 1980, Congress attempted to tighten control over covert operations by adding a new title to the National Security Act of 1947, creating a process requiring the president to sign a "finding." The new controls made it clear that "the president may not authorize the conduct of a covert action by departments, agencies, or entities of the United States government unless the president determines such an action is necessary to support identifiable foreign policy objectives of the United States and is important to the national security of the United States."[7] An executive order also established the president's Foreign Intelligence Advisory Board (PFAIB), and within it the Intelligence Oversight

Board for conducting ad-hoc oversight of intelligence activities by the executive branch. The new oversight arrangements presented hurdles but not roadblocks, and it took only six years for the committees to discover (through the foreign press not through their own diligence) that President Reagan had signed a finding secretly authorizing arms sales to Iran as part of a strategy to free American hostages in Lebanon. This was contrary to public policy, and the decision to use the proceeds to arm the Nicaraguan Contras violated the Boland Amendment prohibiting funds to the Contras, as the world now knows. Theodore Draper famously observed at the time, "If ever the constitutional democracy of the U.S. is overthrown, we have a better idea of how it is likely to be done."[8]

251

It was not until 1991 that Congress bothered to define "covert action." By this time the Association for National Security Alumni, a reform-minded group of former intelligence officials and national security professionals, estimated that six million people worldwide had been killed in connection with secret operations undertaken or supported by the United States since World War II. Under the new law, covert action would not only continue to be possible, the Senate Intelligence Committee's report on the Intelligence Authorization bill declared its intention "to provide general statutory authority for the president to employ overt actions to implement U.S. foreign policy by covert means." President George H.W. Bush nevertheless vetoed the bill over provisions including one requiring notification of Congress either before an operation begins or "within a few days" after the initiation.

Bush also objected to a requirement that the use of third parties in the operation be specified in the finding. "It remains administration policy that our intelligence services will not ask third parties to carry out activities that they themselves are forbidden to undertake," he said in his veto statement, but the broad definition of covert action covering requests to a foreign government would have a "chilling effect" on diplomatic discussions involving national security. The definition of covert action established, and still in effect, is "an activity or activities of the United States government to influence political, economic, or military conditions abroad, where it is intended that the role of the United States government will not be apparent or acknowledged publicly."[9] Third parties, which were central to the Reagan administration's strategy to circumvent Congress in Iran-Contra, are now specified in findings, and the president must show how a covert operation is necessary to support "identifiable foreign policy objectives," but the meaning of "timely notification" remains unresolved. Even more importantly, as the Senate committee confessed in its report, Congress knowingly allows many covert activities to not legally be defined as such because "it would be impractical to seek presidential approval and report to Congress." In these cases, findings may not even be issued, thus defeating the entire purpose of creating a mechanism for making covert action compatible with democratic government.

252   Through the findings process, the president becomes a broker between illegitimacy and the law. The statutory definition of covert action codifies the principle of plausible denial, "a doctrine which encouraged the invention of false information or lies which will be acceptable to other government agencies, the courts, the public, and competing or uninformed groups within the secret agencies themselves."[10] It provides a legal shield for otherwise illegal activities and relieves any agency authorized to carry out a covert action from the burden of being honest. This fog protects the agency that is authorized by a finding to carry out a covert operation. In a political system where the veracity of information is deemed unimportant to public inquiry, there is no agreement on the definition of truth, and truth becomes related to the goals it serves rather than as an end in itself or a prerequisite for citizen action. A failure of American democracy today, then, is the acceptance of an incomplete picture as a basis for participation in politics and society. Americans demand politicians to be honest about their sex lives but not about the threats on which defense budgets are supposedly based, or about an assassination attempt disguised as a retaliation bombing. While Executive Order 12333 states, "No person employed by or acting on behalf of the United States government shall engage in, or conspire to engage in, assassination," the public permits state-sanctioned murder to continue as long as the target is suitably "bad" and the bullet is sufficiently undiscriminating that the public can take comfort in the official deception. Various plots hatched during the Clinton administration to eliminate Saddam Hussein, for example, were not opposed by the House and Senate Intelligence Committees.[11]

LEAVING THE GAO IN THE COLD

Congress's power to appropriate under Article I, Section 9 of the Constitution is its ultimate check on executive excesses, and one of its most important tools for undertaking this duty is the Government Accountability Office, formerly the General Accounting Office (GAO). As the investigative arm of Congress, the GAO has broad authority to investigate receipt and use of public money, to evaluate the programs of federal agencies, and conduct audits. This authority gives it access to government records that pertain to the "duties, powers, activities, organization, and financial transactions of the agency" and to compel such government records through civil action if necessary.[12]

However, the GAO is frequently left in the cold when it knocks on the CIA's door, due to extraordinary exemptions. Under Executive Order 12333, the GAO's virtually unrestricted right of access does not extend to activities the president designates as foreign intelligence or counterintelligence activities. Under the Central Intelligence Agency Act of 1949, "sums made available to the agency by appropriation or otherwise . . . may be expended without regard to the provisions of law and regulations relating to the expenditure of government funds." Some of these funds "of a confidential, extraordinary, or emergency nature" may be accountable only to the DCI, who also has the statutory responsibility to protect "intelligence sources and methods." Finally, the GAO Act of 1980 explicitly states, "nothing in this subsection shall be construed as affecting the authority contained in section 8(b) of the Central Intelligence Agency Act of 1949." The GAO testified in July 2001 it has have generally not sought to address these limitations in their authority "because of limited demand from Congress, particularly from the intelligence committees."[13]

According to a Congressional Research Service study prepared for Congressman John Conyers (D-MI) in 1997, the CIA at first invited the GAO to conduct periodic site audits until disputes arose in 1962 over the type of access granted to the auditors. "Since then," the report says, "GAO audits or reviews involving the CIA have been few, sporadic, ad hoc, and limited in scope. It appears from the public record, moreover, that, where GAO has initiated inquiries that involved the CIA, its cooperation has been less than comprehensive or nonexistent." In effect, a government agency with a multibillion dollar annual budget has not been audited in four decades.

The need for regular audits of the national security bureaucracy is obvious. The National Reconnaissance Office (NRO) managed to keep the construction of a lavish $310 million complex secret from the Senate. That scandal led to revelations that first revealed the NRO had hoarded $1 billion, then the number was increased to $2 billion—this occurred during a time of budget cuts throughout the government.[14] "What they counted on was the laxity of this body's supervision," said Congressman Barney Frank (D-MA) during the debate for a failed amendment to freeze the NRO's budget. "They counted on being able to put that money away so they could in effect supplement their own appropriation. These people have invented the new parliamentary device, the autonomous supplemental appropriation."[15] Without the means (in the case of the CIA) or the will (in the case of the NRO) of carrying out this duty regularly and vigorously, the power of the purse is no more than a limp threat to the arbitrary spending powers of the National Security State.

PROBLEMS OF CO-OPTATION AND COOPERATION

Weakening the GAO's power undermines the shared responsibility within Congress to monitor the national security establishment, an authority vigorously opposed since the inception of the intelligence committees. At a 1976 Senate hearing discussing the creation of the committees, then-DCI George Bush, Sr., went so far as to suggest that all congressional powers over the CIA be vested in one chairman of a joint committee.[16] The committees received sweeping jurisdictions but the responsibility to oversee intelligence agencies is supposed to extend beyond the intelligence committees as well. The House rules for the 109th Congress, for example, state: "Nothing in this clause shall be construed as prohibiting or otherwise restricting the authority of any other committee to study and review an intelligence or intelligence-related activity to the extent that such activity directly affects a matter otherwise within the jurisdiction of that committee." Rule X further makes clear that all relevant committees should have access to "the product of the intelligence and intelligence-related activities of any department or agency."

This broad authority, exercised properly, could serve as a check against co-optation, but the committees have sought to undermine this shared authority; not only do they want to protect their jurisdiction (like all congressional committees do), they want to protect and insulate the agencies they oversee. For example, when the Fiscal Year 1990 Intelligence Authorization Act established a statutory inspector general at the CIA, it made clear that the IG's reports are sent only to the intelligence committees. Most recently, a little noticed change in the House Rules in the 107th Congress gave HPSCI the exclusive jurisdiction to review and study the "sources and methods" of the intelligence community. The committee then used this power to stifle inquiries by other important committees. When the Republican chair of the Government Reform Subcommittee on Government Efficiency, Financial Management, and Intergovernmental Relations asked DCI George Tenet to testify in 2001, he offered the terse retort, "I regret to say that neither I nor any CIA representative will testify" because the HPSCI chair had encouraged him not to comply.[17] Another little-noticed change in the rules practically grants the HPSCI chair the extraordinary authority to *require* the Speaker of the House to refer legislation to his committee.

CONGRESS AS A PART OF THE SECRECY SYSTEM

The narrowing of legislative jurisdiction over the national security bureaucracy has corresponded with more and more intelligence products being shared with Congress, especially since the 1970s. However, this has allowed intelligence organizations to distinguish between oversight activities and providing intelligence products, a distinction made explicit by a "bright line" drawn by the CIA in 1994. The CIA and other intelligence agencies now have thousands of meetings on Capitol Hill each year. These briefings purchase congressional loyalty to the system, and other times they are simply less accurate than open sources, and deliberately misleading. In November 1999 the State Department and the CIA attempted to dissuade a congressional staff delegation from traveling to Iraq by describing threats to Americans. As it turned out, nongovernmental organizations on the ground (especially those not receiving any financial assistance from the U.S. government) provided more reliable information than the official story.

255

The briefing was designed not to inform Congress of the actual situation on the ground or to assist the delegation with timely and relevant information but to protect the policy in place, highlighting the critical distinction between Congress as a consumer of intelligence and Congress conducting oversight.

By becoming a consumer of secret information, members of Congress are constrained by burdensome regulations and laws limiting disclosure. The rules of the House and the Senate presume not the necessity of public knowledge but the protection of secrets. Indeed, in recent years the rules have made it even more difficult for members of Congress to openly discuss national security matters. In 1987 the Senate established a security office within the Office of the Secretary of the Senate to promulgate uniform standards, applicable to all senators and staff, for handling and protecting classified information. In 1993, the House passed an amendment to the Intelligence Authorization Act prohibiting executive-branch agencies from supplying information to members who had not signed a secrecy oath.[18] Then, in 1995, the House of Representatives modified its Code of Official Conduct with almost no debate or information, adding a clause to Rule XLIII requiring a new oath to protect secrecy in addition to the oath to "support and defend the Constitution" that has been in use for more than two hundred years. When a member later that year disclosed information that a Guatemalan army officer on the CIA payroll had ordered the murder of an American citizen and the husband of an American citizen, he was threatened with sanction for violating this oath. Remarkably, the scandal centered more on the disclosure by the member, Representative Robert Torricelli (D-NJ), than on the facts of criminal complicity by an agency of the United States government.[19]

The treatment of Torricelli was far from unusual and fits the standard pattern following confrontations with the National Security State:

- In 1974, Representative Michael Harrington (D-MA) wrote a private letter to a colleague about the CIA's involvement in the overthrow of the democratically elected government of Salvador Allende in Chile a year before. Before giving him the information, the Armed Services Committee had him sign a statement of nondisclosure. After the press learned of the CIA's outrageous role in the Chilean coup, Harrington lost his access to classified House files. He was later denied a position on the special committee set up to investigate the findings he brought to the attention of the House leadership.[20]

- In 1985 Senator Dave Durenberger (R-MN) said Bill Casey "does not feel that the intelligence agencies should be accountable to the American people." The DCI immediately accused the senator of "repeated compromise of sensitive intelligence sources and methods." A year later, the intelligence agencies fed stories to the conservative *Washington Times* that Durenberger was a security risk. That same year the senator and his Republican colleagues asked the president about covert paramilitary operations he was planning in Libya, and Reagan ignored the questions. Iran-Contra was the last straw. In April 1987 Durenberger said Reagan "is the worst source of information on Iran and Nicaragua." The administration and its allies on the Hill eventually neutralized Durenberger when they filed an ethics complaint after he mentioned the U.S. had had an American intelligence agent in Israel several years earlier.[21]

- Senator Patrick Leahy (D-VT) provided a copy of the intelligence committee's draft report on Iran-Contra to the media in 1987. Even though it contained no classified information, the disclosure violated the committee's rules, and the committee chairman promptly accepted Leahy's self-censuring act of resignation.[22]

- Representative George Brown (D-CA), a member of the House Intelligence Committee, gave a series of speeches in 1987 calling for broader use of military satellites for civilian applications such as crop photos and urban planning. Although his floor speeches relied entirely on unclassified public information, the chairman of the committee and the NRO suggested Brown was compromising secrets. Calling it "one of the most irrational things I've ever seen," Brown resigned in protest rather than face an ethics probe.[23]

All of these incidents center not on a failure to uncover the truth. Instead, they illustrate how information is treated as a commodity to be protected instead of a necessary ingredient for deliberation that informs the democratic process. A proven violation of secrecy rules and laws is not even necessary for the secrecy system to enforce loyalty. This is true not only with examples such as Congressman Brown's, but also with the even better known case of a speaker of the House, Jim Wright (D-TX).

Speaker Wright had met with Nicaraguan government officials and opposition Contra leaders numerous times in 1988 to encourage both sides to renew their efforts for a negotiated solution to the conflict. The CIA had been waging a covert war against the Sandinista government but had recently assured HPSCI that it would not be involved in demonstrations to provoke the Sandinistas into overreacting; other U.S. elements in Nicaragua had apparently continued this role, though. Wright told a group of Contra leaders interested in renewing negotiations that the CIA could not be involved in provoking the Sandinista government in order to help the Contras' negotiating position. Further, Wright had been actively seeking the release of activists jailed at one such protest in Nandaime in the hopes that their release would be a good faith gesture by the Sandinistas. The Contra leaders subsequently met with State Department officials who persuaded them to tell the *Washington Times* that in their meeting, Wright said he was opposed to the release of the prisoners and *had* told them that the CIA had fomented the protest in Nandaime.

At a press conference several days later, a *Times* reporter repeated the State Department's garbled version of the story. Wright delicately pointed out that the conversation had said much the opposite. The CIA's past efforts to provoke the Sandinistas (which had already been publicly exposed in testimony offered by David MacMichael, one of the CIA's senior estimates officers for Latin America), had been counterproductive, Wright thought. These earlier revelations had of course led to the House Intelligence Committee's chair asking and receiving assurances from the CIA that it would no longer be involved in fomenting such provocations.

Wright was immediately accused of divulging a sensitive covert action and implicitly linking the CIA to the Nandaime riots. Then-Congressman Dick Cheney and leading Republicans quickly filed an ethics complaint against Wright for disclosing classified information, and the White House levied similar charges. Even without a formal ethics investigation Wright eventually resigned, even though the leak had emanated from the State Department, essentially in an effort to embarrass the Speaker. None of the debate centered on the more important question of whether the CIA had actually played a role at Nandaime; nobody ever actually denied that the CIA or the U.S. Embassy had tried to "provoke a CIA overreaction."[24]

These examples raise the question of who the congressional intelligence oversight committees serve: the public or the national security establishment. The House and Senate Intelligence Committees are required to make periodic reports to their respective chambers, but even when Congress wants to disclose information it feels may be in the public interest, the procedure is circuitous and presumes a need to "protect national security." The original resolution chartering SSCI, drafted by Senator William Brock (R-TN) in connection with a key recommendation of the Church Committee, required annual reports and information on intelligence funding to be made available to the public.[25] An amendment by Senator Robert Taft abandoned this key recommendation of the Church Committee and put in place the current rules (nearly identical to those in the House). Under those rules, the intelligence committee notifies the president of its intent to disclose classified information. If the president objects in writing within five days, a majority of the committee may refer the matter to the whole chamber for consideration in executive session. Then, following these secret deliberations, the question is voted on without divulging the vote's subject matter. According to the Center for National Security Studies, no president has ever filed a formal objection because a compromise has always been agreed to in advance.

The rationale for these rules is to protect sensitive information, and they do sometimes serve this purpose. But they also allow members of Congress to avoid facing moral choices that should be deliberated in public, and they replace the delicate art of good political judgment with an ossified national security impulse. One result is a profound evasion because it is in the members' interest. A second result is that Congress is unable to counter the executive branch's use of leaks with its own disclosures; the system not only undermines public knowledge, it gives the executive exclusive use of a modern tool of public policy, since most leaks originate in the executive branch.[26] Secrecy becomes a blunt tool for selling predetermined policies, promoting loyalty, and dodging debate.

HOLDING DEPARTMENT OF DEFENSE'S FEET TO THE FIRE

By using loopholes or by securing multiple sources of authority for the same purposes, unelected officials in other areas of the national security bureaucracy are able to operate with little supervision and limited public debate. Ongoing military training programs, weapons sales and grants, and long-term troop deployments throughout the world form the cornerstone of U.S. national security strategy and are all areas where this occurs.

The U.S. is by far the world's leading weapons exporter (accounting for a majority of arms exports worldwide), and each year every country in the Western Hemisphere except Cuba participates in military training with American troops. These operations continued (and in many cases escalated) after the end of the Cold War and because their planners in the National Security State apparatus have been able to protect the underlying goals of military and political control from criticism of the means used to achieve them. A good example is military training carried out by the U.S. Army School of the Americas (USARSA) in Fort Benning, Georgia.

The Army described USARSA to Congress in 1998 as "a key component in our nation's commitment to extending democratic ideals in the Latin American region" and noted that it "is recognized by the Army and Department of Defense as a center of excellence for human rights."[27] When the school faced congressional criticism in 1996, the Department of Defense (DoD) released seven training manuals that showed that students were taught murder, torture, and extortion techniques as standard parts of the curriculum.

The Pentagon responded in several ways, with the objective of convincing the critics that USARSA had reformed itself. First, DoD ordered a review by its inspector general, who claimed, among other things, the manuals were not cleared and that Army personnel were unaware they were contrary to army policy. A report issued by Congressman Joseph Kennedy (D-MA) in March 1997 proved that these claims were untrue and pointed out that the IG's report further made clear that no one was going to be held accountable. Second, the Pentagon continued to claim that the violations were unusual cases, when in fact two-thirds of those listed in the United Nations Truth Commission Report on El Salvador were USARSA graduates.

Similarly, the 1999 Guatemalan Truth Commission Report concluded that military forces and state controlled paramilitaries committed 93 percent of the human rights abuses and that U.S. counterinsurgency training from centers such as USARSA had "a significant bearing on human rights violations." Finally and most importantly, supporters of the school claimed its problems were behind it, ignoring the fact that information from the 1998 and 1999 State Department Annual Human Rights Reports and a February 2000 Human Rights Watch Report implicated the school's graduates in new violations involving murder, kidnapping, and torture. The latest reform package, proposed by the Pentagon in 2000, solved these problems by changing the name of the school to the Western Hemisphere Institute for Security Cooperation.

261

USARSA is only one part of the package, though. Other military training occurs under International Military Education and Training (IMET), created in 1976 for "traditional" military training; Expanded-IMET, created to provide noncombat training; and the Joint Combined Exchange Training (JCET), which grants ambassadors and regional military commanders the authority to order special forces training and deployments. State Department oversight of these programs, all of which are implemented by DoD, is supposed to ensure that they remain consistent with foreign policy objectives and meet human rights standards. But when Congress banned IMET assistance to Indonesia in 1992 due to human rights violations by a commando unit receiving the training, DoD simply continued it under JCET instead of terminating the program. The Pentagon claimed the continuation of the training under another name was legal because it was funded by a different pot of money, a loophole also used in Rwanda, where it gave marksmanship training to soldiers accused of participating in massacres.

Expanded-IMET and JCET were both created in 1991, and that year's Defense Authorization Act (Public Law 101-510) added new authority under Section 1004 for the Pentagon to finance and train foreign units if they are involved in counternarcotics operations. This authority created a loophole that enabled Colombia to receive military training for years despite a near total ban on military assistance. According to the Latin America Working Group, a Washington, D.C.-based coalition of human rights and advocacy organizations, this authority also allowed the Pentagon to start training counter-narcotics battalions a year before it formally requested the money.[29] Jean-Jacques Rousseau warned in *The Social Contract* that "Legislation is made difficult less by what it is necessary to build up than by what has to be destroyed" (Book II, 10). This was clearly the logic motivating the Pentagon. With the training already in place even before the policy was discussed, the DoD then went to Congress for money to equip the battalion it had trained with helicopters. National security managers committed the country's military to a dangerous mission requiring a long-term commitment before it even felt obligated to advance vague justifications for its involvement.

"A popular government without popular information or the means of acquiring it," wrote James Madison, "is but a Prologue to a Farce or a Tragedy or perhaps both." By overlooking instead of carefully overseeing the construction of the postwar foreign policy architecture and the domestic laws that supposedly bound it, Americans have routinized and, to some extent, legitimized the formulation of public policy through increasingly less public means; a dangerous precedent has been set. Accountability will remain elusive as long as the nation submits to parallel systems of truth: one public, based on shared histories and competing ideas, and the other private, based on the goals of unelected managers who put national myths at their service. The former seeks to live up to the promise of "ambition made to counter ambition," while the latter threatens the very notion of popular sovereignty. So what options does Congress have?

THE LEGISLATIVE BRANCH'S LAST RESORT

Because Congress does not know whether it owes its allegiance to the executive in matters of security and war or to the public at large, it will accept the judgments of the executive. This happens because the executive has control of most of the information and is in a position to generate lies and misstatements (as the recent case of the Iraq War demonstrates). Secondly, it is able to send forces to different parts of the world—often into battle—without congressional accountability or in anticipation of *post hoc* authorizing. Constant war and incursions put members in the position where they can be accused of not supporting the armed forces in battle or when they are in harm's way.

So where does the power of Congress derive and who is it serving? Although Congress is given the power to regulate the Army and Navy—and by extension the armed forces—this power was surrendered when Theodore Roosevelt used the fleet without authority of Congress at the beginning of the twentieth century, thus establishing a precedent. Congress did use its appropriations power to cut off increased funding to the South Vietnamese armed forces, although this occurred with the complete agreement of the Defense department; indeed there is evidence that the DoD realized that funds were being wasted. So the question remains: how to ensure personal accountability? One is through passage of a personal accountability act similar to the one introduced during the Watergate period by thirty-nine members of Congress to internalize the standards of the Nuremberg judgments into American law. Another option is through the use of impeachment. The impeachment provision of the Constitution is in the ultimate control of Congress. It is the provision that forces a change in leadership constitutionally, without waiting for elections, which in themselves may be tainted. And it serves as the message to the executive that its interest is not in being part of a national security system that dooms the American people to continuous war and breach of international law.

When should a president and officers of his government be impeached? When should Congress move to initiate impeachment proceedings against a sitting president? This question is raised more times than it is answered. And as Professor Cass R. Sunstein has said, there have been examples where impeachment could have been introduced but it was not.[30] Members of Congress fear retaliation against themselves in future elections if they raise the issue. Others fear that the orderly processes of government will be disrupted by impeachment proceedings. They claim that the consequences of such disruption are far worse than the results of a successful impeachment. Thus, legal authorities such as Sunstein remind us of the importance of stability and control over political appetites in heated moments when vengeance grips the citizenry against a sitting president. Their claim is that for the purpose of the health of the republic, impeachment should be considered only as a last resort against a president who has willfully overstepped his authority. Simplifying their view would apply a "smoking gun" standard. They would interpret their metaphor and the constitutional phrase treason, bribery, high crimes, and misdemeanors to

263

mean actions that are undeniable and easily proved. In this meaning one would think that impeachment should be brought where the security and well-being of the citizenry is radically degraded by the offenses of an officer of the United States. As in the case of Richard Nixon, one might accept the smoking-gun metaphor but apply it differently, linking it more closely to violations of separation of powers clauses of the Constitution on questions that are not trivial and in fact go to the character of the state itself.

The most egregious example of this case is that of a president who usurps the authority of Congress to make and declare war and in the process breaches international laws and obligations to which the United States is a signatory. This is the argument one former attorney general, Ramsey Clark, makes against President George W. Bush. His war in Iraq, according to this point of view, was predicated on a series of misstatements and lies that breached domestic and international laws and treaties, with the result that great harm came to American citizens. But is impeachment the proper remedy, and can it effectively end such violations given their gravity and the ambiguity of the impeachment clause?

There is no doubt that impeachment is a political matter, and in a constitutional system it means the protection of an institution's prerogatives, responsibilities, and the fundamental protections of the nation. These are more than niceties because they have very profound long-term consequences. This is not to say that the impeachment clause should be applied with abandon. Because it is a political matter, moods and concerns of congressional members, having heard from their constituents, over time will change. That is why impeachment is an issue dependent on a sitting Congress whose concerns need not carry over to a new Congress. As one distinguished former member, President Gerald Ford, said in his attempts to have Justice William O. Douglas impeached, impeachment is whatever Congress says it is and it may vary from Congress to Congress. Nevertheless, if the impeachment clause and process is more than a political poison pill to be used at will for the basest reasons, we must hold its use to situations where there is egregious violation and where, irrespective of an election, impeachment should be initiated. We must look analytically at it and the implications of when it is used, or for that matter, when not used and when indeed it should be used.

The problem of making war and authorizing it goes to the heart of the republican system of governing. And if a democratic republic is to be sustained, impeachment and conviction must have a central role as it relates to war-making. It must become a modern-day guide for governing and personal accountability, given the potentially catastrophic consequences in situations where a president believes there are no constitutional limits to his behavior, especially in the war-making arena. The relevance of the impeachment clause must be read in light of present-day conditions. While one shouldn't underestimate the importance of misdemeanors in high office, the twenty-first century political condition for the United States goes far beyond the problem of misdemeanors and peccadilloes.

265

★

Impeachment and conviction is seldom used against American public officials. In some cases the very mention that it will be applied has caused the alleged miscreant to resign from office. However, the sparing use of the impeachment clause may be a thing of the past not relevant to present conditions. In the twenty-first century, the damage a president is able to do is beyond anything imaginable in the eighteenth century, save the treasonous behavior of a president who would surrender the United States to a foreign power for personal gain. It is at least arguable that the use of nuclear weapons falls in the same category as actions destructive of the nation and the Constitution and by its nature is a treasonable offense as Arthur Miller has argued. (In the history of the American presidency, bribery has played a minimal part. Even in the presidencies of Grant, Harding, and Nixon, bribery in the usual sense did not apply. However, it should be pointed out that Vice President Spiro Agnew accepted bribes in the Executive Office building of the White House.[31] Such concerns, while important do not go to the systemic agony that faces the U.S. in the twenty-first century.)

Since various leaders undertook to turn the United States into an imperial power, in fact if not in name, the meaning of impeachment needs an update. Popular and congressional concern should center on the following:

(1) The weakness of Congress and the public in inhibiting or stopping the executive from initiating aggressive war. Congress cannot protect its power to declare war, a power not given constitutionally to the president except in the case of repelling an attack on the United States. The result is that the United States is engaged in continuous undeclared wars. Note, for example, President Bill Clinton who as president was not perceived as a warrior president although his use of military force including American troops outside of the Constitution was little short of breathtaking. The War Powers Act has been a dead letter because presidents have refused to recognize its authority, while at the same time sending Congress "courtesy letters" of notification.

(2) The National Security State organizes covert operations throughout the world intended to violate the sovereignty of other nations. The actions that have been taken in the past have included assassination, extortion, use of drugs, and bribery. The result is that the president, by his role in an imperial order, takes on an unconstitutional character. He becomes a broker between legal and illegitimate or criminal activities. The examples during the Cold War are legion. In the Cold War, spying, and covert operations were more than window peeping. While the CIA says that only its failures are known, not its successes, the extreme likelihood is that their "successes" have led to long- and short-term deleterious consequences, whether in Latin America, Africa, or Southeast Asia. One need only mention Guatemala, the Congo, and Indonesia.

(3) The question of weapons of mass destruction also raises the issue of how or whether the electorate is able to make its will known beyond supine acceptance to nuclear arming for war and claims that the common defense is protected through aggressive war.

As a constitutional matter, the stubborn fact is that there are no controls over a president in terms of the use of nuclear weapons. That is to say, the most dangerous weapons constructed could be ordered for first-strike use by any president without advice or approval by Congress against any target, whether out of presidential whim or aggressive

266

intention. The use of such weapons is not by consensus or constitutional procedures. To stop a president from ordering the use of nuclear weapons would be tantamount to a *coup d'etat* under present custom. This means there is a serious defect in the present system that requires correction. The impeachment clause, properly construed, can act as a deterrent against their use. The irony is that President Kennedy feared that he would be impeached if he was not prepared to use nuclear weapons against the Soviet Union during the Cuban Missile Crisis. But it is also true that impeachment can go the other way if the public fears an attack on U.S. soil. Thus President Kennedy thought he could be impeached if he was not prepared to use nuclear weapons to defend the U.S. from attack.[32]

A moment's reflection will lead one to conclude that there are deep flaws in American governing procedure. Something has to give. Either the imperial system is dropped, or the Constitution is dismantled. New documents would either directly eschew imperialism and executive war, or in the alternative, the United States would consciously embrace imperialism and war as the bedrock of a new American Constitution. These will be the choice unless the impeachment clause becomes an integral part of the calculus of going to war. Without clarity, war imperialism will trump Congress and turn it into a rubber stamp.

Professor Sunstein claims that applying the impeachment clause to presidents with regularity would increase instability and delegitimate the constitutional system. He applies the restraint that "cooler heads" have governed when the issue of impeachment was raised. But "cooler heads" have it backward. Obviously the impeachment clause should not be used lightly or for the wrong reasons, as it was in the case of President Clinton. But when it is introduced for matters that rise to the very fabric of the republic, then the impeachment clause, when it is invoked, becomes the constitutional surgical instrument to burst the boil that is poisoning the nation. Thus, in the case of Clinton, Congress could have impeached him, as Louis Fisher and David Gray point out, for "using military force on Baghdad, combat in Somalia, the Haiti occupation, air war in Bosnia, and dispatch of 20,000 troops there."[33] Instead, other grounds were used, which avoided the major issues of usurpation of constitutional authority as they related to war and war making.

The clause of impeachment is not the cause of instability. Its purpose is quite the reverse. The best use of the impeachment clause is as the protection against such actions as undeclared war, which a usurping president has no interest in surrendering. It should be noted that the war powers resolution passed in 1973 has been thought by all presidents to be a violation of their inherent power. It should be noted that Congress effectively surrendered its power to declare war in that resolution by giving a president the power to send troops for a "limited" period of time before obtaining ratification from Congress—that is, not a declaration of war. That was not good enough for Nixon and his successors. Instead, Congress and the public are to take at face value whatever is told to them. The intended result is that both the public and Congress accept roles as a manipulated mass to be "guided" by the whim of the executive. Resolutions are argued in Congress that are meant to give the appearance of participation but in fact are irrelevant to decisions already taken by the executive.

There is another way of applying the Constitution and executing the laws. Upholding the Constitution and the oath of office requires that officials accept limits to their office. Impeachment is the rifle on the wall to be sure that government officials do not undertake frolics of their own, aggressive war, or conduct war crimes. Impeachment is meant as the legal means to ensure that the nation is whole and that its leaders, whether judges, cabinet officials, the president, or vice president, perform according to the Constitution's deepest and widely held convictions, which will ensure freedom in the boundaries of law. To put this in a more homely way, the impeachment clause is not a straitjacket. It is, however, a set of clothes that all government officials are expected to wear. It should be noted that the trial of the Nazi leadership at Nuremberg was predicated on exactly this sentiment. And it was championed by the United States. But an expansionist nation seems to be bound not by law but the use of power in which law and constitution are afterthoughts, useful as a way to keep scholars and publicists chattering but having little, if any, effect on the operations of government.

We may note here several cases of importance from American history. Each of them suggests when impeachment should or should not be raised. In one case the impeachment went to the very nature of American life and its result dictated a malign conclusion for seventy-five years. The case of Andrew Johnson is instructive. Johnson's failure to be convicted in the Senate has been hailed by scholars and lawyers as a great victory for the constitutional system and prudence. One must wonder at such an interpretation of this event, for failure to convict shaped race relations in the United States for well over hundred years.

The political reason for his impeachment was that Johnson favored the Southern plantation owners after the civil war in getting and keeping property over the needs of the freed slaves whom he claimed should never be citizens. He kept blacks from participating in the conventions to redefine state constitutions in the Southern states, which would have allowed them full citizenship in the affairs of the Southern states. His failed conviction had the long-term policy effect of consigning blacks to a condition of legal servitude. However, it strengthened the power of the president in matters of appointment. Johnson had fired Stanton as secretary of war because he favored a comprehensive program to aid the freed slaves and saw no value in re-creating the antebellum conditions in the South. Radical Republicans championed this point of view and despaired at Johnson's neoslavery policies. Johnson replaced Stanton with a more pliable general. This enraged the radical Republicans and the tangled skein of constitutional politics brought a new constitutional crisis. The Senate claimed that Johnson had violated the Tenure of Office Act, which specifically stated that the president could not rid himself of an officer of the executive without agreement from the Congress where consent had been given to the appointment by Congress. The radical Republicans, led by Stevens and Sumner, saw Johnson, a Democrat, as attempting to undercut the power of Congress and squeeze it into a dependent and not a coequal branch. As important as this issue was, the more immediate and more profound issue came down to whether the former rebels would be reinstated in the Confederate states as they reentered the United States, permitting them the exercise of the electoral franchise to the exclusion of freed male slaves. In other words, would the ten rebel states when they returned to the Union be run by the Confederate forces that broke away from the Union? Would the Democratic Party take the entire South to its bosom and thereby assure the election of Johnson in 1868? The radicals feared the answer and ten articles of impeachment were brought against Johnson that passed the House.

In the Senate, Andrew Johnson won by one senator's vote with the result that the habit of mind of black oppression and exploitation would continue. The impeachment intervention was defeated. This meant that an attempt to bring about through the constitutional process, a means of reconstituting the union through constitutional means, expanding democracy, and articulating the purpose of the Civil War as an antislavery war lost operational legitimacy. The loss of this legitimacy meant that the post–Civil War reconstruction would, within a decade, be dominated by the slaveholders as the several thousand Union troops were withdrawn from the South in exchange for the Democrats supporting Hayes for president.

The failure of the Senate to convict emboldened returning Confederate soldiers to take their vengeance and defeat against the freed slaves, who had no place to go or turn. And by 1877 it was clear that the federal government would abandon blacks, turning them over to the states for disposition. In other words, Johnson's success and the failure of the radical Republicans resulted in massive misery for millions of Americans.

The unsavory arrangement that gave Rutherford Hayes the presidency over Samuel Tilden led to the buildup of American imperialism abroad, as it was taken for granted that the white-dominated version of manifest destiny could cross oceans to other lands.

The enlargement of the presidency, as Rexford Guy Tugwell called it, had baleful effects on the power of Congress and the long-term viability of the Constitution. His belief was that the presidency had to be expanded to match its imperial "responsibilities."[34] This imperial expansion can be seen in the structure of the presidency itself. During the Civil War, Lincoln had only a half a dozen advisors outside of the cabinet in the White House. Whether the Constitution would have proved to be more viable, and whether the nation could have remained a constitutional republic with a smaller government is arguable in the face of enormous problems of an economic, political, and social kind in the twentieth century especially given U.S. commitments to intervention. Thus, there were some who claimed that the United States should not invade the Philippines or invade Nicaragua, Guatemala, or Haiti. Given that these were small states that were not thought of as "white," there was little opposition to this form of blatant imperialism, which had no constitutional underpinning. Since the unelected President Johnson escaped conviction in the Senate, it would hardly have been fair for future presidents if they were impeached for sending troops to put down insurrections by nonwhite populations on their own authority. Even if there were no insurrections in Central America, from time to time they needed a spanking through the use of the military to be sure the poor nation paid its bills.

The great constitutional scholar Edward Corwin claimed that FDR had overstepped his authority by helping the British in direct violation of the neutrality acts. Leaders of the Senate (namely Charles McNarney, the Republican senator from Oregon) told Roosevelt that he should undertake the exchange of destroyers for bases with the British on his own authority because he would not receive the support from the Senate for that purpose; the move violated the neutrality act. This issue washed away with the destruction of part of the American fleet when the Japanese attacked Pearl Harbor and their ally Germany declared war on the United States. World War II enhanced the Constitution, although two steps were taken that had important effects. In expanding democracy, Roosevelt successfully urged the passing of legislation that would allow soldiers at the front to vote. Black soldiers who thought they were flying under the flag of freedom and democracy had a hard time surrendering that flag after the war when they returned home to South Carolina, Mississippi, or, for that matter, Detroit. The soldier's right-to-vote legislation had a powerful political effect as well, guaranteeing Roosevelt's reelection to a fourth term. War became, for some, a ticket to first-class citizenship in the American body politic and imperialism the means to ensure the kind of power wartime presidents take for themselves.

For example, Roosevelt, frustrated by a wartime Congress, put forward a series of proposed laws that Congress at first refused to pass. He responded with a threat. Unless Congress passed these bills, he would go ahead and enforce them in any case. Here again we see the expansion of the presidency; a way of organizing and implementing the office that had its roots in Jefferson's decision to acquire the Louisiana Territory outside of methods prescribed by the Constitution. Obviously there are many examples of this behavior, including Polk's war to acquire Mexican territory and Lincoln's support for one of his generals who had a congressman (Clement Vallingdham, D-OH) arrested for exercising his right of free speech when he spoke against Lincoln in the Civil War.

Arguably these events were individual actions. They did not reflect a sustained and continuous presidential pattern that grew out of an imperial thrust that became pathological during the Cold War.

What might have been a case of "forbearance and restraint" has reached an unconscionable level of congressional irresponsibility when not bringing forward impeachment charges on fundamental issues that cannot be resolved through election but which go to the very heart of the Constitution's obvious intention; namely, that initiating wars are not an executive's prerogative. It is in this context that the impeachment clause becomes the ultimate instrument to ensure legal behavior on the part of a president.

272

A second example of impeachment, the case of Richard Nixon is instructive in this regard. The House Judiciary Committee did not vote an article of impeachment against Nixon for engaging in a secret war against Cambodia. Nor did it vote to indict for tax evasion. Instead, its articles were narrowly drawn. Attempting to escape the humiliation of a Senate trial, Nixon resigned after the Judiciary Committee voted its impeachment recommendations. The three major claims against Nixon concerned: breaking into the Democratic party headquarters and attempts to cover up his role in the break in; use of various governmental agencies such as the FBI and Secret Service against citizens thereby violating their rights; and refusal to turn over papers that would have served as an evidentiary basis for the resolution of questions concerning Nixon's approval and knowledge of certain acts considered impeachable.

From the perspective of Nixon there was nothing he did that was different—and there is certainly substantial evidence to support his view that other presidents since the New Deal conducted themselves in similar fashion. All participated in military activities outside of the Declaration of War Clause, or, in the case of his successors, the War Powers Act. All assumed the right to use military power as they saw fit. All assumed that the impeachment clause did not touch activities performed as the commander in chief. And all believed that in the name of "national security" deception was not only permissible but necessary, either by the respective president's government or by the president himself. Certainly Eisenhower had no problem lying about the U2 matter, or sending troops on his own initiative to Lebanon. And certainly there was no authority for Kennedy supporting a U.S.–funded invasion of Cuba, just as there had been no such authority for Eisenhower's coup-induced activity in Guatemala. In Nixon's case, he believed that his activities as a warrior president would insulate him from constitutional attack. But his problems extended beyond his role as commander in chief. Perhaps because he overwhelmed George McGovern in the election of 1972, Nixon thought that he could successfully purge the government bureaucracy and castrate the East Coast establishment, which he believed held him in contempt. For Nixon, the impeachable issues were also dirty tricks and corruption, hardly a new feature of government, although they certainly fit within the traditional meanings of impeachment.

273

The irony was that Nixon and his band were not impeached for overthrowing the duly elected government of Chile, nor was there concern about the Christmas bombings, or the destruction of the dikes and harbors in Indochina ordered by Nixon. And yet these were political acts that fit well in the category of aggressive war, and were, therefore, impeachable offenses.

It is important to remember that the UN Charter remains the highest form of treaty adopted by the U.S. Senate (with one no vote). It became the law of the land at the end of World War II. The Charter argued in specific terms when a nation could go to war, and under what conditions. Aggressive war was the proscribed instrument. And under any disinterested reading of the charter and the American Constitution, Lyndon Johnson's wars had no constitutional authority. His coups and direct wars in Indonesia, Indochina, and the Dominican Republic fell exactly into the constitutional definition of the abuse of public power.

Throughout the period of the Cold War, managers of national security institutions were given the license or took the license to operate outside the law. This fact had two effects opposite in nature. On the one hand, national security managers saw no limits except those imposed upon themselves as to what they could do internationally, and even domestically, as the COINTELPRO program showed. Their arrogance was great because there was no personal accountability system in place, and there was no fear of impeachment, if for no other reason than that their activities were carried out secretly. The political reality was that unless the actions were so public and egregious, the will to impeach was not present. And when the impeachment instrument was used, it trivialized its high purpose. Yet it remained the best hope of constitutionalists; that is, of those who cared about political crimes. Obviously there can be abuses, once President Ford's standard is applied with prurient and vengeful abandon.

The successful indictment and failed conviction of President Clinton reflects the most foolish use of the impeachment power. That Clinton lied was obvious. And that he did so about his affair with Lewinsky was no different than what an ordinary married citizen might have done in similar circumstances, fearful of embarrassment before his wife and young daughter. But these cannot be construed as political crimes. As one of the founding fathers, James Wilson of Pennsylvania, aptly pointed out, the impeachment clause was to apply to political crimes carried out as president, and therefore is a political punishment. And here is the irony. To make the point clear: Clinton was not impeached for ordering the bombing of a medicine factory in the Sudan, nor for the egregious use of the military in combat during peacetime without the prior consent of Congress.

The distinction between George H.W. Bush and George W. Bush in the use of troops abroad is instructive and shows the complexities of what should or should not be an impeachable offense. The invasion of Panama falls well within the category of impeachable offense if we are to be constitutionalists. On the one hand, George H.W. Bush had done all he could to covertly restore suzerainty over Panama. When a coup against General Noriega failed on October 3, 1989, Bush approved a new $3 million covert action to overthrow the government. The Senate Intelligence Committee confidentially inquired of the executive about whether an operation that might result in the murder of Noriega would be a new, looser interpretation of the executive order prohibiting assassinations. Then–Defense Secretary Dick Cheney went on the offense for the administration, testifying that the restraints were too stringent. To improve its bargaining position, the White House went public, accusing Congress of "micromanaging" foreign policy; not unlike the case of Speaker Wright, it was the executive branch that leaked classified information to advance its policy.[35] On the other hand, Bush sought and received support for war against Iraq from the UN on the basis that Iraq had invaded Kuwait. Bush sought a franchise for war from the UN, which he received. Thus, he was seen as a law abider, even though as vice president he knew of and helped formulate the Iran-Contra trade in violation of the Boland Amendment.

274

The case of his son, George W. Bush, is significantly different. The attack with our own commercial airliners on New York, Pennsylvania, and Virginia allowed President George W. Bush three opportunities. By declaring that the United States effectively was in a war without end, various civil liberties could be violated or scaled back as they invariably are during wartime. The internment of Japanese Americans during World War II proves this point. Under George W. Bush, preventive detention has become a fact of American criminal law. Secret courts and wiretaps instituted under Clinton were greatly expanded, and military tribunals were refashioned for a new America continuously at war. The effect of this policy has meant the further centralization of power in the executive.

Ironically, prior to 1940, the Republican Party had been a peace party. Once the Cold War began, its old principles were pulled up by their roots and discarded, and it was easy for George W. Bush to be contemptuous of congressional prerogatives. Thus, he made war on Afghanistan to punish a gang of zealots. In the case of Haiti, the government brought down Aristide, in effect ordering the duly elected president to leave the country. In George W. Bush's first term, he invaded Iraq on the grounds that Iraq posed an imminent threat to the United States. Thus hundreds of thousands of people ended up being engaged in an undeclared war based on a series of lies. That an unelected president should have taken upon himself such a foreign and national security policy is an example of the type of political hubris, high crimes, and misdemeanors the impeachment clause could be used to proscribe—but only if the clause is taken seriously.

Some may wonder why this issue should be raised after President Bush's re-election in 2004. Impeachment goes beyond any particular election. It goes to the validity of congressional power, per se. It goes to the question of war making and other international acts, which have long been considered outside the ring of comity among nations. In this sense the impeachment clause, raised at the time of an election—or any time for that matter—where there is usurpation of the war-making power by the executive, is a political necessity if constitutional attention to freedom and separation of powers is to be sustained. It is the fundamental way to confront those institutions and habits of mind that have served the American people and the world very badly indeed. The question to ask is whether the United States is a warrior state, always at war, and if that is the state the American people are to live within. Not many in the course of American constitutional law have challenged this claim of vicious Hobbesianism.[36]

If the impeachment clause is not applied to egregious violations having to do with undeclared wars and activities attendant to them, it is well that we recognize the present Constitution is being scrapped. The executive branch as it relates to war, covert war, and nuclear war lives lawlessly, with little or no accountability. Presidents do not mind that situation since, as they say, they can make it up as they go along. Whatever the "it" is, wars by whim backfire, shaking the very foundation of democracy, causing the Constitution to become a mere artifact.

NOTES

1 These exemptions can be found at 8 U.S.C. 1427(c), 5 U.S.C. 305 and 5331, 16 U.S.C. 1536(j) and (k), and 42 U.S.C. 290dd-1 and 290ee-1, and 5 U.S.C. 2302(a).

2 See Fred Kaiser, "The Watcher's Watchdog: The CIA Inspector General," *International Journal of Intelligence and Counterintelligence*, no. 1 (spring 1989), 55–75.

3 "The Official Story: What the Government Has Admitted About CIA Ties to Drug Dealers," A Special Report of the Institute for Policy Studies, Washington, DC. The House oversight committee echoed the IG's conclusion in a report released May 11, 2000.

4 *Washington Post*, April 7, 1998, A10. See also Ralph McGehee, *Deadly Deceits: My 25 Years in the CIA* (New York: Sheridan Square Press, 1983)

5 Cited in Britt Snider, "Sharing Secrets with Lawmakers: Congress as a User of Intelligence," Center for the Study of Intelligence, Monograph No. 97–10001, Central Intelligence Agency, February 1997.

6 *Legislative Oversight of Intelligence Activities: The U.S. Experience.* Report Prepared by the Select Committee on Intelligence, S. Prt. 103–88, October 1994.

7 Intelligence Authorization Act for Fiscal Year 1981. Public Law 96-450 at 50 U.S.C. 413b.

8 Theodore Draper, *A Very Thin Line: The Iran-Contra Affairs* (New York: Hill and Wang, 1991).

9 Memorandum of Disapproval for the Intelligence Authorization Act, Fiscal Year 1991, November 30, 1990. Intelligence Authorization Act for Fiscal Year 1991 (Public Law 102–88 at 50 U.S.C. 413b).

10 Marcus Raskin, *The Politics of National Security* (New Brunswick: Transaction Books, 1979, 93). On the president as a broker, see Marcus Raskin, *Notes on the Old System: To Transform American Politics* (New York: David McKay Company, 1974).

11 "Saddam Hussein's Death Is a Goal, Says Ex-CIA Chief," *Washington Post*, February 15, 1998, A36.

12 Title 31 U.S.C. 716. See also 31 U.S.C. 712, 717, 3523, and 3524.

13 Statement by Henry Hinton of the GAO before the Subcommittee on Government Efficiency, Financial Management, and Intergovernmental Relations, and the Subcommittee on National Security, Veterans Affairs, and International Relations of the Government Reform Committee. July 18, 2001.

14 John Diamond, "Senate Votes to Halt Spending of $310 Million Spy Building," *Associated Press*, August 11, 1994; "The Spies Who Lost $4 Billion" *George*, October 1998; Pat Cooper, "U.S. Lawmakers Probe NRO Accounting Woes," *Defense News*, January 29–February 4, 1996; Tim Weiner, "A Secret Agency's Secret Budgets Yield 'Lost' Billions, Officials Say," *New York Times*, January 30, 1996.

15 *Congressional Record*, May 22, 1996, H5426.

16 Angus Mackenzie, *Secrets: the CIA's War at Home* (Berkeley, Los Angeles, and London: University of California Press, 1997).

17 Letter from DCI George Tenet to Chairman Stephen Horn, July 17, 2001 available at http://www.fas.org/irp/congress/2001_hr/071801_horn.html.

18 Glenn R. Simpson, "House Votes to Require Members' Secrecy Oaths," *Roll Call*, August 19, 1993, 12.

19 Dana Priest, "Torricelli Admits Violating House Secrecy Oath," *Washington Post*, April 8, 1995, p. A7.

20 Thomas Oliphant, "Punishing the Messenger," *Boston Globe*, April 11, 1995, 15. See also Frank J. Smist, *Congress Oversees the United States Intelligence Community, 1947–89* (Knoxville: University of Tennessee Press, 1990).

21 Philip Shenon, "Senator Durenberger Stirs New Concern with Outspokenness," *New York Times*, April 8, 1987, B6. Steven V. Roberts, "Congress: More Lessons in the Secrecy Trade," *New York Times*, April 10, 1986, B10.

22 Stephen Englemberg, "Iran-Contra Hearings: Senator Leahy Says He Leaked Report of Panel," *New York Times*, July 29, 1987, A1.

23 Jeffrey Richelson, *America's Secret Eyes in Space: The U.S. Keyhole Spy Satellite Program* (New York: HarperCollins, 1990). Also interviews with former congressional staff.

24 Jim Wright, *Worth It All: My War for Peace* (Washington and New York: Brassey's, 1993, 206–212). And telephone interview with Wright, August 17, 2001.

25 Loch Johnson, *A Season of Inquiry: The Senate Intelligence Investigation* (Lexington, KY: University of Kentucky Press, 1985).

26 For references on this, see Loch Johnson. *America's Secret Power: The CIA in a Democratic Society* (New York: Oxford University Press, 1989).

27 Statement by Major General Carl Ernst, U.S. Army, before the Readiness Subcommittee of the House National Security Committee, March 16, 1998.

28 Tim Weiner, "U.S. Training of Indonesia Troops Goes on Despite Ban," *New York Times*, March 17, 1998.

29 See also "Beyond the School of the Americas: U.S. Military Training Programs Here and Abroad," report by the World Policy Institute, May 2000.

30 References to Professor Sunstein are in response to his article, "Impeaching the President," found at 147 *University of Pennsylvania Law Review*, 279 (1998).

31 See Marcus Raskin, *Notes on the Old System* (New York: David McKaye and Company, 1974).

32 See McGeorge Bundy, *Danger and Survival: Choices About the Bomb in the First 50 Years* (New York: Random House, 1988).

33 Louis Fisher and David Gray Adler, "The War Powers Resolution: Time to Say Goodbye," *Political Science Quarterly* 113, no. 1 (Spring 1998), 1–20.

34 Rexford G. Tugwell, *The Enlargement of the Presidency* (Garden City, NJ: Doubleday, 1960).

35 Tom Kenworthy and Joe Pichirallo, "Bush Clears Plan to Topple Noriega; CIA Can Spend $3 million to Recruit Panama Rebels, Sources Say," *Washington Post*, November 17, 1989, A1. Ruth Marcus and Ann Devroy, "Bush Faults Rules Governing Covert Action Against Noreiga; 'Ambiguities' Could Require Giving Warning," *Washington Post*, October 23, 1989, A1.

36 See *New York Life Insurance Co. v. Bennion*, 158 F2nd260 (266) 10th circuit (1946). Contra analysis in Bernard Schwartz, *The Powers of Government*, Vol 2, 209 (New York: MacMillan, 1963).

278

15

MYTH VERSUS HYPOTHESIS

Norman Mailer

Since his reelection, George W. Bush has been more impressive in his personal appearances, more sure of himself, more—it is an unhappy word in this context but obligatory—he seems more authentic, more like a president.

I would warrant that before this last election he has always been the opposite of what he appeared to be, which is to say that he has worked with some skill to pass himself off as a facsimile of macho virtue. That is not unlike a screen star who has been alcoholic but is now, thanks to AA, a dry drunk who is able to look tough and ready on the screen. He never wavers when in peril. He is inflexible.

I would assert that inflexibility is not actually at the root of the president's character. Inflexibility serves, instead, to cover any arrant impulses that still smoke within. Of course, to keep all that stuff to oneself is not a happy condition for a commander in chief.

This speech, delivered in Cambridge at the 2004 Nieman Conference on Narrative Journalism, was sponsored by the Nieman Foundation for Journalism at Harvard University.

If we contrast George W. to his parents, it is probably fair to say that his father was manly enough to be president, but seemed unable to escape his modesty. Indeed, for all one knew, it was genuine. He must have sensed that he was not quite bright enough for the job. Barbara Bush had, doubtless, more than enough character to be first lady, yet so long as she was obscured by the obliterative shadow cast by Nancy Reagan, she was seen as not elegant enough. In turn, their oldest son, George, in contrast to his father, was neither an athlete nor a fighter pilot. He was a cheerleader. That, in itself, might have been enough to drain some good part of his self-respect. It is not easy to be surrounded by football players when you are just as tall and large as most of them, but are not as athletic. The son, out of necessity perhaps, developed his own kind of ego. He turned out to be as vain as sin, and as hollow as unsuccessful sin.

If this sense of Bush's character is well-based, then one must accept the increment of strength that victory offers to such a man. He now feels as entitled to national respect as the dry-drunk screen star after a box-office smash. One can see the magnitude of George W's personal happiness now. The smirk is gilt-edged these days.

In contrast, the woe one encounters among Democrats is without parallel. Just as no president, not even Richard Nixon, was so detested, so was the belief implicit, just the week before the election, that no matter how deadlocked the polls, it was inconceivable that Bush could triumph. This conviction was most intense among the young. Now, the prevailing mood among many young Democrats is not unlike the disbelief that attends the sudden death of a mate or a close friend. One keeps expecting the deceased to be sitting at the table again. Or, the door-bell will ring and there he will be. But, no, he is not there. Bush is the victor, not Kerry. It is analogous to the way people who have been kidnapped by the intensity of a dream have to keep reminding themselves on awakening, "I am not in Katmandu. I am in my own bedroom. There will be no deliverance from George W. Bush. I will ḥ̶ve to see his face for the next four years."

Of course, if Kerry had won Ohio and so had become president ẹ̶ a deficit of several million votes, the situation down the road ṿe proved disastrous for Democrats. Kerry, given his 50-50 ̶̣he war, would have had to pay for all of Bush's mistakes in

Iraq. He would then have inherited what may yet be Bush's final title: Lord Quagmire!

The truth is that neither candidate proved ready to say why we are really there. Indeed, why? Why, indeed, are we in Iraq? It is likely that a majority of Americans are looking for that answer, no matter whom they voted for.

Undeniably, I am one of them. I have probably spent a fair part of the last two years brooding over this question. Like most large topics which present no quick answers, the question becomes obsessive.

This afternoon, let me make one more attempt. I would ask, however, that you allow me to do it through the means by which I think. I do not come to my conclusions with the mental skills of a politician, a columnist, a journalist, an academician in foreign relations or political science, no, I brood along as a novelist. We novelists, if we are any good, have our own means.

What may establish some mutuality with this audience, however, is that we do have one firm basis in common. Good novelists and good journalists are engaged, after all, in a parallel search. We are always trying to find a better approach to the established truth. For that truth is usually skewed by the needs of powerful interests.

Journalists engage in this worthy if tricky venture by digging into the hard earth for those slimy creatures we call facts, facts that are rarely clear enough to ring false or true.

Novelists work in a different manner. We begin with fictions. That is to say, we make suppositions about the nature of reality. Put another way, we live with hypotheses which, when well-chosen, can enrich our minds and—it is always a hope—some readers' minds as well. Hypotheses are, after all, one of the incisive ways by which we try to estimate what a reality might be. Each new bit of evidence we acquire serves to weaken the hypothesis or, to strengthen it. With a good premise, we may even get closer to reality. A poor one, sooner or later, has to be discarded.

Take the unhappy, but super-excited state that a man or woman can find themselves in when full of jealousy. Their minds are quickened, their senses become more alert. If a wife believes her husband is having an affair, then every time he comes home, she is more aware of his presence than she has been in previous weeks, months, or years. Is he guilty? Is the way in which he folds his napkin a sign of some unease? Is he being too accommodating? Her senses quicken at the possibility that another woman—let us call her Victoria—is the object of his attention. Soon, the wife is all but convinced that he is having an affair with Victoria. Definitely. No question. But, then, on a given morning, she discovers that the lady happens to be in China. Worse. Victoria has actually been teaching in Beijing for the last six months. Ergo, the hypothesis has been confuted. If the wife is still convinced that the husband is unfaithful, another woman must be substituted.

The value of an hypothesis is that it can stimulate your mind and heighten your concentration. The danger is that it can distort your brain. Thoughts of revenge are one example. The first question may be: Am I too cowardly to exercise this revenge? One can wear oneself down to the bone with that little suspicion. Or, one's moral sense can be activated. Does one have the right to seek revenge? Hypotheses on love usually prove even more disruptive. The most basic is, of course: Am I really in love? Is this love? How much am I in love? What is love, after all? To a family man, the question can become: How much do I love my children? Am I ready to sacrifice myself for them? Real questions. Questions that have no quick answer. Good hypotheses depend on real questions, which is to say questions that do not always generate happy answers.

Patriotism offers its set. For some, it is not enough to wave a flag. The people in fascist countries always wave flags. So, some Americans are still ready to ask whether it is false patriotism to support our country under any and all conditions. Others, a majority, no doubt, seem to feel that one's nation demands an unquestioning faith, and so you must always be ready to believe that the people of our nation are superior— by their blood alone—to the people of other nations. In that sense, patriotism is analogous to family snobbery. Indeed, one can ask whether patriotism is the poor man's equivalent of the upper-class sense of inbred superiority.

These questions can provoke us to ask: What is the nature of my
 now? Do we have the right to be in Iraq? Why are we there?
we look at the familiar answers that have been given to us by
ration, the media, and the opposition, allow me an excur-
ntrigues me most about good hypotheses is that they
elation to good fiction. The serious novel looks for

situations and characters who can come alive enough to surprise the writer. If he or she starts with one supposition, the actions of the characters often lead the story some distance away from what was planned. In that sense, hypotheses are not only like fictions but can be compared to news stories—once the situation is presented, subsequent events can act like surprisingly lively characters ready to prove or disprove how one thought the original situation would develop. The value of a good hypothesis, like a good fiction, is that whether it all turns out more or less as expected, or is altogether contrary, the mind of the reader as well as the author is nonetheless enriched.

A good novel, therefore, like a good hypothesis, becomes an attack on the nature of reality. (If attack seems too violent a notion here, think of it as intense inquiry.) But the basic assumption is that reality is ever-changing—the more intense the situation, the more unforseeable will be the denouement. Reality, by this logic, is not yet classified. The honor, the value of a serious novel rests on the assumption that the explanations our culture has given us on profound matters are not profound. Working on a novel, one feels oneself getting closer to new questions, better ones, questions that are harder to answer. It's as if in writing novels, you don't assume there are absolutes or incontrovertible facts. Nor do you expect to come to a firm or final answer. Rather the questions are pursued in the hope they will open into richer insights, which in turn will bring forth sharper questions.

Let me then repeat the point. Novelists approach reality, but they do not capture it. No good novel ever arrives at total certainty, not unless you are Charles Dickens and are writing *A Christmas Carol.* Just so, few hypotheses ever come to closure. Not every Victoria teaches in China.

This much laid out, I am almost ready to leave this long introduction to what I have yet to say. But for the sheer fun of the next notion, let me present it as a lagniappe, not necessary for my argument, but there for its flavor. So I would claim that one more interesting bond between hypothesis and serious fiction is that they both have something to say about the living forms of sex. For a long time, I've amused myself with the notion that the poem, the short story, and the novel can be compared to phases of sex. The short poem, certainly, is analogous to a one-night stand. It may come off as brilliant, or it can be a bummer. A love affair of reasonable duration is, all too often, like a short story. What characterizes most short stories is that they look to suggest something forthright by the end. In their crudest form, when young men write their early pieces, the last sentence almost always has its echo of: "He felt old, and sad, and tired." By analogy, it may be fair to say that few affairs come to an end without being characterized—usually uncharitably—by the participants. Marriage, however, like a novel, is closer to a metamorphosis of attitudes. The end of one chapter may leave the husband and wife ready to break up; they cannot bear each other. In the morning, which commences the next chapter, they discover to their mutual surprise that they are back in the sack. Reality varies from chapter to chapter.

284

I wonder if I have used this to suggest that many of us who do not hold fundamental beliefs approach our sense of reality, therefore, by way of our working hypotheses, even by our larger literary forms. It is certainly true that on the road to Iraq, we were offered more than a few narratives for why we were so obviously hell-bent for war.

In the beginning, some said that George W. Bush, was trying to validate his father by occupying Baghdad—others argued that he wished to appear superior to George H.W. Two opposed hypotheses. Each made a neat one-page article for one or another magazine.

Another hypothesis which soon arose was that such a war would be evil. Shed no blood for oil. That became the cry. Quite likely, it was correct in part, at least, but it was as harsh in argument as the prose of any ill-written tract. Others offered a much more virtuous reason: Conquering Iraq would democratize the Middle East. Problems between Israel and Palestine could be happily settled. In the event, this proved to be nearer to a fairy tale than a logical proposition.

In its turn, the administration presented us with weapons of mass destruction. That lived in the American mind like an intelligence thriller. Would we locate those nightmares before they blew us up? It became the largest single argument for going to war. Colin Powell put his political honor on the chopping block for that assertion.

There were other hypotheses—would we or would we not soon find Osama bin Laden? Which became a short story like "The Tiger and the Lady"—no ending. On the eve of war, there was a blood-cult novel in the night. It was Shock and Awe—had we driven a quick stake through the heart of Saddam Hussein? Good Americans could feel they were on the hunt for Dracula.

Vivid hypotheses. None held up. We did not learn then and we still do not begin to agree why we embarked on this most miserable of wars. Occam's razor does suggest that the simplest explanation which is ready to answer a variety of separate questions on a puzzling matter has a great likelihood of being the most correct explanation. One answer can emerge then from the good bishop's formula: it is that we marched into a full-sized war because it was the simplest solution the president and his party could find for the immediate impasse in which America found itself. (Besides—a war would authenticate his Florida presidency.) Yes, how much we needed a solution to our developing problems.

The first problem, which could yet become the most worrisome, was that the nation's scientific future, and its technological skills, seemed to be in distress. American students at STEM studies— S.T.E.M., science, technology, engineering and mathematics—no longer appeared to be equal to those Asian and European students who were also studying advanced courses at our universities. For pleasure-loving American students, STEM subjects may have seemed too difficult, too unattractive. Moreover, the American corporation was now ready to outsource its own future, even eager to do so. Given drastically lower factory wages in Third World countries, there may have appeared no alternative to maintain large profits. All the same, if American factory jobs were now in danger of disappearing, and our skills at technology were suffering in comparison to Europe and to Asia, then relations between American labor and the corporation could go on tilt. That was not the only storm cloud over the land.

Back in 2001, back before 9/11, the divide between pop culture and fundamentalism was gaping. In the view of the religious right, America was becoming heedless, loutish, irreligious, and blatantly immoral. Half of all American marriages were ending in divorce. The Catholic Church was suffering a series of agonizing scandals. The FBI had been profoundly shaken by moles in their woodwork who worked for the Soviets and a Mafia killer on close terms with their own agents on the scene.

Posed with the spectre of a superpower, our own superpower, economically and spiritually out of kilter, the best solution seemed to be War. That would offer an avenue for recapturing America—not, mind you, by unifying the country, not at all. By now, that was close to impossible. Given, however, that the country was deeply divided, the need might be to separate it further in such a way that one's own half could become much more powerful. For that, Americans had to be encouraged to live with all the certainties of myth while by-passing the sharp edge of inquiry implicit in hypothesis.

The difference is crucial. An hypothesis opens the mind to thought, to comparison, to doubt, to the elusiveness of truth. If this country was founded in great part on the notion that enough people possessed enough good will, and enough desire for growth and discovery to prosper, and this most certainly included spiritual and intellectual discovery, then, or so went the premise, democracy could thrive more than monarchy or theocracy.

Of course, all these political forms depend on their myths. Myths are tonic to a nation's heart. If abused, however, they are poisonous. For myths are frozen hypotheses. Serious questions are answered by declaration and will not be re-opened. The need is for a morality tale at a child's level. Good will overcome a dark enemy. For the Bush administration, 9/11 came as a deliverance. The new myth even bore some relation to reality. There was no question that Islamic terrorists were opposed to all we stood for, good or bad. They did not call us the Great Satan for too little. Nonetheless, the danger presented by this enemy had to be expanded. Our paranoia had to be intensified. We were encouraged to worry about the security of every shopping mall in America. The overriding myth was not merely the implacable danger of Islam, but its nearness to us. To oppose the fears we generated in ourselves, we would call on our most dynamic American myths. We had had, after all, a lifetime of watching action films.

The possibility of weeding terrorists out through international police action never came into real question. We needed much more than that. War is, obviously, a mightier rallying ground than a series of local police actions. Yet, half of America was opposed to our advance toward war with Iraq. Half of us were asking one way or another: "How much goodness has America brought to the world? How much has it exploited the world?"

The president, however, had its own imperatives. Keep America fixed on myth. He went all the way back to Cotton Mather. We must war constantly against the invisible kingdom of Satan. Stand at Armageddon and battle for the land. It was fortified by a belief which many Republicans, some of the most intelligent and some of the most stupid, accepted in full. It was the conviction that America was exceptional, and God had a special interest in America. God wanted us to be a land superior to other nations, a realm to lift His vision into greater glory. So, the myth of the frontier, which demanded a readiness to fight without limit, became part of our exceptionalism. "Do what it takes." No matter how deeply one was embedded in near to inextricable situations, one would complete the job, "Bring 'em on!" The myth was crucial to the Bush administration. The last thing it needed was to contend with anything like a real approach to reality.

This attempt to take over the popular American mind has certainly not been unsuccessful, but it does generate a new and major hypothesis which would argue that the people of the U.S. were systematically, even programmatically, deluded from the top down. Karl Rove was there to recognize that there were substantial powers to be obtained by catering to stupid stubborn people, and George W. Bush would be the man to harvest such resources. George W. was not stupid, but he understood stupid people well. They were not dumb, their minds were not physically crippled in any way. They had chosen to be stupid because that offered its own kind of power. To win a great many small contests of will, they needed only to ignore all evidence. Bright people would break down trying to argue with them. Bush understood this, and he knew how to use this tool. With a determination that only profound contempt for the popular mind can engender, we were sold the notion that this war would be honorable, necessary, self-protective, decent, fruitful for democracy, and dedicated to any and all forms of human goodness. I would suggest that there was close to zero sincerity at the top. The leaders of this country who forced the war through, were neither idealistic nor innocent. They had known what they were doing. It was basic. Do what it takes. They had decided that if America was to be able to solve its problems, then the country had to become an empire. For American capitalism to survive, exceptionalism rather than cooperation with other advanced nations had become the necessity. From their point of view, there had been ten lost years of initiatives, ten years in the cold, but America now had an opportunity to cash in again on the great bonanza that had fallen its way in 1991 when the Soviet Union went bankrupt in the arms race. At that point, or so believed the exceptionalists, America could and should have taken over the world and thereby safeguarded our economic future for decades at least with a century of hegemony to follow. Instead, these exceptionalists had been all but consumed with frustration over what they saw as the labile pussyfooting of the Clinton administration. Never have liberals been detested more. But now, at last, 9/11 had provided an opportunity for America to resolve some problems. Now, America could embark on the great adventure of empire.

These exceptionalists also happened to be hard-headed realists. They were ready to face the fact that most Americans might not have any real desire for global domination. America was pleasure-loving, which, for exceptionalist purposes, was almost as bad as peace-loving. So, the invasion had to be presented with an edifying narrative. That meant the alleged reason for the war had to live in utter independence of the facts. The motives offered to the American public need not have any close connection to likelihoods. Fantasy would serve. As, for example, bringing democracy to the Middle East. Protecting ourselves against weapons of mass destruction. These themes had to be driven home to the public with all the paraphernalia of facts, supposed confirmative facts. For that, who but Colin Powell could serve as the clot-buster? So, Powell was sold a mess of missile tubes by the CIA. Of course, for this to work, the CIA also had to be compromised. That was there to be done. Most people in the CIA are career-motivated. Advancing one's career does not often have much to do with getting the right stuff in intelligence. Successful people in the Agency, as in many another bureaucracy, get to where they are by knowing what is wanted at the top. While intelligence, in itself, is ideally an ascetic activity, it can, like most ascetic endeavors, be miserably corrupted. Doubtless, that is true of every intelligence agency in the world. They end up producing what they feel is needed for their country, for their own career, or just for their next step. When such factors are at odds with each other, Intelligence pays the price. So the CIA was abominably compromised by the move to go to war with Iraq. Most analysts who had information that Iraq had very little or nothing in the way of WMD gave it up. The need at the top of the Agency to satisfy the president cut them off. So we went forward in the belief that Iraq was an immediate threat, and were told that hordes of Iraqis would welcome us with flowers. Indeed, it was our duty as good Americans to bring democracy to a country long-dominated by an evil man.

Democracy, however, is not an antibiotic to be injected into a polluted foreign body. It is not a magical serum. Rather, democracy is a grace. In its ideal state, it is noble. In practice, in countries who have lived through decades and centuries of strife and revolution and the slow elaboration of safeguards and traditions, democracy becomes a political condition which can often withstand the corruptions and excessive power-seeking of enough humans to remain viable as a good society.

It is never routine, however, never automatic. Like each human being, democracy is always growing into more or less. Each generation must be alert to the dangers that threaten democracy as directly as each human who wishes to be good must learn how to survive in the labyrinths of envy, greed, and the confusions of moral judgment. Democracy, by the nature of its assumptions, has to grow in moral depth, or commence to deteriorate. So, the constant danger that besets it is the unadmitted downward pull of fascism. In all of us there is not only a love of freedom, but a wretchedness of spirit that can look for its opposite—as identification with the notion of order and control from above.

The real idiocy in assuming that democracy could be brought to Iraq was to assume that its much-divided people had not been paying spiritually for their compromises. The most evil aspect of fascism is that all but a few are obliged to work within that system or else their families and their own prospects suffer directly. So the mass of good people in a fascist state are filled with shame, ugly memories of their own small and occasionally large treacheries, their impotence, and their frustrated hopes of revenge. Willy-nilly, their psyches are an explosive mess. They are decades away from democracy. There is no quick fix. Democracy has to be earned by a nation through its readiness for sacrifice. Ugly lessons in survival breed few democrats.

It is all but impossible to believe that men as hard-nosed, inventive, and transcendentally cynical as Karl Rove or Dick Cheney, to offer the likeliest two candidates at hand, could have believed that quick democracy was going to be feasible for Iraq.

We are back to oil. It is a crude assertion, but I expect Cheney, for one, is in Iraq for just that reason. Without a full wrestler's grip on control of the oil of the Middle East, America's economic problems will continue to expand. That is why we will remain in Iraq for years to come. For nothing will be gained if we depart after the new semi-oppressive state is cobbled together. Even if we pretend it is a democracy, we will have only a nominal victory. We will have gone back to America with nothing but the problems which led us to Iraq in the first place plus the onus that a couple of hundred billion dollars were spent in the quagmire.

Let me make an attempt to enter Cheney's mind. I think, as he sees it, it will be crucial to hang in at all costs. New sources of income are going to be needed, new trillions, if for nothing else than to pay for the future social programs that will have to take care of the humongously large labor force that will remain endemically jobless because of globalism. That may yet prove to be the final irony of Compassionate Conservatism. It will expand the role of government even as it searches for empire.

Cheney's looming question will be then how to bring off some sizable capture of Iraq's oil profits. Of course, he is no weak man, he is used to doing what it takes, no matter how it smells, he is full of the hard lessons passed along by the collective wisdom of all those Republican bankers who for the last hundred and twenty-five years have been foreclosing on widows who cannot keep up with the mortgage on the farm. Cheney knows. You cannot stop a man who is never embarrassed by himself—Cheney will be full of bare-faced virtue over why—for the well-being of all—we have to help the Middle East to sell its oil properly. We will deem it appropriate that the Europeans are not to expect a sizable share since, after all, they do not deserve it, not given their corrupt deals with Hussein under so-called UN supervision. Yes, Cheney will know how to sell the package for why we are still in Iraq, and Rove will be on his flank, guiding Bush on how to lay it out for the American people.

It seems to me that if the Democrats are going to be able to work up a new set of attitudes and values for their future candidates, it might not be a bad idea to do a little more creative thinking about the question for which they have had, up to now, naught but puny suggestions—which is how do you pick up a little of the fundamentalists' vote.

If by 2008, the Democrats hope to come near to a meaningful fraction of such voters, they will have to find candidates and field workers who can spread the word down south—that is, find the equivalent of Democratic missionaries to work on all those good people who may be in awe of Jehovah's wrath, but love Jesus, love Jesus so much

more. Worked upon with enough zeal, some of the latter might come
to recognize that these much-derided liberals live much more closely
than the Republicans in the real spirit of Jesus. Whether they believe
every word of Scripture or not, it is still these liberals rather than the
Republicans who worry about the fate of the poor, the afflicted, the
needy, and the disturbed. These liberals even care about the well-being
of criminals in our prisons. They are more ready to save the forests,
refresh the air of the cities, and clean up the rivers. It might be agonizing for a good fundamentalist to vote for a candidate who did not
read the Scriptures every day, yet some of them might yet be ready to
say: I no longer know where to place my vote. I have joined the ranks   291
of the undecided.

More power to such a man. More power to all who would be ready
to live with the indecision implicit in democracy. It is democracy,
after all, which first brought the power and virtue of good questions to
the attention of the people rather than restricting the matter to the
upper classes.

Long may good questions prevail.

★

CONCLUSIONS

16

OUT OF THE SHADOWS

Marcus G. Raskin

In the late spring of 1961, just a few months after the disastrous Bay of Pigs, I attended a civil defense meeting in the White House that deserves some retelling. The meeting with President Kennedy was staged for a group of governors chaired by Pat Brown of California. But the most concerned and outspoken of the committee was Governor Nelson Rockefeller, who had pressed for a comprehensive civil-defense-shelter building program that would include blast shelters. There was a political subtext to the discussions.

The White House staff believed that Rockefeller was the likely presidential candidate of the Republican Party in 1964, and so members of the staff—and the president—listened carefully to his views. Nelson and David Rockefeller had just sponsored a series of studies on "the American Purpose." In 1960 elites were concerned that the United States had no national purpose to mobilize around—a requirement of any self respecting state, it was thought. These well-publicized studies on America's purpose had included special reports on defense, national security, and foreign policy. That part of the study was prepared by Henry Kissinger, a rising star in the national security firmament. For the members of the study committee, the twin pillars of American power were its imperial military thrust, which some White House advisors believed would be tested in Indochina and internal economic growth, which would be enhanced through military Keynesianism. So it was not surprising that the question of civil defense, especially after the Bay of Pigs fiasco, and the American mission in the Far East would be discussed. For some among the less informed, the civil defense fallout shelter program was thought to be a protection of the population against nuclear attack. But this was naïve. This view was correctly thought to be impossible by those aware of the nuclear arsenal of the Soviets. For others, civil defense was thought about in psychological terms. It was a "will stiffener" that would grant the president the tool of flexibility because the populace would think of themselves as safe. As President Kennedy and Ted Sorensen, his advisor, came to understand, this was an absurd idea. Indeed, the Soviets would fear that the United States was preparing for a first strike, which would cause them to increase their missile program. It would mean that the United States would be prepared to risk the lives of millions of its own citizens, even in a first strike against Soviet military bases. (Such notions were framed in the phraseology of preemptive and preventive attacks.)

In fact the idea of civil defense shelters inspired conflict and fear in the American public; the white South did not want to share public fallout shelters with blacks, and those with fallout shelters threatened to shut out interlopers from neighboring states. The report on civil defense was given by General Overbeck, who stated that we could not leave our CONU.S. (translation: continental United States) "naked to attack," a phrase that resulted in some smiles at what seemed to be a double entendre dropped into the discussion by Dr. Strangelove. (Needless to say, the different color schemes of the current Bush administration's Homeland Security chief were reminiscent of the Kennedy period and his flirtation with fallout shelters.)

Another briefing was presented at the meeting that turned out to be more telling because it showed the various sides of America both in one man and in what the United States believed its role in the world was to be. In 1961 the Deputy Director of the Central Intelligence Agency was Robert Amory; his briefing was chilling. Diem, we were told, the head of South Vietnam, handpicked by the United States. Under U.S. guidance, he sought to centralize his authority and power.

The Vietcong and the "locals" were unceremoniously assassinating the Diem men; apparently the villagers wanted to choose their own village chiefs. This part of the equation was not shared with the governors. As Amory spoke, Governor Rockefeller interrupted with a note of exasperation and disgust about the Vietcong and their tactics. He contributed his analysis by saying, "Those dirty guys. Why don't they fight fair?" and no more than a few minutes went by when Rockefeller interjected again: "Mr. President, why don't we use tactical nuclear weapons on them?" The idea of nuclear weapons use in high policy circles was standard fare although this time it was gently dismissed by Kennedy. The Rockefeller notion was resurrected and seriously considered during the battle of Khe sanh where nuclear weapons were rejected during the Johnson presidency as tactically impractical.

Some believed the American mission was a religious one, blessed with nuclear weapons. Because the United States, it was said, had no ulterior or crass interests, it was allowed to use any weapons in its armamentarium and enter or make wars of its own choosing. Since the successful tests in the New Mexico desert in 1945, nuclear weapons were like a brooding omnipresence, just as the secrecy system and the attendant military plans included ways to fight nuclear and nonnuclear war on someone else's soil. This was understandable given the frightful cost brought to the United States in terms of wounded and dead as a result of the Civil War.

The underlying assumptions were that questions of national security and foreign policy had to be decided by elites who would speak with one voice, and whose task was to "educate" the American people.[1] Obviously, from time to time, golden lies would have to be told and criminal actions would have to be hidden under the name of national security, which was thought to be of a "higher nature," involving interests and purposes beyond any particular group. Elites knew how to take care of us and, where necessary, take account of our material needs. But this book and the half dozen years of seminars prior to its conception contradict that conceit. While most of us live within the cocoon of national security, few know what the contours of that cocoon are. This is tragic, for Americans do not know how to assess their collective public experience in a way that illuminates and demystifies what is going on, what are offered as facts, what the bills are for, mistakes, and who pays for them. The result is that when the structure

297

is found wanting, we merely build on the old structures and assumptions. As citizens we romanticize and deceive ourselves, believing in authority and accepting the secrecy of the bureaucracy and political leadership. We are quick to forget and suspend our disbelief to evade what the United States government does in the name of the American people. But while facts may be more malleable than we like to believe, they cannot be denied or explained given their consequences, as for example in the case of the Indochina War, where illusion and self-deception could no longer be held in the face of stubborn reality. If, as these essays show, our established analysis of the Cold War policies and institutions, as well as habits of mind that emerged from them, are flawed, and, as I have said, even criminal in many cases, then we must be mindful of not repeating the dreary reality of the past century: a century that many look upon with yearning and clarity. But that is not the reality, and if we insist on thinking about those days uncritically as our halcyon period, the twenty-first century will bring dismal days. Indeed we will miss the profound positive changes that did come about in the twentieth century.

In our attempts at romanticizing the past, we forget that Nixon was spat upon in Venezuela when he visited there because of American policies in Latin America; the United States ratcheted up the arms race with thermonuclear weapons construction; it encouraged rebellion in Hungary and then backed away from supporting the rebels; American nuclear weapons were lost at sea; leaders, experts, and journalists believed that deterrence was a costless strategy for the United States. Not many cared to see that this "costless" deterrence strategy of over $5 trillion has deadly consequences when we tally the quantity of nuclear waste material that hangs on humanity like a huge noose for the next few thousand years. Perhaps it is unimportant that tens of thousands of scientists and technologists around the world used their lives in doing work that should not have been done in the first place. In the United States, defense appropriations became (and remain) a giant cash cow for defense corporations and congressional districts having no relationship to any sober analysis of defense needs. Disarmament as an alternative strategy was not able to withstand the drumbeat of war and war preparation presented as defense. Disarmament without government planning meant loss of jobs, contracts, and status for hundreds of thousands. There seemed to be no workable plan as an alternative to the National Security State–Cold War syndrome that could gain traction with members of Congress. In short spurts there were moments when comprehensive disarmament seemed necessary and realistic, whereas the continuation of the arms race and pursuing unilateral strategies was the foolish dream of imperial utopians. It is true that an incrementalist approach to the arms race was negotiated. It was arms control that pitted the United States with the Soviet Union as *de facto* and *de jure* partners who would arm together but not present a systemic alternative. Partial and highly technocratic treaties were negotiated, which effectively kept the American people, indeed the world's people, out of the debate and the process of systemic change. Military technology was expanded under arms control, with attendant sky rocketing costs. For the United States, that increasingly sophisticated military technology and increased troop size would justify its expense in any kind of war American leaders, more specifically the president and his entourage, or the national security bureaucracy, might care to fight. All manner of war was prepared for, including fighting two and a half wars simultaneously, one of which would be nuclear, others would be limited and nonnuclear as well as covert. Before the Cuban Missile Crisis, which frightened the leaders of the United States and the Soviet Union into a measure of sanity, the world lumbered ever closer to nuclear disaster even as it does now with American leadership believing it has finally achieved single superpower status.

Such policies have been ill-conceived and often went unchallenged in civil society, that is in the universities, the labor unions, and the media. Events since 1945 stand as a warning to the United States that its policies were ill-conceived. The result was that the state apparatus it was building would give rise to hysteria and Manichean beliefs of good and evil, which exempted the United States from critical assessment of its own policies and directions. For much of the Cold War period, oaths of loyalty to the government and the state apparatus were the price of employment in universities and government. It was the loyalty oaths in government or industry, which preceded McCarthyism, that caused civic fear and suspicion to spread through the society like an uncontrolled flu epidemic.

There were thousands of events and judgments, big and small, which comprised the framework of thought and action during the Cold War. Each built on another and each became like a skyscraper built on sand. Even Cold Warriors were not beyond investigation and the thrust of paranoia. Thus, when wisdom and attention to the facts were crucial, the diplomatic service was being reviled and shredded. State Department officials who knew something about China and the Chinese revolution were purged because they had the audacity to have nuanced views on the Chinese revolution, and for that matter the Kuomintang. Even American imperialists did not escape the lash. A prominent Cold Warrior, William Bundy, almost lost his position in the CIA because he had given $400 to the defense of Alger Hiss. (He did so because his law partner in the corporate law firm of Covington & Burling was Hiss's brother, Donald Hiss.) Allen Dulles, the head of the CIA, had to grovel before Senator McCarthy, an act that Dulles surely must have found distasteful. He had little choice because the populist, right-wing Catholic correctly suspected that the CIA housed many former communists, social democrats, and upper-class agents who might or might not have withstood the investigation or defamation.

In Democracy's Shadow points to when the Cold War could have ended, when disengagement could have taken effect, which, according to George Kennan and Senate liberals, would have freed Eastern Europe of the Soviet Union and resulted in radical changes of that benighted system. Given the fact that most American scholars, political scientists, social scientists, and many physicists had made their Faustian bargain with the National Security State by 1949, ideas offending the Cold War had little currency. The critical faculties of the professoriat were dulled by the flush of defense contracts and attacks from the right. Upon reflection, the Cold War decisions made by American politicians and the national security bureaucracy catered to fear and did not serve the people's interest. Instead of a critical look at our past, the government and most organs of opinion developed a civil mantra. We tell each other that we are a nation of the future, a civilization that does not look back. It is a waste of time to cry over spilt milk, and so it is natural that American leadership seldom apologizes for their mistaken or criminal judgments. (Of course it is true that leaders of other nations gag at the thought of apology, but there is something special about American culture in this regard.) We expect our leaders to "tell us the truth" as President George W. Bush said in the election campaign of 2004. One feature of our self-deception is that leaders such as presidents are the servants of the people. And, of course, servants always tell the truth to their masters. In the politics of war, presidents don't complain and don't explain the language of obfuscation and secrecy. "Collateral damage" describes the killing of innocent civilians; "body count" is the grisly instrument of Pentagon officials to define success and failure; taking out a city is masking language for criminal plans and mass destruction. The twentieth century, of course, was the age of the slogan, just as the twenty-first century appears to be the age of the "fleeting image." But in a democracy this is corrosive because civil servants and the citizenry alike tend to talk to each other in coded, seemingly neutral objective language to mask from themselves what they are doing.

It would seem that, although we are a religious nation, if one judges by the large numbers of people who attend church services, there does not seem to be very much shame or guilt about what we as a people do; no doubt some would demur and they would be correct. The internment of 120,000 Japanese Americans at the beginning of World War II was finally acknowledged as a mistake, which in human terms meant compensation dozens of years after the event. On the other hand, the decision to drop the atomic bombs on Japan has by and large been praised as proof of American military supremacy, moral will, and military necessity. The voice of Mahatma Gandhi was not heard very far when he said, at the dropping of the bombs, that the Japanese had lost the war and now the question was whether the United States had lost its soul. Such words could only have been said by a man who believed in the power of nonviolence. There was a less severe but nevertheless uncompromising standard that could have been followed.

The American prosecutor at Nuremberg claimed that the decisions taken against the German leadership would and should be made applicable to leaders irrespective of national origin. Indeed, in 1973, as the Indochina war was drawing to an ignominious close, with tens of thousands still to die, thirty-nine members of Congress introduced a far-reaching bill intended to write the standards laid out by the courts in the Nuremberg cases into American law, excluding death penalty verdicts for the guilty. (The executive objected to the bill and it died in committee.)

The consequences of the Cold War, hubris, and faith in military technology should have fallen to the ground with the failed military adventure in Indochina, collapse of the Twin Towers, and the other disasters that befell the United States on September 11. But that has not been the case. There were those eager to overcome the "Vietnam syndrome" and return to the days of war and intervention, and those who believed that "terrorism," which became the post–Cold War replacement of communism, would be overcome with the destruction and reconfiguration of Muslim-oriented nations.

Defense and national security budgets at the beginning of 2005 will climb to well over $550 billion while internal public expenditures decline, and other nations such as China, Japan, and those of Western Europe move their investment funds elsewhere, forcing cuts in Social Security, variations of either a national sales tax or a flat tax, or borrowing from rich bondholders at high interest rates. The United States is carrying most of the burden in two wars, with casualties in both continuing to mount to the point where the language of self-deception will no longer be sufficient. *Prudent imperialists* and *national triumphalists* alike will say that our soldiers will not have died in vain in these wars. They will say that abstract ideals such as democracy were worth fighting and dying for, and furthermore deaths and casualties attendant to the war increased our national nobility and morality. It will be taken for granted that American reconstruction in Afghanistan and Iraq requires a continuous military and economic presence to ensure geopolitical goals, such as the control over oil resources and pipelines in the former Soviet Union. The hard-headed realists will say that this is a down payment for the costs the U.S. incurred in making the Middle East "free." And the planners and progressives in Congress will wonder whether the U.S. can leave militarily if a civil war might result, spreading war to other nations, with Israel threatening to use nuclear weapons in a preemptive strike against Iraq, thereby blackmailing the U.S. as its protector.

It is ironic how a superpower is exposed, and the more it seeks to prove its power and credibility, the more exposed it becomes. Its leadership, can no longer weigh courses of action that at one time would have been obvious but can no longer be seen inside the cocoon of elite leadership, whether in the Republican or Democratic Party. Some prudent imperialists will call for the old British way. That is, keep authority and power while hiring local constabularies loyal to the United States, giving them weapons but controlling spare parts. Leaders come to believe that others can be forced or seduced into doing the bidding of the imperial nation. Thus, prudent imperialists in Washington and in the think tanks that service the government believe that local constabularies can be used to carry out the will of the United States much in the way it was done during the Cold War, with U.S. military assistance, training in weaponry, and organization. Clever tactics conflates wisdom with hiring local agents, but no one is fooled after generations of "clever," prudent imperialism. And as for sophisticated military technology? Not even Robert McNamara, the former secretary of defense, would claim that military technology breeds wise choices, or for that matter, victory. Certainly at the beginning of the twenty-first century, few would claim American leaders have the quantum of wisdom as against other nations. Just as absolute power corrupts, a belief in attaining absolute power makes those who strive after it dumb or quite mad. They are given to fantasy and grandiose dreams for which an uninformed populace is expected to suffer the consequences.

303

When a nation is in its infancy, the entrepreneurial instinct, whether in war or business, certainly holds an attraction, for both are permeated with the cliché "no pain, no gain." Official national security and economic reports claimed that while the imperial reach expanded and the national security state grew, the markets would solve any perturbations with only the minimum of interruption. Of course the reality has given us different lessons. National security emulating one aspect of markets is predicated as much on crisis as on stability.

Markets value throwing the "weak" and "inefficient" aside in favor of what is thought to be profitable, especially for the few. This idea of free-market capitalism stands alongside the closed markets of military contracts and spending, and yet they complement each other in practice—especially in the emergence of international markets, where anything can be bought and sold, from heroin to "outmoded" military equipment, and, ultimately, parts for nuclear weapons. Permanent wars became a stopgap solution.

PART II

In the twenty-first century, can the United States wean itself from being the dominant warrior nation, which balances itself on the steep ledge of fear, omnipotent fantasy, decline, and destruction? Can it escape its propaganda of self-deception? Can the nation escape the trap of imperialism and the narcissism of "single superpower responsibility?" Because of the official response to September 11, some would say that the trapdoor has closed for American democracy, since the trap infects the public institutions of American life, from the military and security systems to the corporations, universities, schools, and media. But are there political disinfectants to this infection?

The more benign view of the United States brings us to a different narrative about its history as well as the history of other nations. That history and political yearning is dearly held by millions of activists, dissenters, and even government officials who have not lost their sense of personal responsibility, courage, and commitment to the public good. For lack of a better phrase, such citizens have sought to link what is most exemplary in the American past and present to policies that reject and condemn the ways of imperialism and aggressive war. Such attitudes bind these Americans to the ideals of the UN Charter, which articulates in its language that threats to the peace and the use of force to either assess or respond are not the sole province of one nation. This idea grew out of a long history that sought to end the war system.

In the twentieth century, substantial numbers of Americans believed in the criminality of war. And a majority of American senators after World War I saw aggressive war as a criminal enterprise. They believed war imperialism to be the excrescence of civilization. Conservatives believed in a small national state claiming that markets were adversely affected by war. Liberals believed that progress and reason required an end to the war system. In other words, there were deep fears from different sectors of American life that were concerned about the effects war and the imperialist path would have on the United States. Thus, the socialist Norman Thomas, the liberal philosopher John Dewey, and the Republican President Herbert Hoover believed that war and imperialism would destroy American democracy and freedom. After fifty-seven million were killed in World War II and the German leaders were held to account personally for aggressive war, the American public (with exceptions from a number of conservatives, notably Senator Robert Taft of Ohio) applauded the Nuremberg Trials.

Liberal realists say that there are circumstances when wars must be fought because there are crimes greater than war itself. Arguably World War II was an exercise in defense. Whatever complaints the

Japanese had against the United States, it was the Japanese government that ordered the pre-emptive attack on Pearl Harbor. Further, while Roosevelt seemed itching to get into the war in Europe it was the Germans who formally declared war on the United States. In the 1990s some human rights advocates called for humanitarian interventions, though likely as not, when they are unilateral, outside of established international law, and the language of the UN Charter, these interventions are ploys for old-style imperialism but with a more humane sounding voice.

Nevertheless, one must give war its due, since it can have the effect of democratizing the warring nation. Thus, World War II was thought of by the allies as a war of necessity that brought progressive change. In Great Britain a conservative government was replaced by a Labor government, which ushered in the welfare state, though the British could no longer keep to their imperial ambitions and found themselves unable to keep control of India. They turned over the reins of government to Nehru and the Congress Party, and their sphere of influence in Turkey and Greece to the U.S. Germany, Japan, and Italy were transformed as a result of allied war efforts. In Italy a communist-led resistance movement, hard fought battles by the United States, and changes in the direction of the Catholic Church, which dropped their affinities for fascism, caused the capitulation of Mussolini's government by 1943. Japan was forced to surrender militarism as a dominant aspect of its policies.

Before the dropping of the atomic bomb, Japan sought a negotiated surrender, attempting to keep Hirohito as the emperor. The U.S. rejected the terms. Once the two bombs were dropped and the Russian invasion of Manchuria occurred, the United States accepted Japanese terms, because neither the Japanese ruling class, nor the Americans, wanted the Soviet Union to occupy Manchuria. That is, it kept the imperial court as a symbol of authority. In the occupation, Japanese political and economic structures bent to the policies of MacArthur, which brought together aspects of the New Deal—for example in land reform efforts and trust busting—with acceptance of traditional structures of political and economic power that had dueled with the militarists before World War II. (Ironically, it was only the Communist Party of Japan that held an anti-imperialist and antimilitarist position in Japan before the war by supporting the Allies. However, with the onset of the Cold War and the war in Korea, the Japanese communists became a "suspect category" to the occupation government.) The Japanese economy was greatly enhanced by the American occupation. Japan became a staging area for the American invasion in Indochina and U.S.-UN led intervention in protection of South Korea. Because they were not burdened with war budgets, Japanese leaders were able to concentrate their resources on domestic reconstruction and world business acquisitions. Germany became a contested area between the Soviet Union and the West during the Cold War. Stalin sought to guide and then control Eastern Europe. He used the catastrophe that had befallen the Soviet republics after the war to regain territories lost to Germany in World War I and to claim the need of a buffer against the West, and specifically Germany. Though it was seen as a moment of great heroism and courage in the Soviet Union, the Soviet people never quite recovered from the shock and trauma of that war. The West, and specifically the United States, was successful in creating West Germany. In collaboration with the Catholic Church, the West fashioned it into a conservative-dominated nation but with significant social democratic roots in the labor movement, which was successful in supplying a safety net for the populace first introduced by Bismarck to inoculate the ruling classes from being overrun by social democracy.

After the Soviet intervention of Hungary in 1956, it was clear that Eastern Europe had become a wasting asset for the Soviet Union. Khrushchev cut the armed forces and pressed for disengagement schemes that would get the U.S. out of Europe in exchange for the Soviets getting out of Eastern Europe. Such was the purpose of the Polish-generated Rapacki Plan.[2]

In the United States women and blacks felt a measure of inclusiveness as a result of their work in World War II. Women had become central to the total war effort, and for a time they received the respect they were due. They were able to obtain jobs in defense plants because men were off fighting wars. The equality of women gained resonance after the war, just as it had after World War I, when arguments were made for democracy and women's rights at home once the slogan of democracy abroad was used to mobilize citizens into the war effort.

Blacks had another challenge. Their victorious return as soldiers from Asia and Europe dictated that they confront the white, often state-sanctioned terror war, which had been carried out against them since Reconstruction. Indeed, they became part of an extraordinary movement of nonviolence that shifted the gaze of people away from claims that it was only through war and revolutionary violence that much, if anything, could be accomplished. The Indochina war was ended by American soldiers not willing to fight. Young men sought innovative tactics to evade the draft, and millions of people on the streets opposed the war.

Muhammad Ali's refusal to be drafted, and his explanation that "No Vietcong ever called me nigger," were not lost on whites in the United States and abroad. And there was positive resonance for the American-led movements across the globe. The world saw the United States not in the values of Nixon, Kissinger, or McNamara, but in those of Martin Luther King, Jr., who sought a path for the United States that would escape the pain of imperialism, prudent or otherwise.

At the beginning of the twenty-first century the conflict for the purposes and practices of the state against itself and others is more palpable, more dangerous, and far more costly than is generally realized. This reality is not the sole responsibility of one political party or one leader. It is not George W. Bush and his coterie alone, for Democrats have been eager, without thinking, to accept assumptions of national security reform that would vitiate the conception of constitutional democracy, except as a fig leaf to adventure and war imperialism. This is not an easy judgment to overcome, for there will be many who say that September 11 changed everything, and that the transformations that have to occur cannot and should not change the pillars of the Cold War, that is, American triumphalism. The U.S. must continue its claims of moral and economic superiority and moral certitude. According to this view, and one finds it in the various reports about reform of the government in light of September 11, the course correction that is necessary is to move from an anticommunist stance to an antiterrorist stance. The new wisdom is that, whereas states were once our enemies, now it is gangs that grow and metastasize. According to the supporters of the *9/11 Commission Report* and defense reformers, it is not only the missions of government that must be changed, but attitudes and structure as well. They claim that extending the National Security State and creating a psychological doctrine of preemption in all matters dealing with personal and national security is "necessary" and if the Constitution must be bent, so be it. The Constitution is not a "suicide pact." In any case, it is claimed that such changes will revitalize government, give civil servants a mission and purpose, and restore patriotism as an instrument for war mobilization.

Adding a new department (Homeland Security) and increasing the armed forces requires deepened relationships with defense contractors and think tanks that are part of the war and security apparatus. In the expanded National Security State, the universities will have their role to play. They will develop new kinds of expertise in language and culture studies, with an eye to nation-building and imperial development. As in the Cold War, they will be charged with the responsibility of keeping track of students and professors alike, working closely with the FBI and other agencies of government. Scientists and technologists will find new support for work concerned with weapons, spying and monitoring citizens in the U.S. and foreign populations. Journalists who, for a generation, prided themselves on independence from the state, will find themselves becoming unwitting (and sometimes witting) agents of it. Curiously, because of signs of independence, the CIA is to be downgraded organizationally, even as the number of its spies is increased. Laws are to be bent to include preemptive strategies (including preventive detention) against American citizens and aliens while adopting preemptive war (really aggressive war strategies) abroad. There is to be a new national intelligence director whose organizational chart is to parallel that of the Department of Defense, and thus will have a huge three-tiered bureaucracy.

Congress is also expected to streamline itself in order to take into account the new post–September 11 reality. It is claimed by a consensus of the 9-11 Commission that the result will be a better America and will lead to a stronger and more cohesive nation capable of fighting the latest war. The task is noble because it is simultaneously triumphal and defensive. The contours of this idea can be assessed as the natural outgrowth of American democracy. But what was and is democracy? Realists will say that the United States is a warrior state, and because of its warrior nature it changed from a restricted republic through war to the beginnings of democracy. Thus, the American Civil War brought about the formal end of slavery, though it took one hundred years to change the mores and regulations of the nation with regard to state-sanctioned racial oppression. That the United States government organized wars of oppression and forms of genocide against American Indians is no longer disputable, and that population removal was "necessary" as an instrument of progress was the preferred mechanism of administrations throughout the nineteenth and early twentieth century. It was necessary to make way for a superior form of technology, worship, and commerce.

The implications of this line of argument have been that war spreads democracy within the imperial nation and that the imperial nation can bring into being new social, political, and economics systems when its leaders have the will and the intention.

But there is a different narrative that is far more persuasive in this epoch of history. The thrust of decolonization, the rhetoric of democracy, and the rhetoric of socialism and capitalism, brought the idea that national self-determination demanded change against tradition and even change against change. Whether it was Mahatma Gandhi, the antimodernist, or Franklin Roosevelt, the architect of the UN, both believed that the war system was played out as a mode of resolving disputes. Western colonialism as well could not sustain itself in Asia or Africa, for that matter. The more benign form of Western colonialism, imperialism, found itself delegitimated by new centers of power and statements of principle, as in the case of the Bandung Conference, where Third and Fourth World nations sought to define their independence from the Cold War. Western words and slogans such as free world, democracy, development, and capitalism were conflated and often resented in the Third World. As the Cold War progressed, the idea that democracy could be shoved down the throats of other nations seemed foolish. Democracy as mediated through war and imperialism was not the idyllic picture of town meetings in Vermont or Norman Rockwell *Saturday Evening Post* magazine covers, but more like the devastation and destruction wrought by the Americans seeking to brand other nations with our stamp of approval. And when the United States, with its nation-building program, supported "moderate" dictators and authoritarians, as it did throughout the world in much of the Cold War, democracy was reduced to a word of cynicism for it meant another form of propaganda that masked oppression—as it did, for example, in the Philippines of Marcos, or the Union of South Africa, or in Indonesia under Suharto. U.S. military aid and most development aid assistance to such nations were bribes meant to secure the loyalty of the few, while talk of building stable middle classes covered brutal oppression. This was the case in Guatemala, and tragically is the case in Iraq now. These and other nations such as Bolivia, the Congo, and Haiti sank into forms of oppression covered by democratic propaganda. The concept of destroying a town or city in order to save it—a phrase made famous by an American major during the Vietnam War—repeated itself in Fallujah and the Sunni-controlled areas of Baghdad. The current Bush enterprise seemed to be nothing more than a crusade, a term first used by George W. Bush in explaining his war policies as the replay of the Inquisition, having nothing to do with democracy or the saving of souls. In the minds of Hamas and al-Qaeda's leaders, the struggle against the United States was between the godly and the godless. And that has certainly been the view of George W. Bush in his approach to religious fundamentalists in the Third World. (A group, in the case of the Taliban, which the U.S. supported handsomely in the Afghan-Soviet War.) As with any "true believers," torture became acceptable if it was for a satisfactory objective, according to John Ashcroft. What civil servants were embarrassed to do became justified in public policy and law. Torture had become the thing to do. Such is the deformation of democracy when the rule of law is compromised for secrecy.

As democracy developed in the sense of process and objective, certain features became obvious and crucial. Thus, for example, secrecy contradicted the essence of democracy, namely free speech and access to information and knowledge that can be disseminated and used by publics to make reasoned judgments about what they should do, individually and collectively. Secrecy reinforced lying to the public and immoral acts that would not be accepted in the public arena.

Freedom of speech and the Bill of Rights assume that in the long run mistakes can be corrected if they are known. But for this to be true, the character and policies of the democracy must be in the right frame of reference, so that if mistakes are made, they will not lead to the destruction of democracy, freedom, or indeed many millions of the innocent. Tragically, we are not in the right frame of reference. Nor were we during the Cold War when one tallies the detritus of that utterly misunderstood fifty-year enterprise of destruction and missed opportunities.

With the assumptions and actions of the second Bush administration, there is nothing to suggest that the deepening of a policy of war without end or curtailing of civil liberties will cause the people to feel more free. There is nothing to suggest that Americans are less at risk than they were before September 11, or for that matter, during the Cold War, when atomic saber rattling caused American children to hide under their desks at school in anticipation of an atomic attack from the Soviet Union. These were empty acts, just as patting down women before they get on airplanes because they might, or might not, have explosives in their bras is an act of fear and desperation. So, in post–September 11, the government has brought us into a new frame of reference, building and expanding the mistakes of the past into mistakes of even greater magnitude. But this is not the sole result of the current Bush administration.

Both major political aspirants for the presidency in 2004 sought to outdo each other in asserting war as the fundamental right and style of American governing. In other words, neither knew, or seemed to care, how a different frame of reference would be created to sustain and enhance democracy. On the one hand, Senator Kerry sought to appear reasonable by talking about frayed alliances that he could repair. He would "listen" to other nations, but this was merely a question of style as one might pay attention to a child and then make the decision irrespective of the child's wishes. This process was little more than "prudent" imperialism, which did not foster democracy or freedom but enhanced the power of the national security state without awareness of the startling and accumulated dangers to freedom, security, and democracy. Senator Kerry complained that only 2 percent of cargo that came into the United States was being inspected. But it was absurd to believe that there could be anything more than random or "inductive and statistical" inspection, unless the United States was prepared, as a practical matter, to slow down and close markets to foreign goods, thereby causing massive global economic and social dislocation.

Of course seeds of triumphant nationalism were present in prudent imperialism throughout American history. The Monroe Doctrine seemed to guarantee U.S. interference militarily in Latin America, and then, as Secretary of State Acheson said, in any part of the world. In the 1960s and early '70s triumphalist tendencies seemed to wane. They were curbed by the American military loss in Indochina, decisions of

311

the Warren Supreme Court, exposes such as those generated by Seymour Hersh, which helped to protect the civil liberties of demonstrators, large demonstrations against war and for equal rights, and Senate investigations into the corrupt and corrupting practices of the various intelligence agencies.

By 1991 ruling elites looked for a new national purpose, much the way such notions gripped ruling elites of the 1950s and early '60s. Triumphalists saw the possibility of tearing the fig leaf from American national security. Aggressive war no longer needed to be secret. Why not remake the world? Why not change other nations through war? Without our power there would be chaos and imperialism was the means to stop chaos if we were willing to be public about our purpose and destiny. President George W. Bush became the vessel for this expanded vision. He saw no value in alliances, unless they were temporary, with the U.S. dominating the alliance. (In this sense, conservatives followed the edict of Washington's farewell address: that the United States should never have permanent attachments to other nations.) Further, the Bush administration sought to implement a position held by many on the right, that the UN had no value and should be disbanded or further neutered. While prudent imperialists saw the UN as useful so long as it was "guided" by Washington, a position held by editorial writers and George H. W. Bush, nationalist triumphalists believed the UN, with its resolutions and international conferences on women's rights, environment protection, and apartheid, could change the moral and political consciousness of the world at the expense of American leadership. Such a danger required more drastic action.

During the Cold War period, the difficulty the UN had collecting past dues from the United States was a signal to the UN that if it objected too strenuously to the U.S. agenda, the UN was in mortal danger of losing the minimum financial support it needed to survive. In this sense the UN Security Council risked the existence of the UN when it voted against the second resolution to support an Iraqi invasion in 2003. It seemed with the second Iraq War that the UN Security Council was not prepared to franchise the UN's name to accord legitimacy to an American-Anglo enterprise. In the minds of the White House the UN's irrelevance was proved, although the question of *American* irrelevance was more than a fantasy, as its economic debts to other nations increased, its wars had no end, and its desires had become unlimited.

As the troubador once said, "There is something blowing in the wind." There is a general recognition, and it can be measured by the size of popular nonviolent demonstrations, that sees economic imperialism, the war system, nuclearism, and internal repression as corrosive to democratic freedom. These demonstrators are saying that the U.S. government must give up selling fear to its own people and the rest of the world, which it does through its internal and national security policies. There is no balance between freedom and security. In a modern democracy, freedom is our security. Alas, this was not the view of the much-praised *9-11 Commission Report.* In its political stance, the commission sought to represent an establishment consensus of prudent imperialism, which would have proper regard for civil liberties just so long as they did not get in the way of the serious business of the state. The final report called for the total revamping of the federal government. It would transcend the National Security Act of 1947, which assumed a mobilized domestic population against a state (the Soviet Union), the expansion of communism, and dangerous movements for self-determination. We learn from *The 9-11 Commission Report* that what is needed for the United States is "more than a War on Terrorism," and that if "the United States does not act aggressively to define itself in the Islamic world, the extremists will gladly do the job for us."[3]

As a carryover from the pre–September 11 prudent imperialist period, the United States showed deep concern with nuclear weapons and other WMD forms. However, the United States is the largest trafficker in arms and has no interest in destroying its nuclear weapons and missiles. Instead, they are to be refurbished and reconfigured. Indeed, the United States, by a very narrow margin in Congress, has committed itself to tactical nuclear weapons: the so-called "bunker busters."

Domestically, the commission took for granted that the previous "wall" between the CIA and FBI should end, pronouncing that policing, detaining, and spying operations should work off a common grid of information exchange at all levels of government and between agencies and local police forces. Such an idea makes sense on the surface, especially when it includes break-ins. But there is a nagging problem. During the Nixon Administration, Nixon offered the Huston Plan, which was deemed illegal and indeed criminal. Even the FBI's J. Edgar

Hoover rejected the plan as illegal. But in the present circumstances, it is meant as a new doctrine to be accepted as a step forward in American politics and jurisprudence. The Patriot Act and likely new sections to it will allow for justifying detention without trial and even the possibility of lifting U.S. citizenship at executive discretion.

Besides calling for a long-term program of reeducation in the Muslim nations, where young people are ostensibly educated to become suicide bombers (or religious patriots depending on one's point of view), the FBI is to be expanded while the CIA is to be downgraded, although it is to retain various intelligence gathering functions. Human intelligence and covert intelligence may be formally separate but not in reality.

Adding a national intelligence director under the president masks the fact that a new layering of bureaucracy expands greatly the National Security State. It is to be infused, organized, and "coordinated" with the ideology of triumphal nationalism as its guiding principle. That is to say, American citizens can be secure by becoming soldiers in a continuous war that requires citizens to accept biometric profiling and all manner of invasion of privacy. In American history there have been invasions of civil liberties such as the McCarthy scare of the 1950s, the Palmer Raids of 1919, and the Federalist Party's use of the Alien and Sedition laws against its enemies under the presidency of John Adams. In the twenty-first century, Americans "enjoy" heightened fears, secret bureaucracy, and increasingly sophisticated technological devices of social control. Immigrants residing in the United States under the new, improved, and sophisticated technologies will be passively or actively surveilled, and minor infractions such as expiration of a driver's license are to be cause for revocation of visa permits, detention charges, and coding into the "black book" of the suspicious. There is little reason to believe that the protection of the United States from terrorists will be greater if control over most of the intelligence budget is taken from the Department of Defense. One thing is certain: intelligence budgets will grow exponentially under a national intelligence director, just as the Homeland Security Department will grow in the second Bush term and beyond.

The commission has used as its model for reorganization the Department of Defense, a gargantuan department of the government, limits on the expansion of which have not occurred since President

Eisenhower warned in a speech of January 17, 1960, against the "potential for the disastrous rise of misplaced power (which) exists and will persist." A vastly different set of ideas is embedded in our consciousness, aching to be realized.

NOTES

1 In fact information was kept by one sector of government from another, though they might be working on the same problem.
2 See Richard Barnet and Marcus Raskin, *After Twenty Years: Alternatives to the Cold War in Europe* (New York: Random House, 1965).
3 One instructive passage from the report states:

315

> Terrorism is a tactic used by individuals and organizations to kill and destroy. Our efforts should be directed at those individuals and organizations.
>
> Calling this struggle a war accurately describes the use of American and allied armed forces to find and destroy terrorist groups and their allies in the field, notably Afghanistan. The language of war also evokes the mobilization for a national effort. Yet the strategy should be balanced.
>
> The first phase of our post-9/11 efforts rightly included military action to topple the Taliban and pursue al-Qaeda. This work continues. But long-term success demands the use of all elements of national power: diplomacy, intelligence, covert action, law enforcement, economic policy, foreign aid, public diplomacy, and homeland defense. If we favor one tool while neglecting others, we leave ourselves vulnerable and weaken our national effort. Certainly the strategy should include offensive operations to counter terrorism. Terrorists should no longer find safe haven where their organizations can grow and flourish. America's strategy should be a coalition strategy, that includes Muslim nations as partners in its development and implementation.
>
> "Our effort should be accompanied by a *preventive* [italics not in original] strategy that is as much, or more, political as it is military. The strategy must focus clearly on the Arab and Muslim world, in all its variety.
>
> Our strategy should also include defenses. America can be attacked in many ways and has many vulnerabilities. No defenses are perfect. But risks must be calculated; hard choices must be made about allocating resources. Responsibilities for America's defense should be clearly defined. Planning does make a difference, identifying where a little money might have a large effect. Defenses also complicate the plans of attackers, increasing their risks of discovery

and failure. Finally, the nation must prepare to deal with attacks that are not stopped. (*The 9/11 Commission Report: Final Report of the National Commission on Terrorist Attacks Upon the United States* [New York and London: W.W. Norton and Company, 2004], 363–64.)

LIST OF NATIONAL SECURITY SEMINAR PARTICIPANTS

George Washington University

Professor Marcus G. Raskin, Convener

The seminar reviewed laws, executive orders, assumptions, and practices that governed the American government during the course of the Cold War. The seminar's objective was to ascertain whether the organizational structures that emerged from World War II needed transformation in a new period of national and world history. The seminar considered the national-threat model of organizing the state and considered a cooperative model that arguably could be more in keeping with the stresses, needs, and hopes of a post–Cold War democratic state.

SOME PAST SPEAKERS OF THE SEMINAR

Kai Bird and Gar Alperovitz
"The Timing and Development of the Nuclear Bomb"

Professor Peter Raven-Hansen and Professor Bill Chambliss, George Washington University
"The National Security State and Law Enforcement"

Greg Bishak, Executive Director, National Commission on Economic Conversion & Disarmament
"Military Keynesianism and Military Corporatism"

Representative Bob Kastenmier and Senator John Culver
"Congressional Complicity"

Scott Armstrong and Seymour Hersh
"Elite-source Journalism"

Steve Schlossberg
"Labor and the National Security State"

Mark Schneider, Asst. Administrator for Latin America, Agency for International Development
"Development in the Post–Cold War World"

Steve Aftergood, Federation of American Scientists
"On Secrecy"

Saul Landau
"Immigration and the National Security State"

Admiral Eugene LaRocque, Center for Defense Information
"For the Common Defense"

John Prados, Author
"A History of the National Security Council"

Bill Maynes, Editor, Foreign Policy
"An Alternative Foreign Policy"

Congressman Barney Frank
"Organizing and Goal Setting for a Model National Security Act"

Marcus G. Raskin, Professor of Public Policy, George Washington University
"The Determinants of a Cooperative Model for National Security" and "Revising the National Security Act of 1947"

APPENDIX

Judge Abner Mikva, former Chief Judge, U.S. Court of Appeals, former White House Counsel
"Moral Aspirations, Expedient and Legal Choices in National Security Policy Making"

Spurgeon Keeny, President of the Arms Control Association, former Dep. Dir., ACDA
"The Inescapable Nuclear Reality and its Effects on New Policies, Laws and Old Agreements"

Ambassador Bob White, President of the Center for International Policy
and
David MacMichael, former Senior Estimates Officer for Latin America, CIA
"Conflicts and Varying Assumptions Among the Covert and Overt in American Foreign Policy"

James Rosenau, University Professor of International Relations, George Washington University
"Towards a Changed Theory of International Relations"

Sarah Nelson
"Problems with Secrecy"

Morton Halperin, former Special Assistant for National Security
"National Security and the Future of American Democracy"

Congressman John Conyers, Jr.
"Secrecy and Justice in America"

Judge Stanley Sporkin, former General Counsel of the CIA, current District Court Judge for D.C.
"The Organizational Wisdom of the National Security State During the Cold War"

Steve Schwartz, Nuclear Weapons Project, The Brookings Institution
"The Real Cost of Nuclear Weapons"

APPENDIX

John Steinbruner, Senior Fellow, The Brookings Institution
"The Problem of Eliminating Nuclear Weapons"

Ernest Fitzgerald, Director, The Fund for Constitutional Government
"Is There Any Military in the Fat Budget?"

John Holum, Director of the Arms Control and Disarmament Agency
"Prospects for Arms Control"

Ambassador Clovis Maksoud, Director, Center for the Global South, American University
"The American National Security State: A View from the Global South"

Congresswoman Elizabeth Furse
"Increasing Economic and Political Literacy for a New National Security Paradigm"

Michael Schuman, Codirector, Institute for Policy Studies
"Local Governments and U.S. Foreign Policy"

The Honorable Hazel O'Leary, former Secretary of Energy
"America's Nuclear Arsenal: Uncovering the Truth and Building a New Policy"

William Blum, author of *Killing Hope: U.S. Military and CIA Interventions Since World War II*
"U.S. Foreign Policy is What U.S. Foreign Policy Does"

Michael Tigar, Professor, Washington College of Law, former counsel to Terry Nichols
"Terrorism, National Security and Civil Liberties"

Kai Bird, Author, *McGeorge Bundy and William Bundy: Brothers in Arms*
"The Responsibility of Government Elites"

Stephen Rosenfeld, Deputy Editorial Page Editor, *The Washington Post*
"Time for an American Truth Commission?"

ABOUT THE CONTRIBUTORS

GAR ALPEROVITZ is the author of *America Beyond Capitalism: Reclaiming Our Wealth, Our Liberty and Our Democracy*, *The Decision to Use the Atomic Bomb*, *Rebuilding America* (with Jeff Faux), *Cold War Essays*, and the critically acclaimed *Atomic Diplomacy: Hiroshima and Potsdam: The Use of the Atomic Bomb and the American Confrontation with Soviet Power*. He is the Lionel R. Bauman Professor of Political Economy at the University of Maryland, and president of the National Center for Economic and Security Alternatives. He is a former fellow of King's College, Cambridge University, from which he received his PhD.

KAI BIRD is a historian and biographer, and most recently the co-author with Martin J. Sherwin of *American Prometheus: The Triumph and Tragedy of J. Robert Oppenheimer*. He is also the author of *The Chairman: John McCloy, the Making of the American Establishment*, and *The Color of Truth: McGeorge Bundy and William Bundy, Brothers in Arms*. He is also the coeditor (with Lawrence Lifschultz) of *Hiroshima's Shadow: Writings on the Denial of History and the Smithsonian Controversy*. He is a contributing editor to *The Nation*.

NORMAN BIRNBAUM is university professor emeritus at Georgetown University Law Center and a member of the Editorial Board of the *Nation*. His most recent book is *After Progress: American Social Reform and European Socialism in the Twentieth Century* (Oxford University Press, 2001).

WILLIAM BLUM is a former State Department analyst. He is the author of *Killing Hope: U.S. Military and CIA Interventions Since World War II* and most recently, *Freeing the World to Death: Essays on the American Empire*. Visit www.killinghope.org.

JOHN BURROUGHS is executive director of the New York–based Lawyers' Committee on Nuclear Policy (LNCP) and adjunct professor of international law at Rutgers Law School, Newark. In 1998, he represented LNCP at the negotiations on the International Criminal Court in Rome, and in 1995, he was the nongovernmental legal coordinator at the hearings on nuclear weapons before the International Court of Justice. He is author of *The Legality of Threat or Use of Nuclear Weapons: A Guide to the Historic Opinion of the International Court of Justice* (Transaction Publishers, 1998), and coeditor of *Rule of Power or Rule of Law? An Assessment of U.S. Policies and Actions Regarding Security-Related Treaties* (Apex Press, 2003).

ANABEL L. DWYER teaches human rights and humanitarian law at the Thomas M. Cooley Law School in Michigan. She has been a defendant and defense attorney in cases of civil resistance to nuclear weapons and is on the board of the Lawyers' Committee on Nuclear Policy.

DAVID J. DWYER is a professor of anthropology and African studies at Michigan State University. He is the author of numerous articles on language and culture, African languages, and the teaching of African languages. He is currently completing an undergraduate textbook on language and culture.

RICHARD FALK is professor emeritus of political science at Princeton University. He is the author, coauthor, editor, or coeditor of nearly fifty books on international law, national security, and human rights. His most recent book is *Human Rights Horizons: The Pursuit of Justice in a Globalizing World*.

SAUL LANDAU is the author of *The Guerilla Wars of Central America*, *Assassination on Embassy Row* (with John Dinges), *The American New Right*, *The Dangerous Doctrine*, and numerous books. He has made over forty films and documentaries, and has taught at University of California, Berkeley, Stanford University, and the University of Maryland. A longtime fellow with the Institute for Policy Studies, he currently serves as chair of Interdisciplinary Applied Knowledge at Cal State Polytechnic University.

A. CARL LEVAN has worked closely with Marcus G. Raskin for over ten years including as the research assistant for the National Security State seminar at George Washington University that formed the basis for this book. He is the former legislative director for Congressman John Conyers (D-MI), and has also worked as a technical advisor to the National Assembly in Nigeria. He was a Visiting Fulbright Lecturer at the University of Ibadan 2003–2004, and is currently completing his PhD in political science at the University of California, San Diego.

JEFFREY LEWIS is a graduate research fellow at the Center for International and Security Studies at the University of Maryland (CISSM), where he works on the space policy component of a project developing Advanced Methods of Cooperative Security. His dissertation from the School of Public Affairs contemplates a new arms control framework for the United States-China relationship. He is also the executive director of the Association of Professional Schools of International Affairs.

NORMAN MAILER was born in 1923 and published his first book, *The Naked and the Dead*, in 1948. *The Armies of the Night* won the National Book Award and the Pulitzer Prize in 1969; Mailer received another Pulitzer in 1980 for *The Executioner's Song*. He lives in Provincetown, Massachusetts, and Brooklyn, New York.

SEYMOUR MELMAN was professor emeritus of industrial engineering at Columbia University's School of Engineering and Applied Science. He wrote widely on economics, defense policy, and engineering. His books include: *Disarmament, its Politics and Economics* (1962), *Our Depleted Society* (1965), *The War Economy of the United States; Readings on Military Industry and Economy* (1971), *The Demilitarized Society: Disarmament and Conversion* (1988), and *After Capitalism: From Managerialism to Workplace Democracy* (2001). Melman passed away in December 2004.

ANNA K. NELSON is Distinguished Adjunct Historian in Residence at American University. She has published more than thirty articles and book chapters on the national security process of the early Cold War. Her most recent book is *Secret Agents: President Polk and the Search for Peace with Mexico.*

TERRENCE EDWARD PAUPP, is national chancellor of the United Stated for the International Association of Educators for World Peace and is professor of politics and international law at National University, San Diego. He is the author of *Achieving Inclusionary Governance: Advancing Peace and Development in First and Third World Nations* (2000) and has published articles on civil rights, human rights, and constitutional war powers in the *Urban League Review* and the *Journal of Contemporary Legal Issues* (USD). Most recently, he contributed to *Rushing to Armageddon: The Shocking Truth about Canada, Missile Defense, and Star Wars* (2004).

MARCUS G. RASKIN is the author or editor of eighteen books on a broad range of topics including national security (*After Twenty Years: Alternatives to the Cold War in Europe, The Politics of National Security*), philosophy (*Being and Doing, The Common Good, New Ways of Knowing,* and *Visions and Revisions*), and American politics generally (*Essays of a Citizen* and *Notes on the Old System*). He has worked in the executive branch as a member of the National Security Council staff and as a consultant to the White House Office on Science and Technology. He cofounded the Institute for Policy Studies in 1963, and at one point served as chairman of the board of SANE/FREEZE. He is currently a professor of public policy at George Washington University and serves on the editorial board of the *Nation*.

PETER RAVEN-HANSEN is the Glen Earl Weston Research Professor of Law at George Washington University and the senior associate dean for Academic Affairs at the law school. He is the coauthor of *National Security Law and the Power of the Purse* (with William C. Banks) and the editor of *First Use of Nuclear Weapons: Under the Constitution, Who Decides?*

ABOUT THE CONTRIBUTORS

JOHN STEINBRUNER is the director of the Center for International and Security Studies at Maryland (CISSM). He is the author of numerous books, including *A New Concept of Cooperative Security* (with Ashton Carter and William Perry) and most recently, *Principles of Global Security*. Before joining the University of Maryland's School of Public Affairs and CISSM, Steinbruner was director of the Brookings Institution's Foreign Policy Studies Program for eighteen years.

PETER WEISS is an attorney and vice president of the Center for Constitutional Rights in New York City, and the author of numerous articles about international law, human rights, and U.S. foreign policy. He is president of the Lawyers' Committee on Nuclear Policy and vice president of the International Association of Lawyers Against Nuclear Arms.

325

ACKNOWLEDGMENTS

This book is a collective effort a decade in the making. We gratefully acknowledge those who lent their intelligence, experience, and imagination to the project. The list of scholars, journalists, and colleagues whose ideas contributed in some way to this book is long and, by attempting to thank them all, we naturally run the risk of excluding a few.

Many distinguished individuals took time out of their busy schedules to present at the George Washington University Seminar on the National Security State or at the National Press Conference on "National Security and the War System" but were unable to contribute to this book. We would like to thank as many of them as possible here.

Senators George McGovern and John Culver spoke on the role of Congress in the National Security State, as did several former and current members of the House of Representatives. Congressmen Barney Frank and John Conyers described their frustrations with the intelligence bureaucracy and were inspired enough to offer amendments to the intelligence authorization shortly thereafter. Congresswoman Elizabeth Furse gave an insider's view of the Armed Services Committee, and shed light on the problem of building a constituency for reforming the national security bureaucracy. Former Representative Bob Kastenmeier was one of our most reliable attendees and we were among his most devoted students.

Judge Stanley Sporkin, the CIA's former general counsel, sparked a memorable debate by offering a vigorous defense of the CIA's Cold War engagements abroad. Morton Halperin from the National Security Council explained the bureaucratic thicket of national security, and former White House Counsel Judge Abner Mikva described the legal framework for covert operations. Ambassador Robert White from the Center for International Policy, and David MacMichael, a former CIA Senior Estimates Officer gave learned responses about the pitfalls of covert operations in Latin America. James Turner, the former staff director for the House Legislation and National Security Subcommittee, described the gap that emerges from the drafting stage to the implementation stage of national security policy.

Many discussions dealt with the problem of the surplus of secrecy in the government. Steve Aftergood of the Federation of American Scientists, and Professor Sara Nelson, a member of the Assassination Materials Review Board, explained why secrecy is costly for policy makers and the private sector. Scott Armstrong and Seymour Hersh argued that openness is more democratic, and arguably just as reliable as classified information. Former Secretary of Energy Hazel O'Leary gave her account of what happens when a member of the cabinet undertakes a policy of pragmatic openness. Sociology Professor William Chambliss and Law Professor Peter Raven-Hansen explained the consequences of secrecy and law making through administrative fiat expands on domestic law enforcement. Michael Tigar, law professor and criminal defense lawyer, explained the broad consequences of the National Security State on civil liberties.

The GW Seminar became home to an ongoing debate about the relationship between the National Security State, capitalism, and markets. Mark Schneider, Assistant Administrator for Latin America at the U.S. Agency for International Development offered one view, while Ambassador Clovis Maksoud from the Center for the Study of the Global South at American University and Saul Landau from California State Polytechnic University offered rather different views. Steve Schlossberg added another dimension to this debate by outlining the labor movement's compromises and concessions during the Cold War. Last but not least, Greg Bischak from the National Commission on Economic Conversion and Disarmament explained the political economy of national security, and helped keep us on track during many seminar discussions.

Another common subject of the seminars was how to shape America's engagement with the world on a model of cooperation rather than the outdated "threat model." John Holum, Director of the Arms Control and Disarmament Agency, and Spurgeon Keeney from the Arms Control Association, offered honest assessments of the feasibility of a disarmament policy that works towards this goal. Steve Schwartz educated us about the ongoing costs of nuclear weapons if we don't work towards this objective. Bill Maynes, the editor of *Foreign Policy*, and professor of international relations James Rosenau, outlined the challenges to achieving a foreign policy built on the cooperation model within the new "globalization system." Michael Schuman pointed out the important role of local governments and grassroots organizing can play a role in shaping the global model. Admiral Eugene LaRocque, the founder of the Center for Defense Information, and General William Y. Smith, former Deputy Chief of Staff of NATO, were both faithful attendees of the seminar. Ernest Fitzgerald and Chuck Spinney gave a different kind of Pentagon insider's view when they explained how waste and fraud becomes institutionalized. Stephen Rosenfeld, editor of the *Washington Post*'s editorial page, Gore Vidal, and the national security historian John Prados offered insights into why it can be difficult to uncover and expose truths about the system and offered thoughtful answers as to why America so easily forgets what truths it might have known. American University communications professor Christopher Simpson considered the question of propaganda in the information age.

MIT Professor Carl Kaysen, former Deputy Advisor to the President on National Security, international law professor Louis Sohn from GW, history professor Carolyn Eisenberg from Hofstra University, and Phyllis Bennis from the Institute for Policy Studies were among those who participated in an all-day seminar on the National Security State at GW. The many familiar faces who regularly attended the monthly GW Seminars and to whom we thank for provoking spirited debates include: Dan Ellsberg, Anna Nelson, Cindy Gritton, Sam Smith, Martha Honey, Paul Churchill, Nick Steneck, Kathy Kadane, Kate Martin, Bob Borosage, Louis Wolf, Anabel Dwyer, David Dwyer, Stuart Umpleby, Bill Arkin, Julia Sweig, and Dean Maurice East. The seminar would not have been possible without the ongoing commitment of Rod French, Don Lehman, David Grier, and President Stephen Joel Trachtenberg.

As always, John Cavanagh, the staff and the fellows of the Institute for Policy Studies contributed to the success of the seminar and the National Press Club conference. Mark DiGiacomo, Kristi Fanelli, Tom Platt, Solveig "Zoe" Ros, and Diane Alonzo provided administrative and research support. Carl wishes to thank IPS for the Seymour Melman Fellowship he received in 2001, which allowed him to begin working on the book. Conrad Martin and Stewart Mott of the Fund for Constitutional Government provided generous financial support for the conference at the National Press Club. We especially want to thank Carl Bromley and Ruth Baldwin at Nation Books for their patience and editorial expertise.

A similar version of the chapter that appears here as "The Centrality of the Atomic Bomb" by Gar Alperovitz and Kai Bird, appeared in *The History Teacher*, Volume 29, Number 3 (May 1996), pages 281–300. This essay was also the basis of their presentation at the University Seminar. A version of Peter Weiss and John Burroughs's chapter, "Weapons of Mass Destruction and Human Rights," appeared in *Disarmament Forum*, Issue #3 (2004). "The Nuclear Legacy and the Cold War," by John Steinbruner and Jeffrey Lewis, is based on an essay that appeared in *Daedalus*, 131, no. 4 (Fall 2002). It appears here courtesy of MIT Press. Norman Mailer's contribution is based on a speech he delivered at Harvard University in 2004.

The sparkle of life and the hope of the future can be experienced at our Sunday brunches where everyone is seen and heard. My love and special thanks go to the participants especially my children, Erika, Jamie, Noah and Eden; their children Emily, Zach, Maggie, Hannah, Tommy, Tabitha, Mariah, and Bo including the other half of the siring team, Keith, Sarah, and Mina. Everyday my beautiful, gifted, and loving wife gently teaches me new things. It is a shock to be married to a woman who means what she says. Someday I will write about these remarkable and gifted people. Keep tuned.

MARCUS G. RASKIN

Family, friends, teachers, and colleagues all played roles in persuading me this book was possible and sometimes reminding me that it was indeed necessary. Allison, Lisa, Mom, and Dad all offered support and encouragement from the start. Moni was also there, patient and loving, as always. Thank you.

A. CARL LEVAN
NOVEMBER 30, 2004

INDEX

Page number 59*n*40 indicates page 59, note 40.